WORK AND SPIRIT

A Reader of New Spiritual Paradigms for Organizations

D1073748

WORK AND SPIRIT

A Reader of New Spiritual Paradigms for Organizations

Editors:

Jerry Biberman,
University of Scranton

Michael D. Whitty,
University of Detroit Mercy

SCRANTON: THE UNIVERSITY OF SCRANTON PRESS

Many of these articles first appeared in two special issues on "Spirituality in
Organizations" published in the *Journal of Organizational Change
Management* ("Spirituality in Organizations," Parts I and II, Jerry Biberman
and Michael Whitty, guest editors, Vol. 12, Numbers 3 and 4, 1999, MCB
University Press, Bradford, UK). Further information on the *Journal of
Organizational Change Management* and MCB University Press may be
found at http://www.mcb.co.uk/.

Library of Congress Cataloging-in-Publication Data

Work and spirit : a reader of new spiritual paradigms for organizations / Editors:
Jerry Biberman, Michael D. Whitty.
    p. cm.
   Includes bibliographical references and index.
   ISBN 0-940866-89-7 (p/b)
     1. Work–Religious aspects. 2. Management–Religious aspects.
I. Biberman, Jerry, 1949- II. Whitty, Michael D., 1942-

   BL65.W67 W68 2000
   291.1'785–dc21

                                00-057718

Distribution:

University of Scranton Press
Linden Street & Monroe Avenue
Scranton, PA 18510
Phone: 1–800–941–3081
Fax: 1–800–941–8804

PRINTED IN THE UNITED STATES OF AMERICA

DEDICATION

In memory of Rev. George J. Schemel, S.J., founder
and director of the Institute for Contemporary
Spirituality at the University of Scranton, and founder
and for 12 years director of the Jesuit Center for
Spiritual Growth at Wernersville, PA.

CONTENTS

The Individual Within Organizations

Organizational and Societal Issues and Applications

The Possible Future

OVERVIEW

Jerry Biberman and Michael Whitty

Spirit matters—in management, economics and in business in general. This reader offers business educators and opportunity to incorporate various aspects of spirit into their teaching and scholarship. Just as the contributing authors have broken new ground in their teaching, training and consulting. We are hopeful the diverse collection of viewpoints presented in this reader will advance the dialogue on the possible meaning and value of workplace spirituality. Our intention is to provide a broad representation of the academic scholarship in the field of spirituality in management/ organizations. No attempt has been made to exclude the overlap between many other closely related fields such as consciousness in business and religion in business. In fact, we have found much of the scholarship to be highly interdisciplinary in its focus. Medicine and psychology may yet prove to be the most initially convincing paradigms for new integral approaches to reinventing work. Individually healthy work lives beget a truly healthy workplace.

Many of the articles in this reader first appeared in special issues of the *Journal of Organizational Management*—which is edited by David Boje and published by MCB Press. We are grateful to MCB Press for allowing those articles to appear in this reader.

We have divided our selections into four main sections. This introduction will give a short introduction to—and description of—each of the articles contained in the four sections of the reader. Each section contains a diverse mix of views and approaches to a subject that can be and is approached from a vast number of often very different directions. We make no final case for any particular approach. We hope that you will find this reader useful in your teaching, consulting, and research. It can be utilized as a supplementary reader in management, organizational behavior, business ethics, business social responsibility, organizational development, business policy, or a course in spirituality at work.

The articles that appear in this reader on work and spirituality join the many articles that are now appearing in various scholarly journals across many disciplines. This interdisciplinary scholarship has appeared not only in the various business disciplines but also in the sciences, the

xi

social sciences, and the humanities. Moreover, academic studies and books reflect a renewed interest in the topic of spirituality and work as it applies to all the professions, institutions of modern life, and the future visions for the global society of tomorrow. The elements of this topic—work and spirituality—are as old as time but equally timely for the new millennium. It will take more than one academic reader on spirituality to begin to explore these topics. The diverse approaches of our authors ensure a uniquely rich list of references and sources for further study and research. This collection of essays is interdisciplinary, attacking this vast topic of work from different vantage points.

Theoretical Perspectives

It has only been within the last decade that serious academic interest has been evident regarding the possible relevance of spirituality to organizations. Now, with the popular business literature awash with pop psychology for business leaders and their organizations, the world of academia recognizes the importance of visionary organizational theory and a deepened view of basic core values. Both mainline consultants and opinion leaders in the popular business culture realize the need for a higher purpose for organizational life than solely acquiring money and power. They have turned, often, to spiritual business philosophy.

This readers' sample of theoretical perspectives on spirituality reveals the diverse approaches to this new discipline of organization theory. The dominant theme is that the search for deeper meaning in work often leads to a spiritual insight or path, and sometimes a renewal or transformation of the work organization itself. New management theory is coming from the fields of organizational psychology, humanistic psychology and a new business philosophy based on environmental management.

Located at the beginning of three sections of the reader are three poems by Tom Brown—"Glow," "Embers," and "Dawn"—from his e-book *The Anatomy of Fire*. The complete book is available online from mgeneral at www.mgeneral.com.

Judith Neal, David Banner, and Benjamin Lichtenstein present a broad, macrocosmic argument for individual, organizational, and societal transformation. They believe a spiritual consciousness of epic proportions is affecting economic rationale. This lead article lays out the leading theories for individual, organizational, and societal transformation. The authors believe individual paradigm shifts occurring among cultural creatives, professionals, and business leaders are affecting the arena of organizational theory—creating a new philosophy of work. They believe human evolution will revise human interaction, reducing organizational and societal dominance over humankind and the planet. This path-breaking essay sets the standard for a post-economic world. It is fitting we open this special issue with something affirming of human evolution toward a higher consciousness. We may not make it in our academic lifetimes, but the goal is worth shooting for.

Len Tischler presents one very reasonable starting point for understanding the growing interest in business spirit—Maslow's notion that we have a basic need for self-transcendence. Tischler posits the notion that the long-term socioeconomic advance of modern society has allowed for an ever more conscious effort at self-actualization and self-transcendence. Thus, Tischler argues, both the modern individual and the evolving organization seek higher-order needs much in line with Maslow's hierarchy of needs. This is a good starting point for the scientific mind—the behaviorists and the mainstream academics who may have their doubts about the possibility of spirit impacting the workplace. The worlds of organizational psychology, self-actualization, and spiritual philosophy are bridged by the work of humanistic psychologists such as Maslow.

Tischler shows us the academic roots of the new interest in higher-order consciousness as the next step in human evolution (once basic human needs are met). Tischler believes conscious evolution can be applied to organizations.

Martin Rutte—in an updated article that first appeared in the popular business book *Heart at Work* by Jack Canfield and Jacqueline Miller —suggests that the nature and meaning of work are undergoing a profound evolution. Much of mainstream business literature, both popular and academic, accepts the thesis of constant change as an aspect of the late twentieth century, and certainly much the same or more so in the twenty-first century. Rutte observes fear in the workplace requiring a psychological and spiritual counterweight in order for people to maintain strength, balance, and meaning in their work. Rutte urges the business world to reinvent itself and provide a place of livelihood for people, rather than simply a job for mere survival. Rutte believes future work could invite people to express their full, creative spirit. This may supply competitive advantage to systems and organizations that unleash this latent potential within each of us.

As if to prove the point on the diversity of assumptions surrounding spiritual values and work, Dan Butts raises the challenge to researchers of the necessity of considering the macroeconomic and political aspects of organizational power. Butts suggests that it is not enough to find personal meaning in work, or for the organization to be a jazzed-up, winning team. The long-term impact on the total society and the planet must be factored into a compete and far-seeing spirituality of work. Few business writers have included these considerations. This short essay invites symposia between organizational theory, business social responsibility, political economy, and a desirable political philosophy for the future. Where do we begin? Maybe with theories of socioeconomic evolution which mold human behavior and consciousness. Maybe by linking the needs of the human community and planet earth with organization vision and goals.

Brenda Freshman has undertaken one of the most extensive analyses in the existing literature of definitions of spirituality, and where and how these terms are used. She uses qualitative analysis procedures, network analysis, and a grounded theory process to explore the relationships between concepts, definitions, and applications of this somewhat new business language. She brings the world of professional psychology to the literature of workplace spirituality. Her work may only begin to satisfy the observer skeptic who requires a highly quantitative approach to all academic subjects. But it is a beginning, and there is much quantitative data that could be included in the shortened paper that is published here. Indeed, she suggests researchers of spirituality in organizations be highly inclusive of virtually all definitions of spirit, remain very open-minded toward all approaches, and recognize that there may not be only one correct answer to the need for spirit in the workplace.

Lois Hogan compares the spirituality and work literature with related themes in organizational development and change management. She suggests a very useful application of spirituality principles into organizational consulting, leadership, and the everyday reality of business as we know it. It may be helpful for academic readers and students to see a thoughtful practitioner access the real-world utility of all this theory and inspiration.

David Boje calls for a new worldview for business and economics. He calls it "festivalism" to distinguish it from the systems of the past and present. Boje believes it is possible and desirable to cultivate the core value of harmlessness or nonviolence toward work and economics.

He believes production and consumption can be more balanced and humane with the principle of harmlessness or "ahimsa." Boje provides a vision for an alternative to our current economic system, an alternative that seems to contain the implicitly selfless, spiritual values implied in most of the visionary essays selected for this reader. Maybe the next step will be to connect the personal, inner work which has motivated much of the early literature in the field of spirituality and work to the cosmological vision of global thinkers, philosophers, and political economists who are attempting to shape the global future. In the end, reinventing the individual, the organization, and the total environment will be integral to the spiritual future of work.

Elmer Burack begins the important task of integrating key behavioral ideas and models, ranging from Maslow to McGregor, with the growing acceptance of the utility of workplace spirituality. Burack addresses the reinvention of organizations and the application of theory Y leadership to organization culture. Case examples are presented from Hewlett-Packard, Tom's of Maine, and the Ford Motor Company. Burack argues that with the pace of workplace design and change initiatives, managers are refocusing on the human aspects of work. He reminds us of the extent of scholarly interest in benchmarking firms which attempt to inject or retain elements of soul in organization—even if it's not actually called that in most cases.

Paul Gibbons provides a working definition of spirituality, along with a discussion of needed measures, assumptions, and validity claims current in this new literature. Gibbons urges more collaboration with other disciplines outside business education to help build better, more complete theoretical frameworks. He also raises many serious questions yet to be thoroughly researched and incorporated into the spirituality paradigm. Could the corporate leadership simply co-opt the workable and exploitive possibilities of work attitude for continued world dominance? Do the post-modernists and scholars in critical management studies have a valid critique of the lack of adequate incorporation of political economy and political sociology into the visionary paradigm of business spirituality? All of these questions suggest the need for more cross-disciplinary research. Can segregated academic disciplines make the necessary connections in theory and research? This reader is a far cry from serious coverage of macroeconomic futures or power structure research.

The Individual Within Organizations

The academic interest in workplace spirituality actually has most of its roots in the vast and longstanding literature of consciousness, self-actualization, and self-transformation. The selections contained in this category reflect the renewed belief in the importance of healthy spirituality to individuals within organizations. This has been increasingly accepted by business leadership and most organizational theorists. Stephen Covey's *Seven Habits of Highly Effective People* is a current, mainstream example of the popularity of this insight. Business higher education has long stressed self-motivation, stewardship, and work as vocation and duty. The case for spirituality as a vital part of individual and organizational health is seen as the key to connecting the cry of the human heart for meaning in work with the soul in organization which is addressed in our third segment of articles.

Sandra King and Dave Nicol have developed a formula for addressing the split between the demands of work and the cry of our souls for life expression. They argue that the requisite organization of the future will require continuing enhancement through recognition of individual spirituality. King and Nicol have drawn on the work of Elliot Jaques, a systems theorist and management guru, and Carl Jung, who championed self-completion in life. They believe that both Jaques and Jung provide complementary insights on how meeting basic human needs for meaning in work results in organizational benefits as well. Jung convincingly establishes our understanding of mans search for meaning throughout work life. Jaques provides a practical, total system for effective managerial organization and managerial leadership for the twenty-first century.

While many of the scholars of this newly developing field such as Neal, Banner, and Lichtenstein suggest that a sweeping paradigm shift is underway, the essay by Gerald Cavanagh, identifies longstanding ways that spirituality enables businesspeople to gain a more integrated life perspective on their work and career. Cavanagh documents the growing interest in this topic among professors, professionals, and business leaders. He argues convincingly that spirituality is a vital asset to individuals, organizations, and society. Simply put, it helps people treat themselves and others properly. That, Cavanagh argues, is why more managers and firms are encouraging spirituality in the workplace. Cavanagh offers a strong case for bridging current ethical concerns in the here-and-now world of business to the higher aspirations of the best in world religion and spirituality. His agenda for business schools includes service learning, justice, spirituality, and faith. He observes that religiously oriented universities may provide a model for integrating spirituality and service into their mission. In this essay the reader can see the interrelationship of spirituality and religion as it plays itself out in work and higher education.

Abbass Alkhafaji discusses the issue of spirituality in the workplace from the point of view of a Muslim. He describes the conflict throughout history between the approaches of rationalists (mind embodied) and traditionalists (soul embodied), and contrasts both approaches with the messages of the divine prophets that call for reforms and a balance of the soul, mind, and body. He then explores how these issues apply to the role of management and to his own individual spiritual practice.

Ultimately, our beliefs and scholarship must be grounded in our teaching and consulting. Andre Delbecq provides a personal reflection on how his beliefs have affected his teaching and scholarship. Delbecq suggests that our deeply held values, often spiritual or religious, provide a foundation for our professional lives. Delbecq believes that his service and sense of mission has been grounded in his spiritual convictions. He believes our core values strengthen our teaching and provide meaning to our working lives. We believe similar essays could be written by faith-based scholars from any of the great spiritual traditions.

Grace Ann Rosile has a very down-to-earth approach to demonstrate the value and practicality of a major theme in almost all schools of spirituality—namely, connectedness. Rosile shows how appreciation of the natural world can improve individual and organizational effectiveness. Rosile shows how raising horses and loving animals provide profound lessons for all aspects of our life. She provides horse sense that any businessperson can understand and apply to their tasks or organization. Rosile offers us a simple, credible metaphor for wholeness in our personal and professional existence as well as the life of the organization. When spirituality is clearly and simply connected to the natural world and to our part in that natural world, we come to see that basic spirituality is just good horse sense.

Organizational and Societal Issues and Applications

Many of the following contributors realize the necessity of societal change as a precursor to macro-organizational changes. Only with a paradigm shift on a global level in economics and business philosophy and values can the assumptions which drive business organization be modified or upleveled to the realms of higher consciousness. Most of the academic writers seem to hold great faith in spiritual evolution creating a new consciousness in human society. Clearly, more inter-disciplinary work needs to be done on the relationship of political economy, global economics and politics, and cultural values as they affect and govern organizational values. Social justice, cosmology, and business ethics need to join the dialogue as well.

Dorothy Marcic argues for the long term desirability, perhaps necessity, of organizational hospitality for the good of humanity. She believes it is imperative for organizations to be hospitable to the human spirit. Marcic is among many of the contributors to this reader who call for a new paradigm in fundamental business values which might be best characterized as looking beyond the bottom line.

James Conley and Fraya Wagner-Marsh describe the basic attitudes and practices which allow the maintenance of a spiritually based culture. These fourth-wave attitudes include the self-awareness and personal development of organizational leaders, a basic honesty with self, and mutual trust and honesty with others. This must be accom-panied by an articulation of the organization's spiritually based philosophy. They illustrate the importance of the selection of personnel to match the corporation's spiritually based philosophy. Conley and Fraya Wagner-Marsh identify the need for organizational commitment to employees, as well as the resultant commitment to quality and service. Most importantly, they remind us that philosophic principles or consciousness and worldview are decisive to the spiritually based firm of the fourth wave.

Jerry Biberman, Michael Whitty, and Lee Robbins use the story of *The Wizard of Oz* as a metaphor to describe how balance and spirituality in an organization can lead to the organizational transformation generally sought by most authors in this new field of spirituality and work. While most writers address spirituality on the individual level, this article addresses spirituality on the macro-organization level by suggesting specific steps organizations can take to promote balance and spiritual values. The authors demonstrate how the ingredients for trans-formation are already available within organizations. Awareness, courage, heart, and will are the keys to success in achieving the paradigm shift sought and predicted by many of the authors in this reader. *The Wizard of Oz* is a metaphor for the human journey through life. If that is so, in terms of basic virtues and life's negative qualities as well, then perhaps, argue Biberman, Whitty, and Robbins, this morality tale can be applied to organizational life as well. To inspire the reader, the authors have focused on positive trends in new work values which offer hope to those seeking a deeper meaning in work than provided by the dominant value system of greed, excessive competition, and alienation from our fellow worker and the world around us. The authors also hope that the use of metaphors and storytelling proves a useful complement to the tidal wave of popular and academic studies currently available to businesses and to higher education. It may take something simple and well understood by all—such as the folk story of *The Wizard of Oz*—to reach the mainstream work culture with the good news. Systems that work in a balanced way with all aspects of human potential and our conscious evolution will best serve the future holistic, sustainable, global economy. Nothing less meets our human destiny and the needs of the planet.

Gregory Konz and Francis Ryan address the question of maintaining organizational spirituality over time. They admit this is no easy task. Konz and Ryan offer existing spiritual work culture as a model for attempted development and maintenance of spirituality. Suggesting that vision and mission are a practical starting point for empirical research into the impact of values on organizational cultures, they have looked at the mission statements of the Jesuit colleges and universities in the United States. While acknowledging the trends in business toward spirituality and the very strong commitment of Jesuit institutions to spirituality, Konz and Ryan remind the reader of the great difficulty in maintaining a convincing spirituality in everyday work life. High-minded theory (and theology) is one thing, but everyday consciousness and consideration is quite another.

Stephen Porth, John McCall, and Thomas Bausch offer a more recent mainstream example of new management paradigms reaching the doorway to spirit in organization. These authors look to the concept of the learning organization as evolving toward themes which are potentially spiritual. They see a convergence between basic ethics and contemporary management theory. The learning organization will arrive at an understanding that organizational virtues make better business sense than allowing negative qualities to grow. Learning common sense in the workplace may reaffirm old values. The theory in business social responsibility literature is that good ethics is good business (at least in the long run). These authors, by using a well-established consultants model—the learning organization—show the mainstream practitioners of these topics a good, realistic point of departure for further study. Organization theory is starting to expand its notion of the possible human, and thereby the possibility of transforming organizational consciousness.

John Milliman, Jeffrey Ferguson, David Trickett and Bruce Condemi provide a concrete expression of community spirit in the workplace. They provide the case study of Southwest Airlines. These authors suggest that inspired leadership, determined to create and sustain community and caring in the workplace, can benefit the organization as well as the individual employee. They present a values-based model which argues that spiritual values can positively affect both employee attitudes and organizational effectiveness. In a very practical manner, they propose that the human resource function and the notion of workplace empowerment be aligned with the spiritual tone of the organizational culture. These scholars suggest that more research be conducted comparing the issues associated with economic performance and employee attitudes and their search for meaning in their work life.

Sandra King, Jerry Biberman, Lee Robbins, and David Nicol provide a brief history of the rising interest in spirituality in the workplace on the external, organizational, and individual levels. These authors argue for its legitimacy as a relevant and worthwhile part of work life. They are bringing this theme into their classrooms in various different ways, using many diverse approaches and techniques. Their surveys show many academics and many leading firms on the same trend line of integrating spirituality into management education and in the constantly changing world of business organizations.

Sandra Waddock provides a concrete application of Butt's thesis. Waddock calls for a basic modification of the competitive systems imbalance and the supremacy of raw, exploitative economics as king in the absence of community or spirit. She boldly suggests that a more humane workplace community will require far more collaboration and interconnectedness than the current hypercompetitive norms. Waddock believes Connectedness and a healthy interdependence are truly part of a communitarian organizational spirituality. That we are all in this together and should always be fully factored into the broader human work culture. Waddock adopts Ken Wilber's integrative framework to argue that we seek deeper meaning in work and that organizations are more successful if they address humankind's search for meaning in community and spirit. Waddock's work contributes to the dialogue seeking the restoration of human community at work and capitalism with a human face.

Dennis Heaton reminds us that a holistic lifestyle will bring many direct and indirect benefits to organizations as well as individuals. Heaton approaches the needs of management, organizations, and their employees from the holistic health perspective. Corporate wellness and health promotion are the terms in current use. Heaton can serve as an example of interdisciplinary scholarship connecting two often separate fields of study—that of health and that of management.

The Possible Future

The possible future is contained in this path-breaking reader. It is one of the first academic collections to thoroughly examine a major trend in human organization occurring in the new century. We may actually be documenting a paradigm shift in basic work values. Large systems and organizational processes have been undermined through cultural pathologies, addiction, and shadow. This is the modern paradigm—toxic stress and inequity in the name of profit. In light of this reality, a growing school of scholars, consultants, business journalists, and visionary business leaders have taken the road least traveled. On this yellow brick road we have encountered many cultural, political, and even technological obstacles. But, we as a business civilization in a new century are overcoming much of this, inch by inch, day by day. It is a process of cultural and societal growth into higher consciousness. Breakthrough points appear on the horizon despite the shadow of this present moment in business history. We are invited to heal the organizations within which we live. A basic workplace spirituality can be the common ground for the new work community. Working people and human evolution itself are constantly seeking meaning, purpose, and a sense of contribution to work life. These needs are best served and deepened when a spiritual paradigm frames the intentions of all stakeholders. Real human nourishment is provided by the soulful organization. Reframing the meaning of work has the support of the servant leaders worldwide who see that a life of service best fits the basic human need for relevance, recognition, meaning, and self-transcendence. These concluding essays are merely representative of a growing literature which advocates and predicts a period of fundamental and continuous change in human organizational values.

Mark Kriger and Bruce Hanson help remind us of the importance of universal core values to humane and trustworthy future organizations. Kriger and Hanson have conducted a survey of selected professionals to determine the basic qualities for healthy organizations. They identify twenty prerequisites for healthy organizations—ranging from honesty, humility, and encouraging liberating visions to honoring the whole person and aligning oneself with the organizational vision. Kriger and Hanson have created a set of normative propositions which make economic sense. They have opened a window to tapping human potential at higher levels than are common even in the most competitive organizational systems.

Jerry Biberman and Mike Whitty report a significant trend in business theory and practice which indicates a possible spiritual future for work. Their essay cites a representative selection of popular business titles and some early academic work which reinforce each other with arguments for the practical benefits of spirit-based core values for organizations. Biberman and Whitty believe the early part of the twenty-first century will witness a paradigm shift in underlying business philosophy. They forecast these megatrends in business and economics to result in a post-modern spiritual future for work.

Elizabeth Guss describes herself as a theologian of the workplace. Guss is a consultant, trainer, and job coach. She has used spirituality as a practical tool in her professional career in Utah. Again, the scholar or student can see a new paradigm from which to do work. A new way of integrating spirituality into our work lives. Guss believes that we gain wisdom when the human spirit is engaged. When both individuals and organizations find an integrated path or vision, each becomes more alive, aware, and effective. Thus, inner victory soon results in outer victory for people and their organizations.

Perhaps this reader will contribute, in some small way, to a paradigm shift in societal values toward a more soulful organizational ethos and ethics in the new century. Conscious evolution is contributing to this jump time in human and organizational transformation. We are all leaders in this jump time of organizational change of heart.

Most of the contributors to this collection come from the perspective of identifying or advocating an oncoming paradigm shift in business values. In the "Another View" piece which follows, David Boje describes the wide range of paradigms and metaphors used in the study of what he calls "Spiritual Capitalism." We share the view that more scholarship is needed to demonstrate the importance of spirituality to organizations, visionary leadership and global economics. We also appreciate the distinctions made by Boje with regard to the study of spirit in organizations. The mainstream business press is awash with the managerialist and free market/fundamentalist perspective on spirituality and religion. This collection breaks new ground and makes valuable contributions to the humanist, ecologist and affirmative postmodernist application of spirituality to the workplace. More work needs to be done by the skeptical postmodernists to be sure that we are not simply returning to Calvinism and he predatory capitalism which both spirituality and religion seek to transcend. Can spirituality give capitalism and its organizations a human face? For the sake of the common good, we hope so.

Special Thank you

We wish to thank Clifford McMurrary for his tireless efforts in preparing the manuscript for publication. Also, we would like to thank Richard W. Rousseau, S.J., Director, John Sinclair, Assistant Director, and Patricia Mecadon, Production Manager of the University of Scranton Press, the publisher of this book.

ANOTHER VIEW

APPROACHES TO THE STUDY OF SPIRITUAL CAPITALISM

David M. Boje

"Spiritual capitalism" is all the rage, but unless rigorous research, theory, and teaching takes place it will fade. Between 1992 and 1999, the *Journal of Organizational Change Management* (JOCM) alone published 68 articles that mentioned spirituality, of which 36 made it their focus (beginning with Bullis & Glaser, 1992).[1] Two of the special issues on spirit at work are included in this anthology. We are all grateful to MCB publishers for their support of this emerging field. In this preface, I would like to briefly list the paradigms and metaphors being applied in these issues and this anthology to the study of spiritual capitalism as affirmative or skeptical.

Let me begin with a 1997 JOCM article by Jerry Biberman and Michael Whitty in which they asserted that various writers were presenting an emergent postmodern management paradigm that emphasizes spiritual principles and practices and would become more widespread each year. They add "that the human relations movement, organization development, and its attendant concepts developed as a reaction to the prevailing modernist paradigm, and existed within it, rather than trying to create a new paradigm." The modernist paradigm has both a "humanist" and "managerialist" focus. Managerialists espouse a functionalist and enlightenment worldview in which even spirituality has its function in making business more profitable. There are other paradigms from which writers look to indigenous spiritual practices to revitalize ecology to erect "spiritual capitalism" in place of predatory capitalism enterprise (Karliner & Karliner; Mokhiber & Weissman, 1999). Steingard and Fitzgibbons (1995), for example, argue

---

[1] This statistic was established using MCB publishers' online search engine using a key word search on "Spirit" (which includes spirituality and reading the context of the 68 articles).

that global capitalism is a spiritually flawed discourse that is not ecologically sustainable. Butts (1997) is outraged at the selfishness, greed, and mean-spirited, winner-take-all scapegoating (class warfare) inflicted on the working class and other disfranchised social groups. And Walck (1995) is cautious about spirituality, reminding us that our global discourse ignores the "spirituality" of the poor. Christian spirituality played a major role in native genocide. It therefore makes sense to look at alternative paradigms to see both the good and evil of any spirituality movement. What I would like to do is arrange several of the paradigms mentioned by these JOCM authors into a map (see Figure 1 below).

FIGURE 1

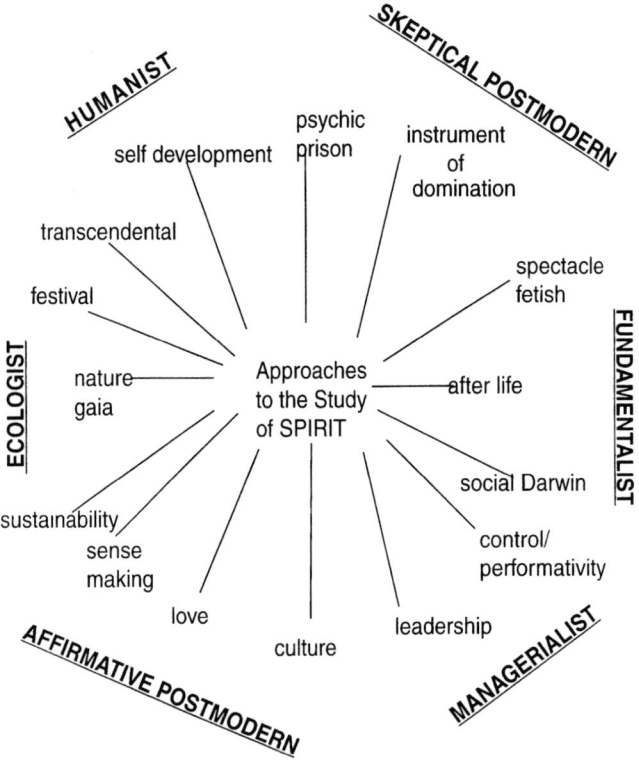

Figure 1. Paradigms and metaphors in the study of spiritual capitalism.

Six of the many paradigms in the study of spiritual capitalism are paired as follows: affirmative and skeptical postmodern, fundamentalist and ecological, and managerialist and humanist (see Figure 1). Each offers different metaphors to spirit. To some spirit is the metaphor of love, festival, transcendence, and self-development (Marcic, 1997). But to other paradigms, spirit is the metaphor of the "psychic prison" and the "instrument of domination" or the privileging of rich over poor class in Herbert Spencer's "Social Darwinism." Höpfl (1994), for example, contends that organizations imitate religious forms and invoke even the "Holy Spirit" to exploit through demands for submission, obedience, and control. She adds "management evangelists and various other prophets of management have engaged in an unreflective or opportunistic rhetoric of change management."

For the affirmative postmodernists, spirit is simply "love" and "sense making" at work. For the skeptical postmodernists, spirit can be a form of "psychic prison" or an "instrument of domination." For the managerialists spirit is a form of "control," a way to increase "performativity" through greater commitment, and something "leaders" do with their sense of vision and mission. To the ecologist, spirit is the "Gaia," the living nature of Mother earth and the cosmos. JOCM writers have posited a relation between environment and the spiritual value of the land as well as the spiritual, not just economic, needs of citizens (Bullis & Glaser, 1992; Stead & Stead, 1994: Upadhyaya, 1995). Christa Walck (1996), for example, writes about organizations being seen through the metaphor of "spiritual places." However, to the religious fundamentalist, spirit is the promise of the "afterlife," or next life and to some it is still a very "Social Darwinian" notion of the blessedness of being born rich and the curse of the poor threatens the survival of the human species. Between these six paradigms, there are metaphors that are between two or more paradigms (e.g., spectacle, culture, transcendental). Spirit is a way to reinvigorate "culture" with a more enlightened capitalism for the affirmative postmodernists. And "culture" is a way to invoke higher levels of functional performance, control, and leadership for the managerialist paradigm. Between affirmative postmodernist and ecologist paradigms is the sustainability movement. And between the humanist and ecologist paradigms is "transcendental" and "festival" metaphors of spirit. And between the skeptical postmodernist and fundamentalist paradigms are the metaphors of spectacle and religious fetish. My point in displaying this array of spirit metaphors and paradigms is to give the reader some idea of the many worldviews that are doing work in the study of spirit in the workplace and in the theater of global capitalism. With this map, I can now say something about the various writings on spirit in JOCM and in this anthology. This book does something important that the mushrooming lists of books on spiritual capitalism are not doing.[2] That is, Gerald Biberman and Mike Whitty have brought together a rich array of paradigms and metaphors on spiritual capitalism.

Of all the metaphors in Figure 1, the "culture" approach to spirituality gets the most play in 1999. Porth and McCall (1999), for example, are almost affirmatively postmodern in seeing some convergence and divergence between the learning organization culture model and traditional spiritual understandings of employees and organizations. King and Nicol (1999) argue a functionalist paradigm in that management can recognize the potential for mutual benefit in the nexus of the individual's spiritual odyssey and the overall health of the organization culture. Milliman, Ferguson, Trickett, and Condemi (1999) look at the cultural spirit of Southwest Airlines culture. In the age of downsizing, Southwest, for example, announced the Love Airline has a no-layoffs policy and integrated what the authors see as spiritual values throughout the corporate culture. Fraya Wagner-Marsh and James Conley (1999) see the bold spiritual corporate culture writers surfing the fourth wave of Peter Vaill's (1989) permanent white water. But Burack (1999), to me, like so many writers of the culture metaphor, seeks to reinscribe Theory Y and Z, Maslow, corporate culture, and everything else with spirituality.

After culture, the humanist position is prominent. Biberman, Whitty, and Robbins (1999) look at the implications of the *Wizard of Oz* story for spiritual transformation. Kriger and Hanson (1999) quest with appreciation inquiry for the value paradigm, positing that a truly healthy organization can overcome the spiritual disease of fanaticism, isolation, separation, and illusion by letting go of delusions and aspiring to enact what is highest and most uplifting to the "human spirit."

---

[2] See, for example, *Servant Leadership* (Greenleaf, 1977; Melrose, 1995), *Spirit at Work or in the Workplace* (Sproul, 1980; Hawley, 1993; Scherer & Shook, 1993; Conger, 1994; Gozdz, 1995; Schechter, 1995; Guillory, 1997), *Leading with Soul* (Bolman & Deal, 1995), *The Soul of a Business* (Chappell, 1993), *Soul in the Workplace* (Briskin, 1996; Canfield & Hansen, 1996; Renesch & DeFoore, 1996), *Managing with the Wisdom of Love* (Marcic, 1997), *The Fourth Wave* (Maynard & Mehrtens, 1993), and spiritual leadership books by Covey (1989, 1994).

While there is much that is affirmative and appreciative in the functionalist, managerialist, ecological, and humanist approaches to spiritual capitalism, there are paradigms that are critical of the nouveau spirituality-based philosophies of business. In particular, the new books and articles of JOCM, as well as other journals and teaching seminars, may offer the aura of spiritual transformation of work and society, while masking the material conditions and three important needs.[3]

Cavanagh (1999), in my view, takes a refreshingly critical view of the spirituality movement. He approaches the skepticism of the critical postmodernist. He sees spirituality growing in emphasis as a backlash to the downsizing craze (as did Burack, 1999), the number of 1960s baby-boomers who are now writing, and our imminent change to a new millennium. Cavanagh is skeptical about mixing the New Age movement in spirituality with the good old-time religions. And he questions how "both Evangelical Christianity and the spirituality in business movements" legitimate a "person-centered individualism." And given the diversity of spiritual practices, from humanist, fundamentalist, to New Age ecologist, in a complex organization, there can be hegemonic consequences as some spiritual practices gain power in the workplace over others. This brings me to three closing challenges to spiritual capitalism writers.

First, there is a need for more basic (I recommend ethnographic as well as additional self-reflective) research before we integrate spirituality with other popular consulting models. Neal, Lichtenstein, and Banner (1999) assert that spirituality can transform and transcend the individual, organization, and society. They posit that incorporating spirituality into our theorizing can improve our explanations. Freshman (1999) is a good example of beginning to do the research. She published the results of an exploratory content analysis of various uses and definitions of the word *spirituality* and used the software program AtlasTI to assist with coding functions and to help draw graphic networks of relationships between her codes. She suggested that more research is needed on the community of scholars who are using the term *spirituality* in so many varied ways. This research is exceedingly rare.

---

[3] There are two journals devoted just to spirit at work *(Spirit at Work* and *Business Spirit).* The 1998 Academy of Management meeting overflowed with spiritual capitalism. Cavanagh (1999) comments that the 1998 theme was "What matters most?" and hosted seven symposia (six were showcase sessions) that explicitly discussed spirituality and/or religion.

Another example is Kaplan (1995), who did a study of the spiritual journey of several women consultants. Other research takes a more self-reflective approach to method and theory. Konz and Ryan (1999) did a study of the mission statements of the 28 United States Jesuit universities and revealed that maintaining an organizational spirituality is no easy task. They argue that both individuals and organizations have spirituality and that "it is easier to maintain the established spirituality of an organization than it is to change an organization's spirituality. At the same time, it is not easy to maintain an organization's spirituality." And besides content and empirical studies, there are important self-reflective studies begun in JOCM. Louis (1994), for example, studied Quaker spiritual practices and was self-reflective of her own Quaker practices. *Spirit Hawk* (1994), the collaborative collective writing voices of Susan M. Schor, Kathleen Kane, and Cindy Lindsay,[4] is as Barrett (1996) comments, "a courageous, revealing exploration into personal transformation and social change." Like Louis, *Spirit Hawk* uses self-reflection to explore and theorize "spiritual deprivation," "feeling from a spiritual center," listening to the "voice of spirit," losing one's "spiritual connection," and bringing spiritual insight and connection into one's daily work life. *Spirit Hawk* succeeded in being self-reflective and cautious. Finally, in this anthology, Butts (1999) speaks to the theory-building issues: "Spirituality at work is an idea of revolutionary potential that requires more clarity and theoretical understanding."

Second, we need to understand why spiritual capitalism is becoming so popular in particular societies. Here, Tischler (1999), using a humanist paradigm, sees the soaring interest in spirituality in business as a phenomenon explainable by Maslow's hierarchy of needs, where self-actualization is a luxury that United States and Euro economies can enjoy while most of the world is caught up in the need to survive. Similarly, Burack (1999) also sees the spirituality movement as a backlash to what he terms the "economic-technological imperative" of downsizing and reengineering and he also embraces Maslow. More research in this area would help.

Third, there is a need to raise questions about teaching spirituality in the business college. Waddock (1999), for example, argues that "if we hope to influence teaching, scholarship, and practice, and if com-

---

[4] As they put it, "The name *Spirit Hawk* is derived from the experience the three of us have with one another which includes our intellectual, physical, emotional and spiritual selves and the presence of hawks flying overhead."

munity is one of the elements on the subjective side of life that reflects spirit, then we need to make it acceptable in our teaching to build small communities." This is easier said than done. For example, Cavanagh (1999) suggests, the service-learning movement, the pet project of the year 2000 Academy, is happening with a missionary zeal that will surely lead to backlash as people see parallels to religious and service missions. Will students understand why they are being sent on such missions? Finally, Delbecq (1999) is among a legion of theorists turned spiritualists. Delbecq uses a Christian, almost fundamentalist definition of spirituality and service that is no doubt a good fit to senior executives in Silicon Valley, but may not be amenable to a wider variety of spiritual practices. His definition of spirituality embeds service in a test: "My test of authenticity is the extent to which progress in the spirit of journey manifests itself in loving and compassionate service." Yet if we hold up the history of capitalism to this same test, I am not sure we would pass. We also need research on how to teach spirituality in non-religious institutions. For teaching spirituality is a bit easier in Jesuit and other religious universities with a spirit mission than in public universities (I can say this from experience).

In conclusion, I am asking for more rigor in the way we theorize, research, and teach spirituality, lest we become a passing fad and do more harm than good. I am excited that JOCM was among the first journals to take spirituality seriously and prouder still to say that collectively this anthology represents a healthy debate among the paradigms and metaphors in Figure 1. As Biberman, Whitey, and Robbins (1999) remind us, "without spirituality the normative purpose of business is profit." Yet spirituality could bring balance to an otherwise predatory capitalism. Namasté!

References not in the 1999 JOCM issues

Barrett, Frank J. (1995), "Finding Voice Within the Gender Order," *Journal of Organizational Change Management 8 (6)*, 8–15.

Biberman, Jerry, & Michael Whitty (1997), "A Postmodern Spiritual Future for Work," *Journal of Organizational Change Management 10 (2)*, 130–138.

Bullis, Connie, & Hollis Glaser (1992), "Bureaucratic Discourse and the Goddess: Towards an Ecofeminist Critique and Rearticulation," *Journal of Organizational Change Management 5, (2)*.

Butts, Dan (1997), "Joblessness, Pain, Power, Pathology and Promise," *Journal of Organizational Change Management 10 (2)*, 111–129.

Höpfl, Heather (1994), "The Paradoxical Gravity of Planned Organizational Change," *Journal of Organizational Change Management 7 (5)*, 20–31.

Kaplan, Kathy L. (1995), "Women's Voices in Organizational Development: Questions, Stories, and Implications." *Journal of Organizational Change Management 8 (1)*, 52–80.

Louis, Meryl Reis (1994), "In the Manner of Friends: Learnings from Quaker Practice for Organizational Renewal." Special Issue, "Spirituality in Organizations." *Journal of Organizational Change Management 7 (1)*, 42–60.

Marcic, D. (1997), *Managing with the Wisdom of Love: Uncovering Virtue in People and Organizations*, Jossey-Bass, San Francisco, CA.

Spirit Hawk (1995), "Three Women's Stories of Feeling, Reflection, Voice and Nurturance: From Life to Consulting." *Journal of Organizational Change Management 8 (6)*, 39–57. Gender and Voices Special Issue.

Stead, W. Edward, & Jean Garner Stead (1994), "Can Humankind Change the Economic Myth? Paradigm Shifts Necessary for Ecologically Sustainable Business." *Journal of Organizational Change Management 7 (4)*, 15–31.

Steingard, David S., & Dale E. Fitzgibbons (1995), "Challenging the Juggernaut of Globalization: A Manifesto for Academic Praxis." *Journal of Organizational Change Management 8 (4)*, 30–54.

Upadhyaya, Punya (1995), "The Sacred, the Erotic and the Ecological: The Politics of Transformative Global Discourses." *Journal of Organizational Change Management 8 (5)*, 33–59.

Walck, Christa L. (1995), "Global Ideals, Local Realities: The Development Project and Missionary Management in Russia." *Journal of Organizational Change Management 8 (4)*, 69–84.

Walck, Christa L. (1996), "Organizations as Places: A Metaphor for Change." *Journal of Organizational Change Management 9 (6)*, 26–40.

Weber, Max (Darth) (1958), *The Protestant Ethic and the Spirit of Capitalism*. NY: Charles Scribner's Sons.

Theoretical Perspectives

GLOW

by Tom Brown

The human race
Now runs in place,
Exclaiming, "Little
We don't know!"

Yet mark its path,
Count all it hath;
One truth's been lost:
We are born to glow.

We started out from land untamed,
From boundless rock and root.
Only man could see
Past trunks of trees,
Through river's roar;
Creating, we did grow.

On farms, in mines,
From seas to timberlines,
We shovelled, cast, and cut,
Our progress never slowed.

Till now.
We've trounced this planet's wealth
And claimed it as our own.

And every house and every car,
Each creature comfort known —
Yes, every shoe and every phone —
Shouts our presence home.

We've made the world
Reflect ourselves:
Our wishes ceaseless flow.
The human mind,

3

Stretched enterprise-wide,
Hungers still to grow.

Then doubt not that —
From infant wiggle
To elder amble slow —
Within each breast
The spark *is* there.
We are born to glow.

The human mark,
How we most shine,
Exceeds accounting line.
Accrue? Create?
Don't hesitate.
We are born to glow.

On mankind's cake
Our time is marked
By candles,
The progress show.

Each new Age
Inspires a wish —
Each wish a gift —
'Cross wax alit,
It blows and blows.

But wax snuffed out
Is not the flame
Tomorrow yearns to know.

What was the wish?
What was the wish?
We are born to glow.

—from *The Anatomy of Fire: Sparking a New Spirit of Enterprise*
by Tom Brown ©2000 by MANAGEMENT GENERAL
http://www.mgeneral.com

SPIRITUAL PERSPECTIVES ON INDIVIDUAL, ORGANIZATIONAL AND SOCIETAL TRANSFORMATION

Judith A. Neal,
University of New Haven

Benjamin M. Bergmann Lichtenstein,
University of Hartford

David Banner,
Renaissance Consulting Associates

Why must anyone seek for new ways of acting? The answer is that in the long run the continuity of life itself depends on the making of new experiments. . . . The continuous invention of new ways of observing is man's special secret of living.
(Young, 1960, quoted in Vaill, 1984: 18)

Management literature is replete with discussions about the need for individual, organizational, and societal transformation (c.f. Adams, 1984; Fox, 1994; Harman & Hormann, 1990; Hawken, 1993; Henderson, 1996; Maynard & Mehrtens, 1996; Owen; 1997, Yukl, 1994). In general these authors argue that the pace of change is increasing, and that in order to keep pace with it, individual, organizational, and global transformation is required. Individual transformation is needed because managers and leaders must be proactive leaders, open to change, and flexible enough to adapt to constantly shifting demands from their organizations. Organizations must transform because of the shift to the global marketplace, increased competitiveness, and the rapid acceleration of change. Societal transformation must occur because of environmental degradation, shifts in economic power, inequalities in distribution of wealth, and unsolved social problems such as discrimination and illiteracy.

5

For all these reasons, interest in transformation has become widespread. For most practitioners and management educators, the focus of interest is economic. In order to justify investing in any transformational processes, most managers focus on the bottom-line effects of transforming their organizations, emphasizing increased performance, increased profits, and reduced costs from transformation. Additionally, empirical research on organizational transformation (e.g., Romanelli & Tushman, 1994) and industry punctuations (e.g., Tushman & Anderson, 1986) has also focused on the performance impacts of transformative change. These perspectives are based on the competitive and economic value of major rapid change at the organizational and industry-wide level.

But is this what really matters most in transformation? Not all management scholars believe so. According to an important and growing stream of research, the core benefits of transformation are not economic, yet are critical to the success of individuals, organizations, and society. It is the non-material, even spiritual qualities of transformation that may be the most profound for individuals, organizations and society. At the individual level, increased attention on personal meaning and transformative leadership has shown striking benefits of integrating personal development and awareness in everyday work (Torbert, 1991; Whyte, 1994). Numerous recent books have emphasized the dramatic increase in interest in incorporating spirituality into management theory, management development, and management practice (Neal, 1997; Renesch & DeFoore, 1996). The titles of some of these books suggest ways in which individual, organizational, and global transformation can be integrated: *Managing with the Heart* (Bracey, Rosenblum, Sanford & Trueblood, 1990); *The Soul of a Business: Managing for Profit and the Common Good* (Chapell, 1993); *Leading with Soul: An Uncommon Journey of Spirit* (Bolman & Deal, 1995); *Managing with the Wisdom of Love: Uncovering Virtue in People and Organizations* (Marcic, 1997).

A similar argument is being voiced at the organizational level. For example, in their longitudinal research on 18 "visionary" companies which have been leaders in their industries for over 50 years, Collins and Porras (1994) show that each company's success was due to a focus on core values, not solely on the bottom line, although the core values of these organizations were based on non-economic beliefs and an empowering culture—in economic terms they outperformed their comparison companies by as much as 16:1. Peters and Waterman (1982) found much the same thing in their research on "excellent" companies. Globally, recent insights from the natural sciences have shown the world to be an individual whole, a web of relationships in which any action has complex, non-linear, and unpredictable effects (Gleick, 1987; Capra, 1996). Accepting the veracity of this research requires a shift in how we perceive and experience our world. This shift brings the values of environmental sustainability, social equality, and global awareness to the forefront of our attention, recognizing that at its essence, management is much more than an economic endeavor (e.g., Gladwin, Kennelly & Krause, 1995). Moreover, spirituality and consciousness, far from being "far out" and irrational, have been found to be at the core of dynamic evolutionary systems, and thus must be included in our analysis and practice of organizational design and change (Ackerman, 1984; Banner & Gagne, 1995).

This paper presents three theoretical perspectives that incorporate a spiritual perspective in understanding transformation processes at different levels of analysis.

Individual Transformation: A Stage Model of Spiritual Evolution

Our model of individual transformation is based on in-depth open-ended interviews with 40 people from different walks of life. These include a coffee grower, a duplicating clerk, a CEO of a non-profit, a female train attendant for Amtrak, a surgeon, a fitness trainer, an unemployed computer programmer, a corporate magician, a dentist and his dental assistant. Some of the questions were:

1. Tell me a little bit about your work background and your career choices. What role, if any, has spirituality played in the career choices you have made?
2. How did you come to be interested in integrating spirituality and work?
3. Tell me about a particularly satisfying or meaningful time when you were able to practice one or more of your principles, values, or beliefs at work.
4. Tell me about a time when you had difficulty integrating your spirituality and your work.

5. What are the costs and benefits to you of focusing more on
    spirituality in your workplace?

Data for this theory also came from a facilitated online discussion
group on spirituality in the workplace that lasted for three years, with an
average membership of 150 people and over 700 informal conversations
with people interested in work as a spiritual path. The majority are from
the United States, but there is also the CEO of Meteorological Services
in New Zealand, a Ninja master from Sweden, and consultants and
academics from Australia, Norway, England, and Canada.

In our qualitative analysis of these data (Strauss & Corbin, 1993),
several themes were revealed. One of the key learnings is the
widespread interest in integrating spirituality and work. This interest
exists in sole proprietorships, small businesses, and at all levels of large
corporations; in non-profit, for-profit, governmental and religious
organizations. It also appears to be occurring in individuals in most of
the industrialized countries and is not just limited to the United States.
The types of careers where it seems to be most widespread are
consulting, education, and health care. In spite of the growing interest,
most of the people who are consciously integrating their spirituality and
their work feel very alone and have difficulty finding others to talk to
about this process.

This model addresses: (1) what seems to trigger a spiritual transformation in people, (2) the process of integrating the transformation
into one's work, and (3) the effects that this transformation has on their
relationship to their work. For example, some of the typical "causal
factors" of spiritual transformation are: a spiritual crisis such as a life-
threatening illness, a divorce, losing one's job, a profound spiritual
experience that is the result of a near-death experience, a personal
epiphany experience related to being in a sacred place, being alone in
silence for an extended time, and being in nature.

According to the data, once a spiritual transformation is triggered
in an individual, he or she seeks to integrate that transformation into
their life. In terms of their work life, the integration of spiritual
transformations appears to unfold in three stages:

1. Dark night of the soul, where previous life anchors no longer
    have any meaning
2. Spiritual searching, a search for new core spiritual principles

3. Spiritual integration, learning to apply those principles in key aspects of one's life, including work

For most people, the effects of this process on their relationship to their work is to find new meaning in their work, a renewed and inspired commitment to performance through service, and a deepening of the valuing of relationships in the workplace. However, for some people the transformation process creates a severe conflict between the culture of the organization and individual needs for spiritual development. In this case people tend to leave their jobs, either physically or emotionally. It appears that an increasing number of those who are leaving are starting their own businesses where they feel freer to live their spiritual principles more openly.

In summary, interest in spirituality in the workplace is fairly widespread; however, there is little empirical research published on this topic. The research reported here begins to provide a basic understanding of specific qualities of individual spiritual transformations, and the process by which individuals integrate these transformations into their work.

Organizational Transformation: The Trans-Rational Logic of Corporate Change

In the same way that individual transformation is often "non-rational" or non-linear, so organizational transformation can display similar characteristics. Although from the outside organizational change may seem to follow a distinct logic that appears orderly, exploring the transformative experience from within groups and organizations provides a much different model. To identify the experiential qualities of major corporate change, a research project was designed to explore the moment of transformation by consultants who have successfully supported organizations in top management teams, business units, and whole companies. In order to understand the commonalities between theory and practice in organizational transformation, the practitioners chosen for the research were individuals who had also developed specific theories of organizational transformation, which they used to guide their practice. In-depth interviews were taken from three practitioner-theorists—Peter Senge, Bill Torbert, and Ellen Wingard—and data analysis focused on each person's logical use of their theory across several interventions, and how that compared with their description of the actual moment of organizational transformation. More details of the study are reported in Lichtenstein, 1997.

Spirit was not at the core of any of their change theory, and none of their case studies was related to spirituality per se. Yet a marvelous if puzzling finding was revealed through qualitative analysis of nearly a dozen specific examples of organizational transformation. In each one, the practitioner/theorist uses their theory to diagnose and design the initial stages of a change process. Their theory provides a rational logic for pushing the organization to the brink of transformation, and the theory offers logical tools to support the overall effort. Yet, in all cases the transformations they helped generate were sparked not through rational efforts at all: the actual "cause" of transformation, according to the data, was expressed by these practitioner/theorists in terms of "grace" (Ellen Wingard), "magic" (Peter Senge), and "a miracle" (Bill Torbert).

How can we explain these findings? By definition the terms "grace," "magic," and "miracles" identify phenomena that cannot be scientifically or logically explained. Formally grace is defined as "unmerited divine assistance," magic means "an extraordinary influence seemingly from a supernatural source," and miracle is defined as "an extraordinary event manifesting divine intervention in human affairs" (Websters, 1996). These words connote a felt sense of going beyond theory and rational action, suggesting that the actual transformation is out of the (rational) control of the practitioner. That is, as the theory is stretched to its limit, what actually sparks the transformation is somehow unreachable through logic, not tied to rationality. What then can be the explanation of this process?

Answering this question is especially crucial, since the widespread expansion of transformation and spirituality at work requires some explanation and theory. One way to understand this combination of rational and "trans-rational" logic is through theories of chaos and self-organization, which provide new ways to model the non-linear, complex behavior of dynamic systems (Gleick, 1987; Goerner, 1994; Goldstein, 1994); they have begun to be extended to organizations (e.g., Thietart & Forgues, 1995; Youngblood, 1997).

Chaos and self-organization can link with more mainstream theories to provide an explanation for the non-material elements of organizational transformation. According to these case studies, there is a logical framework that produces rational actions in the first stages of an intervention effort. However, at a critical threshold it is non-linear logic and spontaneously felt action—what these individuals termed "grace," "magic," and "miracles"—that actually supports organizational (and personal) transformation. Theories of chaos and self-organization can integrate the deductively logical and non-linear aspects of this process, through understanding the dynamics of far-from-equilibrium dynamical systems. These complex systems show how seemingly random events occur as high degrees of order, and why unexpected events can become amplified into new regimes of order that increase the capacity and functionality of the organizational system.

As such, these new models may also suggest a response to the question of whether economics or spirit is more important in organizational transformation. Namely, the cause of transformation may indeed be spirit, yet the result may indeed be an increase in effectiveness and productivity within the system.

Transformation at the Societal Level

The two previous sections of this paper focus on the micro (individual) and group (organizational) process of transformation. Now, let's look at the macro (societal) perspective. At this level of analysis, we can say that the "building blocks" of societal transformation are individual and group transformation. One way to describe this process of aggregation from individuals and organizations to societal transformation is through the "hundredth monkey" phenomenon (Keyes, 1983). According to this research, in 1952, a group of scientists were providing a group of Japanese monkeys (macaca fuscata) with sweet potatoes dropped in the sand. The monkeys liked the sweet potatoes, but disliked the grit of the sand. So, one monkey took the potatoes down to the stream and washed them off before eating them. The monkey taught this trick to her mother, and so it went . . . monkey after monkey teaching other monkeys to wash the potatoes before eating.

Then, an amazing event occurred. After a certain critical mass of monkeys were washing their potatoes (say, 99 monkeys), the next monkey to learn this process caused it to instantaneously be transmitted not only into the entire monkey tribe on that island, but to all monkeys in nearby islands. The added energy of this "hundredth monkey" somehow created a breakthrough of transformational proportions. Dr. Rupert Sheldrake has proposed a theory to explain this phenomenon (Sheldrake, 1986). Collective belief patterns form what he calls "morphogenetic fields," which are actually habits of thought, and these maintain a relative permanence through what he calls "morphic resonance," i.e., people agreeing with the belief add strength to the pattern and it becomes "fixed." But, if a critical mass of people begin thinking a different way, then a new field of belief is created and instantaneously transformation in thought (and therefore behavior) can occur. This work by Sheldrake is controversial within his discipline (biology), but it does give a new way to look at a process which often occurs outside the range explained by conventional change theory.

As mentioned earlier, chaos theory, systems theory, and the "new physics" have begun to inform management theory and practice (Senge, 1990; Jaworski, 1996; Wheatley, 1992; Youngblood, 1997). Terms such as dissipative structures, synchronicity, self-organizing systems, connectedness, and wholeness are becoming commonplace in management thought and practice. David Bohm uses these ideas in his description of physical reality as an "unbroken, seamless whole" where our perception of separateness is merely a habit of thought (Bohm, 1983). In other words, modern physics says we are part of a larger whole, interconnected with all life, but we experience ourselves as separate from each other and from Nature itself (Capra, 1996). So, the nature of "objective reality" in a very real sense is not the crucial issue—what matters most is our experience of reality. And that experience is created by our individual (and shared) paradigms (Morgan, 1986).

A culture promotes a particular cultural paradigm in its socialization processes. Once learned, this cultural paradigm becomes "the ways things are" and, as such, is basically unquestioned and assumed to be true (Banner & Gagne, 1995). Cognitive theory and Eastern mysticism have converged to declare that we, in fact, create our collective reality by agreement in thought, i.e., we see what we believe (Castenada, 1974; Dyer, 1993). So, a good question to ask at this point is this: What is the nature of the dominant societal belief pattern that has created our experience of reality?

Four main beliefs tend to dominate our cultural paradigm and, therefore, our experience of reality (Hotchkiss, 1996). These beliefs are: (1) I am a body (our main focus is on health, feeling good, avoiding disease, etc., and my experience of life is dominated by my experience of my body and its limitations); (2) I am guilty (either due to religion —"original sin"—or through guilt programming from parents and others, we get the idea that we are deeply guilty); (3) I am separate (we believe that we as individuals are set loose at birth to fend for ourselves in a hostile universe); and (4) I am incomplete (in and of ourselves, we are inadequate and we need to add material possessions, degrees, titles, etc., or a marriage partner to make ourselves whole). These dominant beliefs lead us to concluding that we are unsafe in the world and that we must control everything to get what we want (or to avoid unwanted outcomes) (Schaef & Fassel, 1988). This control assumption leads us to addiction and to what writers are now calling the power-over or dominance paradigm (Banner & Gagne, 1995; Breton & Largent, 1996). Up until the fairly recent influence by chaos theory, systems theory, and the "new science," management thought has been dominated by the assumption that the job of the manager is to control everything so that things turn out "right," i.e., according to plan (Mintzberg, 1994).

But recent writing about the New Management Paradigm is suggesting alternatives to this notion of command and control. For example, Hench (1998) has described a new view of management as "a continuous learning process for creating meaning and value through service with and for others." In contrast to the model of Plan, Lead, Organize, and Control, he has identified a new model of Experiment, Serve, Self-organize, and Learn (Hench, 1998: 9). The overall view is of non-linear, emergent change in dynamic self-organized contexts, which is precisely the focus on the theories of chaos and self-organization in management literature (e.g., Youngblood, 1997).

In a similar way, Banner and Gagne (1995) have described the new assumptions of a transformational paradigm. These include an assumption that everything is connected, that the whole organizes the parts, that we are co-creators with life, that harmony and integration follow alignment with life, and that the paradigm shift is now (Banner & Gagne, 1995: 47–54). Based on these new assumptions they create a transformational model of organizing in society, in which the level of cause is shifted to individuals, and elements of organizational structure or social context emerge based on long-term social interactions. By identifying causality at the level of shared beliefs, attitudes, and values, there is a recognition that when enough individuals make the shift to a new paradigm—and as more and more organizations do also—there is higher likelihood that society will transform as well. This social transformation then is not based on an overarching economic benefit to the culture, but on the realized shifts in individuals and organizations as they become more attuned to spiritual principles and issues.

According to New Paradigm writers, our propensity to trust only our physical senses and what we can measure with our sciences is related to our need to dominate and control. Thus, societal transformation will occur when a critical mass of individuals decide to let go of the control imperative and trust the design and control inherent in life itself. All of this is not saying that we should give up on controlling anything, but, rather, that we should be aware of invisible fields of thought and belief that govern our experience and be ready to loosen our grip on "reality" in order to let new wisdom come in. In this way, paradigm shifts can occur (and societal transformation can take place) to propel us into our next stage of collective evolution.

Summary

In this paper we have explored three different perspectives on the transformational process, at the individual, organizational, and global level. Each of these theories postulates that the transformation process is non-linear and non-rational and yet that there are some underlying patterns that describe the phenomena associated with transformation. The first step in extending this work is to accept that there are invisible fields of thought and reality that affect us in the everyday world. We must, indeed, transform our understanding of research, data collection, and knowledge. We propose that the management field will benefit greatly from incorporating a spiritual perspective into our theories as well as into our research and theory development processes.

References

Ackerman, L. (1984), *The Flow State: A New View of Organizations and Managing*, Miles River Press, Alexandria, VA.

Adams, J. (1984), *Transforming Work*, Miles River Press, Alexandria, VA.

Banner, D., & E. Gagne (1995), *Designing Effective Organizations: Traditional and Transformational Views*, Sage, Thousand Oaks, CA.

Bohm, D. (1983), *Wholeness and the Implicate Order*, Routledge Publications, London, England.

Bolman, L., & T. Deal. (1995), *Leading with Soul: An Uncommon Journey of Spirit*, Jossey-Bass, San Francisco, CA.

Bracey, H., Rosenblum, J., Sanford, A., & Trueblood, R. (1990), *Managing from the Heart*, Dell Paperback, New York.

Breton, D., & Largent, C. (1996), *The Paradigm Conspiracy,* Hazelden, Center City, MN.

Briskin, A. (1996), *The Stirring of the Soul in the Workplace,* Jossey-Bass, San Francisco, CA.

Canfield, J., & Hansen, V. (1996), *Chicken Soup for the Soul at Work,* Health Communications, Inc., Deerfield Beach, FL.

Capra, F. (1996), *The Web of Life,* Anchor Books, New York.

Castenada, C. (1971), *A Separate Reality,* Bantam Books, New York.

Chappell, T. (1993), *The Soul of a Business: Managing for Profit and the Common Good,* Bantam Books, New York.

Collins, J., & J. Porras (1997), *Built to Last: Successful Habits of Visionary Companies,* HarperBusiness, New York.

Csikszentmihalyi, M. (1990), *Flow: The Psychology of Optimal Experience,* Harper and Row, New York.

Dyer, W. (1993), *Real Magic,* Harper, New York.

Fox, M. (1994), *The Reinvention of Work: A New Vision of Livelihood for Our Time,* Harper San Francisco, San Francisco, CA.

Galen, M., & K. West (1995), "Companies Hit the Road Less Traveled: Can spirituality enlighten the bottom line?" *Business Week,* June 4: 82–84.

Gilligan, C. (1982), "In a Different Voice: Psychological theory and women's development," *Harvard University Press,* Cambridge, MA.

Gladwin, T., Kennelly, J., & Tara-Shelomith, K. (1994), "Shifting Paradigms for Sustainable Development: Implications for Management Theory and Research." *Academy of Management Review 20,* 874–907.

Gleick, J. (1987), *Chaos; Making a New Science,* Penguin, New York.

Goerner, S. (1994), *Chaos and the Evolving Ecological Universe,* Gordon & Breach.

Goldstein, J. (1994), *The Unshackled Organization.* Productivity Press, Portland, OR.

Goldstein, J. (1995), "Unbalancing Psychoanalytic Theory: Moving beyond the equilibrium model of Freud's thought." In R. Robertson & A. Combs (eds.), *Chaos Theory in Psychology and the Life Sciences,* Lawrence Erlbaum, NJ.

Harman, W. (1993), "Approaching the Millennium: Business as a Vehicle for Global Transformation," in M. Ray & A. Rinzler (eds.), *The New Paradigm in Business: Emerging Strategies for Leadership and Organizational Change.* Jeremy Tarcher, New York.

Harman, W. & J. Hormann (1990), *Creative Work: The Constructive Role of Business in a Transforming Society*, Knowledge Systems, Inc., Indianapolis, IN.

Hawken, P. (1993), *The Ecology of Commerce: A Declaration of Sustainability*, HarperBusiness, New York.

Hawley, J. (1993), *Reawakening the Spirit in Work: The Power of Dharmic Management*, Berrett-Koehler, San Francisco, CA.

Henderson, H. (1996), *Building a Win-win World: Life Beyond Global Economic Warfare*, Berrett-Koehler, San Francisco, CA.

Hench, T. (1998), "Getting Beyond 'Planning, Leading, Organizing and Controlling': A nonlinear framework for organizing." Paper presented at the Sun-Break Conference: Non-linearity in Organizations. Las Cruces, NM, February, 6, 1998.

Hubbard, M. B. (1998), *Conscious Evolution: Awakening the Power of Our Social Potential*, New World Library, Novato, CA.

Isaacs, B. (1993), *Taking Flight: Dialogue, Collective Thinking, and Organizational Learning*. Organizational Dynamics, New York.

Jaworski, J. (1996), *Synchronicity: The Inner Path of Leadership*, Barrett-Koehler, San Francisco, CA.

Kanter, R. M. (1977), *Men and Women of the Corporation*, Basic Books, New York.

Kantrowitz, B., King, P., Rosenberg D., Springen K., Wingert P., Namuth T., & Gegax T. (1994), "In Search of the Sacred," *Newsweek* (November 28), 52–62.

Keyes, K, Jr. (1983), *The Hundredth Monkey*, Vision Books, Coos Bay, OR.

Kiefer, C., & Senge, P. (1984), *Metanoic Organizations*, in J. Adams, *Transforming Work*, Miles River Press, Alexandria, VA.

Kuhn, T. (1970), *The Structure of Scientific Revolutions*, University Press, Chicago, IL.

Laszlo, E. (1987), *Evolution: The Grand Synthesis*, Shambhala, Boston, MA.

Lichtenstein, B. forthcoming. "Valid or Vacuous: A definition and analysis of the new paradigm in management," *Behavioral Scientist*.

Lichtenstein, B. (1997), "Grace, Magic, and Miracles: Toward a 'chaotic' logic of organizational transformation," *Journal of Organizational Change Management, 6*.

Lichtenstein, B. (1997), "Grace, Magic & Miracles: A 'chaotic logic' of organizational transformation." *Journal of Organizational Change Management, 10 (5)*, 393–411.

Marcic, D. (1997), *Managing With the Wisdom of Love: Uncovering Virtue in People and Organizations*, Jossey-Bass, San Francisco, CA.

Maynard, H. & Mehrtens, S. (1996), *The Fourth Wave: Business in the 21st Century*, Berrett-Koehler, San Francisco, CA.

Mintzberg, H. (1994), *The Rise and Fall of Strategic Planning*, Free Press, New York.

Morgan, G. (1986), *Images of Organization*, Sage Publications, Newbury Park, CA.

Nair, K. (1997), *A Higher Standard of Leadership: Lessons from the Life of Gandhi*, Berrett-Koehler, San Francisco, CA.

Neal, J. (1995), "Employees Seek Jobs that Nourish Their Souls," *Hartford Courant*, August 8, A12.

Neal, J. (1997), "Spirituality in Management Education: A guide to resources," *Journal of Management Education, (21) 1*, 121–139.

Neal, J., Lichtenstein B., & Banner, D. (1998), "What Matters Most in Transformation: Economic and spiritual arguments for individual, organizational and societal change," presented at the National Academy of Management, San Diego, CA.

Noer, D. (1993), *Healing the Wounds: Overcoming the Trauma of Layoffs and Revitalizing Downsized Organizations*, Jossey-Bass, San Francisco, CA.

Owen, H. (1997), *Expanding Our Now: The Story of Open Space Technology*, Berrett-Koehler, San Francisco, CA.

Peters, T., & Waterman, R. (1982), *In Search of Excellence: Lessons From American's Best-run Companies*, Harper and Row, New York.

Ray, M. & Rinzler, A. (1993), *The New Business Paradigm*, Tarcher, LA.

Renesch, J. & B. DeFoore (eds.) (1996), *The New Bottom Line: Bringing Heart & Soul to Business*, New Leaders Press, San Francisco, CA.

Romanelli, E., & Tushman, M. (1994), "Organizational Transformation as Punctuated Equilibrium: An empirical test." *Academy of Management Journal, 37,* 1141–1166.

Russell, P. (1998), *Waking up in time: Finding Inner Peace in Times of Accelerating Change*, Origin Press, Novato, CA.

Schaef, A. W. & Fassel, D. (1988), *The Addictive Organization,* Harper and Row, San Francisco, CA.

Schaefer, C., & J. Darling. (1997), "Does Spirit Matter? A look at contemplative practices in the workplace," *Spirit at Work* (July): 6–8.

Senge, P. (1990), *The Fifth Discipline: The Art and Science of the Learning Organization,* Doubleday, New York.

Sheldrake, R. (1986), *A New Science of Life,* Bantam Books, New York.

Stacy, R. (1995). "The Science of Complexity: An alternative perspective for strategic change processes," *Strategic Management Journal 16,* 477–495.

Steinem, G. (1983), *Outrageous acts and everyday rebellions,* Holt, Rhinehart and Winston, NY.

Strauss, A., & Corbin, J. (1993), *Basics of Qualitative Research,* Sage Publications, Newbury Park, CA.

Thietart, R., & Forgues, B. (1995), "Chaos Theory and Organization" *Organization Science 6,* 19–31.

Torbert, W. (1991), *The Power of Balance,* Sage, Newbury Park, CA.

Tushman, M., & Anderson, P. (1986), "Technological Discontinuities and Organizational Environments" *Administrative Science Quarterly 31,* 439–465.

Vaill, P. (1984), "Process Wisdom for a New Age," in J. Adams, *Transforming Work,* Miles River Press, Alexandria, VA.

Waterman, R. H., Waterman J., & Collard B. (1994), "Toward a Career-Resilient Workforce," *Harvard Business Review,* July–August: 87–95.

Wheatley, M. (1992), *Leadership and the New Science: Learning about organizations from an orderly universe,* Berrett-Koehler, San Francisco, CA.

Whyte, D. (1994), *The Heart Aroused,* Currency/Doubleday, New York.

Wilber, K. (1996), *A Brief History of Everything,* Shambhala, Boston, MA.

Young, J. (1960), *Doubt and Certainty in Science,* Galaxy Books of Oxford University Press, New York.

Youngblood, Mark D. (1997), *Life at the Edge of Chaos,* Perceval Publishing, Dallas, TX.

Yukl, G. (1994), *Leadership in Organizations,* Prentice-Hall, Englewood Cliffs, NJ.

THE GROWING INTEREST IN SPIRITUALITY IN BUSINESS:

A LONG-TERM SOCIO-ECONOMIC EXPLANATION

Len Tischler,
University of Scranton

Introduction

There are so many new management ideas and practices occurring in businesses today that it is hard to keep up with them. It seems that almost every year or two there is another "new" way to run a company. Just this decade we have gone from quality to reengineering, to an out-ward-looking, proactive resource-based view of strategizing for the firm, to information system-based strategies, to EVA, MVA, and share-holder value approaches, to human resource-based strategies. We have moved from the many unrelated diversification mega-mergers of the 1980s to the even larger core-business-centered mergers of the 1990s. There seem to be ever-increasing moves from the real and concrete to the virtual and knowledge-based, and from the independent to the inter-connected in every aspect of running a business. Workers and managers alike are becoming more like independent brokers of their services and knowledge, and are not only looking for money but increasingly for other values such as meaning, personal and professional growth, and even spiritual growth (Drucker, 1993; Renesch & Defoore, 1996; Schmidt & Posner, 1983).

It is this last change that sparked an interest in the topic of this paper. What underlying theory might explain such a movement, espe-cially to spirituality? Why are societies in economically developed countries seeming to move away from a strict focus on money and economic stability and toward also allowing focuses on human growth in a variety of areas? Even more, why are calls for such new focuses being heard and experimented with in businesses? The focus of this paper is to delineate a theory that could explain this trend, especially to spirituality. The theory is based on Maslow's (1943) theory of a hierarchy of needs.

Maslow's (1943) theory of a hierarchy of needs stands the test of time as one of the major theories of motivation in our management and psychology textbooks (Wahba & Bridwell, 1976). Whatever the reasons for its weak empirical showing, the theory seems "obvious" to those who read it, whether school children or sophisticated social scientists. This paper is intended to take Maslow's theory into new territory: the paper will apply the theory to the social level of activity rather than the individual—as a theory of *social* consciousness and motivation. The proposed theory is: as the majority of citizens in any society can be freed from the lower levels of concern, they can, as a society, shift their concern to higher-order needs.

This paper will proceed as follows. First it will review the basics of Maslow's hierarchy of needs theory. Second it will give a brief history of the progress and impacts of the industrial revolution in economically "developed" countries. Third, it will show that there appears to be a relationship between broad economic prosperity and the hierarchy of needs at the social level. Finally it will conclude about implications of this theory.

Maslow's Hierarchy of Needs

There are five basic levels of needs in this theory (Maslow, 1943): physical or survival needs, security needs, social needs, achievement needs, and self-actualization needs. The hierarchical part of the theory is that until an individual is freed from concern about a lower level (order) of need, he cannot be effectively or consistently focused on a higher-order need. Thus, according to the theory, if a worker lives a close-to-subsistence life outside of work, he will work primarily for pay (food, shelter) and will have little motivation or interest in any other kind of human resources benefits or programs. As long as he is intensely concerned for his and his family's daily survival, he cannot have much concern for developing refined social graces, sophisticated language skills, higher-order (and longer-term) achievement skills, or any other higher-order growth. Once freed from such lower-order concerns, however, he can and will begin to explore his higher-order growth needs.

The History and Impact of the Progress of the Industrial Revolution

In America and Europe the industrial revolution has evolved over approximately two hundred years. One way to view the quintessential element of this evolution is to focus on its consequent development and spread of economic prosperity: economically "developed" societies have evolved from having most of their population living in almost daily concern about physical survival to having most of their population being free from such concerns. In America and most of Western Europe in the 1990s, even when laid off, most people are not going to starve to death if they are out of work for several months or even for a year or more.

Many elements led to this kind of change: Machines were invented which allowed more goods to be made, transported, and sold at significantly lower costs. Business learned how to plan, organize, lead, and control work and enterprises so that the economy could grow. Social movements grew to try to equalize the power between the wealthy and the masses, leading to unions, anti-trust regulation, the development of corporate and governmental safety nets for workers, and movement toward corporate social and environmental responsibility. We progressed largely with a machine orientation: management reacted to the changing technologies of the time, setting up organizations and practices that matched the technologies (machines), and social movements reacted to management practices that strained people in order to accommodate the technologies or enrich only the few. Additionally, we moved from living in small, self-sufficient communities that changed little, to creating mass societies with rapid change, leading to the need for national-level governmental safety net and responsibility programs to ameliorate the negative impacts of individual economic dislocations and of society-wide and environmental effects (Drucker, 1993; Galbraith, 1967; Reich, 1991).

Recently we have been evolving into a "post-industrial," "information," or "knowledge" age. The hallmarks of this shift appear to be a focus on each individual who is a part of the economy and on the betterment of society. For example, we have increasing empowerment and participation within the company coming from the quality revolution (Deming, 1993; Juran, 1992), from a corporate application of Eighteenth century political theory (Pinchot & Pinchot, 1993), from an insightful understanding of knowledge (as opposed to machines, money, or labor) as the true basis for economic growth (Romer, 1990; Toffler, 1980), from a social conscience (Boje & Dennehy, 1993), and from a hard-nosed understanding of what will make a company more "sustainable" (Magretta, 1997). In addition, we have increasing social voice outside the company with a heavy emphasis on accommodating to customer wants (Deming, 1993; Juran, 1992), increasing private- and public-sector monitoring of safety, quality, and environmental standards (e.g., ISO 9000, ISO 14000, Sierra Club, FDA, OSHA), and a budding social interest in sustainable products and practices (e.g., MADD, SADD). Moreover, we have grown from a recognition that people's perceptions and feelings can affect their work (productivity and quality; Roethlisberger & Dickson, 1966), to a variety of social and technical approaches to try to ameliorate or inspire feelings in ways that will improve productivity and quality (e.g., the human relations and behavioral science approaches). Systems theorists have evolved from a sole focus on quantitative techniques to an equal or primary focus on the human element in business (Deming, 1993; Hammer & Stanton, 1995). We have also moved from "one size fits all" approaches to contingency approaches, which themselves have evolved from only a few macro contingencies to understanding that although there are patterns to be understood, each person and situation is unique (deserves individual attention and respect).

We seem to be moving toward an era of emphasizing that a business does better for its survival and profitability when it creates an environment (culture) that emphasizes "teamwork, customer focus, fair treatment of employees, initiative, and innovation" (*Fortune*, 1998: 218); that emphasizes the betterment of society and the environment (Gardner, 1990; Greenleaf, 1973; Magretta, 1997; Renesch & Defoore, 1996); and that understands that human motivation is mainly intrinsic (Deming, 1993; Kohn, 1993; Senge, 1990). This last point emphasizes that merely using the old approaches to worker motivation, coercion, or bibery (pay and incentives), will no longer work; it is also becoming necessary for sustainable company growth to offer employees inspiring work and to help employees grow in ways that are best for them. In fact, a growing number of business leaders seem to be wanting to move us toward an era that emphasizes individual self-actualization as both the ultimate human end goal and as the best means to creating even more success and wealth for individuals and companies (Bolman & Deal, 1995; Hendricks & Ludeman, 1996; Herman, 1994; Jaworski, 1998; Renesh & Defoore, 1996).

What we have seen over the past two hundred years, then, is an evolution

- *from* an agrarian society of little change for the majority of people
- *through* an industrial society that through a machine orientation created
- comparatively enormous wealth for most people in developed countries,
- a mass society with attendant changes in social structure, and social consciousness, and
- an unimaginably faster and increasing pace of change
- *to* a post-industrial society that focuses on individual achievement and self-actualization growth for as many people as possible in a socially, economically, and environmentally sustainable and responsible manner.

Economic Prosperity and the Hierarchy of Needs

Another way to view this evolution is through the lens of a hierarchy of human needs. In the agrarian age most people spent their entire lives daily focused on their physical survival and security. Many of the five to ten percent of each society's elite could spend some of their time on higher-order needs (social, esteem, self-actualization), but most people did not have that luxury.

As the industrial revolution created wealth for more people, increasing numbers of people had time and money to spend on more than their survival and security needs. Although most people have not yet gained this extra time, the 1960s generation began to look beyond the "work for money" ethic. They experimented with new types of human relationships (e.g., "free love," communes, co-ops), new ways to build self-esteem (other than business or money achievement), and various approaches to self-actualization (e.g., meditation, yoga, etc.). Their experiments did not directly or quickly infiltrate the business world; rather, they were an early part of the gradual transition from the industrial age to the post-industrial age. The 1960s youth of America and Europe were the first generation in history in which the majority of a society were pretty well assured of physical (economic) survival, stability, and growth. They didn't know hardship, depression, or the ravages of war or major disease. They were free to dream dreams that their parents could not relate to and that horrified their grand-parents.

They were being accused of trying to tear down the very fabric of society that led to and underpinned modern prosperity and freedom.

Meanwhile, two concurrent forces arose. As workers became increasingly aware that survival was assured even if they lost their jobs, many, especially educated workers, began to want more than just money from their jobs (Drucker, 1993; Galbraith, 1967). They craved more affiliation and esteem values; some even craved self-actualization growth. Moreover, as knowledge has become an increasingly important competitive factor (Davis & Davidson, 1991; Romer, 1990), companies have had to increasingly offer their educated employees many new kinds of opportunities and benefits. Continuous learning, formal and informal, is needed to stay on the cutting edge in each field of knowledge. Broader and freer access to in-house and external information is needed. Broader and richer kinds of affiliations are needed: collaboration across internal departments and specialty areas, affiliation with external professional and industry groups, teamwork, open, trusting work with suppliers and customers, etc. (Senge, 1990; Wheatley,1992)

More than this, workers who have broken their dependence on an almost exclusive money orientation at work are increasingly intrinsically motivated (Deming, 1993; Kohn, 1993; Senge, 1990). This has brought about the need for a proliferation of job design elements and their integration (Hackman & Oldham, 1980) and of organizational structures (Galbraith & Lawler, 1993; Levy, 1998), as well as for a new understanding of human behavior (Argyris, 1993; Kohn, 1993; Vaill, 1996). As workers decreasingly look to outer situations, people, and structures to motivate their behavior and impact their feeling and thinking, they look increasingly inward for direction, esteem, and the creation of their own happiness.

Most recently, during the past decade or so, there has been a rising call to include spirituality in our workplaces. In response, for example, the Transcendental Meditation movement of the 1960s and 1970s has developed the "Maharishi Corporate Development Program" for the 1990s (Maharishi Center for Excellence in Management, 1997). The number of conferences about spirituality in business has gone from none to almost a dozen per year in the United States alone in 1998, and several throughout the rest of the world. Books on personal growth and spirituality have continued to proliferate this past decade; the remarkable part of this trend is that many have moved from an exclusive focus on personal, individual growth to bringing this growth into the workplace and to corporate transformation using similar approaches or principles (Bolman & Deal, 1995; Hendricks & Ludeman, 1996; Herman, 1994; Jaworski, 1998; Renesh & Defoore, 1996; Wheatley, 1992).

Conclusion and Implications

In summary, we have seen that as the industrial revolution progressed in societies, it produced widespread prosperity. As a large portion of a society becomes free from the need to focus almost exclusively on physical and security needs for survival, it appears that the society as a whole can move in the direction of focusing on the higher needs: social, esteem, and self-actualization, including spirituality. We have seen this occur so far in the United States and in the economically "developed" countries of Europe. This trend seems to point to a hierarchy of human needs at the social level. Such a theory of social change can offer us new ways to understand many of the social changes of our time, including our rising interest in spirituality in business.

This theory can also shed light on some of the difficulties of the less economically developed societies that are trying to move up the economic ladder. The spread of wealth in a society does not immediately change social outlooks and attitudes; social changes seem to lag behind economic prosperity by a generation or two. Trust must evolve over time that the system will support the population economically even in hard times. In addition, it is not the overall wealth of a society that leads to social change toward higher-order levels of concern, but the spread of wealth to a majority of the society's people over time.

This theory can also help us to predict conditions that would lead to a deterioration of a society from a higher-order focus to a lower-order focus: when economic conditions deteriorate dramatically, or when the economy shifts so that wealth is again hoarded by a few, and the majority are back to worrying about their short-term survival. On the other hand, it could be possible that if a society can spread and sustain its higher-order mentality long enough, a new, higher-order consciousness could develop which locks the society into this mentality and in return supports the continuation of an economy that sustains the majority of the society's people.

References

Argyris, C. (1993), *Knowledge for Action: A Guide to Overcoming Barriers to Organizational Change*, Jossey-Bass, San Francisco, CA.

Boje, D. M., & Dennehy, R. E. (1993), *Managing in the Post Modern World: America's Revolution Against Exploitation*, Kendall/Hunt, Dubuque, IA.

Bolman, L. G., & Deal, T. E. (1995), *Leading with Soul: An Uncommon Journey of Spirit*. Jossey-Bass, San Francisco, CA.

Davis, S., & Davidson, B. (1991), *2020 Vision*, Fireside, New York.

Deming, W. E., (1993), *The New Economics for Industry, Government, Education*, MIT Center for Advanced Engineering Study, Cambridge, MA.

Drucker, P. F., (1993), *Post-capitalist Society*, HarperBusiness, New York.

Fortune (1998), "What Makes a Company Great?" October 26, p. 218.

Galbraith, J. R., Lawler, E. E., & Associates (1993), *Organizing for the Future: The New Logic for Managing Complex Organizations*, Jossey-Bass, San Francisco, CA.

Galbraith, J. K. (1967), *The New Industrial State*, Houghton Mifflin, Boston, MA.

Gardner, J. W. (1990), *On Leadership*, The Free Press, New York.

Greenleaf, R. K. (1973), *The Servant as Leader*, Center for Applied Sciences, Peterborough, NH.

Hackman, J. R., & Oldham, G. R. (1980), *Work Redesign*, Addison-Wesley, Reading, MA.

Hammer, M., & Stanton, S. A. (1995), *The Reengineering Revolution: A Handbook*, HarperBusiness, New York.

Hendricks, G., & Ludeman, K. (1997), *The Corporate Mystic: A Guidebook for Visionaries with Their Feet on the Ground*, Bantam Books, New York.

Herman, S. M. (1994), *The Tao at Work: On Leading and Following*, Jossey-Bass, San Francisco, CA.

Jaworski, J. (1998), *Synchronicity: The Inner Path of Leadership*, Berrett-Koehler, San Francisco, CA.

Juran, J. M. (1992), *Juran on Quality by Design: The New Steps for Planning Quality into Goods and Services*, The Free Press, New York.

Kohn, A. (1993), *Punished by Rewards: The Trouble with Gold Stars, Incentive Plans, A's, Praise, and Other Bribes*, Houghton Mifflin, Boston, MA.

Magretta, J. (1997), "Growth Through Global Sustainability," *Harvard Business Review*, Jan–Feb 1997, 75 (1), pp. 78–88.

Maharishi Center for Excellence in Management (1997), "The Maharishi Corporate Development Program," *Web*: www.tm.org/mcdp/index2.html

Maslow, A. H. (1943), "A Theory of Human Motivation," *Psychological Review*, 50, pp. 370–396.

Pinchot, G., & Pinchot, E. (1993), *The End of Bureaucracy & the Rise of the Intelligent Organization*, Berrett-Koehler, San Francisco, CA.

Reich, R. B. (1991), *The Work of Nations: Preparing Ourselves for 21st Century Capitalism*, Alfred A. Knopf, New York.

Renesch, J., & Defoore, B. (eds.) (1996), *The New Bottom Line: Bringing Heart and Soul to Business*, New Leaders Press, San Francisco, CA.

Roethlisberger, F. I., & Dickson, W. I. (1966), *Management and the Worker*, Harvard University Press, Cambridge, MA.

Romer, P. (1990), "Endogenous Technical Change," *Journal of Political Economy*, 98 (5) Part 2, pp. 71–102.

Schmidt, W. H., & Posner, B. Z. (1983), *Managerial Values in Perspective*, American Management Association, New York.

Senge, P. M. (1990), *The Fifth Discipline: The Art and Practice of the Learning Organization*, Doubleday Currency, New York.

Toffler, A. (1980), *The Third Wave*, William Morrow, New York.

Vaill, P. B. (1996), *Learning as a Way of Being*, Jossey-Bass, San Francisco, CA.

Wahba, M. A., & Bridwell, L. G. (1976), "Maslow Reconsidered: A review of research on the need hierarchy," *Organizational Behavior and Human Performance*, 16, pp. 212–240.

Wheatley, M. (1992), *Leadership and the New Science: Learning About Organization from an Orderly Universe*, Berrett-Koehler, San Francisco, CA.

SPIRITUALITY IN THE WORKPLACE

**(This is an updated version of an article that first
appeared in the popular business book, *Heart at Work*,
by Jack Canfield & Jacqueline Miller.)**

The nature and meaning of work are undergoing a profound evolution. Two forces are helping to catalyze the momentum of this process —fear and the emergence of both a more personal and widespread spirituality.

The fear is about losing our job and having to do more with less. And the emergence of spirituality in the workplace points to the desire that there be more to work than just survival. We yearn for work to be a place in which we both experience and express our deep soul and spirit.

Fear in the Workplace

There are several factors causing an increase of fear in the workplace.

The first is massive corporate downsizing. The benefit of downsizing is that it does increase profits. Moreover, it cuts the fat and the excess while streamlining the organization. But downsizing also has a downside. It causes pain and suffering. In addition to the pain felt by those people who have been let go, those who are still left are asked to increase production with less resources, in the same amount of time, and for the same pay.

They feel stressed out and bone-tired. They are anxious about the security of their job and often are resentful. And most painful of all, they don't see any light at the end of the tunnel.

Downsizing works in the short term; in the long term, what's lost is loyalty, engagement, experience, creativity, and the full expression of spirit.

A second factor is that more work is moving offshore. Years ago, it was just manufacturing work. Now it's also service jobs. India and Israel, for example, are becoming key sites for the development of computer software. We thought that there were certain types of work that would always remain in the developed world—that these were "our jobs," like service and new technology development—it's just no longer so.

And what about successful companies laying people off? That's never happened before. The understanding used to be that when a company was in fiscal trouble it would lay off people, and when the company was successful, it would keep and even hire people. But with reengineering and new advanced technology, there is a need for less people, so successful companies are downsizing.

When you put all these factors together, you're taking the work contract—the implicit agreement that I would come to work for you for life, the belief in security of employment—and smashing it. The message is crystal clear: "You don't have a secure job anymore." And that causes insecurity, it causes anxiety, and it causes fear.

There is a growing sense of "dispiritedness" in individuals and in the overall workplace. The spirit has been shut down. It can't fully express itself. There is a sense of disengagement. It may not be completely quantifiable, but people can and do feel the lack of spirit in their workplace.

All of this doesn't need to paint a completely bleak picture. We can look at these very same factors from another, more useful perspective—the spiritual. The security we thought we got from the corporation is a myth. Real security comes from a connection to that which is truly secure—the spirit. We are in the process of moving from "dependent children" at work, with the parental company looking after us, to really coming into our full, adult Selfhood. From this new reality we can begin exploring and expressing more of our true spiritual selves.

The Emergence of Spirituality

In addition to fear, there is a compelling inner longing for spiritual fulfillment. There are several factors present in society reflecting the emerging desire for personal and collective spirituality.

The baby-boomer generation is now entering its 50s. People are reaching mid-life and looking at those issues that are characteristic for this age—issues such as: "What is my legacy?"; "What are the long-term values that I want to leave behind?"; "In what other arenas of life do I want to invest my energies now that I've reached the peak of my career?"; "What is really important to me as I begin to see my parents, aunts and uncles start to die?" These kinds of thoughts are usual for people in mid-life. What is unusual, however, is that the baby-boomer generation is so large. When it begins to think about these issues, then society follows. As spirituality emerges for baby boomers, the whole of society is affected.

Concern and involvement with the bio-environment also reflect an emerging sense of the spiritual. The environment is both life supporting and gives us an awareness and consciousness of the whole. It reveals to us how we are interconnected and interdependent. And when you think about that, that's a very spiritual metaphor.

> When the concept of human spirit is understood
> as the mode of consciousness in which the
> individual feels connected to the Cosmos as a
> whole, it becomes clear that ecological
> awareness is spiritual in its deepest sense.
>   —Fritjof Capra

Yet another factor is the maturing of the scientific paradigm. We thought we could solve all the world's problems with science. We thought we could eventually understand everything through science. But the more we know, the more we find out we don't know. Science has been divorcing itself from the spiritual for several hundred years. However, science without spirituality is like a wave without the ocean. A growing number of scientists realize this and are moving more into spiritual exploration.

These three factors are indicative of the overall emergence of spirituality in our time. Popular culture also reflects this in the growing number of books, movies, and TV programs about spirituality. And spirituality in the workplace is part of this phenomenon.

What Is Spirituality?

I've found that when people ask me the question "What is spirituality?" what they're really concerned about is "Will I have 'the Answer'"? or some other dogmatic response. They're afraid that I've already got spirituality defined and that they will disagree with my definition, which will then cause separation. People are afraid that I (or anyone else speaking about spirituality) will shove a particular point of view down their throats. This approach offers the listener no opportunity to search for his/her own truth.

The journey is not about spirituality as "the answer," but about spirituality as "the question." A question allows you to look more deeply. It allows you to search for what's true for you, and in so doing, deepen your own experience. But ultimately, what moving from answer to question does is make it safe and permissible to explore this territory in a way that is useful.

What is spirituality for you? Where is spirit or spirituality not showing up in your workplace? Where is it flourishing? Explore these kinds of questions, at work, for yourself, your relationships, your division, and your company. And in this questioning, in this exploration, notice the deepening of your own experience of spirituality at work.

Spirituality in the Workplace

What would a more spiritual workplace mean for people? It would mean that work would move from merely being a place to get enough money to survive—from just earning our daily bread—to being a place of livelihood. By livelihood I mean a place where we both survive and are fully alive. We are alive in that our spirit fully expresses itself. And through our contribution, we allow other people's spirits to be nourished and to flourish. Livelihood has, at its core, three meanings for work: survival (you're alive), enlivening of the individual Self (you're aliveness), and enlivening of the collective Self (their aliveness).

What are the benefits of a more spiritual workplace? One of the primary benefits is that people are more in touch with the Source of creativity. As businesspeople, we realize the value of creativity and innovation. Creativity is a cornerstone of business. It allows us to come out with new products and services that really are of service. It allows us to do more with less. In essence, creativity leads to more efficient contribution.

As we move more into a service and technological economy, we want to continually expand innovation and creativity. But you can't demand that of people. "Human capital" has to be treated differently than "financial capital." You have to create an atmosphere in which creativity and innovation flourish; and that is accomplished through the bountiful expression of spirit. When we are more in touch with the Source of creativity, there is also revitalization, renewal, and resilience.

Another benefit is increased authenticity in communication. A lot of the work I do as a consultant is to create a "safe space" in which people feel permission to talk about their truth without fear of reprisal. Businesses aren't accustomed to doing this as a matter of normal everyday practice. However, when the truth is allowed to be safely and respectfully spoken, old problems clear up, new possibilities emerge, and people feel more aligned. They work together in a trusting team.

Increased ethical and moral behavior is yet another benefit. But who cares if a company is ethical? Isn't business just a place where you see how much you can get ahead? In a word, no. An important value of ethical behavior for a business is the development of trust. We trust people who operate in an ethical framework. Employees trust employers. Employers trust employees. And customers who trust a company stay customers longer.

Spirituality in the workplace also promotes the expression of talent, brilliance, and genius—talent in the sense of our Divine gifts; brilliance in terms of our intellect and the intensity of the light we have to shine; and genius not as a scarce commodity, but as something that everyone has. Our true job is to connect with that genius. And moreover, spirituality in the workplace also leads to increased self-fulfillment, contentment, and a deep sense of belonging.

In most businesses today, spirit and spirituality aren't talked about. The first thing that needs to happen is to make it safe and permissible to talk about it, as normally and as naturally as the many other conversations we have at work, such as profitability, innovations, and personnel issues.

We start this simply by beginning. Talk to those you trust, talk to others in business, talk to your colleagues, but begin to talk about it. There may be an initial fear, but after a while, the momentum will be unstoppable.

Managing in the New Spiritual Workplace

Today, we live in the transition period between the old definition of work as survival and the new definition of work as livelihood. New management techniques and new organizational structures are needed to handle this emerging context.

Management in the survival mode has been based on command and control. The way you get people to produce is by telling them what to do and making sure it gets done. But in a spiritual workplace, productivity is achieved through nurturing the expression of the self and the spirit. Our job, as leaders, is to facilitate the discovery of spirit, to esteem it, to celebrate it, and to hold others accountable for their expression of it. Support your employees and colleagues in being clear that part of their job responsibility is to fully express their spirit, their life purpose, and their gifts.

A senior vice-president of a large utility company told me that one of the roles of companies in the future will be to help employees discover their life purpose and to make sure that their work is consistent with and demanding of that purpose. "Imagine what would happen," he said, "if you had a company in which all the people were doing their life's work. You would have more loyalty, more resilience, more creativity, more innovation, and a deeper sense of self-reliance, self-renewal, and self-generation."

Another new management function will be helping people unleash and express their full, creative spirit. One of the ways to do this is to reconnect people with their artistry, whether that's music, painting, dancing, poetry, or cooking. Poet David Whyte, author of *The Heart Aroused*, goes into companies and reads poetry. Boeing Aircraft is one of his ongoing clients. The managers he works with begin to realize other aspects of themselves. Poetry helps them delve more deeply into their creative self, and it helps contribute to new insights, both personal and corporate. (Another great way for you and your employees to reconnect with your creativity is to read and do the exercises in *The Artists Way*, by Julia Cameron.)

An Invitation

The next phase of the evolution of work has begun. Spirituality is becoming more openly recognized as an integral part of work. If this is something that speaks to you, that you want more of in your workplace, I invite you to jump in!

SPIRITUALITY AT WORK:

AN OVERVIEW

Dan Butts, Health Psychologist,
Columnist on Social Issues

In the past decade there have been a torrent of thoughtful papers, as we have in this journal, dealing with the role of spirituality at work. Three of the many excellent books on different aspects of this enormously rich, complex, and often confusing topic are: *The Soul of a Business: Managing for Profit and the Common Good* by Tom Chappel, President of "Tom's of Maine"; *The Reinvention of Work: A New Vision of Livelihood for Our Time* by Matthew Fox, ex-priest and founder of Creation Spirituality; and *The Fourth Wave: Business in the 21st Century* by consultant Herman Bryant Maynard, Jr., and trend analyst Susan E. Mehrtens.

What then is spirituality? What goes on in church? New age religions? A set of impractical beliefs? A private experience with little value in working? A state of consciousness? Soul work? Contemplative practices like meditation or prayer? Time-honored principles and tools for living and working with more joy and success? A transpersonal state of human development (beyond individual, skin-encapsulated ego) with new values, priorities, and skills, which is also laying a foundation for a new bottom line?

What's needed is sufficient clarity and theoretical understanding of the meaning of spirituality and how it can apply to work, especially in terms of personal satisfaction, peak performance, and overall business success that can also enrich communities, cultures, and the Earth itself. Business owners, managers, policymakers, and academic researchers all need to remember, as many surveys indicate, that tens of millions of world citizens are hungering for transmaterial, mind-expanding, soul-enriching, and heart-centered (spiritual) values.

Thomas Moore, popular writer of several books on the soul such as *Care of the Soul: A Guide for Cultivating Depth and Sacredness in Everyday Life* (1992), points in the right direction by telling us how to add spirituality and cultivate soul through more depth, meaning, and the restoration of the sacred in our everyday lives.

Ultimate Values

One useful way of integrating spirituality in the workplace is through *sacred/ultimate/whole-system values* which enable the human spirit to grow and flourish. These time-honored, life-affirming, and unifying values, which can also enhance profit and productivity, include truth and trust (which liberate the soul), freedom and justice (which liberate creative and co-creative genius), creativity (innovation), collective harmony and intelligence (wholeness, synergy), deeper meaning, and higher purpose. Peters and Waterman (1982) reported that employees perform most energetically, creatively, and enthusiastically when they believe they are contributing to a higher purpose.

Optimal Human Development

Full or optimal human development, or, to use current business terms, maximizing human capital, is another direction for spirituality at work. Social psychologist Abraham Maslow's "hierarchy of human needs" suggests that if work helps to fulfill personal survival and security needs, and social, self-esteem, and ego needs, then employees would tend to become more oriented toward higher self-actualization and being (spiritual) needs. Maslow (1970) also wrote on human values and peak experiences.

Early in the 1990s, Peter Senge (1990, 1993) introduced the model of the learning organizations new workplace paradigm that provides a fertile landscape for the cultivation of soul and spiritual values. Senge, the director of the Center for Organizational Learning at MIT's Sloan School of Management, has a model and popular training program consisting of five disciplines (skills and tools) for creating a highly effective organization: shared vision, personal mastery, new mental models, team learning, and systems thinking.

Social psychologist Daniel Goleman (1995, 1998) has developed the idea of *emotional intelligence*, which integrates a range of skills in three critical areas of soul development and practice at work and in life. This model is also consistent with the emerging team-based organizational paradigm which requires that managers and workers develop a higher level of self-discipline, interpersonal and ethical skills (emotional intelligence): knowing one's emotions (self-awareness); managing emotions (self-control and resilience); self-motivation (creativity); recognizing emotion in others (empathy); handling relationships (social and organizational skills, handling diversity, resolving conflicts, transformational leadership).

Transcendence in the Workplace

Psychologist Mihaly Csikszentmihalyi (1990), in his 25-year research on optimal *experience (flow)*, has identified the characteristics of work (and life) experience that can liberate human spirit and creativity. In his research with surgeons and other groups, he found clear goals, total immersion in the activity, transcendence of ego boundaries and merging with the environment, and high levels of motivation, self-confidence, competence, enjoyment, and other intrinsic rewards.

For the past two decades, enlightened companies have encouraged employees to participate in various human potential programs or what could be called psychospiritual disciplines or technologies. Meditation, prayer, and guided imagery (visioning or "futurizing") are three of the more common practices. Course on Miracles, shamanic journeying, and various yogic paths are also of growing interest in corporate America.

There are six essential elements, all of which are important at work, "that constitute the heart and *art of transcendence*" in all major religions and spiritual growth traditions: "ethical training; development of concentration; emotional transformation; a redirection of motivation from egocentric, deficiency-based needs to higher motives, such as self-transcendence; refinement of awareness; and the cultivation of wisdom" (Walsh & Vaughan, 1993).

Emotional transformation involves releasing destructive emotions such as fear and anger, and cultivating positive emotions such as equanimity, joy, love, and compassion. Ethics is widely regarded as an essential foundation of mental training and transpersonal (spiritual) development. Unethical behavior both stems from and reinforces destructive mental factors such as greed, anger, and hatred. Conversely, ethical behavior dissipates these and cultivates positive mental factors such as calm, kindness, and compassion (ibid., pp. 48–50). Ultimately, after transpersonal maturation occurs, ethical behavior is said to flow spontaneously as a natural expression of identification with all people and all life (universal, cosmic, or Christ consciousness).

Spiritual Psychologies

Transpersonal psychology, which began about 25 years ago as an extension of humanistic or existential psychology, encompasses authentic living and working, realms of consciousness far beyond ordinary waking consciousness, soul-liberating disciplines like meditation, and transpersonal experiences extending beyond (trans) the individual or personal to embrace wider aspects of humankind, life, psyche, and cosmos. Jungian psychology reminds us of the archetypal depths and power of the collective unconscious and the therapeutic potency of images, myths, and symbols.

Asian systems such as Buddhist, yogic, Vedantic, and Taoist psychologies complement Western approaches by describing stages of transpersonal development and providing techniques for realizing them. Taoism, for example, is based on the integration of the yin and the yang, or the female and male energies or principles of consciousness (or leadership). Yoga psychology recognizes seven chakras, or subtle energy systems, that have various correspondences including personality type and levels of consciousness. Buddhist psychology recognizes that all our individual and social (and work-related) pathologies are based on aversions, addictions, delusions, and dualisms.

In future issues of the JOCM, we will explore other critical dimensions of spirituality at work including ethics and community, the essential organizational context for both learning and spiritual growth (see *Community Building: Renewing Spirit & Learning in Business* edited by K. Gozdz, 1995).

References

Chappell, T. (1993), *The Soul of a Business: Managing for Profit and the Common Good*, Bantam Books, New York.

Csikszentmihalyi, M. (1990), *Flow: The Psychology of Optimal Experience*, Harper & Row, New York.

Fox, M. (1994), *The Reinvention of Work: A New Vision of Livelihood for Our Time*, HarperCollins, New York.

Goleman, D. (1995), *Emotional Intelligence: Why it can matter more than IQ*, Bantam Books, New York.

Goleman, D. (1998), *Working with Emotional Intelligence*, Bantam Books, New York.

Gozdz, K. (Ed.) (1995), *Community Building: Renewing Spirit & Learning in Business*, New Leaders Press, San Francisco, CA.

Maslow, A. (1970), *Religions, Values, and Peak-Experiences*, Viking Press, New York.

Maynard, H. B., & Mehrtens, S. E. (1993), *The Fourth Wave: Business in the 21st Century*, Berrett-Koehler, San Francisco, CA.

Moore, T. (1992), *Care of the Soul: A Guide for Cultivating Depth and Sacredness in Everyday Life*, HarperCollins, New York.

Peters, T., & Waterman, R. H. (1982), *In Search of Excellence: Lessons from America's Best-Run Companies*, Harper & Row, New York.

Senge, P. (1990), *The Fifth Discipline: The Art & Practice of the Learning Organization*, Currency Doubleday, New York.

Senge, P., et al (1994), *The Fifth Discipline Fieldbook: Strategies and Tools for Building a Learning Organization*, Currency Doubleday, New York.

Walsh, R., & Vaughan, F. (Eds.) (1993), *Paths Beyond Ego: The Transpersonal Vision*, Tarcher/Pedigree, Los Angeles, CA.

AN EXPLORATORY ANALYSIS OF DEFINITIONS AND APPLICATIONS OF SPIRITUALITY IN THE WORKPLACE

Brenda Freshman,
California School of Professional Psychology

In the twenty-first century, the contemporary work force is faced with escalating ambiguity and chaos. Information technology and globalization are forcing organizations to respond with increasing flexibility (Hitt, Keats, & DeMarie, 1998). Contemporary theorists (Harmon, 1992; Ray, 1993; Wheatly, 1994) call for new and/or different ways of viewing organizational systems. Michael Ray (1993) describes this response: "Throughout the world, people in business— including owners, managers, and employees—are changing the way they think and work. They are engaged in a transformation, that some have said is as great as any in history." Michael Gorbachev puts it this way: "It is time for every individual, nation, and state to rethink its place and role in world affairs. We need an intellectual breakthrough into new dimensions where the human spirit is paramount" (1995). Correspondingly, Conger (1994) asserts that there is a current surge in the search for spirituality in the workplace and in our daily lives. Reflecting this sentiment has been a noticeable (to those interested in such topics) increase in publications and conferences on "Spirituality in the Workplace" and spirituality in daily life (Austin, 1995; Conger, 1994; Chappell, 1994; Frederic & Brussat, 1996; Lee & Zemke 1993; Jones, 1995; McAteer, 1995; McCormick, 1994; Moore, 1992; to name a few publications). In response to this growing attention, the primary endeavor of this study is to investigate contemporary definitions and applications of "spirituality in the workplace."

"Spirituality in the workplace" often conjures up a flood of images, with positive and negative associations. My personal experience is that people's reactions to the "S" word associated in the workplace run the gamut, from a wild thirst for knowledge, to skepticism and confusion, to fear. Some of my friends in the "rat race" have expressed that the concepts of "business/work" and "spirituality" are diametrically opposed. A recent quote from a conversation I was having with a New York–based media entrepreneur provides an example. With a chuckle and smirk he quipped, "The only thing spiritual about my work is the bottom line." Other folks I have met are afraid to discuss spiritual issues in the work-place for fear of being persecuted. However, there have also been many people I have met who have an enthusiastic interest in spirituality in the workplace. Don McCormick (1994), in his article titled "Spirituality and Management," captures the vast array of thoughts and feelings on the matter by deducing, "Definitions of spirituality abound." Hence rather than specifically defining "spirituality in the workplace" in a conclusive way, this study attempts to answer the question, "What are people writing about when they refer to 'spirituality in the workplace'?"

Emerging new paradigms of research have allowed investigators to methodologically examine complex social constructs from multiple perspectives, thus enhancing understanding (Rowen & Reason, 1981). This requires new ways of thinking about data collection and analysis. In order to capture a snapshot image of definitions which are admittedly varied and in flux, this study has set the intention to explore rather than conclude. Starting from the assumption that definitions and applications are numerous and diverse (McCormick, 1994), the attempt is made to document the terrain currently being traversed in the area of "spirituality in the workplace." The emergence of this explication occurs through a grounded theory process. Grounded theory is focused on the organization of ideas by thorough analysis using systematic and microscopic comparisons (Strauss, 1984). Comparisons and contrasts of the data from the three different text sources employed the qualitative techniques of thematic categorization and network analysis. The three sources were, (1) e-mail discussion group on the topic of "Spirituality in the Workplace"; (2) Questionnaire on "Spirituality in the Work-place"; and, (3) literature search on "Spirituality in the Workplace" and revealed related topics. The results of this process lead to sense-making and model construction.

Method

Text Sources

Three sources of text were used for analysis. E-mail messages from the on-line discussion group "Spirit at Work" were one source. One hundred e-mail messages were selected at random out of a sample of 362 e-mail messages gathered over a 3-month period. The second text sample source was a survey administered to this and other discussion groups and bulletin boards on-line. The inquiry asked the two direct questions below.

1. What does "spirituality in the workplace" mean to you?
2. How do you apply/practice spirituality in your workplace?

After the questionnaire responses and e-mail messages were collected, the sample text passages were entered into the *AtlasTI* program and underwent a coding process. This procedure analyzes the text and tags constructs with one-word code labels. Relationships between codes were documented with symbol links. The most frequent codes and topics that emerged were used as a basis for a literature search to obtain additional text samples. These codes were [Goals], [Intuition], [Authenticity], and [Awareness]. A variety of literature resources were explored by cross-referencing these four most frequent codes with "spirituality in the workplace." In addition, the key words and "spirituality in the workplace" were used in an on-line data search employing internet search engines. Text passages from the books and on-line search were entered into the program and subjected to analysis.

Technology

The software program, *AtlasTI*, published by Thomas Muhr (1993) in Berlin, was used in the qualitative analysis process. This program assists with coding functions and has the capability to draw graphic networks of relationships between codes. A PC laptop computer was used for all electronic gathering and coding processes.

Design and Procedure

The research and analysis in this project took place in several steps. First, the data samples (text sources) were collected and analyzed, generating codes and identifying relationships. Next the data were arranged into network views, displaying codes by source and revealing relationships to prepare for further interpretation. Then a comparative analysis of the three network views revealed four "Family" categories (actions, nouns, qualities, and theories). The next step arranged the composite data into network views based on the four "Families" and sentence interpretations were formed (see results section). The final step organized the findings into a flexible model with the ability to expand and allow for multiple interpretations and additions while still maintaining a semblance of structure. Each one of these steps is described in more detail.

Step 1

Text passages from the e-mail discussion group and surveys were entered into the computer, read, and analyzed for content meaning. The examiner reviewed the text line by line, within paragraphs asking the following questions of the data: (1) What is the intent of the message (i.e., to help, to ask a question, to respond, to vent—release tension and anxiety by sharing, to announce events . . . etc.)? (2) What is the content of the message (i.e., the subjects involved, the actions reported or expressed, the reactions of the parties involved)? (3) What are the relationships between ideas or concepts expressed (i.e., connections, assumptions, conclusions, associations)?

Each time an answer to question #1 (intent) or #2 (content) was established, the text section that expressed that answer was then labeled with a code(s) that reflected the intent and/or content of the message. Text segments that reflected question #3 (relationships between ideas) were identified as "relationships" and were documented by creating a link between codes in a text segment. Some examples of these links are: is associated with; leads to; is about; is an aspect of; supports; influences. To illustrate, the following statement, "[Meditation] enhances my [connection] to my [higher self]," would be documented as a text statement with three codes (in brackets) with a relationship link of positive influence. The same idea could take place over a longer paragraph or story form, "I often think that my daily [meditation] practice somehow brings me closer to my [higher self], I remember once when I was up to over 30 minutes a day on a very regular basis . . . I felt so [connected] then . . ."

A frequency count was taken on all the codes generated from the two sources. The top four codes in the frequency count ([Goals] [Intuition] [Authenticity] [Awareness]) were then used as a basis for the literature search. The text passages found were then entered into the Atlas software program and underwent the same "coding" processes described above that were conducted on the e-mail and questionnaire sources. A list of codes by source was generated and displayed in Table 1.

Table 1

Codes common to all three sources	E-mail only	E-mail and survey	Survey	Literature and survey	Literature only	Literature and e-mail
Acceptance	Abundance	Choice	Acknowledgment	Beyond	Model	Alignment
Applied spirituality	Active receptivity	Ethics	Attention	Caring	Depth	Appreciation
Authenticity	Age	Fear	Backlash	Critical-		Attitude
Awareness	Androgyny –	Holistic	Demonstration	Skepticism		Balance
Compassion	masculine –	Humor	Dignity	Growth		Change
Creativity	feminine	Listening	Dialogue	Respect		Chaos theory
Culture	Angels	No harm	Innovation	Service		and self-organ-
Development	Announcements	Reflection	Light			izing systems
Diversity	Conformity	Support	Safety			Commitment
Goals	Conflict		Unconditional			Communication
Higher purpose	Death		love			Community
Integrity	Downsizing					Control
Learning	Discrimination					Connecting
Meditation	Home Office					Corporate
Personal	Information					Entrepreneur
Spirituality	Technology					Effectiveness
Stories	Internet					Faith
Trust	Interdependence					Forgiveness
Truth	Knowledge workers					God concept
Unity	Labyrinth					Inspiration
Values	Language					Intuition
	Nature					Leadership
	NLP					Management
	Protection					Meaning
	Questions					Motivation
	Re-engineering					Nurturing
	Responsibility					Openness
	Searching					Organization struc-
	Surrender					ture
	Teaching					– size
	Tools					Organization bene-
						fits
						Organization learn-
						ing
						Partnership
						Path
						Paradigm shift
						Play
						Purpose
						Rational
						Stress
						Survival
						Uncertainty
						Visualizations

Phase one results   Codes generated from data analysis of three text sources on "spirituality in the workplace"

Step 2

Network views from each of the three sources—e-mail, question-naire, and literature—were generated to view the relationship links between "spirituality in the workplace" and the codes revealed.

At this point the data were sufficiently coded and displayed to allow the investigator to observe themes and/or patterns. This exami-nation was assisted by the use of a grouping heuristic. Specifically, when investigating the coded relationships within and between the source network views, the examiner reflected on the following three questions: "What are the categories or patterns present?" "How do the codes relate to each other?" "How do the codes relate to the base code of 'spirituality in the workplace'?" This reflection process led to the formalization of the following four "families" and their explanations as defined by the researcher: (1) Nouns (persons, places, or things), tangi-bles, entities; (2) Actions—things that can be done, verbs, activities; (3) Theories—interpretations, assumptions, beliefs, value- added thoughts; and, (4) Qualities —experiences, feelings, attributes, adjectives, non-tangibles.

Step 3

Next, the codes unveiled in step 1 were reviewed and categorized into one of the four family categories (nouns, actions, theories, and qualities). The researcher then constructed a network image for each one of the four families. The network images were constructed by placing the code symbol for "spirituality in the workplace" in the center and then instructed the community to pull up the respective family codes and links. The images were visually scanned and reviewed for comparisons.

Step 4

To gain clarity and to lead to possible applications the views were re-interpreted into clauses. Codes that are linked together are used as subjects and objects in sentences where relationship symbols provide nouns and prepositions. Sentence translations for each of the four views (actions, nouns, qualities, and theories) were generated to form paragraphs.

Results

Results unfold at each phase of the study and culminated with the sentence interpretations and discussion below. Each step contributes to answering the question, "What do people write about when they refer to spirituality in the workplace?" Step 1 compiled Table 1, which shows all the tagged codes by source. Step 2 resulted in the emergence of the four family groupings (nouns, actions, theories, and qualities). These four categories then became the basis for four more network views. Step 4 reinterpreted the views into sentences that reflect the links expressed in the data. The network views are visual distillations of the concepts ([codes]) and relationships (links) revealed in the sample text passages without the descriptive, personal examples. The sentence interpretation paragraphs below are the result of re-interpreting the views into text clauses. For the sentence interpretations below, "spirituality in the workplace" is represented as a topic code = [Spirit@Work].

Action Family View: Sentence Interpretations

[Acceptance] of [diversity] is a resultant action of [Spirit@Work]. [Understanding] and [acceptance] of [diversity] helps with [conflicts]. [Applied spirituality] is an activity of [Spirit@Work]. [Community] applied to [work] (in the work setting) is an action of [Spirit@Work]. [Development] of perception is an example of [Learning]. [Learning] is an action of [Spirit@Work]. [Intuition] supports [work] and [spirituality]. [Awareness] is an aspect of [spirituality]. [Personal] [development] leads to [spirituality]. [Religious practice], [visualizations], and [meditation] are examples of [applied spirituality]. [Searching] for [truth] is an aspect of [spirituality]. [Storytelling] is an action of [Spirit@Work] that influences [culture] and helps with the manifestation of [purpose]. [Storytelling] has [management] applications. [Teaching] about [compassion] as an aspect of [Spirit@Work] is occurring. [Work] as an action of [Spirit@Work] is an application of [service].

Noun Family View: Sentence Interpretations

[Goals] associated with [higher purpose] lead to [Spirit@Work]. When [Management] [communicates] about [values] which are related to aspects of the [paradigm shift], this helps/supports [Spirit@Work].

[Organizational Structure] and [leadership] influence [culture], which in turn influences [Spirit@Work]. [Management] applies [storytelling] to influence [culture]. [Personal] [relationships] are actions of [applied spirituality]. A [home office] is an example of an [authentic] [path].

Qualities Family View: Sentence Interpretations

[Authenticity] is an aspect of a [God Concept]. [Authenticity] is a [path]. [Awareness] is a quality of [Spirit@Work]. [Awareness] is an aspect of [intuition]. [Awareness] leads to [creativity]. [Creativity] supports [learning] about [community]. [Intuition] leads to [creativity]. [Creativity] is a quality of [Spirit@Work]. [Compassion] is a quality of [Spirit@Work]. [Compassion] and [wisdom] are aspects of the [new paradigm]. [Diversity] is a quality of [Spirit@Work]. [Flexibility] is a quality of [applied spirituality]. [Integrity] is a quality of [Spirit@Work]. [Integrity] is applied to [leadership]. [Integrity] is [energizing]. [Personal] is a quality of [Spirit@Work]. A property of a [spiritual] [path] is that it is [personal]. [Trust] is a quality of [Spirit@Work]. [Trusting] [relationships] help to build [community]. [Searching] for the [truth] is a [quality] of [Spirit@Work]. The [integration] of [truth] and [self] helps [unity]. [Unity] is a quality of [Spirit@Work]. [Unity] is [omnipresent] and [beyond].

Theories Family View: Sentence Interpretations

[Diversity] leads to [organization benefits] and when applied to [leadership] can influence [culture] and assist [management] with [perceptions] that lead to [learning]. [Spirituality] is a theoretical aspect of [Spirit@Work]. [Spirituality] is a [personal] [connection] to [God]. The [Path] of [spirituality] is an aspect of [Spirit@Work]. [Values], [ethics] and [volunteer work] are aspects of [spirituality]. [Spirituality] is not [religion]. [Higher purpose] is a theoretical aspect of [Spirit @Work]. [Higher purpose] leads to [guidance]. [Intuition] leads to [higher purpose]. [Higher purpose] has aspects that are [beneficial] and [beyond] the physical. [Service] is an example of [higher purpose]. [Truth] about [reality] is [unity]. [Truth] is an aspect of [Spirit@Work].

Discussion

Discoveries have been made in reference to the opening question of this paper, "What do people write about when they refer to 'spirituality in the workplace'?" As projected in the introduction, not any one, two, or even three things can be said about "spirituality in the workplace" that would include the universe of explanations. The data collected and analyzed here reflect the diverse nature of the concept. New challenges arise in my mind. Is there an inclusive way to approach the complexity of the results that will lead to some practical applications and/or increased knowledge in the area? And more specifically, is anything useful to be made of the clauses? These statements are certainly not intended to be taken as "facts" or even statistically significant relationships (although in future research this might be possible). Rather, definitions and applications of "spirituality in the workplace" of an involved population are revealed. Fortunately, it is the similar and diverse perceptions of employees that often matter most in change management processes. A possible next step in an organizational context would be to feed the findings back to the group members as part of an unfolding participative process inviting "spirituality in the work-place."

A next step in the present context is to highlight themes and practical applications reflected in the results. One of the predominant motifs is the presence of diversity as a beneficent contributor to "spirituality in the workplace" across each of the family interpretations. Specifically, a "qualities" family sentence states, "[Diversity] is a quality of spirituality in the workplace." A theories clause asserts, "[Diversity] leads to [organization benefits] and when applied to [leadership] can influence [culture] and assist [management] with [perceptions] that lead to [learning]." Clauses reinterpreting the "activities" network give some examples of possible organizational benefits: "[Acceptance] of [diversity] is a resultant action of spirituality in the workplace," and "[Understanding] and [acceptance] of [diversity] helps with [conflicts]." These concepts appear relevant and practical since cultural pluralism is "an integral part" of today's society (World Commission for Culture and Development, 1996).

Possibly contributing to the pluralistic aspect of "spirituality in the workplace" is the emphasis on the uniquely personal aspect of spirituality. This point is also echoed several times in the sentence reinterpretations. Specifically, a theories sentence states that, "[Spirituality] is a [personal][connection]," in the qualities family, "[Personal] is a quality of spirituality in the workplace," and "A property of a [spiritual] [path] is that it is [personal]." From the action clauses, "[Personal][development] leads to [spirituality]." Previous emphasis has been made on the personal and diverse attributes of spirituality in a work setting. Specifically, Vaill (1996) suggests that dialogue rather than debate is more productive when dealing with the diversity arising from multiple personal perspectives on spirituality.

The code [intuition] was also involved in multiple statements: "[Intuition] supports [work] and [spirituality]; [Intuition] leads to [creativity]; [Awareness] is an aspect of [intuition]; [Intuition] leads to [higher purpose]." Practical intuition is considered to be an integral aspect of emotional literacy, which is a key skill for organizational leaders (Cooper & Sawaf, 1997).

Another recurring theme in the data is the multiple appearance of [learning] and [development]. Example clauses are: "[Learning] is an action of [Spirit@Work]; [Development] of perception is an example of [learning]; [Creativity] supports [learning] about [community]; [Personal] [development] leads to [spirituality]." Strategic continual learning has been suggested to be an adaptive strategy for individuals (Vaill, 1996) and organizations (Collins & Porras, 1994; Senge, 1990) in dealing with the current turbulent conditions of contemporary workplaces.

A suggested practical use of this information would be to help individuals reflect on what emerges as possible next steps in their own self-development. To explain, for those people interested in increasing their active experience of "spirituality the workplace," a look at the phrases in the "actions" family could provide some suggestions and/or stimulate other ideas. Similarly, to gain clarity of one's own definitions and associations of "spirituality in the workplace," a review of the "theories" and "qualities" sentence interpretations, coupled with self-observation (inner listening), could lead to personal insight.

Perhaps the most useful part of what has been demonstrated here is that there is no "one answer" to the question "What is spirituality in the workplace?" but rather a framework is presented with opportunities for exploration and discovery. In a sense, this study is an attempt at operationalizing the quote from management professor Don McCormick (1994), in the opening paragraphs of this paper, "Definitions of spirituality abound." The researcher further asserts that when investigating "spirituality in the workplace," the process benefits by being as inclusive as possible with respect to the diversity of definitions held by the specific population involved. It is also strongly recommended that any organizational interventions around "spirituality in the workplace" treat all employees and their beliefs with respect. Any effort to do otherwise would not only miss the point but also miss the opportunity for learning and growth and could possibly do more damage than good.

This study has attempted to reflect the expansiveness of the topic is motivated by a "Social Constructionist" orientation. "Social Constructionism views discourse about the world not as a reflection or map of the world but as an artifact of communal interchange" (Gergen, 1985). This intent was reflected by the collection of data from the writings of people who were actively engaged in discourse on "spirituality in the workplace." The current author further asserts that definitions and applications of "spirituality in the workplace" are unique to individuals. One must be careful not to presuppose otherwise. Therefore, when planning any group or organizational intervention around the topic, again the suggestion is made to derive definitions and goals from the participants themselves.

In conclusion, to say that the definitions and experiences of "spirituality in the workplace" are limited to what is presented here would be a disservice and a misrepresentation. Multiple perspectives and understandings of the topic can contribute greatly to its comprehension. The sentence interpretations and following discussion are presented, not as a summation, but rather as an invitation to reflect on interrelated concepts associated with "spirituality in the workplace." An inclusive framework is most efficiently achieved through the use of methodologies that can handle pluralistic concepts. Martin Rutte (1995) has stated, "Spirituality in the workplace is not an answer, but rather a way to ask the questions." The methodological applications and results of the current study are presented as only one of many possible ways to understand such a complex and diverse area as "spirituality in the workplace."

References

Argyris, C. (1976), "Leadership, Learning, and Changing the Status Quo," *Organizational Dynamics*, 29–43.

Austin, N. K. (1995), "Does Spirituality Work?" *Working Woman*, 88.

Brussat, F., & Brussat M. A. (1998), *Spiritual Literacy*, Scribner, New York.

Chappell, T. (1994), "The Soul of a Business," *Executive Female*, 17, 38.

Collins, J. C. & Porras, J. I. (1994), *Built to Last*, HarperCollins, New York.

Cooper, R. K., & Sawaf, A. (1997), *Executive EQ*, Grosset-Putnam, New York.

Conger, J. (Ed.) (1994), *Spirit At Work*, Jossey-Bass, San Francisco, CA.

Corbin, J., & Strauss, A. (1990), "Grounded Theory Research—Procedures, Canons and Evaluative Criteria," *Qualitative Sociology*, 13.

Debats, D., Drost, J., & Hansen, P. (1995), "Experiences of Meaning in Life; A combined qualitative and quantitative approach," University of Groningen, Department of Clinical Psychology, Academic Hospital, Oostersignel 59, 9713 EZ Groningen, The Netherlands.

Freshman, B. L. (1995), "Spirituality in the Workplace: An exploratory literature analysis and preliminary model structuring," Unpublished manuscript, California School of Professional Psychology at Los Angeles.

Gergen, K. (1985), "The Social Constructionist Movement in Modern Psychology," *American Psychologist*, 40, 266–275.

Gorbachev, M. (1995), "A Call for New Values," *Noetic Sciences Review*, 12–13.

Harman, W. W. (1992, October), "Signs of a Shift in World View: Potential resolution of the world dilemma," Presented at the Planet in Change Symposium, Johannesburg, South Africa.

Haskell, L. (1995), "90 Decisions: The entrepreneurial model," *Indianapolis Business*, 16, 14.

Hitt, M. A., Keats, B. W., & DeMarie, S. M. (1998), "Navigating in the New Competitive Landscape: Building strategic flexibility and competitive advantage in the 21st century," *The Academy of Management Executive, 12(4)*, 22–42.

Klemke, E. (1981), *The Meaning of Life*, Oxford University Press, New York.

Lee, C., & Zemke, R. (1993), "The Search for Spirit in the Workplace," *Training*, 21–28.

McCormick. D. W. (1994), "Spirituality and Management," *Journal of Managerial Psychology, 9 (6)*, 5–8.

McAteer, M. (1995), "Banking on spirituality," *Toronto Star*, April 15, Canada.

Miles, M., & Huberman, A. M. (1994), *Qualitative Data Analysis,* Sage Publications, Thousand Oaks, CA.

Moore, T. (1992), *Care of the Soul,* HarperPerennial, New York.

Ray, M., & Rinzler, A. (Eds.) (1993), *The New Paradigms in Business,* Tarcher/Putnam, New York.

Rowen, P., & Reason, J. (Eds.) (1981), *Human Inquiry,* Wiley & Sons, New York.

Rutte, M. (1995, September), "Spirituality in the Workplace," *Spirituality in the workplace,* Symposium conducted at the California School of Professional Psychology, Los Angeles, CA.

Senge, P. (1990), *The Fifth Discipline,* Doubleday, New York.

Strauss, S. (1984), "Qualitative Analysis in Social Research—Grounded Theory Methodology (Part Two)," Hagen: FB Erziehungs—und Sozialwissenschaften der Fernuniversitt Hagen.

Vaill, P. B. (1996), *Learning as a Way of Being,* Jossey-Bass, San Francisco, CA.

Wheatley, M. J., & Kellner-Rogers, M. (1996), *A Simpler Way,* Berrett-Koehler, San Francisco, CA

World Commission for Culture and Development (1996), Our Creative Diversity, URL:http://kvc.minbuza.nl/kvcframe.html?/boekteksten/chapter2.html

Zohar, D. (1997), *Rewiring the Corporate Brain,* Berrett-Koehler, San Francisco, CA.

A FRAMEWORK FOR THE PRACTICAL APPLICATION OF SPIRITUALITY AT WORK

Lois Sekerak Hogan,
Consultant in Organizational Strategy,
Change & Communication

Despite growing interest in spirituality and work, its study and practical application has been constrained by a number of factors. Among these factors are a lack of agreement on the definition of spirituality and limited theoretical and empirical literature on the topic, although it is represented by a wide variety of primarily anecdotal perspectives in the popular business press. Perhaps the biggest constraint is that there are few coherent conceptual frameworks that organize the literature. Like the proverbial blind men and the elephant, each writer presents a particular perspective revealing various aspects of the topic, but there have been few attempts to suggest a larger view of its overall nature. The topic has only very recently begun to be addressed in the academic literature, though scholarly interest is on the rise.[1]

Much of the literature that could contribute to an understanding is related conceptually, but may utilize other terminology or exist in diverse disciplines such as business and management, philosophy, religious studies, psychology, and social science. As noted by Dehler and Welsh (1994), the literature on spirituality and work has been inadequately integrated with other organizational concepts. One attempt of this article is to look across disciplines for points of convergence that can better illumine the ways in which the concept of spirituality and work can be operationalized. In this article, a differentiation is made

---

[1] The *Journal of Organizational Change Management* published two special issues on the topic in June and July 1999, and the Academy of Management has seen an increase in sessions with a spiritual theme. Increase in scholarly interest is also evidenced by approximately 30–50 dissertations in progress on the topic as estimated by Judith Neal, editor of the online newsletter *Spirit at Work* and a clearinghouse for information on the topic.

between spirituality and religion, following McCormick (1994), who argued that spirituality is a more universal experience, unbounded by any particular belief or dogma.

A Proposed Framework

Based on a review of representative literature[2]—both that which directly refers to spirituality and work and those that indirectly relate as extrapolations of themes—this article proposes a preliminary framework that organizes the thinking on spirituality and work into four themes. The framework evolves from the transition from a modern, positivist industrial-era paradigm to a postmodern, postindustrial paradigm—a transition often referred to in the spirituality and work literature (e.g., Biberman & Whitty, 1997; Briskin, 1996; Handy, 1990, 1994; Harman, 1991; Mollner, 1991; Ray, 1991; Wheatley, 1992). The intention is not to discredit industrial-era contributions; rather the purpose is to suggest that the domination of traditional business goals such as profitability and productivity is being supplanted by complementary themes that extend the role of work and business into new areas.

The four themes of the proposed framework shown in Table 1 below include: (1) the transition from an emphasis on fragmentation to a concern for wholeness; (2) the shift from self-absorption to a relationship focus; (3) the progression from an emphasis on primarily materialist values to include spiritual values; and (4) the evolution from the instrumental to the developmental purpose of work.

TABLE 1: Four Dimensions of Spirituality and Work	
Old Paradigm	Emerging Paradigm
Fragmentation	Wholeness
Self-absorption	Relationship Focus
Emphasis on Material Values	Inclusion of Spiritual Values
Instrumental Purpose of Work	Developmental Purpose of Work

---

[2] Because the framework considers broadly cross-disciplinary information sources, the article does not provide exhaustive references, but examines representative literature from various disciplines.

To elaborate the framework, I next provide examples of various individual and organizational activities that suggest ways each of the themes can be operationalized within the workplace.

Dimension 1: Shift from Fragmentation to Wholeness

Industrial-era attempts made to better measure and control output resulted not only in workplace practices that fragmented the experience of work but that subordinated the soul to the needs of productivity and efficiency (Briskin, 1996). In fairness, industrial-era practices benefited culture in many ways; however, the general tendency to separate and divide perpetuated fragmentation as a general cultural theme, resulting in a number of dichotomies or splits between various aspects of work. Table 2 identifies various ways in which fragmentation is experienced at work and contrasts these themes with ways in which a sense of wholeness can be restored to the work experience.

TABLE 2: The Shift from Fragmentation to Wholeness	
Fragmentation	Wholeness
Compartmentalization of work and personal life	Integration of work and personal life, e.g., Work/Life initiatives
Emphasis on rationality and devaluation of non-rational	New appreciation for the role of emotion, intuition, love, and other "non-rational" experiences in the work setting
Chasm between workers and management	Employee empowerment
Division of work into small pieces or "jobs"	Systems or integrative approach to work and product design
Spirituality as separate from work	Spiritual practices and concepts applied in the workplace

(a) Integration of Work and Personal or Family Life

The difficulty many workers experience in trying to balance work and personal life is an issue gaining momentum and credence (Friedlander, 1992, 1994; Friedlander & Delberg, 1995). The desire for more balance is particularly evident among the younger generation. For example, the *Wall Street Journal* reported that corporate recruiters note a trend in undergraduate recruiting in which questions about work/life balance are becoming more common, suggesting a major change in values in this generation (Shellenbarger, 1997, January 29). Rather than seeing work and personal needs as being mutually exclusive, managers and employees in many organizations are collaborating to achieve work and personal objectives to everyone's benefit (Friedman, Christensen, & DeGroot, 1998). Among the numerous work/life initiatives underway in United States corporations are: childcare; eldercare; work sharing; flexible scheduling; self-renewal through sabbaticals; leave for new parents, schooling, or family illness; exercise programs; etc.

(b) New Appreciation for "Non-rational" Experience in the Workplace

Cartesian mind-body dualism elevated the importance of rationality within work environments, while correspondingly devaluing non-rational experience such as emotion and intuition, among others. Yet, bringing out these parts that do not "belong" in the workplace preserves a sense of soul in the workplace (Whyte, 1994). As an example, the reclamation of emotion at work is a frequent theme in the spirituality and work literature. Dehler and Walsh (1994) argued that despite the emotional nature of work, emotion has not been adequately considered by management theory and is a missing element in organizational change efforts. Pleas are made for working with passion (Anderson, 1984), managing from the heart (Bracey, Rosenbloom, Sanford, & Trueblood, 1993), encouraging the heart of employees (Kouzes & Posner, 1999), and nurturing emotional intelligence as a leadership skill (Goleman, 1995, 1998).

(c) Employee Empowerment

Organizational consultant Burkard Sievers (1986) observed that because the planning and managing of work have become separated from its execution, the division of labor has resulted in one set of people handling the machines while the others are privileged to think about work. However, the chasm that sometimes exists between the planning and execution functions of work is changing to some extent as organizations reorganize, reengineer, and decentralize power from higher to lower levels. Despite being driven by economic goals, one effect of flattening the managerial hierarchy within business is the creation of empowered workers, thereby advancing the view that workers can manage themselves and that self-management and execution can be combined. Jaffe and Scott (1998) have identified empowerment of all employees as an aspect of spirit at work. Among the various characteristics they associate with empowerment are whether employees behave in a self-managing way and can really make change, and whether they have input into corporate policies.

(d) Systems Approach to Work and Product Design

Although the fragmentation of work into smaller steps through "jobbing" made complex tasks more manageable, some thinkers— particularly Marxists (e.g., Braverman, 1974; Marcuse, 1964)—argued that the assembly line and other divisions of labor also created a gulf between the worker and the end result of the work, making it less meaningful. In the language of spirituality and work, such work became lacking in "soul." In contrast, designing work to provide a broader perspective through job enrichment or work redesign creates opportunity for a more fulfilling work experience (Hackman, Oldham, Janson, & Purdy, 1975; Hackman & Oldham, 1975; Lawler, 1994/1973). As an example, the revolutionary team production process at Ford Motor Company's Saturn manufacturing plant was designed to provide workers with an opportunity to be engaged in the whole process thereby also enabling a greater sense of satisfaction and meaning in the work. While the literature on job enrichment and work redesign has not been linked to the spirit and work literature, its intention of making work more meaningful is a theme that is found repeatedly (e.g., Mitroff & Denton, 1999; Naylor et al., 1996; Vaill, 1989).

(e) Spiritual Practices and Concepts Applied in the Workplace

Though the traditional separation of church and state in the United States has made the integration of spiritual practice within the workplace somewhat controversial (see Cavanagh, 1999), in many organizations managers are gaining a whole new role as spiritual guide, for example, by unleashing spirit and potential, and by helping employees find purpose and meaning in their work (Konz & Ryan, 1999). Organizations report a variety of activities that have a spiritual theme. As examples, AT&T and Boeing, among others, invited poet David Whyte to speak to managers and employees about "The Preservation of Soul in Corporate America" (Whyte, 1994). A group of World Bank employees initiated a "Spiritual Unfoldment Society" that met periodically for conversations on awakening higher consciousness and integrating spiritual values into their work (Barrett, 1996). *Business Week* (Galen & West, 1995) reported that Lotus Development created a "soul" committee to reexamine the company's management practices and values in order to build a strong culture. Consultants with the Australian branch of the international consulting firm of McKinsey & Company reported improvements attained in customer service delivery for a client by attending to the workers' spiritual experience (Rennie & Bellin, 1998). *Industry Week* profiled eight successful CEOs who follow spiritual guidelines in running their businesses (Braham, 1999).

Individuals also describe various ways in which they privately incorporate their personal spirituality into their work. As examples, participants in one study (Darling & Schaefer, 1998) reported using a variety of approaches including: active/deep listening, affirmations and visualizations, meditation or centering processes, aligning their values with work, etc.

Dimension 2: Shift from Self-absorption to Relationships

A second dimension of spirituality at work concerns the shift from organizations being predominantly interested in institutional goals and needs to recognition of the value and importance of collaboration, community, and relationships. Related themes in the literature include: viewing a central aspect of spirituality as the desire to go beyond one's self-interests (McKnight, 1984; Ray, 1991); linking spirituality with having a sacred attitude toward relationships (Neck & Millman, 1994); defining spirituality as a transcendent connection to a larger world (Conger, 1995); and depicting society as moving from a material age into a relationship age in which the recognition of connection between others will drive more cooperation (Mollner, 1991).

Physicist Gary Zukov (1995), who has applied ideas from quantum physics to understand the evolution of business, believes that work change will be characterized by a shift from exploiting and manipulating to creating mutually beneficial relationships with key stakeholder groups. Examples of the ways in which organizations are recognizing the importance of relationships are summarized in Table 3 and elaborated in the text.

TABLE 3: Shift from Self-Absorption to Relationships	
Self-absorption	Relationship Focus
Emphasis on the organization and its needs	Emphasis on stakeholder relationships
Employees seen as a means to an end	Building workplace community
Corporate self-interest dominates	Corporate citizenship, ethics, and socially-responsible business practices
Command and control management styles	Participative processes

(a) Emphasis on Stakeholder Relationships

Organizations today are viewed as existing in a web of relation-ships between and among various stakeholder groups (Atkinson, Waterhouse, & Wells, 1997). Having a stakeholder strategy is viewed as a responsible business practice as well as making good business sense (Svendsen, 1998). As an example, innovative business entrepreneur Tom Chappell, founder of the personal care products company Tom's of Maine, has written extensively about the necessity and power of relationship in creating spirited and soulful organizations (1993). Similarly, in building her international chain of retail stores called The Body Shop, founder Anita Roddick has emphasized the importance of relationships to her employees, customers, and to the world at large (Roddick, 1991; Wheeler, Sillanpaa, & Roddick, 1998).

(b) Building Community in the Workplace

The metaphor of community in a workplace context implies an appreciation of mutual goals and needs, individual differences, and the value of an endeavor characterized by fellowship (Autry, 1991). Be-cause community emphasizes connectedness and interdependence, it has been seen as an essential element of spirituality (Waddock, 1999). Community at work is essentially the recognition of being aligned around a common purpose, which has been described as "metanoic organizations" (Kiefer & Senge, 1984). Workplace community has become a recent topic of exploration in the management literature (Goffee & Jones, 1996; Gozdz, 1995; Wheatley & Kellner-Rogers, 1995). The results are clearly more than relational, as can be seen in a case study documenting the experience of one organization making a conscious transition to corporate community (Brown, 1991). The results for this organization included significant reductions in cycle time for new product development, accident rates, employee absenteeism, turnover and healthcare costs, and customer complaints, as well as improvements in productivity.

(c) Corporate Citizenship, Ethics, and Socially Responsible Business Practices

Social responsibility is a repeated theme in organizations that are operating with a spiritual perspective. Chappell (1990) said, "The ultimate result of a business with soul is . . . a way of doing business that can analyze and strategize—but always with an eye on the common good" (p. 214). Organizations are beginning to take a broader perspective concerning their responsibility to society through the use of socially responsible business practices (Makower, 1995), corporate citizenship efforts (Tichy, McGill, & Clair, 1997), and by using spirituality—rather than legal requirements—as a foundation for principles of international business ethics (Jackson, 1999). The socially responsible organization acts as a "steward," placing an importance on service over exclusive self-interest (Block, 1993). To demonstrate social responsibility, workplace efforts include activities such as giving employees time off for community service, employee volunteer programs, donating a portion of organizational profits to non-profit causes, responsible investment, environmental accountability, as well as involvement in major global issues.

As with other initiatives introduced thus far in this article, there is evidence that socially responsible business practices positively impact financial performance (e.g., Makower, 1995; Preston & O'Bannon, 1997). As Peters and Waterman (1982) noted, when employees believe they are contributing to a larger purpose, they generally invest more energy, creativity, and enthusiasm into the work.

(d) Participative, Consensus-based Decision-making Processes and Listening Opportunities

In describing various types of "soul work" within organizations, Mirvis (1997) described many ways in which companies are engaging stakeholders in conversation as a way to engage more people and widen perspectives. Numerous innovative designs have emerged that involve large groups of stakeholders in collaborative discussion and decision making (Bunker & Alban, 1992, 1996), for example: the Future Search process (Weisbord & Janoff, 1995); Open Space Technology (Owen, 1993); and Real Time Strategic Change (Dannemiller & Tyson, 1990). Other processes, such as Dialogue (Bohm, 1989; Gerard & Teurfs, 1994; Isaacs, 1993), engage participants in conversation and active listening, often without explicit purpose other than to come to an appreciation of different points of view.

Dimension 3: Beyond Materialist Values to Include Spiritual Values

The third theme of spirituality and work concerns the shift from a dominance of materialist values to include more comprehensive values, many of which address more humanistic or spiritual concerns (Chappell, 1993; DeFoore & Renesch, 1995; Kriger & Hanson, 1999; Roddick, 1991). Business is being asked to play a more constructive role (Harman & Hormann, 1990), especially as the shift to a post-industrial society calls into question industrial growth–era values, attitudes, and expectations (Kiefer & Senge, 1984). The new values indicate a shift away from survival strategies and lifestyles focused on consumerism toward a life that is centered on ethics and sustainability (Elgin, 1996; Ray, 1996). Yankelovich (1981) characterized it as a cultural shift from an ethic of instrumental values to sacred/expressive ones. Though many human values have been seen as antithetical to the more short-term profit motives of organizations (Friedlander, 1994), an emphasis on core values—not merely on the bottom line—was linked to the success of the 18 "visionary" companies studied in Collins and Porras's (1997) longitudinal research. All of the companies have demonstrated long-term financial success, despite having value priorities that are non-economical.

The Global Paradigm Report (Elgin, 1996), which went beyond the United States to survey emergent world values, noted a shift in values toward personal rather than institutional authority, a continued swing toward democratic participation and gender equality, and added that there is a core group that is pioneering new ways of living that bridge the inner world (with emphasis on psychological and spiritual growth) and the outer world. Table 4 contrasts the differences between material and emerging spiritual values.

TABLE 4: Beyond Material Values to Include Spiritual Values	
Material Values	Spiritual Values
Business as a competitive war for profit	Business as a cooperative force for good
Business goals drive leadership & culture	Values-based leadership and culture
Emphasis on financial data	Recognition of a "new bottom line"

(a) Business as a Cooperative Force for Good

While profitability and productivity are still essential for success in the competitive global market, exclusive emphasis on these goals is discouraged by more spiritually attuned organizations. Instead of viewing business as a competitive war for profit, these enterprises view it as a cooperative force for good. As one example of the difference in thinking, futurist Barbara Marx Hubbard (1998) suggested that instead of a "war room" where some companies track their competition, "peace rooms" should be created where attention is paid to what is working in the organization (e.g., tracking energy, creativity, emerging innovations, successes, and breakthroughs). Among the many values that are becoming more evident in the workplace are harmony, trust, honesty, compassion, and cooperation (Ray, 1991); right-conduct, nonviolence, love, inner peace (Miller, 1991); social responsibility, respect for nature and for all relations, meaningful work, and employees bringing their whole selves to work (Chappell, 1993); global citizenry, sharing prosperity, empowering employees and treating them with dignity, educating and raising the consciousness of employees, customers, and the larger society, bringing and expressing passion in work, making a place at work for love, intuition, truth, and authenticity, admitting mistakes, and a keen sense of responsibility to the environment and ecological balance (Roddick, 1991).

(b) Values-based Leadership and Culture

Emphasis on values-based management and leadership is found in both the spirituality and work literature (e.g., Barrett, 1998) and the more traditional business literature (e.g., Blanchard & O'Connor, 1997). For example, *Business Week* (Galen & West, 1995) claimed that AT&T is helping managers define their values in order to be better leaders.

While having clearly articulated values does not necessarily imply a spiritually motivated organization, specific values are sometimes identified as crucial for managers, such as "authenticity" and "caring" (Autry, 1991; Covey, 1991; DePree, 1989; Koestenbaum, 1991; Vaill, 1998).

(c) The Growth of Non-financial Indicators in Business Reporting

Within the spirituality and work literature, reference is often made to looking beyond the bottom line (Makower, 1995) or to a "new" bottom line, suggesting that organizations have responsibilities to more than just increasing profit for the shareholder or owner benefit. Among the suggestions is the idea that financial statements of socially responsible organizations should report on five kinds of capital, which in additional to financial capital include: human and intellectual, social, natural, and consumer capital (Leaver, 1995). Simultaneously, research from a number of business and financial sources has criticized the use of financial indicators alone as an insufficient measure of an organization's health, performance, or future success (Stewart, 1998). For example, a recent Brookings Institution report asserted that as little as one-third to one-half of most companies' stock-market value is accounted for these days by hard assets such as property, plant, and equipment. Instead, a growing share of value is attributable to so-called "soft" assets, which have traditionally been excluded from financial accounting methods (Shellenbarger, 1998, July 22). In addition to the traditional financial measures, such approaches also look at intangible assets such as employee morale, satisfaction, and retention; customer satisfaction and brand loyalty; investments in employee learning and growth; community relations; and other such factors. Though the development of non-financial measures was driven by the desire to meet the information needs of creditors and investors rather than being spiritually motivated, the effort may have the unintended effect of focusing attention on relationships and other attributes that are often associated with work and spirituality.

Dimension 4: From an Instrumental to a Developmental Purpose of Work

Public opinion trend-watcher Daniel Yankelovich claimed that instrumentalism, which views material possessions as the instruments for generating satisfaction, is gradually being supplanted by a "sacred" outlook that seeks intrinsic value in the workplace (cited in Kiefer & Senge, 1984, p. 69). While others argue that, for many, work remains a primarily economically motivated activity and not one where the fulfillment of higher-level needs is sought (e.g., Brief, Konovsky, Goodwin, & Link, 1995), many thinkers (e.g., Anthony, 1980; Fox, 1994; Harman & Hormann, 1990; Naylor, Willimon, & Osterberg, 1996) have suggested that work has a developmental role. As an example, organizational psychologist Marsha Sinetar (1987) predicted that the worker's need for self-actualization would be a key management issue by the year 2000.

The movement from an instrumental to a developmental view of work can be compared to Abraham Maslow's (1968) *Hierarchy of Needs* in which higher developmental needs—including the spiritual—are attended to once more basic survival needs are met. Because the "basic" needs of a large extent of the population in Western culture are met, work needs may be shifting into higher-order needs (Tischler, 1999). The demand for developmental work may reflect a critical mass within the world's population that is evolving to a new level of needs. Table 5 introduces themes in the shift between an instrumental and a developmental view of work.

TABLE 5: From the Instrumental to the Developmental Purpose of Work	
Instrumental	Developmental
Work as a means of livelihood	Work as an opportunity for self-development
Spiritual development and meaning sought outside the workplace	Work as a path for spiritual growth or meaning sought in work

(a) Work as an Opportunity for Self-development

Harmon and Hormann (1990) stated, "In a technologically advanced society where production of sufficient goods and services can be handled with ease, employment exists primarily for self-development, and is only secondarily concerned with the production of goods and services" (p. 26). Included in their definition of self-development are such things as personal and professional development, quality relationships, and meaningful service to others. Outside of the spirituality and work literature, numerous studies have demonstrated that people choose to work, even when it is not economically necessary, because it gives them a sense of purpose and opportunities for personal creativity and fulfillment (Gini & Sullivan, 1987; Morse & Weiss, 1955; MOW International Research Team, 1987; Vecchio, 1980)— characteristics also found in the literature on spirituality and work.

(b) Work as a Path for Spiritual Growth or Meaning Sought in Work

The desire for work to be meaningful is a frequent theme found in the spirituality and work literature (Briskin, 1996; DeFoore & Renesch, 1995; Fox, 1994; Handy, 1990; McKnight, 1984; Mitroff & Denton, 1999; Moore, 1997; Naylor et al., 1996; Richards, 1995; Secretan, 1996; Vaill, 1989). Though existential issues such as meaningful work have tended to be ignored in organizations, organizational existentialist Thierry Pauchant (1995) noted that a number of his colleagues as well as other influential management thinkers have begun to address this issue (e.g., Warren Bennis, Frederick Herzberg, Ian Mitroff, and Henry Mintzberg). The Institute for the Future, a research firm that does trend forecasting, has predicted that the issue of meaning will become more and more important in companies (Galen & West, 1995). In a 1991 survey of 7,200 business managers by the American Management Association, nearly half of the respondents reported that for them success is increasingly measured in terms of greater job satisfaction and more meaningful work (Goddard, 1991). Managerial recognition of the need to create meaning and purpose for employees has been linked with the current emphasis on values-based business (Leigh, 1997). Writing for the *Harvard Business Review*, Martha Nichols (1994) predicted that creating meaning might be the most important managerial task of the future. Workers want to know how their work contributes to the organization, and companies will need to have ways of answering this question to attract bright and dedicated employees (Herman & Gioia, 1998). As management consultants Peters and Waterman (1982) said, "We desperately need meaning in our lives and will sacrifice a great deal to institutions that will provide meaning for us" (p. 56).

The popular literature on soul, spirit, and meaning suggests several other concepts about what constitutes meaningful work, some of which view work as a spiritual path. These include: (a) the idea of work as a "calling," which suggests being strongly guided to or having a passion or deep intention for a particular type of work (Ferguson, 1980; Finney & Dasch, 1998; Hillman, 1996; Moore, 1997; Whitmyer, 1994); (b) work imbued with transcendent purpose, i.e., when a person feels a part of some larger purpose (Conger, 1995; McKnight, 1984); (c) ideas arising from the Buddhist idea of Right Livelihood in which spirituality is unalterably linked to one's work (Phillips, 1994; Sinetar, 1987; Whitmyer, 1994); and (d) becoming so absorbed in the work that it approximates a meditative experience such as found among many Eastern spiritual traditions including Buddhists, Sufis, and Hindus.

Summary

Based upon a broad review of topics discussed in the spirituality and work literature and conferences, this article has proposed a framework for organizing these topics into four themes: wholeness, relationship focus, emerging values, and the developmental purpose of work. Within each theme, examples were given to illustrate how the theme could be operationalized in the workplace. By elaborating the themes, the examples included various other organizational activities and initiatives that otherwise might not be appreciated as related to spirituality.

There are several limitations of the framework that warrant mention. First, there may be more than four dimensions that could have been considered. Second, the framework does not purport to cover every theme mentioned in the spirit and work literature; many important ones are not addressed, for example, new approaches to leadership and management (Autry, 1991; Barnett, 1985; Bolman & Deal, 1995; Greenleaf, 1993; Vaill, 1989, 1998; Wheatley, 1992), personal, organizational, and societal transformation (Adams, 1984; Neal, Lichtenstein, & Banner, 1999; Owen, 1987), and new forms of ownership and wealth distribution (Harman & Hormann, 1990)—to name a few. Third, some may protest that these ideas are merely old concepts in new spiritual clothes. While this may be partially true, it may also be the case that a synchronistic convergence is occurring between activities and initiatives in the workplace and with the themes promulgated by the spirituality and work literature. Fourth, moving beyond an abstract discussion of spirituality and work to suggest concrete, actionable ideas that individuals and organizations can implement raises a concern about the commodification of the concept, which would make it a management fad. Similarly, some may view the example actions described as a formula for implementation of spirituality at work. Both of these reactions are examples of using the right ideas for the wrong reasons (i.e., to assuage employees, to pay lip service to popular ideas, or to use them for primarily self-serving interests). It cannot be emphasized strongly enough: intention is essential to the essence of spirituality integrated with work. Moreover, despite the evidence demonstrating positive impact on financial performance and productivity,[3] it cannot be assumed that this is a universal result for organizations implementing these ideas. There are also other drawbacks; for those interested in pursuing the integration of work and spirituality, it is essential to review other criticism of the integration of spirituality at work, though that is outside the scope of this article.[4] Finally, there is a somewhat unsatisfying reaction in taking a profound topic such as spirituality and attempting to reduce it to various elements appropriate for a secular setting; spirituality is a highly personal and perhaps irreducible experience and—without question—more than the sum of its parts. Ultimately, it must be considered that the challenge is not to answer the question "What is spirituality and work?" but to continue to live in the question and keep it alive.

References

Adams, J. (Ed.). (1984), *Transforming Work: A collection of organization transformation readings*. Alexandria, VA: Miles River Press.

Anderson, N. (1995), 2nd edition. *Work with Passion: How to do what you love for a living*. New World Library: New York.

Anthony, P. D. (1980), Work and the loss of meaning. *International Science Journal, 32*(3), 416–426.

---

[3] For example, see Barrett (1998) and Collins and Porras (1997).

[4] Critics of spirituality and work integration argue that it blurs the line between spirited and spiritual and allows management to potentially interfere with employees' personal lives (Peters, cited in Galen & West, 1995) or that passion and spirituality might be used to promote excessive commitment to work, causing workers to ignore the negative effects on health, family, and community (Caproni, 1997). Nancy Austin (1995) has labeled the integration of spirituality at work as "neospiritualism," criticizing that it goes beyond the unorthodox; it is crazy.

Atkinson, A. A., Waterhouse, J. H., & Wells, R. B. (1997), A stakeholder approach to strategic performance measurement. *Sloan Management Review* (Spring), 25–37.

Autry, J. A. (1991), *Love and Profit: The art of caring leadership*. New York: Morrow.

Barnett, J. H. (1985), A business model of enlightenment. *Journal of Business Ethics, 4(1)*, 57–63.

Barrett, R. (1996), A corporate values revolution. www:corptools. com/text/corpvals.html. Waynesville, NC: Richard Barrett & Associates LLC.

Barrett, R. (1998), *Liberating the Corporate Soul: Building a visionary organization*. Boston: Butterworth Heinemann.

Biberman, J., & Whitty, M. (1997), A postmodern spiritual future for work. *Journal of Organizational Change Management, 10(2)*, 130–138.

Blanchard, K., & O'Connor, M. (1997), *Managing by Values*. San Francisco: Berrett-Koehler.

Block, P. (1993), *Stewardship: Choosing service over self-interest*. San Francisco: Berrett-Koehler.

Bohm, D. (1989), On dialogue. Paper presented at the Seminar by David Bohm at Ojai Foundation, Ojai, CA.

Bolman, L. G., & Deal, T. E. (1995), *Leading with Soul: An Uncommon Journey of Spirit*. San Francisco: Jossey-Bass, Inc.

Bracey, H., Rosenbloom, J., Sanford, A., & Trueblood, R. (1993). *Managing from the Heart*. New York: Delacourt Press.

Braham, J. (1999, February 1), The spiritual side. *Industry Week, 248*, 48–56.

Braverman, H. (1974), *Labor and Monopoly Capital: The degradation of work in the twentieth century*. New York: Monthly Review Press.

Brief, A. P., Konovsky, M. A., Goodwin, R., & Link, K. (1995), Inferring the meaning of work from the effects of unemployment. *Journal of Applied Social Psychology, 25(8)*, 693–711.

Briskin, A. (1996), *The Stirring of Soul in the Workplace*. San Francisco: Jossey-Bass, Inc.

Brown, J. (1991), Corporation as community. In J. Renesch (Ed.), *New Traditions in Business: Spirit and leadership in the 21st century* (pp. 130–137). San Francisco: Sterling & Stone.

Bunker, B. B., & Alban, B. T. (1992), Editors' Introduction: The large group intervention—a new social innovation? *The Journal of Applied Behavioral Science, 28(4),* 473–479.

Bunker, B. B., & Alban, B. T. (1996), *Large Group Interventions: Engaging the whole system for rapid change.* San Francisco: Jossey-Bass.

Cavanagh, G. F. (1999), Spirituality for Managers: Context and critique. *Journal of Organizational Change Management, 12(3),* 186–199.

Chappell, T. (1993), *The Soul of a Business: Managing for profit and the common good.* New York: Bantam Books.

Collins, J., & Porras, J. (1997), *Built to Last: Successful habits of visionary companies.* New York: HarperBusiness.

Conger, J. A. (1995), Moved by the Spirit: Leadership and spirituality in the workplace. *OD Practitioner, 27(1),* 46–51.

Dannemiller, K. D., & Tyson, C. (1990), Interactive Strategic Planning: A Consultant's Guide. Ann Arbor, MI: Dannemiller Tyson Associates.

Darling, J., & Schaefer, C. (1998), Spirituality in the Workplace. *Lapis,* 63–67.

DeFoore, W., & Renesch, J. (Eds.) (1995), *Rediscovering the Soul of Business: A renaissance of values.* San Francisco: New Leaders Press.

Dehler, G. E., & Welsh, M. A. (1994), Spirituality and Organizational Transformation: Implications for the new management paradigm. *Journal of Managerial Psychology, 9(6),* 17–26.

DePree, M. (1989), *Leadership is an Art.* New York: Doubleday.

Elgin, D. (1996), *The Global Paradigm Report.* San Francisco: Fetzer Institute.

FASB. (1998), Business reporting research project. www.fasb.org: Financial Accounting Standards Board.

Ferguson, M. (1980), *The Aquarian Conspiracy: Personal and social transformation in the 1980s.* New York: St. Martin's Press.

Finney, M., & Dasch, D. (1998), *Finding Your Calling, Loving Your Life.* New York: Simon & Schuster.

Fox, M. (1994), *The Reinvention of Work: A new vision of livelihood for our time.* San Francisco: HarperSanFrancisco.

Friedlander, F. (1992), Work and family: Is it simply a balancing act? *Vision/Action,* 4–7.

Friedlander, F. (1994), Toward whole systems and whole people. *Organization, 1(1),* 59–64.

Friedlander, F., & Delberg, A. (1995), Strategies for personal and family renewal: How a high surviving group of executives cope with stress and avoid burnout. *Journal of Management Inquiry,* September 1995.

Friedman, S. D., Christensen, P., & DeGroot, J. (1998) Work and life: The end of the zero-sum game. *Harvard Business Review* (Nov/Dec).

Galen, M., & West, K. (June 5, 1995). Companies hit the road less traveled: Can spirituality enlighten the bottom line. *Business Week,* 82–85.

Gerard, G., & Teurfs, L. (1994), Explorations in dialogue: What works, what does not. *Vision/Action: The Journal of the Bay Area OD Network, 13(2),* 19–24.

Gini, A. R., & Sullivan, T. (1987) Work: The process and the person. *Journal of Business Ethics, 6(8),* 649–655.

Goddard, R. W. (1991), A new view of work. *Supervision, 52(4),* 14–16, 26.

Goffee, R., & Jones, G. (1996), What holds the modern company together? *Harvard Business Review* (November-December), 133–148.

Goleman, D. (1995), *Emotional Intelligence: Why it can matter more than IQ.* New York: Bantam Books.

Goleman, D. (1998), What makes a leader? *Harvard Business Review* (November-December).

Gozdz, K. (Ed.) (1995), *Community Building: Renewing spirit and learning in business.* San Francisco: Sterling & Stone.

Greenleaf, R. K. (1993), The leader as servant. In C. Whitmyer (Ed.), *In the Company of Others: Making Community in a Modern World* (pp. 56–64). New York: Jeremy P. Tarcher/Perigree Books.

Hackman, J. R., Oldham, G., Janson, R., & Purdy, K. (1975), A new strategy for job enrichment. *California Management Review,* Vol 17, No. 4 (Summer 1975), p. 57.

Hackman, J. R., & Oldham, G. R. (1975), Development of the job diagnostic survey. *Journal of Applied Psychology, 60, 2,* 159–170.

Handy, C. (1990), *The Age of Unreason.* Boston: Harvard Business School Press.

Handy, C. (1994), *The Age of Paradox.* Boston: Harvard Business School Press.

Harman, W. (1991), *A Re-examination of the Metaphysical Foundations of Modern Science.* Sausalito, CA: Institute of Noetic Sciences.

Harman, W., & Hormann, J. (1990), *Creative Work: The constructive role of business in a transforming society.* Indianapolis, IN: Knowledge Systems.

Hawley, J. (1993), *Reawakening the Spirit in Work: The power of dharmic management.* San Francisco: Berrett-Koehler.

Herman, R., & Gioia, J. L. (1998, December). Making work meaningful: Secrets of the future-focused corporation. *Futurist, 32,* 24–26.

Hillman, J. (1996), *The Soul's Code: In search of character and calling.* New York: Random House.

Hubbard, B. M. (1998), Conscious evolution: Awakening the power of our social potential. Puerto Vallarta, Mexico: International Conference on Business & Consciousness.

Isaacs, W. (1993), Taking flight: Dialogue, collective thinking, and organizational learning. *Organizational Dynamics,* 24–39.

Jackson, K. T. (1999), Spirituality as a foundation for freedom and creative imagination in international business ethics. *Journal of Business Ethics, 19(1),* 61–70.

Jaffe, D., & Scott, C. (1993), Building a committed workplace: an empowered organization as a competitive advantage. In M. Ray, and A. Rinzler (Eds.), *The New Paradigm in Business.* New York: G. P. Putnam's Sons, pp. 139–196.

Kiefer, C. F., & Senge, P. M. (1984), Metanoic organizations. In J. D. Adams (Ed.), *Transforming Work: A Collection of Organizational Transformation Readings* (pp. 141–147). Alexandria, VA: Miles River Press.

Koestenbaum, P. (1991), *Leadership: Inner side of greatness.* San Francisco: Jossey-Bass.

Kouzes, J., & Posner, B. (1999), *Encouraging the Heart: How leaders can inspire others to consistently extraordinary performance.* San Francisco: Jossey-Bass.

Kriger, M.P., & Hanson, B. J. (1999), A value-based paradigm for creating truly healthy organizations. *Journal of Organizational Change Management, 12(4),* 302–317.

Lawler, E. E., III. (1994/1973), *Motivation in Work Organizations.* San Francisco: Jossey-Bass, Inc.

Leigh, P. (1997), The new spirit at work. *Training & Development, 51(3),* 26–33.

Makower, J. (1995), *Beyond the Bottom Line: Putting social responsibility to work for your business and the world.* Touchstone Books, New York.

Marcuse, H. (1964), *One-Dimensional Man*. Boston: Beacon Press.

Maslow, A. (1968), *Toward a Psychology of Being* (2nd ed.). New York: D. Van Nostrand Co.

Mavrinac, S. C., Jones, N. R., & Meyer, M. W. (1995), *Competitive Renewal Through Workplace Innovation: The financial and nonfinancial returns to innovative workplace practices*. Washington, DC: U. S. Department of Labor.

McCormick, D. W. (1994), Spirituality and management. *Journal of Managerial Psychology, 9(6)*, 5–8.

McKnight, R. (1984), Spirituality in the workplace. In J. D. Adams (Ed.), *Transforming Work* (pp. 139–153). Alexandria, VA: Miles River Press.

Miller, W. C. (1991), How do we put our spiritual values to work? In J. Renesch (Ed.), *New Traditions in Business: Spirit and leadership in the 21st century*. San Francisco: Sterling & Stone.

Mitroff, I., & Denton, E. (1999), A study of spirituality in the workplace. *Sloan Management Review, 40(4)*.

Mollner, T. (1991), The 21st-century corporation: The tribe of the relationship age. In J. Renesch (Ed.), *New Traditions in Business: Spirit and leadership in the 21st century*. San Francisco: Sterling & Stone.

Moore, T. (1993, March/April). The soul of work. *Business Ethics, 7*, 6–7.

Moore, T. (1997), *Meaningful Work* [Cassette Recording]. Boulder, CO: Sounds True.

Morse, N. C., & Weiss, R. S. (1955), The function and meaning of work and the job. *American Sociological Review, 20(2)*, 191–198.

MOW International Research Team, (1987). *The Meaning of Working*. New York: Harcourt Brace Jovanovich, Publishers.

Naylor, T. H., Willimon, W. H., & Osterberg, R. (1996), *The Search for Meaning in the Workplace*. Nashville, TN: Abingdon Press.

Neal, J., Lichtenstein, B.M., & Banner, D. (1999), Spiritual perspectives on individual, organization and societal transformation. *Journal of Organizational Change Management, 12(3)*, 175–185.

Neck, C. P., & Milliman, J. F. (1994), Thought self-leadership: Finding spiritual fulfillment in organizational life. *Journal of Managerial Psychology, 9(6)*, 9–16.

Nichols, M. (1994), Does new age business have a message for managers? *Harvard Business Review* (March/April).

Owen, H. (1987), *Spirit: Transformation and Development in Organizations*. Potomac, MD: Abbott Publishing.

Owen, H. (1993), *Open Space Technology: A user's guide*. Cabin John, MD: H. H. Owen and Co.

Pauchant, T. C. (Ed.). (1995), *In Search of Meaning: Managing for the Health of Our Organizations, Our Communities, and the Natural World*. San Francisco: Jossey-Bass, Inc.

Phillips, M. (1994), The social dimensions of "right livelihood." In C. Whitmyer (Ed.), *Mindfulness and Meaningful Work: Explorations in Right Livelihood* (pp. 111–116). Berkeley, CA: Parallax Press.

Preston, L., & O'Bannon, D. (1997), The corporate social-financial performance relationship. *Business & Society, 36, 4* (December), 419–430.

Ray, M. L. (1991), The emerging new paradigm in business. In J. Renesch (Ed.), *New Traditions in Business: Spirit and Leadership in the 21st Century* (pp. 33–45). San Francisco: Sterling and Stone.

Ray, P. H. (1996), The rise of integral culture. *Noetic Sciences Review* (Spring), 4–15.

Renesch, J., DeFoore, B., & Peters, T. J., (eds.), (1997), *The New Bottom Line: Bringing heart and soul to business*. Pleasonton, CA: New Leaders Press.

Rennie, M., & Bellin, G. (1998), Raising the consciousness and profits of business. Puerto Vallarta, Mexico: International Conference on Business & Consciousness.

Richards, D. (1995), *Artful Work: Awakening joy, meaning, and commitment in the workplace*. San Francisco: Berrett-Koehler Publishers.

Roddick, A. (1991), *Body and Soul*. New York: Crown Publishers, Inc.

Secretan, L. H. K. (1996), *Reclaiming Higher Ground: Creating Organizations that Inspire the Soul*. Toronto: Macmillan Canada.

Shellenbarger, S. (1997, January 29). New job hunters ask recruiters, "Is there life after work?" *Wall Street Journal*. New York: Dow Jones & Company.

Shellenbarger, S. (1998, July 22), Companies are finding it really pays to be nice to employees. *Wall Street Journal*. New York: Dow Jones & Company.

Sievers, B. (1986), Beyond the surrogate of motivation. *Organizational Studies, 7(4)*, 335–351.

Sinetar, M. (1987), *Do What You Love and the Money Will Follow*. New York: Dell.

Svendsen, A. (1998), *The Stakeholder Strategy: Profiting from collaborative business relationships*. San Francisco: Berrett-Koehler.

Tichy, N. M., McGill, A. R., & Clair, L. S. (Eds.) (1997), *Corporate Global Citizenship: Doing business in the public eye*. San Francisco, CA: New Lexington Press, Edition: 1st ed.

Tischler, L. (1999), The growing interest in spirituality in business: a long-term socio-economic explanation. *Journal of Organizational Change Management, 12(4)*, 273–279.

Vaill, P. (1989), *Managing as a Performing Art: New ideas for a world of chaotic change*. San Francisco: Jossey-Bass.

Vaill, P. (1998), *Spirited Leading and Learning: Process wisdom for a new age*. San Francisco: Jossey-Bass.

Vecchio, R. (1980), The function and meaning of work and the job: Morse and Weiss. *Academy of Management Journal, 23(2)*, 361–367.

Waddock, S. (1999), Linking community and spirit: a commentary and some propositions. *Journal of Organizational Change Management 12(4)*, 332–344.

Weisbord, M., & Janoff, S. (1995), *Future Search: An action guide to finding common ground in organizations and communities*. San Francisco: Berrett-Koehler.

Wheatley, M. (1992), *Leadership and the New Science*. San Francisco: Berrett-Koehler Publishers.

Wheatley, M. J., & Kellner-Rogers, M. (1995), The paradox and promise of community. In F. Hesselbein, M. Goldsmith, R. Beckhard, & R. F. Schubert (Eds.), *The Community of the Future* (pp. 9–18). San Francisco: Jossey-Bass.

Wheeler, D., Sillanpaa, M., & Roddick, A. (1998), *The Stakeholder Corporation: The Body Shop: Blueprint for maximizing stakeholder value*. London: Financial Times Management.

Whitmyer, C. (Ed.) (1994), *Mindfulness and Meaningful Work: Explorations in right livelihood*. Berkeley, CA: Parallax Press.

Whyte, D. (1994), *The Heart Aroused: Poetry and the preservation of soul in corporate America*. New York: Currency (Doubleday).

Yankelovich, D. (1981), Toward an ethic of commitment. *Industry Week, 209*, 62–66.

Zukov, G. (1995), Evolution and business. In B. Defoore & J. Renesch (Eds.), *Rediscovering the Soul of Business: A renaissance of values*. San Francisco: New Leaders Press.

FESTIVALISM AT WORK:

TOWARD AHIMSA IN PRODUCTION AND CONSUMPTION

David M. Boje,
New Mexico State University

My spiritual teacher, Gurudev Chitrabhanu, is a Jain monk who worked alongside Gandhi and spent twenty years walking about India with a message of non-violence. He now spends half his time in Mumbai and the other leading and inspiring the Jain communities in the United States. In November 1997, I toured India with my wife Grace Ann Rosile and Gurudev Shree Chitrabhanu. As I saw India, I was even more resolved than before, that world capitalism is a tragic coevolutionary play led by the spectacle of inhumanity to all sentient beings. I saw the world's future if we are not able to coevolve in more sensitive ways; it was written all over the streets of Mumbai, in people and animals sleeping in doorways, in the faces of starving children. Gurudev is a former Jain monk, now a spiritual teacher of non-violence. Gurudev says, "the decision is up to us to be violent or non-violent." He vows no harm to any sentient being.

Satish Kumar, also a Jain monk, after walking halfway around the world promoting peace and disarmament, settled in England. Satish founded Schumacher College, named after E. F. Schumacher, the author of *Small Is Beautiful*. Schumacher's (1973) book, *Small Is Beautiful: Economics as If People Mattered*, challenges the concepts of unlimited growth, predatory competition, and violent forms of production and consumption. In bringing Jain teachings of non-violence to Western countries, both Satish and Gurudev have endured much criticism. Decades ago, it was considered highly inappropriate for Jain monks to use modern transportation systems and travel abroad. Both speak to the discontent people in the West experience with a crisis of identity and meaning, from spectacle lifestyles of over consumption and violent production. Both spend hours each day in meditation to separate from the influences of what I call spectacle. Ahimsa teaching has had a profound impact on major figures.

Reverend Martin Luther King Jr., for example, applied Ahimsa nonviolent teachings of social change. His nonviolent Civil Rights marches, open prayers, and other forms of protest captured the imagination of millions who did not realize that there were violent racial relations all around them. Nonviolent action brings about awareness, and it is then up to people to make their own choices. But, spectacle does not reform so easily. It is able to appropriate a reform movement and make it part of spectacle appeal. For example, Cohen and Solomon (1995) comment on how Martin Luther King's life story has become part of the annual media spectacle of his ritualized annual holiday television consumption.

> What TV viewers see is a closed loop of familiar file footage: King battling desegregation in Birmingham (1963); reciting his dream of racial harmony at the rally in Washington (1963); marching for voting rights in Selma, Alabama (1965); and finally, lying dead on the motel balcony in Memphis (1968).

Spectacle is selective in its storytelling. What the ritualized King spectacle leaves out in its annual tributes is how in the last years of his life Reverend King turned his attention to the growing gap between rich and poor. King observed that a majority of Americans below the poverty line, and these were mostly white folks. The year of his assassination, he was calling for radical changes in the distribution of wealth and proposing a poor man's march on Washington, D.C. Ahimsa and Gandhi influenced these three spiritual leaders.

Mahatma Gandhi was also deeply influenced by the Ahimsa philosophy. Ahimsa is part of the three-millennia Jain philosophy of India (Yashovijayji, 1974). To Gandhi "not to hurt any living thing" is an important part of Ahimsa, but not the most important element.[1] The important elements are to avoid hatred, lying, wishing ill, and to realize that millions of microorganisms live in and around us. Ahimsa is not just non-violence; it is unconditional love combined with self-control.

> To hear suggestive stories with the ears, to see suggestive sights with the eyes, to taste stimulating food with the tongue, to touch exciting things with the hands, and then at the same time expect to control the only remaining organ is like putting one's hands in the fire, and expecting to escape being burnt.[2]

---

[1] Gandhi's Non-Violent Resistance, p. 41.

[2] Ibid, p. 45.

Gandhi's choice was to be celibate to sustain his self-control. Gandhi sought alternatives to silk production, a process that kills the silk worms during the manufacturing process. I attended the Gandhi Institute and observed one of his inventions, a cotton spinning machine that any person with a bit of training and patience can operate. He distributed the spinning machines to create an alternative to the then British controlled manufacture of cotton and the nation's dependency on silk garments. My friend Susan Segall brought back this factory in a box machine so that I might also meditate while I spin threads. It takes a lot of patience and higher levels of skill than I now possess. It does allow me to meditate on non-violent options in my own production and consumptive practice. I am eager to find non-violent patterns of living in a world saturated with violence. In what follows I want to apply Ahimsa philosophy to a different understanding of what I study as "spectacle and festival."

Spectacle is above all a legitimating narrative for social engineering and social control masking the violent (non-Ahimsa) acts of production and consumption. By spectacle I mean Debord's (1967) *Society of the Spectacle*, the often violent and oppressive social control that masquerades as a celebration of betterment by recycling pseudo-reforms, false desires, and selective sightings of progressive evolution, never devolution. By violent I mean the willful and careless and often unnecessary disruption or extinction of the life of another, including the life of non-human species. "The spectacle is the moment when the commodity has attained the *total occupation* of social life" (#42). "In particular the ways in which technical development becomes a substitute for natural development" (#24, 36). "Last year, Americans, who make up only five percent of the world's population, used nearly a third of its resources and produced almost half of its hazardous waste" (Affluenza, 1997). The Situationaliste answer to the ideological social control of spectacle is festival, by which we self-manage and self-produce our own production and consumption practices. In this way we redefine our needs and desires.

Festival is the "very keynote of the life" I see beyond a critique of spectacle . . . *Play* is the ultimate principle of this festival, and the only rules it can recognize are to live without dead time and to enjoy without restraint (Situationist International, 1966: 14). Many cities and nations still conduct annual festivals, a tradition that goes back centuries in many parts of the world. Yet, the festivals have taken on thick outer spectacle shells, becoming gaudy consumption rituals, without much referentiality to what makes a festival festive in the first place. Most organizing attempts of festival find they are mutating due to their organizing situations into bizarre affairs. The Pittsburgh Irish Festival, for example, features a Bingo Tent, Dog Tents, and a Gaelic Mass. Is this a strange or suitable organization? Perhaps it is a collage of spectacles more than a festival. Or, perhaps it is the bizarre juxtaposition that keeps it festive. Festival was once about narratives and theatrics that reversed or otherwise parodied the portrait of power. On Fool's Day, the peasants became magistrates, clergy, and nobles, while all these elites took on lesser positions. In the Tomato Festival, people tossed tomatoes at everyone and on the next day life went back to its normal spectacle routines.

The pre-capitalism festival ways of life were appropriated and transformed by spectacle capitalism. Festival has been replaced by spectacles of theatrical consumption (the mall and the stores in the mall) as well as by spectacular organizations (producers of spectacles and themselves spectacles). The peasant is everywhere, composing as much as two-fifths of the world's population, many working at slave wages to provide the spectacle to the advantaged. The peasants sit on the margins of spectacle, ready to reclaim cyclical time and local spaces, and perhaps replace spectacle with festival.

The festival had something to do with one's conscious awareness, and with a focusing of that awareness. Festival is defined as expressing inner happiness in a context of social activity. Spectacle is defined as material displays of happiness in a context of over consumption. When festival is more about materialism than play, self-reflection, and social commentary, it becomes disempowered, just another spectacle. When the message of festival is in the externalities, the inner spirituality of the event is suspect.

Consider the similarities. Both spectacle and festival combine theatrics, storytelling, crafts, and other arts into a community of performance. Both festival and spectacle incorporate food, story, theatrics, music, art, and other entertainment. I want to open up the question of what is festival for more rigorous exploration. They are oftentimes found together, occupying the same time and place. The same work organization has both festive and spectacle garniture. Two people can be in the same organization, doing the same job, for the same boss. One sees festive situations; another sees spectacles of misery, self-indulgence, and addictions to overproduction and conspicuous, even eco-destructive consumption. One will experience a sense of joy; the other will find only frustration. Many events with the label "festival" do not appear to be festivals at all to all of the participants. I want to show the basis of festive and spectacle processes in modern organizations. Shakespearean Festivals, Renaissance Festivals, Craft Festivals, Harvest Festivals (dates, chili, wine, apple, etc.), Film Festivals, and Music Festivals are all the rage. They define the community, but so do spectacles. Disneyland, a modern organization spectacle, defines Los Angeles County, though it is really located in Orange County. Renaissance Festivals, oftentimes, reenact fifteenth and sixteenth century Europe as a celebration of cyclical time and a local reverence for place, even though they are reenacted outside of Europe, in places like Kansas and Idaho. Yet most of festival is not separate from spectacle. It seems every state in the Union and most countries have their festivals and their spectacles, without much differentiation between what is one and the other.

What is a Festival Organization?—Be it simple or complex, behind the festival stalls, booths, theater, exhibitions, and merchandising, there is the festival organization, and perhaps a spectacular one masquerading as festive. Some festival organizations construct fictive fantasies of the good olds days of King Arthur Knights of the Round Table or Elizabethan splendor in a Renaissance Festival. Spectators are invited to come dressed as princesses, wenches, noblemen, and barbarians, as they enjoy the jousting and feasting. Others go to great length to make the historical period become "living history." They re-create the architecture, dress, and customs of a particular epoch. Yet, in many cases, they are no more authentic than the Pirates of the Caribbean or the Haunted Mansion at Disneyland are. The sense of "authenticity" of a festival, be it a Renaissance Faire, Shakespearean Theater, or Bluegrass Music Festival, varies from one situation to the next. The name "festival" in the title of the event is not a way to tell its pedigree.

There is much contemporary spectacle mixed into the festival. For example, the Colorado Renaissance Festival advertises that for a price you and fifty guests can be part of a Royal Wedding. For just $2,500 you can have the fairy tale wedding managed by expert wedding coordinators, complete with the melodious murmur of the King's bagpiper, escorting you to the newly refurbished Canterbury Chapel where you will be a player in an Elizabethan Wedding Ceremony. A King and Queen wedding feast follow this wedding. Costuming and wet bar are extra. Is there something in Jain philosophy that can help us sort this out?

In Jain teachings there is a story about a prince who is about to marry. Just before the wedding feast, he observes the preparations. He sees a courtyard full of cages of all the various animals about to be slaughtered for his wedding feast. The moment is transformative. He decides to become a monk, and seeing his example, his bride elects to become a nun. They each lived lives of renunciation. To me, the meaning of the story is that the couple developed conscious awareness of the difference between a festival and a spectacle. They developed conscious awareness of a spectacle of material celebration and saw that this path would not lead them to attain higher spiritual values. Instead, they chose to renounce material possession and material violence in favor of non-violence and simplicity.

Ahimsa is a modification and reform of spectacle, a way to live spectacles that are non-violent. Festival can be antispectacle; it can lie beyond spectacle, in ways that I envision being non-violent. Festival is not an escape from spectacle. The practical concern of Ahimsa is with worker and community health and safety; alternatives to child labor and prison labor; living wages; enlightened work conditions; freedom of worker association; ecological sustainability; globally equitable production and consumption practices; future generations. Festival is doing something proactive about inequality. Two hundred twenty-five billionaires now have more annual income than half the planet's 6.1 billion population. The festival is an attempt to make leisure more important than work.

TABLE 1: Spectacle and Festival	
Spectacle	Festival
1. Work	1. Play
2. Work or play time	2. Work and play
3. Imposed patterns of behavior	3. Freely constructed behavior
4. Dead time	4. Live time
5. Religions of consumption	5. Self
6. Pseudo-desires	6. Transparent desires
7. Pseudo-needs	7. Transparent needs
8. Loss of self	8. Self-management
9. Colonized spaces	9. Free spaces
10. Spectator	10. Participant/co-designer
11. Functionary	11. Self-managed
12. Survival of the fittest/richest	12. Coevolution and co-survival

We do not see the spectacles we grow up in, we do not see who makes our products, and we do not even glimpse how violent the production process has become. All we see are the glitzy lights at the mall, the sexy displays of TV ads, and the corporate claims to excellence on all web sites.

On the Relations of Violence to Spectacle—the Society of the Spectacle desensitizes its participants to violence, in what Whitmer (1997) calls the "Violence Mythos." The myth here is a self-sealed logic of violence legitimation. Violence is everywhere, in the streets, in schools, in the workplace, and in the home. Our children scream if we deny them a Nintendo kill-game of "realistic" violence. Beneath the spectacle illusion of progress through technology and gadget accumulation-equals-happiness lies the brutality and cruelty to animals, humans, and mother earth to sustain our lifestyles. I seek to enter the festive world, to walk and breathe real life "situations" as an active yet non-violent participant, not a passive spectator in everyday life space. I was socialized to accept and tolerate violence and to consume violence willingly as leisure.

It is often assumed that the most technologically advanced economies are the least violent. The United States is the most violent of all industrialized nations on the planet with the least safe places to live and work. According to a 1994 Justice Department report, nearly one million violent crimes occur in the workplace each year. There were more than 6,200 deaths on the job due to traumatic injuries in the United States in 1997. The death toll from work-related disease is nearly 10 times higher (Weissman, 1999). There were more than 6 million work-place-related injuries and illnesses recorded in 1997, with more than 1.8 million of them causing time lost from the job. The United States has the highest rates of childhood homicide, suicide, and firearms-related death among all of the industrialized countries. In 1995 alone, 35,957 Americans were killed with firearms, in homicides, suicides, and accidents (National Center for Health Statistics, 1997). Every day in 1994, 16 children aged 19 and under were killed with guns (National Center for Health Statistics, 1994). Firearms kill more people between the ages of 15 and 24 than all natural causes combined (National Center for Health Statistics, 1994).

Empirical research is consistent in its findings. According to the American Psychological Association's 1993 report, "Violence and Youth: Psychology's Response," there are not just one but four long-term effects of viewing violence:

1. Increased aggressiveness and anti-social behavior
2. Increased fear of being or becoming a victim
3. Increased desensitization to violence and victims of violence
4. Increased appetite for more and more violence in entertainment and real life

The long-term impact of children growing up watching thousands of hours of violence is that they role model what they see in the spectacle of violence. The Center for Media and Public Affairs reports that the total number of violent scenes in entertainment programming increased by 74% in three years—from 1,002 in 1992 to 1,417 in 1994, to 1,738 in 1995—reaching an average of nearly 10 incidents of violence per channel per hour during the most recent season, even after excluding commercials and all non-fiction programming.[3]

Violence is also increasing among spectators. After the Vancouver Canucks lost the Stanley Cup, 70,000 mad fans took their violence to the streets, amid clouds of tear gas. Some 200 people were injured including two with critical head injuries.[4] After the Detroit Tigers won the 1984 World Series, United States fans in Detroit and Chicago took their violence to the street, again destroying property and one another. Seventy-three University of Wisconsin students were crushed against a fence after a 13–10 win over Big Ten rival Michigan.

Violence is not only increasing in frequency in TV and movies, it is also increasing as a way of advertising. Violence in commercials also rose 30% since 1992. The 948 violent scenes tabulated during commercials in 1995 nearly equaled the 1,002 violent scenes recorded during all entertainment programming in 1992. Ads have a few moments to show something interesting enough to attract the viewer. The easy way out is to show something violent.

"Land Ethic" and Non-Violence. There is a close parallel between Leopold's "Land Ethic" and Ahimsa. Both see ignorant interference in the evolution of other species as a form of violence. Leopold's "biotic pyramid" defines ecology as an interdependent web of life, which includes the land.

---

[3] Center for Media and Public Affairs. "Study Finds Rise in TV Guns and Violence Cable Movies and Cartoons Are Culprits, Not the Networks." September 11, 1996 http://www.cmpa.com/archive/viol95.htm

[4] Robert Lee "Fan sports violence also common in United States" July 7, 1994 http://beaconwww.asa.utk.edu/issues/v66/archives/www/v66/n11/violence.111.html

Larger Carnivores
Omnivores—bears, racoons, man
Herbivorous mammals
Insect-eating birds and rodents
Plant-eating insects
Plants
Soil

Leopold contended that undisciplined human technology (e.g., guns, strip mining tractors, and laws allowing for mass extermination of wolves and other species) resulted in violence to the biotic web of life. Leopold's (1949) "Land Ethic" can be stated very simply: "A thing is right when it tends to preserve the integrity, stability, and beauty of the biotic community. It is wrong when it tends otherwise." The contemporary result of land ethics is the bioethics movement (Koch, 1992):

Through technology, we are rapidly changing the earth. These changes have accelerated as man moved from a hunter/food gatherer to a member of an agricultural society and finally into the industrial age. Many of the present technological changes are irreversible, damaging to the land and clashing with our increasing scientific knowledge of how biotic communities function. Individuals are faced with a moral environmental responsibility.

Ahimsa; is not about blame, it is about finding alternatives to violence, and letting people find their own way. Ahimsa, for me, recognizes that you just do not wake up one morning and turn off the television, turn vegetarian, and the next morning awaken in a non-violent world. Rather, it is a matter of cultivating a taste for non-violence in a spectacle that encourages just the opposite. It is the path of non-violent resistance, not blame and judgment.

The Web of Life. In sum, the Ahimsa worldview encompasses the nonviolence philosophy of Gandhi, Chitrabhanu, Kumar, King Jr., and Leopold. It applies to issues such as gun violence, domestic violence, TV violence, animal violence, and other aspects of a world nurtured in the spectacle of production and consumption.

People do resist spectacle—there is hope for spectacle transformation. There are eco-teams forming in Europe and North America to look at ways to cut back on our over consumption patterns. Consumer groups are forming that resist shopping addictions, credit-card addiction, workaholism, and television/Nintendo/Web cyber dependency. Turning Point, for example, runs full-page ads to raise questions about the impact of technology and transnational corporate strategies on the environment and the ability of nations to sustain growing populations with a quality of life for their people (Murphy, 1999: 1).

Table 2 contrasts spectacle and more Ahimsa Festival assumptions. In particular, there are differences in how progress, happiness, and spiritual value are defined.

Table 2 is focused on simplicity. Simplicity is a movement to cut out unneeded consumption and production in the hopes that others on the planet will have the means to live. Jain teachings apply to simplicity. The monk does not store possessions, has no roof over his head, and some do not wear clothes or own anything at all. He seeks simplicity in his daily life and equality with his fellow human beings. Merchants are encouraged not to stock products of animal sacrifice and consumers are galvanized not to consume such products.

TABLE 2: Assumptions of Spectacle and Ahimsa Business Practices

Spectacle Assumptions	Ahimsa Festival Assumptions
✓ Progress defined as material accumulation	✓ Progress defined as spiritual accumulation
✓ Material accumulation = happiness	✓ Self-awareness = happiness
✓ Spectacles of production and consumption grow by resource use	✓ Planet has finite and dwindling resources to be preserved
✓ Economic productivity	✓ Eco-sustainable productivity
✓ Material values	✓ Spiritual values and awareness
✓ Work that is drudgery	✓ Work that is ennobling/ actualizing
✓ Business that pollutes	✓ Business is non-polluting
✓ Technology advances to sustain competitive progress	✓ Technology used sparingly to sustain natural splendor
✓ Survival of the fittest = richest	✓ Survival of the cooperative
✓ Consume for immediate gratification; live for today	✓ Consume in ways healthy for our offspring; live for their future
✓ Conspicuous consumption = good	✓ Frugal consumption = good

Let no one run away with the idea that this type of merchant exists only in my imagination. Fortunately for the world, it does exist in the West as well as in the East. It is true, such merchants may be counted on one's fingers' ends, but the type ceases to be imaginary, as soon as even one living specimen can be found to answer to it (Gandhi, *Non-Violent Resistance*, p. 49).

To the Jain businessperson, we are in the initial stages of transforming the old Spectacle assumptions into the new Ahimsa assumptions of what makes for an enlightened business organization. I think it takes daily meditation and critical awareness of the violence of the production and consumption spectacles, as well as the opportunities to make Ahimsa choices. The New Testament says, "to be as harmless as doves and wise as serpents in our actions." Harman (1994: 48) argues "we are moving from a culture dominated by materialistic values to one that recognizes the role of deep intuitive wisdom in guiding our collective future." The Ahimsa business paradigm would transform spectacles of production and consumption:

1. Engage in business practices that are non-violent to other species.
2. Limit economic growth to what is ecologically sustainable.
3. Develop ecological awareness through reduce, recycle, and reuse practices.
4. Cultivate personal self-development through servant leadership, introspection time, and community service.

Festival means cutting back on an over consumptive and conspicuous production lifestyle. Materiality does not bring happiness. It also means overcoming societal addictions to violent entertainment. Festival is taking a critical look at commodity and production needs that are inherently artificial prescriptions for the happy person in the happy society. Part of Ahimsa philosophy is to treat all living beings as equal to one's own self. This means not interrupting or degrading the evolution of plants, animals, and humans. While not everyone can make such a commitment or make it all at once, the challenge is to encourage more people to behave with less violence. This would necessitate a critical look at animal rights, the living planet, and ways in which we are tampering with all species in the Biotech Century. It means looking at the coevolution of humans, their technology, animals, and planets.

I would like to look at Ahimsa as a non-violent way of doing business, an alternative philosophy to late modern capitalism and state socialism. Both it seems to me to enact manic consumption habits. Spiritualism and Marxism are opposed, as are capitalism and postmodernism. Marxism seeks to reform and transcend the violence of capitalism and capitalism sees itself as a competitor and successor to (state) Marxism. The festival is, for me, a middle ground, at the center of capitalism, Marxism, spiritualism, and postmodernism. It is my attempt to open the flow of non-violent practices of production and consumption that can coexist with other capitalisms, post-Marxists, spiritualities, and postmodernisms. The critical postmodern and Marxist approaches allow a critique of capitalist spectacle and Pollyanna or capitalist spiritualism in order to find where festival is sustainable. A critique of techno-determinism, linear progress, and evolutionism in capitalism is necessary. As is a critique of the technocratic and teleology of Marxism. I seek the "life capitalism" of festival. Without the critique the festival quickly reverts to spectacle.

In affluent pockets of economies, we the affluent can design a story for our lives in which we design ourselves as the main character using a variety of scattered and disconnected elements and fragments. We can design our body, our career, our environment, and live a life of simulation, playing virtual and theatric games, and never touch real at all. What is "authentic" in a world in which every aspect of spectacle is by designer choice.

Spectacle is ubiquitous to both market capitalism and state socialism. Beyond the extreme, an often-violent (to humans and ecology) spectacle of "free market" capitalism and "state bureaucratic" communism, there is a third path I call festivalism. Festivalism is both post-capitalism and post-communism because there is a resituation of both these violent extremes in favor of non-violence.

Is it possible to transition capitalism and state socialism to a higher stage of development? Whereas free capitalism adheres to free market to distribute resources, the mechanism of state socialism is one of central planning to equitably distribute resources. Each views the other as an exploitative apparatus. The "affluent monster" in both systems continues to outstrip the earth resource base and widens the gap between rich and poor (Marcuse, 1969: 7). I view Ahimsa and festival as a different moral aesthetic and transcendent value system that will change work and consumption practices.

Festivalism makes five assumptions. First, festival assumes we can create companies that earn a capitalist profit and maintain non-violent ecological and social practices. Second, festival assumes local stakeholder groups of workers, citizens, and managers can balance the burgeoning power of global corporate monopolies by expressing their non-violent preferences through their market behavior. Third, festival assumes the myopic corporate focus on short-term accumulation could be abandoned when there is an understanding of the living whole. Fourth, when festival citizens recognize the difference between living to work versus working to live, then they will be able to tame their shopaholic and addictive consumption appetites, thereby letting others live. Fifth, non-violent work, fun, and leisure are possible. In sum, *Festival is defined as the pragmatics of long-term sustainability in a non-violent culture, in balance with the whole planet.*

The spectacle employee. It takes many employees to produce spectacles for others to consume. The employees are separated one from the other, and do not always see how their respective tasks make up the spectacles being produced for consumption. Each task may appear totally and completely non-violent. The spectacle employee is sometimes, maybe often, the distracted workaholic, the sacrificing breadwinner, never seeing how little leisure is left, or their children growing up without them.

The spectacle consumer. We are taught to be spectators, to look, but not to see, to be a spectator but not to be an active participant when we consume. Firat and Dholakia (1998), in marketing, are also writing about "theaters consumption" —that is, becoming more interactive, blurring the line between producer and consumer, by allowing consumers to self-design their experience. They argue the separation between production and consumptive activities is changing, but corporate control remains. The Jain monk leaves spectacle altogether, in some cases forsaking even clothing, along with all worldly possessions. Jain lay people, in particular businesspeople, do not forsake all spectacles. They only seek involvement with the least violent forms of spectacle and the most minimal forms of accumulation.

I am learning that each of my possessions—my car, my books, my computer, my house, my furniture, my tools, etc.—is an attachment, a weight on my life. With each possession comes the attachment of caring for it. At work, each project, each conference, each dissertation committee, each class, each student, each e-mail is also an attachment. I live in a whole web of material and social attachments. I am learning slowly to choose my attachments, to decide how I spend my time and energy, caring for relationships or caring for material possessions.

"The celebrity" says Debord (#60) is "the spectacular representation of a living human being, embodies this banality by embodying the image of a possible role." Corporations such as Disney, Nike, IBM, Toyota, Intel, and Microsoft also become celebrities. In the Jain philosophy, each person must find their own uniqueness instead of emulating their fantasy about being the copy of another. Spectacles provide a mirage, a phantasm, and an illusion that allows us to safely avoid looking beneath the fabricated images, product stars, and corporate icons.

There are also those who see a future of spectacles that will be as nightmarish as Metropolis, Bladerunner, and the many sour predictions of the Biotech Century (Rifkin, 1998). To read spectacles of production and consumption requires a theory of spectacle. We are taught to not read and to ignore the "technical apparatus of contemporary" spectacles, "the means and methods power employs, outside of direct force, which subject individuals to societal manipulation, while obscuring the nature and effects of capitalism's power and deprivations" (Best & Kellner, 1997: 84).

Spectacle, says Debord, is an opium that allows us to sleep-walk, as if drugged, stumbling blindfolded through a devolving landscape of ecological and human horror, while cocooned in artificiality and illusion, mind-numbed by cyber media into passive stupefied spectators. This is why it is not easy for people socialized in spectacles and consumption images of the good life through consumption to step outside of its mechanisms of persuasion and see its impact on nature, social systems, and the manipulation of our own desires. Our life is just too "saturated with spectacles" and we are too pacified in their "permanent opium war" (Debord, 1967: #44).

In the postmodern condition, spectacle and festival intermingle and we are left to live in their nexus. For example, on July 23, 1964, the first Meadow Brook Music Festival was held, featuring the Detroit Symphony Orchestra. The Meadow Brook Music Festival staged its first ballet in 1968. The first laser show was Starship Encounters in 1978. The festival features choral company, ballet, and symphony music. In 1980, the types of music expanded to include Jazz. In 1982, there were Fourth of July fireworks. In 1984, there were performances of the Marine Band and bluegrass groups. In 1990, the festival included the nights of laser shows to attract a more family audience. In 1992, Dolly Parton and the Mormon Tabernacle Choir launched the Music Festival. In 1993, there was a more diverse or fragmented schedule including "Bugs Bunny on Broadway," James Brown, Dwight Yoakum, 10,000 Maniacs, Peter Paul and Mary.

Some of the postmodern festivals have an activist agenda. For example, the Amnesty International Film Festival takes on a more activist role than most other film festivals. They actively deconstruct the rhetoric and propaganda of governments violating human rights by putting their reports side by side with the oppressor claims that there are no such violations. Another type of activism is represented in the International CRÈCHE Festival. They present an interesting purpose:

> Organizations in many nations are addressing the issue of the loss of biological diversity on this planet. Our organization attempts to speak to the loss of cultural diversity. We are attempting, in one small way, to help the folk artists of the world gain recognition of their arts and crafts and help them find a global market for their work at a fair price. If the folk artist cannot survive neither can the folk arts.[5]

This particular festival advocates that the artist receives a fair price for their labor. Other festivals and craft associations are not so equalitarian.

Conclusions

Guy Debord (1967) sought to abolish (modern) spectacle, to smash the spectacle in avant-garde revelation, *not* to transform or reform it. Yet modern spectacle is everywhere. A group of students (SI, 1966) had the vision of festive play, as a dream beyond the spectacle. Yet spectacle is everywhere. Debord called himself a Situationist (#191) because he wanted to replace the spectacle of official illusion with a deep awareness of the situation of violence, and how spectacle inverts reality.[6] If we are to dissociate festival from spectacle, we must begin with awareness.

In the postmodern, any line between festival and spectacle gets quite blurred. The 1998s Edinburgh Festival Fringe was a cyber-festival, filled with "frivolities and finito," including festive chat rooms with comedy stars.[7] The cybertech world affords us new art, new virtual forms of interaction, and new ways to live out our fantasies.

---

[5] Source, http://www.creche.org
[6] Numbers refer to paragraph numbers in Guy Debord's *Society of the Spectacle* (1967). La Société du Spectacle was first published in 1967 by Editions, Buchet-Chastel (Paris); it was reprinted in 1971 by Champ Libre (Paris). The full text is available in English at http://www.nothingness.org/SI/debord/index.html
[7] Source, http://www.comedyzone.beeb.com/edinburgh98/

REFERENCES

Affluenza (1997), "Running Out of Time." Affluenza is a production of KCTS/Seattle and Oregon Public Broadcasting: A PBS Special http://www. pbs.org/kcts/affluenza/show/about.html.

American Psychological Association Report on Violence and Youth (1993). "Is Youth Violence Just Another Fact of Live?" From the American Psychological Association, Commission on Violence and Youth. Violence & Youth: Psychology's response (Vol 1). Washington, D.C.

Best, Steven, and Kellner, Douglas (1997), The Postmodern Turn. New York/London: The Guilford Press.

Boje, David M. (1999), Spectacle and Festival of Organization: Managing Ahimsa Production and Consumption. Book being published at Hampton Press (CA), expected release is 2001.

Center for Media and Public Affairs. "Study Finds Rise in TV Guns and Violence Cable Movies and Cartoons Are Culprits, Not the Networks." September 11, 1996.

Chitrabhanu, Gurudev Shree (1977), The Philosophy of Soul and Matter. Clare Rosenfield (ed.). New York: Jain Meditation International Center.

_____. (1980), Twelve Facets of Reality: The Jain Path to Freedom. Clare Rosenfield (ed.). NewYork: Dodd, Mead & Company.

Debord Guy (1967), Society of the Spectacle. La Société du Spectacle was first published in 1967 by Editions, Buchet-Chastel (Paris); it was reprinted in 1971 by Champ Libre (Paris). The full text is available in English at http://www.nothingness.org/SI/debord/index.html

Firat, Fuat A., and Nikhilesh Dholakia (1998), Consuming People: From Political Economy to Theaters of Consumption. London/New York: Routledge.

Gandhi, Mohandas K. (1957), Gandhi, An Autobiography: The Story of My Experiments with Truth. Boston, MA: Beacon Press.

____. (1951), Non-Violent Resistance (Satyagraha). New York/London: Schocken Books.

Harman, Willis (1994), "The New business of business: work as if the earth and people mattered." Interview edited by Ronald S. Miller, Science of Mind 67(9), 38–49.

Ismat, Abdal-Haqq (1989), "Violence in Sports," http://ericps.crc.uiuc. edu/npin/respar/texts/ teens/violence.html

Koch, Carl (1992), "In Search of a Land Ethic." Woodrow Wilson Biology Institute. http://www.gene.com/ae/AE/AEPC/WWC/1992 /land_ethics.html

Lee, Robert (1994), "Fan Sports Violence Also Common in United States," July 7, 1994, http://beacon-www.asa.utk.edu/issues/v66 /archives/ www/v66/n11/violence.111.html

Leopold, Aldo (1949), *A Sand County Almanac and Sketches Here and There*. New York, Oxford University Press.

Marcuse, Herbert (1969), *"One Dimensional Man: Studies in the Ideology of Advanced Industrial Society."* Boston, MA: Beason Press.

Murphy, Pat (1999), "Campaign to Change the World." Environmental News Network, November 1, Retrieved September 7, 2000, from the World Wide Web: http://www.enn.com/enn-features-archive/ 1999/11/110199 /turning_6583.asp

Nakhre, Amrut W. (1982), *Social Psychology of Nonviolent Action: A Study of Three Satyagrahas*. Delhi, India: Chanakya Publications.

National Center for Health Statistics (1994) Summary: Firearm-Related Deaths and Hospitalizations Wisconsin. 1994, Firearm-Related Deaths and Hospitalizations Continued Firearm-related injuries. Report retrieved September 7, 2000, from the World Wide Web: http://www.cdc.gov/mmwr/PDF/wk/mm4535.pdf

National Center for Health Statistics (1997) "Report on Nation's Health Documents Toll of Injuries in U.S. Firearm Mortality Down 11%, Traffic Fatality Rates up 2%, 1993–1995" News Release dated July 24, 1997. Retrieved September 7, 2000, from the World Wide Web: http://www.cdc.gov/nchs/releases/97news/hus96rel.html

Rifkin, Jeremy (1998), *The Biotech Century: Harnessing the Gene and Remaking the World*. New York: Tarcher/Putnam.

Rosenfield, Clare, & Segall, Linda (undated) *Ahimsa Is Not a Religion, It Is a Way of Life*. New York: Jain Meditation International.

Situationalist International Strasbourg Pamphlet (1966), "On the Poverty of the Student Life." This pamphlet was a prelude to the May 1968 revolt in France and has been translated into more than a dozen languages and reprinted in over half a million copies. Ken Knabb's English translation is at http://www.slip.net/~knabb/ SI/poverty.html

Weissman, Robert (1999), "Want to kill somebody and get away with a slap on the wrist?" *Corporate Focus Newsletter* (April 27, 1999, e-mail newsletter) - Focus on the Corporation columns available at rob@essential.org

Whitmer, Barbara (1997), "*The Violence Mythos.*" New York: State University of New York Press.

SPIRITUALITY IN THE WORKPLACE

Elmer H. Burack,
University of Illinois, Chicago

Introduction

This paper focuses on newer work life and organizational culture arrangements which improve the human experience and thereby help to achieve longer-term enterprise stability, growth, and profitability. Relational terms such as credibility, trust, wisdom, and ethics are used to describe these approaches. These discussions are based on the writer's years of research and corporate experiences as well as thoughtful analyses, examples, and discussions of other social scientists. The scope and complexity of this area is suggested by other papers in this special Journal issue. Thus this paper represents but one modest part of the whole.

Current progress in defining and creating a more hospitable worklife environment and enriching human experience is too frequently taken to mean soft or devious management or a thinly veiled attempt at a religious renaissance in corporate America. The former is wrong and the latter point valid only in a very general sense. In truth some commonly used terms and descriptive titles use meanings, values, and experiences from quite different contexts. Some examples include "spirituality," "soulfulness," "rediscovering the soul," and "managing with love." I suspect that it will be some years yet before these terms gain general usage in business. Regardless, they are used in this paper, albeit selectively.

Bases for this paper's approach to workplace spirituality represent the initial discussions. Next, a diverse group of organization application examples suggests the broad utility of these approaches. Since some readers are likely to be interested in various theoretical models and concepts underlying these discussions, the following section provides several "wiring" diagrams or models and a brief explanation of these. The final section includes some of my speculations as to possible future directions.

For paper purposes, the following concepts of spirituality in the workplace will be used:

1. Spiritual growth and advancement of the human experience involve mental growth—problem solving and individual learning will often be the main vehicles of individual development.
2. Spiritual growth reflects the gratification of individual needs, especially "belonging" and those of a higher order such as a sense of achievement. The individual's context for these is broadly encompassing work-family connections and work-place settings.
3. Spirituality in the workplace is communicated and reinforced through the institution's leaders, organizational culture, policies, and work design among other factors. Sensitivity to and interest in the person (employee) must be common to all approaches.

Workplace Spirituality: Why the interest?

The fast-growing interest in and durability of workplace spirituality stems largely from two mainstream business developments. One is termed the "economic-technological imperative." The other one is simply described as "people-centered management." The foundation for the latter approach will be described as "Theory YZ" in recognition of two of its early contributors.

The *economic-technological* imperative has been a part of the business scene from the very beginning. Economic or technological considerations in the past were the major driving forces for introducing major changes which led to new economies of scale or higher productivity. More recently, the scenario would be as follows. "Downsizing and reengineering are now a way of life for us. However, we seem to be confronted with decreasing economic returns and competition has caught up, and we now are doing similar things in a technologically driven environment. We concluded that it is people who now will make the difference." Their numbers are growing fast, albeit their commitment to people-centered approaches is more tenuous. Ford Motor Company is an outstanding example of a firm that made a complete turnaround in favor of people-centered approaches (Burack, 1993). Now in force for some two decades, its people-driven approaches are viewed as the main contributing factor to their outstanding performance in the highly competitive automotive industry according to a recent *Wall Street Journal* article (July 16, 1998: A1).

EXHIBIT 1

LEADERSHIP AND WORKPLACE SPIRITUALITY

New Economy ⇨ Strategizing Workplace ⇨ Characteristic Workplace
Leadership   Spirituality   Factors and
                                                           Organizational Practices*

*Characteristic Focus Areas
  • Employee participation in creative problem solving
  • Encouraging continuous learning
  • Developing people-friendly work spaces
  • Facilitating employee welfare
  • Encouraging community support
  • Consistent trustful relationship
  • Regard for the human spirit

The *people-centered* premise served as the central foundation for what to date has been quite a different group of firms. This organizing principle drove workplace practices, policies, process, and culture. Some business owners and founders such as those at Hewlett-Packard and Fel-Pro were committed to these practices from their beginnings or shortly thereafter.

TheoryYZ and the Spiritual Legacy: A Personal View

I believe that the world we live in is governed by various physical and spiritual "laws." Plane flight, cellular biology, and the essential goodness of many people are examples of things I don't fully understand. But I don't have to because they are there and they work and form an essential part of our lives (Marcic, 1997: 2–44). Also, after years of research and consultive experiences, I have concluded that growing numbers of organizations are moving toward work arrangements which are described in this paper as "spiritual" (see Exhibit 1). This is quite a generalization, so let me be more specific.

1. Some companies have been people oriented and quite profitable for many years. They thoughtfully *balanced* various business and work dimensions to achieve high productivity and profit-

ability (Vaille, 1989). Some were built on people-centered principles from their beginning. The critical elements balanced were: *physical* (e.g., equipment, pay, and safety); *intellectual* (e.g., leveraging available knowledge and capabilities, learning, and planning); *emotional* (e.g., interpersonal relationships and communications, teaming, feedback, and emotional development); *volitional* (e.g., willingness to change and good adaptability to new demands or conditions); and *spiritual* (e.g., concern with ethics, empathy for people, justice, and individual dignity). These dimensions are highly interdependent and must be dynamically balanced for enterprise success in response to fast-changing circumstances (Marcic, 1997: 31–43).

2. Some companies were managing with "spirituality" from their founding. Others were drawn to this organizational and managerial mode at a relatively early point in their history. In more recent years, increasing numbers have been drawn toward these approaches based on much more pragmatic considerations: their version of theory X (people as work instruments, centralized direction, etc.) didn't work anymore; technology, process reengineering, and restructuring still didn't do "it"; or more generally, all of the accouterments of high efficiency were installed including individual empowerment, but authenticity and trust were still missing.

3. Many companies have been rated in national surveys as among the "best places to work" and are also good to highly successful long-term profit performers (Burack & Mathys, 1998).

4. Some companies, perhaps a relatively large number, are still anchored to Theory X. I believe that these will continue to thin out in numbers as more and better alternatives appear and employees increasingly exercise their employment preferences for whom they are willing to make a high performance commitment (Burack, 1993; Burack and Singh, 1995; Meyer and Allen, 1997).

A New Role for Spirituality in the Workplace

Newer organization types are emerging which are much flatter than classical pyramidal structures and which emphasize increasingly empowered and collaborative employment relationships. Personal contacts among employees and between employees and managers are often brief, transitory, or even non-existent (Shaw, 1997). Trust, a belief that those on whom we depend meet our positive expectations of them (Shaw, 1997: 21), assumes a new and critical role. A new employment relations compact is being defined between workers and management (Burack and Singh, 1995). The rapid reinvention of organizational form and function has been driven directly by widespread downsizing and more generally a fast-changing competitive environment of global dimensions.

The newer work environments place a premium on employee qualities best described as conscientiousness. They are called on to do much more problem solving, adapt quickly and learn rapidly, often work longer hours, and gain newer capabilities derived largely from job-related experiences (Behling, 1998: 82–84). Unfortunately, employee respect and confidence in management is being eroded based on data from the International Research Corporation as reported in *Business Week* (June 28, 1998: 72). Distrust has grown (Shaw, 1997: XI).

Distrust leads to unclear performance targets and generally disrupts critical organizational communications, processes, and relationships. Advice giving is avoided and internal communications are viewed suspiciously. Relationships and communications become more perfunctory and people cooperate by the rule book, necessitating extensive negotiation and perhaps coercion. The promise of a learning organization is dimmed and fast response to environmental change suffers (Shaw, 1997: 11–14).

Spirituality and Work: A Contemporary View

The traditional notion of spirituality has been enlarged much beyond its anchorage in religious traditions. Transformations in religious and philosophical thought over the millennia have led to numerous applications in work life and organizational settings. M. Scott Peck (1980) makes no distinction between mind and spirit; thus the process of achieving spiritual growth is "one and the same" as achieving mental growth (p. 11). Life takes on meaning through the process of meeting and solving problems (p. 11). Since work comprises so much a part of everyone's life, organization practices can contribute greatly to spiritual (mental) growth. For example, problem-solving processes which call forth creativity or challenge conventional thought patterns, or which lead to workable or new solutions, result in additional learning and thus we experience spiritual growth.

There are other important ideas related to spirituality which have come to define a modern idea of spirituality in the workplace. One dispirited leader, seeking something more than a good bottom line, discovered his soul and learned how to be kind to his spirit and that of the organization. In the book *Leading With Soul* (Bolman and Deal, 1995) typical prescriptions include developing more hospitable work spaces, rendering services to both the organization and community, and facilitating in the workplace while strengthening organizational objectives and performance (Conger, 1989). Dorothy Marcic (1997) reinforced the idea that successful businesses may in part contribute to their financial success by facilitating the realization of spiritual values in organization life. She provides numerous examples which are compelling and underscore the importance of spiritual analysis and thinking in the work setting.

Abraham Maslow's (1962) widely acknowledged work on motivation systematically delineated higher states of mental health and possibilities for individual accomplishment. Implicit within his theorizing is the notion that organizations which can assist people in achieving their possibilities thereby become instrumental to their own improved economic bottom line. Maslow argues that all people operate out of an "inborn hierarchy of needs." Creating the culture and organization for gratifying lower-order needs—physical safety and belonging—is in itself an accomplishment. Even in the downsizing era of the 1990s, an important degree of security is provided to people who have been helped to develop transferable skills and for whom thoughtful counseling has been provided. At the same time, when these lower-order needs are satisfied (Exhibit 2), the person is in a position to move to higher-order needs where selflessness, loyalty, and public-spiritedness increasingly manifest themselves. Perhaps only a small minority will achieve their higher-order possibilities, but the needs hierarchy does suggest another tangible path for enlarging upon spirituality in the workplace. This approach is also likely to open doors to unprecedented levels of work and enterprise accomplishment. Other work design avenues to achieving higher levels of individual motivation (for performance) via self-realization of individual needs are beyond the scope of this paper. However, two important points need to be made regarding spirituality approaches described here before preceding further.

EXHIBIT 2

THE NEWER ORGANIZATIONAL IMPERATIVES

Global Competition Tight Labor Markets Merger of Acquisition Activity	⇨	Need for Rapid Adaptation and Change	⇦	Downsizing Reengineering Reinventing Organization Structure, Role, and Culture	⇨	A New Employment Relations Compact: *Mutual Commitment Organization and Employees

Ultimately the individual and a sense of spirituality at "*true work*" comes from one's own being (Fox, 1994). In this view, goodness and being are interchangeable (p. 81). In the last analysis, it is the person who takes on the expression of spirituality, albeit the organization culture or environment is conducive to this process. When the inner self connects to one's work, work and the inner self seem to know no limits; the highest level of work is spiritual "because it challenges the limits of being and stretches for the . . . spiritual horizon" (Fox, 1994: 82).

The other point concerns the organization's economic imperatives. In the spirituality approaches described here and for the organizations cited, profitability is seen as a key but not the sole outcome of business activity. Even in wholly owned private businesses, where much more latitude exists for the leader/owner, spirituality thinking is viewed as a way to help assure long-run profitability, bolster shorter-run returns, and establish a more harmonious tone in the organization.

The Reinvention of Organizations—Focus on Work Life and Spirituality

Dramatic environmental changes underway for better than a decade have drastically altered the business setting and thus led to radical shifts in organizational structure, process, and focus. Globalization, competition, diversity, aging populations, and environmental pollution are among the widely acknowledged factors (Exhibit 3, step 1). These developments have led to a reinvention of organizations (Exhibit 3, step 2) involving architecture (systems and processes), job/works, life features, and the focus of decision making (Burack, 1993). Human resource roles and relationships have taken on new importance (step 3), which are people centered and built on empowerment and team-centered activity (Ulrich, 1998; Ulrich and Associates, 1997; Jaffe, Scott, & Tobe, 1997). Leadership (step 4, Exhibit 1A) has assumed a new and critical role in these reinvented business settings. Credibility of the leader's actions, organizational policies, and far-flung business practices assume new importance in bottom-line results (Fitzenz, 1997; Kouzes and Posner, 1993). The newer systems, fast-changing conditions, the people dependency of empowerment and team-oriented activities, and increased work demands place a new premium on gaining employee commitment (Conger, 1989; Meyer and Allen, 1997; Schuster, 1998; Wood and Bandura, 1989).

EXHIBIT 3

THEORY YZ: A JOINT MANAGEMENT–EMPLOYEE APPROACH FOR HIGH COMMITMENT AND PERFORMANCE

| Organization Leadership ⇨ | Creating a Culture and Spirit of High Commitment and Performance ⇨ | Fashioning a New Employment Compact ⇨ | Newer Bottom Lines *Financial *Productivity *Welfare of People |

The scope and complexity of organizing and managing the new systems rests importantly on the quality of past relationships (step 5, Exhibit 2) and the type of organizational culture created. Leadership's actions and organizational practices will be reviewed (step 6, Exhibit 2) in the light of: managerial and leadership acumen displayed (e.g., in decision-making, innovation) and adherence to core values, ethics, and integrity. Leadership will be expected to foster individual and group learning, and shape on a newer basis for employment relationships under greatly changed environmental conditions. Creating and reinforcing a sense of spirituality in the workplace is necessary for achieving a unified whole. For the purposes of this paper, these approaches are based on Theory YZ (Exhibit 2). This theory reflects the contributions of Douglas McGregor (1960: Theory X and Theory Y) and Bill Ouchi (1980: Theory Z). The critical elements of Theory YZ include:

1. Recognition of the worth and value of people—pursuing an employee-centered management approach
2. Desire to create high-integrity work climates
3. Establishing a foundation of trust, faith, justice, respect, and love (Marcic, 1997)
4. Fostering organizations which jointly meet ownership's economic and individual needs

Needless to say, where the quality of relationships has been poor, management faces a daunting task in establishing or restoring a trustful climate (DeFoore and Renesch, 1995; Shaw, 1997).

A final point concerns the hoped-for outcomes of applying a Theory YZ approach to create a sense of workplace spirituality (Exhibit 2). Perhaps these are most easily thought of as concerned with four different but highly interrelated outcomes:

a. Leadership and the organization demonstrated concern for employees, respect for others, consistency of actions and demonstrated acumen.
b. Employees conscientious (e.g., quality, cooperation), continuing skill and knowledge advancement, adaptability and high sustained performances.
c. External (strategic constituents) quality, consistency, environmentally aware, and a responsible community member.
d. Mutual trust and shared responsibilities for joint benefits.

Organization Demographics, Culture, and Workplace Spirituality

The particular features of workplace spirituality are shaped by the organization's defining vision of its work life and what it is all about. These are influenced importantly by such key factors as work, technology, competition, organization size, and other basic features of structure and process. Thus, for example, a spirituality dimension such as *worker opportunities to identify with and shape their work* varies greatly in specifics for engineering units in comparison with production units. Differences would also rise because of size c enterprizes of 100 employees versus say 10,000 employees. The above notwithstanding, organization culture embodies the values, beliefs, and attitudes of the enterprise's defining vision. It encompasses the entire organization. Organization culture becomes the "biblical mobile ark" of what is stood for, the presence of which is felt throughout the organization. The litmus test of functionality becomes the extent to which the espoused values, beliefs, and attitudes are reasonably enacted in workplace design, communications, and interpersonal relationships. Ongoing indications of workplace spirituality are then registered by the employee's sense of credibility, trust, and personal fulfillment opportunities regarding enterprise leaders, managers, and work associates. Some short corporate case summaries follow which help to illustrate this rather complex picture. Details of designing for workplace spirituality are presented in a concluding section.

Hewlett-Packard and the H-P Way

H-P's presence among the small circle of "most esteemed" companies in the United States largely reflects the entrepreneurial spirit and vision of its founders Bill Hewlett and Dave Packard. Prior to 1970, H-P was a highly successful manufacturer of precision measuring instruments. In the decades following, it reinvented itself completely to become a world-class computer leader in the 1990s. However, in the decades after its founding (1939), the H-P way (its culture) continued to provide an overarching presence shaping workplace attitudes, relationships, compensation systems, communications, and employee initiatives and fulfillment opportunities. The founders erected a management by objectives type framework which incorporated both long- and shorter-term goals and permitted a highly decentralized management style. This facilitated many autonomous employee opportunities. Highlights of H-P's culture and its enactment are presented in Exhibit 4.

EXHIBIT 4

THE NEWER LEADERSHIP IMPERATIVES

Organizational Leadership	⇨	Envisioning Multiple Bottom Lines	⇨	Fashioning a High Commitment-Performance Culture	⇨	Empowered and Collaborative Employment Relationships
		* Productivity		* Foster Workplace Spirituality		
		* Financial Performance		* Continuous Learning		
		* Welfare of People				

The items listed in Exhibit 4 provided direction for organization design and the fleshing out of relationships and workplace policies. The

"H-P way" set out mutual understanding and respect as basic to its cooperative relationships and achieving and sustaining leadership in creative products and manufacture. These understandings came to characterize its operations. H-P became one of the first organizations to introduce flextime, which represented top management's vote of confidence in its employees and recognition of widely differing individual needs rather than a "one style fits all" approach.

A final point regarding the H-P way concerns their employment and staffing policies in periods of financial adversity or business downturns. Temporary economic downturns were handled through attrition and shortened work weeks (shared by all). Longer-term business downturns were handled through early retirements, buyouts, and attrition. Downsizing, was easily the most severe threat in terms of numbers affected and loss of one's livelihood. When confronted with the need to downsize in the early 1990s, the numbers affected were substantially reduced because of long-term human resource planning and staffing approaches.

Tom's of Maine

Organizations with less than 250 employees and often under 100 employees are far more characteristic of United States companies and thus spirituality opportunities in the workplace or enterprise. Tom's of Maine provides a highly interesting and informative scenario because it provides one of the few documented examples of "the middle way," living its values and being successful financially (Chappell, 1997). Here the middle way is the Buddhist notion—a special type of "balance." This was an organization which is perhaps best described as living paradoxically. This meant combining reflection and action; being severe but strong and connecting reflection and action; and communicating faith, integrity, honesty, and passion to people and its products while sustaining a healthy regard for making money.

The value of Tom's experience to the tens of thousands of other small firms (and large ones too!) is the fact that its mission evolved over a long gestation period. Initially it was a typical entrepreneurial start-up by a husband and wife team. It sold various personal care household products featuring environmentally friendly, natural ingredients. The leaders' preoccupation with survival and growth largely resulted in bottling up personal and strongly held values as these might become an integral part of the business. Put another way, creating, manufacturing, marketing and distributing a unique family of products was highly demanding—and not surprisingly they fell much short of creating an organization that evidenced these values. For more than four years, Tom Chappell relentlessly pursued the challenge of fully identifying their passionately held values and beliefs and then achieving an organization design, policies, and relationships that fully represented these—while becoming financially sound and achieving an enviable bottom line. His process of self-discovering included a four-year stint at Harvard's Divinity School. His "sabbatical" and change process included numerous give-and-take sessions and retreats involving their board, senior managers, employees, friends, and various professionals.

Central to their eventual success was the role of leadership. Tom, as the president and main stockholder, had the faith and the strong convictions and passions needed to carry them through many trial-and-error episodes and traumatic experiences and head encounters with possessors of conventional wisdom and believers in command and control tactics. The essence of the company, its "soul," was to be found in its core belief and values structure. Highlights of these included:

- Mind and spirit can work together for market share.
- One can do well (economically) by doing good.
- An enterprise can be socially responsible and environmentally sensitive and still make a (good) profit.
- Heart and head have to be united in ways that meet the need of the company and the person.

- Corporate identity is found in the quality of relationships of their main constituencies.
- People have a high capacity for creativity and excellence and it is an organization's responsibility to unlock these for the benefit of the enterprise and person.
- Products can be conceived and marketed which embody their core value.

Achieving these values and beliefs meant that they had to create an organization staff with people who espoused these and a willingness to grow. A high level of individual competence would be necessary to achieve these, but the people in turn had to have confidence in the leadership's acumen; they had to experience this new leadership model and examples of support that would make success for the individual and business realistic. One example of corporate actions supporting employee confidence and trust was the recall of some 400,000 units of product at a critical period in their growth—because the product was not as good as it should be.

Management's credibility and trust was established over an extended time period through numerous actions. A representative group of these included: child care facilities, a viable retirement plan, placing fruit snacks out in the plant, and picnics and other employee get-togethers. Additional company actions included tithing 10 percent of profits for worthy charities and providing for employees to take 5 percent off on company time for worthy community and charitable work projects! Tom's of Maine is an outstanding example of a company that *chose to do good.* They created a morally and socially responsible company which also was profitable.

The Ford Motor Company Experience

Better than 20 years ago, the Ford Motor Company "discovered" downsizing in order to survive. By the early 1980s they had accumulated financial losses of almost $3 billion and had reduced their North American workplace by several hundred thousands (Burack, 1993: Chapter 6). The (radical) reinvention of the company, requiring some 10 to 15 years, witnessed a complete scraping of a "Theory X" management style. This "X" style dated back to the early years of the century and reflected the philosophy of (the senior) Henry Ford. "Theory X," the view of people as essentially non-thinking tools requiring much direction and close control, was gradually replaced with a newer vision of human resource potential. This was considered as a "work-in-process" which took years to work out because of its scope uniqueness and customized fit to Ford circumstances. This concept, critical to the process of reinventing the company, rested squarely on two key assumptions:

1. Corporate credibility with workers and the consuming public had to be addressed and progress achieved before survival, let alone future growth was assured.
2. Long-term business success would be the consequence of consistent progress as measured by *two* bottom lines—one financial and the other people.

Trustful relationships between the management and the workers (and union), a key achievement in their attaining high performance, required meeting the antecedent condition of credibility.

Their new vision of work-life and employment relationships represented a new social-psychological contract. It was truly a work-in-progress since few functional models existed and there were none which even approximated the scale and the radical changes which eventually took place.

Conclusions

There is no question in my mind that profound changes are taking shape in the workplace and that spirituality will be one of the main themes. The critical ingredients for accelerating and sustaining change are now in place: a critical mass of solid scholarship and research; widespread, numerous and growing writings well divided among scholarly and popular publications; expressed needs by individuals; numerous and successful organizations for brushmaking; and last but not least, an even widening proof of top executives and owners who are convinced of the merits of these approaches. More and more managers will be seeking information to guide interval design and change initiations.

References

Barrick, M R., and Mount, M. K. (1993), "Autonomy as a Moderator of the Relationships Between the Big Five Personality Dimensions and Job Performances," *Journal of Applied Psychology*, 81: 474–482.

Behling, O. (1998), "Employee Selection: Will Intelligence and Conscientiousness Do the Job?" *Academy of Management Executive, 12(1)*, 77–86.

Bolman, Lee G., and Deal, Terrence E. (1995), *Leading With Soul*. San Francisco: Jossey-Bass.

Burack, E. H. (1993), *Corporate Resurgence and the New Employment Relationships*. Westport, CT: Quorum.

Burack, E. H., and Mathys, N. (1996), *Human Resource Planning.* 3rd ed., Rev, Northbrook, IL: Brace-Park.

Burack, E. H., and Mathys, N. (1998), "Employee Oriented Cultures and Performance," Working Paper, University of Illinois at Chicago, College of Business Administration.

Caridas, E (1995), "Creating Optimal Performance in the Workplace," in DeFoore, Bill, and Renesch, J. (eds.), (1995), *Rediscovering the Soul of a Business*. San Francisco: Sterling & Stone, Inc.

Champy, J. (1996), *Beyond Reengineering*. New York: HarperCollins.

Chappell, T. (1994), *The Soul of a Business: Managing for Profit and the Consumer Good*. New York: Bantam-Doubleday.

Conger, J. A. (1989), "Leadership: The Art of Empowering Others," *Academy of Management Executive, 3(1)*, 17–34.

Conger, Jay A., Ed. (1997), *Spirit at Work*. San Francisco: Jossey-Bass.

Csikszentmihalyi, M.(1993), *The Evolving Self*. New York: Harper-Collins.

DeFoore, B., and Renesch, J., Eds. (1995), *Rediscovering the Soul of a Business: A Renaissance of Values*. San Francisco: Sterling & Stone, Inc.

Dorfman, R. A. (1994), *Aging into the 21st Century*. New York: Brunner-Mazel.

Emery, F., and Emery, M. (1993), *Participative Design for Participative Democracy*. Australian National University, Centre for Continuing Education.

Fitz-enz, J. (1997), *The 8 Practices of Exceptional Companies: How Great Organizations Make the Most of Their Human Assets*. New York: AMACOM.

Fox, Matthew (1994), *The Reinvention of Work*. San Francisco: Harper.

Fukuyama, F. (1995), *Trust: The Social Virtues and Creation of Prosperity*. New York: Free Press.

Hosmen, L. Tune (1995), "Trust: The Connecting Link Between Organizational Theory and Philosophical Ethics," *Academy of Management Review 20(2)*, 379–403.

Jaffe, D. T., Scott, Cynthia D., and Tobe, Glenn R. (1997), *Rekindling Commitment*. San Francisco: Jossey-Bass.

Kouzes, J. M., and Posner, Barrz Z. (1993), *Credibility: How Leaders Gain and Lose It, Why People Demand It*. San Francisco: Jossey-Bass.

Marcic, Dorothy (1997), *Managing with the Wisdom of Love*. San Francisco: Jossey-Bass.

Maslow, Abraham (1962), *Toward a Psychology of Being*. Princeton, New Jersey: Van Nostrand.

McGregor, Douglas (1960), *The Human Side of Enterprise*. New York: McGraw-Hill.

Meyer, J. P., and Allen, Natalie J. (1997), *Commitment in the Workplace: Theory, Research and Application*. Thousand Oaks, CA: Sage.

Ouchi, B. (1980), *Theory Z*. New York: Doubleday.

Packard, David (1995), *The H-P Way*. New York: HarperCollins.

Peck, M. Scott (1980), *The Road Less Traveled*. New York: Touchstone, Simon & Schuster.

Schuster, F. (1998), *Employee-Centered Management: A Strategy for High Commitment and Involvement*. Westport, CT: Quorum.

Shaw. *Trust in the Balance* (1997), San Francisco: Jossey-Bass.

Ulrich, D. (1998), *Human Resource Champions: The Next Agenda for Adding Value and Delivering Results*. San Francisco: Jossey-Bass.

Ulrich, David, Losey, Michael, R., & Lake, Gerry (eds.), (1997), *Tomorrow's HR Management*. New York: Wiley.

Vaille, Peter (1989), *Managing as a Performing Art: New Ideas for a World of Chaotic Change*. San Francisco: Jossey-Bass.

Wood, R. E., and Bandura A.(1989), "Impact of Conceptions of Ability in Self-Regulation Mechanisms and Complex Decision Making." *Journal of Personality and Social Psychology 56*, 407–415.

SPIRITUALITY AT WORK:

DEFINITIONS, MEASURES, ASSUMPTIONS, AND VALIDITY CLAIMS

Paul Gibbons is an independent consultant
on Spirituality and Work. His recently completed
thesis entitled *Spirituality at Work: A Pre-theoretical
Overview* is available from pauligibbo@aol.com.

Introduction

We who research and practice in the area of Spirituality at Work have a vital mission: we are custodians of a fledgling discipline that might be a powerful force for good in the lives of people. For helping individuals integrate their work and spiritual lives might mean that the 100,000 or so hours that an individual will work in their lifetime are more joyful, balanced, and meaningful and nourish their spirit rather than drain it. These more fulfilled individuals might then return to their families and communities contented, refreshed, and ready to contribute rather than escape. Because of this integration, one might expect these people might be more ethical or more productive workers—which would benefit their employers. Moreover, Spirituality at Work might help businesses to become humane, socially active, and environmentally responsible. If that were the case, it might be the most important task our society faces in the first decades of the new millennium.

But even without this optimistic view of spirituality, Spirituality at Work is worth serious academic and practical consideration. Ninety-four percent of Americans say they believe in God (Emmons & Crumpler, 1999), and 74% consider themselves both religious AND spiritual (Pargament, 1999). Since 1990, "spirituality and religion" has been among the fastest-growing segments of the book market. More and more people construct themselves as spiritual. Therefore, on a phenomenological or constructivist basis alone, spirituality is worth incorporation into our models of human and organizational behavior. Furthermore, even the most secular individual has unconscious theories-in-use about whether

111

humanity is fundamentally sinful or good, whether the world is essentially safe or hostile, whether systems are naturally chaotic or ordered, or whether our own agency or our circumstances determine our future. These beliefs may play out in not too subtle fashion, say during a performance appraisal, or while managing a complex project.

In summary, there are many compelling academic and practical benefits to a deeper understanding of Spirituality at Work. However, marshaled against our efforts is an array of forces including:

- A rift between spiritual and scientific discourses creating "a joint denial of significance and validity" (Wilber, 1998)
- A techno-economic context where short-term financial measures (i.e., corporate earnings and GNP) are pursued obsessively, while longer-term non-material outcomes (human or societal or environmental welfare) struggle to find voice
- A socio-cultural system geared toward instant gratification and consumption and where individual achievement is frequently measured in material terms or by advancement within structured hierarchies

Therefore, the adoption of concepts and practice from Spirituality at Work seems likely to be resisted by the academic and business "establishment" on a number of grounds. Among the challenges will be that our findings are not "real world," or are not "rational." Other challenges may be of a more emotional nature, resulting from the threat that Spirituality at Work may pose to established "knowledges" or power structures (in the Foucauldian sense). Still other challenges may come if our work resembles "old wine in new bottles" or has the appearance of yet another fad.

In my opinion, the implications for academics and practitioners are:

1. We who work in the field of Spirituality at Work must be even more rigorous with our theoretical frameworks (definitions, measures, assumptions, and truth claims) than researchers in more "rational" areas of organizational science, or than we have been to date.
2. In order to do this, we must seek a level of integration and collaboration with other disciplines that we have not, to date, attempted.
3. We must be wary of the "fad" phenomenon and seek to maintain a level of distinctiveness and rigor of Spirituality at Work.

This paper suggests gaps and weaknesses in our definitions, measures, assumptions, and truth claims that integration with other disciplines may help to address, then considers what we might do to prevent Spirituality at Work from becoming a fad.

Definitional Difficulties

So, while we must avoid too much indefiniteness and abstraction on one hand, we must also avoid hard and fast definitions on the other hand. For no words in our human language are adequate or accurate when applied to spiritual realities.
                              (Evelyn Underhill, *The Spiritual Life*, p. 23)

For some, like Underhill, the ineffability of spirituality precludes definition, while others have attempted to characterize and define it at length. For example, *World Spirituality: An Encyclopedic History of the Religious Quest* (Cousins, 1986) reaches to 25 volumes. Today, spirituality covers an increasingly wide range of belief systems and practices, rendering its elaboration as a concept challenging. Spirituality, once an aspect of religion, has turned the linguistic tables and religion is now seen as one of many possible spiritual paths. Once spirituality was a path to deep communion with God. Now God, for many, is no longer the object of their spiritual search: the path is one of communion and connectedness with many other transcendent conceptions.

Bauman (1998) echoes Underhill's thoughts from a post-modern perspective, saying that definitions of terms like spirituality "conceal as much as they reveal, and maim and obfuscate while pretending to clarify and straighten up." But he continues by saying "if we fail to coin a 'rational definition,' we would enter the post-modern world ill-prepared to tackle the [essential research] questions." In our case, what is the "spirituality" that is talked about in Spirituality at Work? How might this spirituality affect organizations, the people in them, and the environment and society? What outcomes do we associate with Spirituality at Work? What mechanisms do we propose for these outcomes? How can these outcomes be facilitated? So while definition and characterization have their limits as ways of knowing, the text below intends to show that the rigor of the definition and characterization process can raise important issues.

In Spirituality at Work texts, one tends to encounter definitions of spirituality that are abstract, universal, and inclusive. These definitions accommodate the many different belief systems and paths that the term represents. For example: *"Spirituality is the search for direction, mean-*

ing, inner wholeness, and connectedness to others, to non-human creation and to a transcendent."[1]

However, this level of abstraction and the universality of its application afford little practical help with understanding the phenomenon, or how the search might be conducted, or about the variety of belief systems that guide the search. Some further elaboration is needed, and one method of understanding the phenomenon is through examining the characteristics of contemporary spirituality, which are typically post-modern. For example, spirituality has always emphasized mystery, denying rationality as the sole source of knowledge. It focuses on subjectivity, both in interpretations of spiritual texts, and in the variety of ways in which spirituality may be experienced. It permits a "willingness to combine symbols from disparate codes or frameworks of meaning, even at the cost of disjunctions and eclecticism" (Hellas, p. 4). It suggests a personal transcendent conception and a personal spiritual journey, and not necessarily a patriarchal God or a scripted spiritual journey. The term has religious roots that inform current understandings, but it rejects religious grand narratives.

Characterizations of this type help one to answer the question: What is the "spirituality" of Spirituality at Work and particularly how does it differ from its pre-modern and modern ancestors? Moreover, all of the attributes of this characterization point toward the pluralistic nature of contemporary spirituality. However, from this fragmented, pluralistic view it is possible to construct a typology (Gibbons, 1999).

This typology would condense the myriad of different "spiritualities" of our time into three types: religious, secular, and mystical. Secular spirituality includes earth-centered, nature-centered, and humanistic spiritualities. The intellectual leaders of this movement are Dewey, Emmerson, Rogers, Schumaker, and Maslow. Its beliefs may be pantheistic and atheistic, and its practices include social and environmental activism. The Body Shop and Ben & Jerry's are corporations that have links to this type of spirituality. The mystical tradition is not only an important sub-discipline within Christianity, Judaism, and Islam, but without this type, most Eastern spiritualities would be omitted from our understanding. Authors and researchers in our field largely ignore this type of spirituality in their measures and models, which is a very significant omission. There are enterprises founded on these principles, and theoretical and empirical links between this type of spirituality and a

---

[1] Based on King (1997, p. 668).

number of desirable organizational outcomes such as task effectiveness and lowered stress (Schmidt-Wilk et al., 1996).

This typology also suggests a close relationship between religion and spirituality, constructing spirituality as the broader term, while defining religion as the most prevalent and "scripted" spiritual path. However, this intellectual accommodation between spirituality and religion does not prevent a great deal of conflict and even animosity between those who see their path as distinct from, and superior to, that of others. With the drawing of a distinction between religion and spirituality, some claim the ascendance of the spiritual. This distinction and this ascendance are problematic to Pargament (1999), who laments, "Religion is associated with the organizational, the ritual and the ideological, and spirituality with the personal, the affective, the experiential and the thoughtful." He observes a tendency to view religion as bad, "restricting and inhibiting human potential," and spirituality as good, "speaking to the greatest of human capacities."

He goes on to establish that this view is not justifiable historically. James (1902) defined religion as "the feelings, acts and experiences of individual men in their solitude." Furthermore, "functional definitions of religion have always been plentiful . . . where there is no mention of gods, higher powers, or supreme beings." Lastly, "not all religion is bad, and not all spirituality is good in terms of its effects on mental health." The relationship between spirituality and religion is a complex one, and it is lamentable that it is so poorly understood. A critical practical question is: Does spirituality at work include religion at work? Some people who I have interviewed are horrified by this thought, yet to exclude religion would exclude the spiritual path of the vast majority, and some of the world's most ancient spiritual teachings. From a practical standpoint, further reconciliation of this relationship is essential if we are to progress.

While spirituality may be better understood by studying its characteristics and types, to understand it fully, one must also inquire into the content of spirituality: that is, specific beliefs, values, and practices. However, it is in this domain that even greater conflict may arise. For example, for some people, belief in God is the *sine qua non* of a spiritual belief system. While for others, supernatural beliefs are irrelevant or even harmful. Certainly, today's spirituality accommodates a diversity of transcendent conceptions, but this diversity troubles some observers. Blond (1998, p. 285) laments that "God has been pluralized into a general spirituality and identified with virtually anything whatsoever," thus creating a "conceptual emptiness." Emmons and Crumpler (1999) question,

"Can one speak of holiness or divinity without God? Wherein would these terms derive their meaning?" These scholars clearly see the content, rather than the process, of the spiritual search as key. In addition, the focus is on the object and not the subject. However their views are at odds with contemporary interpretations, which focus on the process ("the journey"). The object has been pluralized, which does pose some problems.

First, this pluralism permits almost anything to be called spiritual. A substantial number of conference presentations on Spirituality at Work talk exclusively about values, having fun at work, or "right-brain" approaches. While these concepts are valuable, they are far from new, and certainly not distinctively spiritual. Second, content-free spirituality does not get one very far practically; one needs definitive beliefs and practices that specify just what one does. For example, in Buddhism, mindfulness, compassion, and meditation, and in Christianity, prayer, church attendance, forgiveness, and brotherly love. In addition, from a research standpoint, the study of a general spirituality may be too difficult. It may be necessary to study specific phenomena, like prayer and meditation, or forgiveness and selfless service.[2]

So we must go beyond abstract and universal definitions and delve into the more conflict-ridden areas of characteristics, types, and specific content. Only by using this range of different definitions can we understand the phenomenon of Spirituality at Work and its relationship to the outcomes that we desire in sufficient depth. Furthermore, by insisting on concrete definitions and focusing more on content and less on process, our field becomes less abstract and more pragmatic. We may then be able to propose specific evidence-based solutions to individuals and organizations interested in integrating work and spirituality.

Defining Spirituality at Work

Just as spirituality may be defined abstractly and in terms of characteristics, types, and specific content, so may we take the same approach to defining Spirituality at Work. An abstract definition of Spirituality at Work is: "*A journey toward integration of work and spirituality, for individuals and organizations, which provides direction, wholeness and connectedness at work.*"

---

[2] For examples, see Schmidt-Wilk et al. (1996) on meditation, or Kurth (1995) on selfless service.

However, as with the definition of spirituality, this level of abstraction does not help us understand, study, or practice Spirituality at Work. Therefore, Spirituality at Work must also be explicated in terms of its different types. Two primary types exist according to level of analysis: individual and organizational. Furthermore, a number of sub-types exist within these types.

Individual Spirituality at Work is journey toward integration of an individual's work and spiritual life. This means having work contribute to the individual's spiritual path, and having the individual's spiritual path contribute to their work. The specific nature of this integrating journey will depend on the individual's spiritual path, but for a Buddhist, it might include practicing mindfulness, compassion, and meditation at work and a career journey that emphasized "right livelihood" (Whitmeyer, 1994). Individual Spirituality at Work also includes work on spirituality and leadership, individual creativity, intuition, and well-being at work.

Organizational Spirituality at Work is the organizational journey toward the spiritual. This can include organizational efforts to nurture individual Spirituality at Work, but also organizational reorientation toward spiritual goals and means. Until recently, this phenomenon was not well described, but Mitroff and Denton (1999) have proposed five sub-types of organizational spirituality. These are the Religious, Recovering, Evolutionary, Socially Responsible, and Value-driven organizations. And as different types of spirituality have different beliefs, practices, and ethical bases, so Mitroff and Denton's typology proposes 30 dimensions of organizational Spirituality at Work.

TABLE 1: Characteristics of the Spirituality at Work Discourse
Predominantly a North American phenomenon.
Largely a grass-roots phenomenon rather than an organizationally orchestrated one (cf. BPR).
The primary texts are popular books whose truth claims are largely assertion.
A pluralistic phenomenon but with some hostility toward traditional/ fundamentalist religiosity.
Literature with an overall optimistic and uncritical tone.

In addition, as with spirituality, a list of characteristics can often help understand a phenomenon. Table 1 contains a list of some of the characteristics that characterize Spirituality at Work. It is important that scholars and practitioners challenge and extend this table, for this self-examination and reflexive inquiry is essential if we are to apprehend and address weaknesses in our discourse. Finally, as with spirituality, Spirituality at Work may be expressed in terms of specific beliefs and practices. Building on the ideas of Wilber (1996) and Gibbons (1999), Table 2 organizes the individual and organizational aspects of Spirituality at Work in terms of their interior and exterior attributes. Exterior phenomena can be measured and observed by empirical methods. However, interior phenomena require phenomenological, narrative, or discursive approaches.

TABLE 2: A Proposed Organizing Framework for Spirituality at Work

	Interior	Exterior
Individual	• Private meditation and prayer • Practicing spiritual attitudes toward work and colleagues • Deep beliefs about the nature of God, the Universe, Humanity, Order/ Chaos, Grace, etc.	• Observable behaviors • Spiritual symbols and talk • Spirituality and leadership development • Spirituality and career development • Empirical research (e.g., well-being, task effectiveness, motivation)
Organizational	• Organizing principles (Mitroff & Denton, 1999) • Values programs • Climate, attitudes • Organizational history and mission • Culture, stories, myths	• Structural features (e.g., hierarchies, reward systems, measures) • Spiritual goals (multiple stakeholders, non-material outcomes) • Spiritual means (participation? no layoffs?) • Boundaries/ statements of policy on Spirituality at Work • Nurturing individual spirituality (e.g., time and space)

This table is far from definitive, but it does point out some gaps in our understanding that are suggestive of a research agenda. For example, while Mitroff and Denton (1999) have proposed certain dimensions along which a spiritual organization may be classified, these are principles and values (i.e., interior). The exterior, structural features of an organization that would promote more spiritual means and outcomes are also worthy of study.[3] These would include identifying reward systems, HR policies, organizing principles (e.g., process versus functional, flat versus hierarchical), connectivity, and physical layout that would nurture individual spirituality at work, and assist the organization toward fulfilling more spiritual goals with more spiritual means.

The content of the tables in this section is preliminary in nature. Clearly more extensive development and elaboration is possible. And while classification and definition are modernist approaches, the process of doing this for spirituality identified the gap in our literature on mystical and Eastern spiritualities. Applying Wilber's four quadrants to Spirituality at Work suggested a gap in our understanding of the lower-right (exterior-organizational) aspects of our field. Furthermore, this definition and classification becomes essential if we are to do more empirical or more rigorous research on Spirituality at Work, for spirituality may be too broad to study as a general phenomenon. It is not that we should endorse chiefly rational methods for understanding the ineffable, but as Wilber suggests, our evolution needs to transcend and include earlier methods of knowing (i.e., modernist approaches and the empirical-rational method), and not reject or abandon them.

Operationalizing Spirituality—on Measuring God?

In operationalizing spirituality, the pluralism discussed in the previous section becomes a serious issue. Not only are there multiple spiritual paths, but even paths which are superficially similar may, on deeper examination, have very different worldviews. For example, "Do you believe in God?" seems an easy place to start. However 95% of Americans say they do (Emmons & Crumpler, 1999) and it is clear that this God means different things to these people. For some, God is real, immanent, omnipresent, and material, but for others, like William James, God is impersonal and less concrete:

---

[3] Milliman et al. (1999) have analyzed this for a single organization—SouthWest Airlines—drawing attention to the possible links between Values, Goals, HR systems, and Outcomes.

I have no living sense of commerce with a God. I envy those who have, for I know that the addition of such a sense would help me greatly. The Divine, for my active life is limited to impersonal and abstract concepts which, as ideals, interest and determine me . . . yet there is something in me which makes response when I hear utterance from that quarter made by others . . . Something tells me—"thither lies the truth"—and I am sure it is not old theistic prejudices of infancy. (James, 1902)

Other diverse views on the nature of God are also evident. For example, God is frequently anthropomorphized as either wrathful or loving. Even within the Judeo-Christian tradition there are diverse beliefs about the nature of humanity (e.g., original sin), the nature and source of salvation (i.e., grace versus works), ethical stances (e.g., laws versus virtues), and the involvement of God in the minutiae of human affairs. Evidence from the Psychology of Religion suggests that one's concept of God has important effects on mental health and ethical behavior (see Gibbons, 1999, for a review). It seems possible to extend this finding further, anticipating that this diversity of views will produce very different attitudes and behaviors at work.

This complexity and diversity of spiritual paths has led some researchers to advocate a discursive, narrative approach (Neal et al., 1999). The advantages of this approach are that it:

- Better reveals the developmental and process aspects of spirituality
- Explores how spirituality expresses itself in context
- May allow study of cognitive structures and schema that would link specific beliefs to behaviors
- More effectively captures the affective nature of spiritual experience

However, the external validity of research findings based on this method is limited, and it seems that the much doctoral research on Spirituality at Work still focuses on the development of measures. (e.g., Beazley, 1997; Perez, 1998) Unfortunately, this has led to an over-abundance of scales that derive from three different research streams: our stream (Spirituality at Work), the Psychology of Religion, and the pastoral professions (nursing/ counseling/addiction recovery). Worse still, Spirituality at Work research reports fail to acknowledge the existence of literally hundreds of well-tested measures within these other two discourses. Of course, accompanying these measures are their associated empirical findings concerning the relationship between spirituality, religion, and a large number of attitudinal and behavioral outcomes. Again, these seem ignored by our researchers. One scholar, Pargament (1999), suggests that most measures of spirituality look very similar to measures of religiosity, and wonders what incremental value our new measures add to our understanding of these phenomena.

To my knowledge, no thorough academic reviews of the importance of spirituality in the pastoral professions exists; however, Fitchett (1997) has prepared a collection of abstracts from these areas. A review of this literature that would seek to uncover measures, insights, or alternative perspectives from this field and ours would seem to be indicated.

An even older discipline is the psychology of religion, which has been studying religiosity using chiefly empirical methods almost since the turn of the 20th century. A recent overview of this literature (Gibbons, 1999) yielded insights that may be critical to our understanding of spirituality at work.[4]

First, how earnestly someone follows a religion (salience) seems more important than the specific content of their beliefs and practices. In summary, the relationship between salience and both well-being and ethical behavior seems curvilinear. In simple terms, the very religious and the non-religious are most happy and most ethical: the mildly religious seem to be the least happy and the least ethical (Spilka et al., 1985).

Second, why someone is religious is critically important. Intrinsic religious people view "faith as a supreme value in its own right," or, "my whole approach to life is based upon my religion." People who are intrinsically religious "internalise their beliefs and live by them." Extrinsic religion is essentially utilitarian. Extrinsically religious people use their religion as a mean of obtaining status, security, self-justification, and sociability. There may be two important sub-orientations of "extrinsics": social (using religion toward social gain) and personal (using religion toward gaining comfort, security, and protection). I-E research shows that "intrinsic" religiosity is much more associated with happiness and life satisfaction and self-esteem than "extrinsic" (Hood,

---

[4] But see Spilka et al. (1985) for definitive material.

1992; Masters & Bergin, 1992). Masters and Bergin also report a variety of empirical research showing that "Intrinsic" religiosity is associated with mental health outcomes such as: an absence of a variety of psychopathologies; competent perception and expression of one's own feelings, and empathy with others' feelings; an active, flexible approach to dealing with life situations and dealing with stress.

These two findings from the psychology of religion seem important, but how might they be relevant to the study of Spirituality at Work? It might be argued that Spirituality at Work will promote a greater degree of centrality of one's spiritual practice through ending the compartmentalization and secularization of one's working life. Therefore, the empirical findings on centrality coupled with the above reasonable (but speculative) interpretation suggest a justification for workers and employers taking an interest in Spirituality at Work.

However, which orientation, intrinsic or extrinsic, might one associate with Spirituality at Work? This question can be interrogated through questioning what is driving the increased interest in Spirituality at Work. My contention is that many of our writings are highly "extrinsic" in stance, extolling the benefits of Spirituality at Work to productivity and self-realization. This news is less encouraging as it suggests that where Spirituality at Work becomes a "project of the ego," or is harnessed for secular outcomes (profit), the desired benefits may not be as expected.

I must emphasize that these two findings are merely representative of the wealth of resources available to our field from the Psychology of Religion discourse. There is more where they came from and a more thorough review of that field might prevent some wheel-reinvention as well as generate critical insights for the study and application of our discipline. The challenge is to build on the research of the Psychology of Religion while maintaining the conceptual distance that post-modern spirituality requires.

Before leaving this section, there is one other glaring weakness with current measurement instruments that merits attention. To understand Spirituality at Work empirically, we are interested in those operationalizations that will best predict work behaviors and mental states. If the "separation thesis" is valid, and some individuals see work as a distinct and secular enterprise, then empirical relationships between spirituality (outside work) and behavior and mental states (inside work) may be weak. Research from the Psychology of Religion suggests that this may be true: individuals do compartmentalize their value systems

(Spilka et al., 1985). While the general level of "communion with God" may be important, the level of communion at work may be more so. Largely, the measures of spirituality that have been developed are context-free. That is, they interrogate general spiritual beliefs and behaviors, rather than those in use in the work context. It seems very likely that to understand Spirituality at Work, we will have to measure spirituality at work.

Assumptions and Validity Claims

Even the most academic and rigorous of our writing seems based on assumptions that are often not held up for examination. Table 3 lists a selection of these.

TABLE 3: Assumptions of Spirituality at Work	
Human nature	• Spirituality is universal and an innate part of our nature.
Work context	• The work context is (a) worsening, (b) changing more rapidly than ever.
	• The work context is injurious to the human spirit.
Work content	• The work content helps determine the individual's experience.

These assumptions are reviewed in detail elsewhere (Gibbons, 1999), but all of them are open to significant challenge. Spirituality need not be conceived of as universal and innate: phenomenological, cultural, and developmental models also allow for the importance of spirituality to some (an increasing number) of individuals without incurring hostility from those for whom spirituality is an irrelevance, or anathema. Assumptions of a worsening or rapidly changing work context may be guilty of romanticism and anhistoricism. Assumptions that work context adversely affects the human spirit deny the role of the individual in creating their reality through enactment and interpretation (Weick, 1995). These assumptions also perpetuate a "victim" mentality that is at odds with some spiritual worldviews. Finally, the importance of the work content is at odds with a number of material and spiritual perspectives—while it probably is important in our culture, in some spiritual perspectives (e.g., Karma Yoga) the attitude that one brings to the work determines one's experience of it: "with love and enthusiasm toward our work, what was once a chore and hardship now becomes a magical tool to develop, enrich and nourish our lives" (Fields et al., 1994).

In summary, many of the assumptions that we seem to take for granted seem very interesting areas for research or scholarly inquiry. Furthermore, if we are to build a case for Spirituality at Work, how much stronger it will be if we are explicit about our assumptions and willing to hold them up for examination.

An analysis of the content themes in our literature, organized into individual, organizational, and societal levels, suggests that Spirituality at Work will positively affect almost every aspect of organizational life. Unfortunately, some claims seem largely unjustified based on the theory and evidence available to-date.

Table 4 summarizes an extensive analysis of the validity claims of eleven outcomes claimed in our texts (from Gibbons, 1999). However, our field is vast and this research may have overlooked significant findings that strengthen the nature of some of these claims. Furthermore, Neck and Milliman (1994) cite research which points to a number of additional outcomes including individual creativity, intuition, organizational innovation, self-actualization, organizational vision, and teamwork. These claims require analysis on a similar basis.

TABLE 4: Spirituality at Work Claims

Claim	Primary Basis of Claim
Vocation choice	Qualitative findings from non-random sample. Potentially important for some people, at some life stages.
Subjective well-being	Empirical evidence. Complex relationship, component elements of spirituality very important.
Motivation	Empirical evidence. Poor theoretical formulation.
Task effectiveness	Empirical evidence. Direct evidence only for mystical spirituality.
Leadership	Normative research. Constructivist arguments much more powerful.
Well-being and task performance	Empirical evidence. Complex relationship at organizational level, indirect effects, e.g., through organizational citizenship behaviors very important.
Climate	Positive. Verification and use of different predictor (not SpWB) indicated.
Culture	Untested assumption. Complex and inverse relationship is more likely.
Culture and financial performance	Empirical and anecdotal research. Likely conflictual and potentially inverse relationship.
Resource acquisition	Argumentation: potentially positive for people, and negative for capital.
Ethical organizations	Empirical research/ argumentation. Complex relationship.

The essence of these arguments is that we must apply much more rigor and critical thinking to our field. We face challenges from the academic and business communities that would label Spirituality at Work as irrelevant or irrational—therefore, to succeed our ideas must appear much stronger than ideas that might be equally new and untested, but that have more face validity in the eyes of academics and practitioners. This could mean more empirical studies such as Trott (1996)[5]; however empirical research (or lack thereof) tends to have little effect on the activities of practitioners and consultants. The gap between theory, research, and practice may be even bigger for Spirituality at Work than it is for mainstream organization science as many of our practitioners are from the "new spirituality" discourse, and not overfriendly to scientific approaches. My experience at numerous conferences suggests to me that in their race away from mechanistic and reductionist thinking, they abandon critical thinking also. Just because science cannot prove everything, does not mean that everything we do works, or works equally well.

Integration Possibilities

The case for deeper study of and integration with the Psychology of Religion was presented earlier, and while our discipline has touch-points with many others,[6] there are two (Business Ethics and Organization Science) that deserve specific mention as they hold the promise of very fruitful collaboration.

Business Ethics can contribute to Spirituality at Work research in a number of ways. First, it provides a body of knowledge that links ethical beliefs, ethical decisions, and ethical actions, and access to the ideas of Aristotle, Plato, Kant, Aquinas, and others. Second, business ethicists have theoretical frameworks and research for resolving the financial and non-financial claims of different stakeholders on the organization (Sims, 1994). Third, business ethicists have theory and empirical research on ethical decision making in organizations (Gellerman, 1989). Fourth, there is a body of case-studies of ethical and

---

[5] Trott demonstrated a positive relationship between Spiritual Well-Being and organizational climate, commitment, and general self-efficacy in a for-profit setting.

[6] One field that may prove an especially fruitful one to review is the Sociology of Religion, in which there is a large sub-discipline on the relationship between religion and capitalism (i.e., Weber, 1935).

socially responsible organizations, some of which is applicable to Spirituality at Work.[7] Lastly, ethics is very much on the organizational agenda (if sometimes only for risk management and compliance reasons). An understanding of the links between spirituality and ethics would provide practitioners in our field a means of contributing to the non-financial goals of the corporation.

Finally, in order to gain wider academic credibility, Spirituality at Work researchers must link their research to organization science and not just to popular management theory. How do these two disciplines differ? Organization science is, overall, more concerned with theory and evidence. For example, popular management theory would hold that values and financial performance are linked and indeed some Spirituality at Work books take that stance. However, research in organization science has had great difficulty proving a link between either specific values and financial performance, or culture strength and financial performance (Siehl & Martin, 1990; Martin, 1999). Furthermore, the relevance of the oft-cited Collins and Porras (1994) research on "core ideologies" to Spirituality at Work is very doubtful as the core ideologies and values (Table 5) of some "visionary companies" are quite different than spiritual values like forgiveness, love, compassion, mindfulness, and balance (Gibbons, 1999).

TABLE 5: Core Ideologies of Visionary Companies

Citicorp	3M	Nordstrom
Expansionism	Innovation	Service to the customer
Being out in front	Integrity	Hard work
Autonomy	Respect	Continuous improvement
Meritocracy	Tolerance	Excellence
Aggressiveness	Quality and reliability	
	Solving problems	

Source: *(Collins & Porras, 1994)*

---

[7] See Hartman (1998) for a graduate level text on Business Ethics. Also see Weaver & Agle (1999) for a model relating religion and ethical decision making.

On Novelty and Fads

Which brings me to my final and deepest concern: Is Spirituality at Work a fad? Could it become one? Human Relations and OD, Socio-technical Systems, TQM, and QWL all had powerful and noble goals. Some of those areas were much better grounded theoretically and more deeply researched than our fledgling discipline can yet claim. But, while the ideas and ideals of these movements have been incorporated selectively into some companies and persist to this day, overall, it can be argued that they have not lived up to their initial promise. Was it the content, the process of adoption, or the socio-technical context that produced the disappointing results for these other disciplines? Spirituality at Work advocates must consider this question if Spirituality at Work is not to meet an identical fate.

Is our content fad-like?[8] Though the words *Spirituality at Work* are new in business discourse, some of the concepts being labeled spiritual bear resemblance to OD concepts such as values, participation, and organizational mission statements. These are sometimes spiritual, but they are not new, nor are they necessarily or distinctively spiritual. In my view this rebranding of older concepts risks debasing the currency of the word *spirituality* and trivializing our content. However, "strong forms" of spirituality are very distinctive indeed. Whether they are of the religious, secular, or mystical types, they represent (in my view) a radical departure from our existing business paradigms.

Spirituality and business are two belief systems with different ultimate goals: profit and God (or the equivalent sacred transcendent conception). Spirituality at Work concerns itself with the coalescing of these belief systems. In this coalescing, some mutual accommodation must take place if these two belief systems are to coexist. However, right now, spirituality is doing most of the accommodating and in the process losing its distinctiveness. In my view, many of our popular books describe a "feel-good" spirituality. Beazley (1997) calls this "bromidic" spirituality "a collection of platitudes without a supporting component mandating self-examination, self-discipline, study and sustained effort." If we are interested in making a significant impact on how people experience their work lives, or organizations conduct their affairs, we need to be careful how much we allow the currency of spirituality to be debased.

---

[8] Trivial, ephemeral, superficial.

How might the "process" by which Spirituality at Work is being popularized turn it into a fad? Gill and Whittle (1992) describe the history of three management fads (MBO, OD, and TQM) whose life cycles took between 10 and 40 years to unfold. "Extravagant claims" and "an absence of critique and a high degree of consensus characterize the early phases" and disillusionment and decline the later ones. These descriptions would seem to apply to many of the popular books on our subject, which is understandable since they are aimed at the mass market. However, as academics we have the opportunity to counterbalance some of their pollyannaism by making sure that we raise theoretical and practical concerns in our literature and that our literature contains appropriate critique and healthy debate.

Finally, we must consider whether our ideas are sufficiently robust in the face of the challenges from the techno-economic and sociocultural context. There are hundreds of books on religion and political economy that might shed scholarly light on the relationship between spirituality, the work ethic, and capitalism: Can Spirituality at Work coexist with the capitalist techno-economic context? Why would organizations consider seriously wider stakeholder and non-material goals? How does institutional theory predict these organizations will fare against their more profit-oriented competitors? Furthermore, some important sociological arguments from critical theory have not yet been exposed to scholarly debate:[9] Is Spirituality at Work another "liberal rhetoric" used to conceal issues of exploitation and "make the intolerable, tolerable"? Is Spirituality at Work an extension of corporate "culturism," or the control systems of modernity? Could Spirituality at Work lead to increased conflict between spiritual worldviews? Between spiritual and material goals? Between worker spiritual lives and greater employer demands for time and effort?

These questions represent an extreme point of view, but it is worth considering whether we have an adequate response. We can ask what can be learned from the sociological "conflict" school without wholly embracing its conspiratorial views of corporate actions.

Spirituality at Work is a powerful force for good and we who are its custodians must ask ourselves what we are doing to ensure that it is taken seriously and to prevent it from becoming a fad. For if it does

---

[9] See Gibbons (1999) for a more detailed description and potential rebuttal of these arguments.

become a fad, individuals will have lost the chance to try to apply some well-tested principles and practices in their work lives and to, perhaps, make those work lives more meaningful and joyful. Researchers will have lost the opportunity to adopt a more holistic approach that would integrate a broad range of thoughtful and scholarly ideas on individual and organizational behavior. And organizations will have lost an opportunity to try and moderate some of the ills that are, today, taken for granted as part of corporate culture: e.g., overwork, commoditization of people, and exploitation of the environment.

It is the responsibility of we researchers, consultants, and practitioners to prevent this from happening. For a topic such as spirituality, we must strive to be even more precise in our definitions, assumptions, theories, and research methods. For if one truly believes in the power of spirituality to effect radical positive change, then the future of that radical positive change depends on the commitment of the people who are studying and practicing Spirituality at Work now to distinctiveness and rigor.

References

Bauman, Z., "Postmodern Religion," In Heelas (ed.), *Religion, Modernity, and Postmodernity*, Blackwell: Oxford (1998).

Beazley, H., (1997), "Meaning and measurement of Spirituality in Organizational Settings: Development of a Spiritual Assessment Scale." Doctoral Dissertation: George Washington University, p. 133.

Blond, P., "The Primacy of Theology and the Question of Perception," In Heelas, P. (ed.), *Religion, Modernity, and Postmodernity*, Blackwell: Oxford (1998).

Collins, J., & Porras, J., *Built to Last: Successful Habits of Visionary Companies*, HarperBusiness: New York (1994).

Cousins, L., (1997), "Buddhism," in Hinnells, J. (ed.). *A New Handbook of Living Religions*, Penguin: London

Emmons, R., & Crumpler, C., "Religion and Spirituality? The Roles of Sanctification and the Concept of God," *The International Journal for the Psychology of Religion 9 (1)*, 17–24 (1999).

Fields, R., Taylor, P., Weyler, R., & Ingrasci, R., "To Work Is to Pray," In Whitmeyer, C. (Ed.), *Mindfulness and Meaningful Work*, Parallax Press: Berkeley (1994).

Fitchett, G., "Screening for Spiritual Risk: A Guide to Selected Resources," Unpublished collection of abstracts, Center for Spirituality and Health, Rush–Presbyterian–St. Lukes Medical Center, Chicago, IL (gfitchet@rpslmc.edu) (1997).

Gellerman, S., "Why 'Good' Managers Make Bad Ethical Choices," In Andrews, K. (Ed.), *Ethics in Practice: Managing the Moral Corporation*, HBR Press: Boston (1989).

Gibbons, P., *Spirituality at Work: A Pre-Theoretical Overview*, MSc. Thesis–Birkbeck College, University of London (Aug. 1999).

Gill, J., & Whittle, S., "Management by Panacea: Accounting for Transience," *Journal of Management Studies*, 30 (1992).

Hartman, L., *Perspectives in Business Ethics*, Irwin McGraw-Hill: Chicago (1998).

Heelas, P., "On Differentiation and De-differentiation," *Religion, Modernity, and Postmodernity*, Blackwell: Oxford (1998).

Hood, R., "Sin and Guilt in Faith Traditions: Issues for Self-Esteem," in Schumaker (ed.), *Religion and Mental Health*, Oxford University Press: Oxford (1992).

Jackall, R., *Moral Mazes: The World of Corporate Managers*, Oxford University Press: New York (1988).

James, W., *The Varieties of Religious Experience*, Penguin: New York (1902).

King, U., "Spirituality," in Hinnells, J. (ed.), *A New Handbook of Living Religions*, Penguin: London (1997).

Kurth, K., "An Exploration of the Expression and Perceived Impact of Selfless Service in For-Profit Organizations." Doctoral dissertation, George Washington University (1995).

Martin, J., personal communication (1999).

Masters, K., & Bergin, A., in Schumaker (ed.), *Religion and Mental Health*, Oxford University Press: Oxford (1992).

Milliman, J., Ferguson, F., Trickett, D., & Bausch, T., "Spirit and Community at Southwest Airlines: An Investigation of a Spiritual Values Based Model," *Journal of Organizational Change Management, 12(3)* (1999).

Mitroff, I. & Denton, E., *A Spiritual Audit of Corporate America: A Hard Look at Spirituality, Religion, and Values in the Workplace*, Jossey-Bass: San Francisco (1999).

Neal, J., Lichtenstein, B., & Banner, D., "Spiritual Perspectives on Individual, Organizational, and Societal Transformation," *Journal of Organizational Change Management 12(3)* (1999).

Neck, C., & Milliman, J., "Thought Self-Leadership: Finding Spiritual Fulfillment in Organizational Life," *Journal of Managerial Psychology 9(6)*, pp. 9–16 (1994).

Pargament, K., "The Psychology of Religion and Spirituality? Yes and No." *The International Journal for the Psychology of Religion 9 (1)*, pp. 3–16 (1999).

Perez, S., *Religious and Non-Religious Aspects of Spirituality and their Relation to Myers-Briggs Personality Typology*. Doctoral dissertation: Georgia State University (1998).

Schmidt-Wilk, J., Alexander, C., & Swanson, G., "Developing Consciousness in Organizations: The Transcendental Meditation Program in Business," *Journal of Business and Psychology 10(4)*, pp. 429–444 (1996).

Schumaker, J., *Religion and Mental Health*, Oxford University Press: Oxford (1992).

Siehl, C., & Martin, J., "Organization Culture: A Key to Financial Performance," *Organizational Climate and Culture*, Jossey Bass: San Francisco (1990).

Sims, R., *Ethics and Organizational Decision Making: A Call for Renewal*, Quorum: Westport (1994).

Spilka, B., Hood, R., & Gorsuch, R., *The Psychology of Religion: An Empirical Approach*, Prentice Hall: New Jersey (1985).

Trott, D. C., *Spiritual Well-Being of Workers*, Doctoral dissertation, University of Texas–Austin (1996).

Underhill, E., *The Spiritual Life*, Hodder & Stoughton: London (1937).

Weaver, G., & Agle, B., "Religiosity as an Influence on Ethical Behavior in Organizations: A theoretical model and research agenda," Paper presented at the Society for Business Ethics annual conference: Chicago (1999).

Weick, K., *Sensemaking in Organizations*, Sage: Thousand Oaks (1995).

Whitmeyer, C., *Mindfulness and Meaningful Work*, Parallax Press: Berkeley (1994).

Wilber, K., *A Brief History of Everything*, Shambhala: Boston (1996).

Wilber, K., *The Marriage of Sense and Soul: Integrating Science and Religion*, Random House: New York (1998).

The Individual Within Organizations

EMBERS

by Tom Brown

That very first day
On that very first job:
The call, the work, the quest —
How you did aspire!

You stormed all tasks,
You donned no masks,
You seldom felt much higher.

The secret to that heady time?
Oh, to be driven by the fire.

No "boss" could make you feel
Like that —
No, not then, not even now.
The pay for you was more than cash:
Striving hard, showing strong,
And pining to achieve.

The advances sought,
The problems caught,
Each improvement wrought —
It was what *you*
Created,
Crafted,
Sired.

The magic of those moments when?
Oh, to be driven by the fire.

How different now,
How sadly less,
It seems your work berates.
The job's all task;
Your smile's a mask;

False starts, you fluctuate.

It doesn't feel so warm inside,
When you're an ember dying.
When wonder's gone,

Is your memory strong?
Oh, to be driven by the fire.

What would it take,
Whom would you need,
To spark that flame again?
Is it leading,
Or being led,
That lacquers a life with glee?

That first day
On that first job:
You knew the answer then.

The future begs; will you recall?
Oh, to be driven by the fire!

— from *The Anatomy of Fire: Sparking a New Spirit of Enterprise*
by Tom Brown © 2000 by MANAGEMENT GENERAL
http://www.mgeneral.com

ORGANIZATIONAL ENHANCEMENT THROUGH RECOGNITION OF INDIVIDUAL SPIRITUALITY:

REFLECTIONS OF JAQUES AND JUNG

Sandra King,
Dave M. Nicol,
Frostburg State University

Introduction

More than ever, individuals find themselves in a world of *permanent white water*, experiencing a lack of meaning in their lives and an attendant sense of spiritual desolation (Vaill, 1989). Consequently, many people are increasingly embarking upon a spiritual journey, seeking to discover their true selves, searching for a higher purpose and meaning to their lives (Conger, 1994). This spiritual journey is not necessarily confined to a religious framework (Conger, 1994) as many might conclude, for, as Patterson (1997) observed, "religions can be viewed as the maps, while you might consider spirituality to be the territory."

What is this sense of desolation that prompts the spiritual journey? For that matter, what is meant by a spiritual journey? Though the words may vary, we found a common thread in the writings of many authors (e.g., Covey, 1989; Mitroff, Mason, & Pearson, 1994; Morris, 1997; Neal, 1997; Peck, 1993; Roof, 1993; Stein & Hollwitz, 1992). In general, they refer to the spiritual journey as a process of focusing within, in order to gain an awareness of *Self*. Only through this awareness of *Self* can individuals become truly actualized and find meaning and purpose in their work and in their lives. This is the individuation process which produces both an interconnection with *Self* and a connection with others, fostering a sense of order and balance in an otherwise chaotic life.

For our purposes, then, the journey toward spirituality represents the quest to unite one's inner and outer world, to provide meaning and purpose to one's life. The search, and consequent realization, provides an individual with a sense of alignment and order—a spiritual cohesiveness, which instills a sense of rightness and well-being. Csikszentmihalyi (1990) describes the experience as a feeling of being in the *flow*. It is a sense of wholeness, a oneness with who we are and an awareness of how we fit with our external environment.

> *Because work is a central part of our existence, much of this spiritual odyssey occurs within the context of the workplace. Yet, when assessing the relevance of its human resources to the effective performance of the organization, few consider the extent to which the organizational environment fosters an individual's spiritual development. It is our contention that this constitutes a costly oversight. We propose that an organization whose work environment responsively supports the quest for individual unity and direction, and fosters spiritual development, will realize heightened individual and organizational performance. As Tom Morris, an author and consultant, states, "Good people in a good environment do good work." (1997:126)*

To realize the organization's benefit potential from such an orientation, management must address attendant challenges and opportunities by learning to understand the relationship between an individual's spiritual quest and the organizational environment. This can produce a previously unrealized synergistic relationship in which management's support of the individual's spiritual quest for meaning and purpose benefits both the employee and the organization.

In this paper, we suggest the combination of Carl Jung's and Elliot Jaques' theories as a valuable construct for attaining that understanding. Carl Jung's theory of the individuation process provides perspective as to how and why individuals behave as they do. Spiritual growth, as described by Jung, entails an inner journey to become an individuated *Self* (Jung & von Franz, 1964). The journey of self-discovery leads to an understanding of *Self* in relation to others and allows individuals to find meaning and purpose in their work.

However, for the individual's efforts toward self-awareness to be fully actualized, it is necessary for the organization to be structured to support the individual's growth. Jaques' Stratified Systems Theory offers a framework consistent with such individual development. An understanding of how the two theoretical frameworks may be linked can enable management to both support individuals in their spiritual journey and fulfill the managerial commitment to optimize organizational productivity.

We begin with a brief discussion of the theoretical framework of Jung and Jaques. We will then amplify on how the application of these theories can enable organizations to support the individual employee's spiritual journey, both as its social duty and for its benefit.

Carl Jung's Theoretical Framework

In Carl Jung's theory of individuation, the individual strives to become whole and distinctive from the collective (Jung, 1933; Jung & von Franz, 1964). In order for an individual to realize her/his specific purpose, connection with one's unique *Self* must be achieved (Eddinger, 1972; Harding, 1965). In this context, *Self* is the whole of the individual, including all aspects of an individual's conscious and unconscious, often referred to as a paradoxical union of opposites (Harding, 1965). The *Self* is superior to the ego and is experienced as the center of the personality (Jung, 1933). Although the path to individuation can be quite different for each person, the process tends to be similar (Singer, 1972). Individuals become conscious of their whole personality, *the Self*, to gain awareness of their higher purposes and potential capabilities.

The Individuation Process

The individuation process occurs as one's ego is initially developed, then challenged, and ultimately subordinated to a more comprehensive psychic entity, the *Self* (Jung, 1933; Singer, 1972). The process constitutes the conscious realization and fulfillment of one's unique being. In the first stage, an individual is without conscious awareness of *Self* (Harding, 1965). The whole of the individual is unified in the unconscious. However, as a child develops a conscious awareness, the ego begins to develop and becomes the seat of one's identity. Through these first stages of development, a child only develops part of the "whole of the personality," leaving the other part lost in the unconscious (Harding, 1965). The conscious personality, the ego, develops as a result of adaptation to parents, environment, and collective expectations. Thus, it reflects factors such as gender, birth order, and personality characteristics. The more disciplined and rigid one's ego becomes in response to external influences, the more difficult it becomes to reconnect with the part lost in childhood (Eddinger, 1972; Harding, 1965). This chasm leaves individuals wandering in a spiritual desert, suffering a sense of alienation and separation from the *Self.*

To emerge from the desert, the individual's *Self* must transform the ego and achieve alignment with its individuality (Eddinger, 1972; Jung and von Franz, 1964). However, the ego fears the loss of what is known —its identity—and resists by struggling with the unknown aspect of *Self.* For example, the ego of entrepreneurs can be so identified with their businesses that they are unable to leave them, even when their *Selves* are calling for something different in their lives. The resistance is so strong because the ego is dependent on the business for a sense of identity. Without the business, the entrepreneurs fear there will be no sense of *Self.* In this context, it is understandable why so many entrepreneurs have difficulty with the individuation process, and, unable to realize their true individuality, often destroy their businesses (King et al., 1996).

Jung believed that the need to reconnect to the *Self* is instinctual; hence, the effort to do so occurs either consciously or unconsciously (Jacobi, 1965). Individuals who continue to be disconnected from their unconscious sides and operate solely from their egos often experience extreme adverse emotions (Eddinger, 1972; Harding, 1965). In fact, if the struggle continues unconsciously, individuals who find themselves unable to fulfill their unique destinies may experience depression (Eddinger, 1972), often with detrimental consequences for their work.

In order to find one's unique path, it is necessary to become aware of the various unconscious aspects of the *Self.* It is through the discovery, affirmation, and integration of these aspects that individuals gradually move toward a higher sense of individuality (Jacobi, 1965; Jung & von Franz, 1964; Singer, 1972). Hence, the struggle between the ego and the *Self* manifests itself through various inner voices reflecting these unconscious aspects (Eddinger, 1972). As individuals become aware of the voices emanating from the undeveloped aspects of their personality, they develop a clearer awareness of *Self* and a greater appreciation of others. The organizational consequences of such a revelation can be quite positive (Stein & Hollwitz, 1992). An individual learns "to hoist one's sail," having achieved an understanding of the "boat" (framework) of her/his life, enabling greater sensitivity to and alignment with the surrounding forces (Singer, 1972: vii). As a consequence, an individual is more likely to value her/his own uniqueness and that of others.

Jung suggested that if an individual's ego becomes too one-sided, with the conscious personality fixated on his/her dominant characteristics, then the repressed unconscious personality characteristics gain expression by being projected onto another (Harding, 1965; Jung & von Franz, 1964; Singer, 1972). It is therefore possible to develop an awareness of one's undeveloped personality by focusing on the nature of relationships with others. Manifestations of an individual's undeveloped personality are often actualized through interpersonal relationships (Jung and von Franz, 1964). For example, when individuals experience extreme psychic energy (e.g., love or hate), they are usually projecting onto another person their own repressed personality. If projections are recognized and confronted, an individual has the opportunity to understand and then consciously integrate those personality characteristics (Harding, 1965).

The most basic of projections is the shadow—the dark side of the personality (Jung & von Franz, 1964). Essentially, the shadow is the personification of that which we deny in ourselves. By projecting our shadow onto others, we are able to reject it, instead of having to take responsibility for it (Harding, 1965). Alternatively, we can accept our shadow's existence, allowing us the opportunity to confront and eventually find a healthy way to integrate the dark side of our personalities into our lives. Through the integration of one's shadow, an individual develops an awareness of his/her connection to other human beings, providing a basis for communication, understanding, and respect.

Another aspect of the unconscious personality is Jung's conception of the Soul, referred to as anima in the male and animus in the female (Harding, 1965). For each individual, the animus/anima corresponds to characteristics which are opposite of her/his biological gender and accompanying culturally determined roles. Hence, animus/anima refers to a woman's unconscious undeveloped masculine side and a man's unconscious undeveloped feminine side. If individuals are able to appreciate and integrate these contrasexual personality elements into their consciousness, they tap into a rich resource for their development.

For example, if courage were associated with maleness, a woman can become more courageous by recognizing and integrating her animus into her life. Conversely, a man who integrates his anima may become more receptive.

Individuals who are unable to confront their animus/anima will project their contrasexual qualities onto others in an attempt to fulfill their unconscious need to develop into whole individuals (Harding, 1965; Jung & von Franz, 1964). This may be illustrated in a woman who constantly looks to her male boss to make decisions that she could easily make on her own. The irony of the projection is that what the woman sees in the man actually originates deep within her own psyche. Unless she can recognize the projection as a mirror image of her own psyche, it will not stop. The recognition and utilization of those projections is important in the process toward individuation and spiritual enhancement.

In business relationships, individuals who are aware of their projections are able to develop an understanding of the source of interpersonal conflicts. As a consequence, they are more objective in assessing situations and making decisions. They are more accepting and less prone to blame others, thereby enhancing teamwork (Stein & Hollwitz, 1992).

Application of Jung's Work in Organizations

The health of the organization is dependent on the quality of its interpersonal relationships. When individuals become emancipated from their projections, they are able to develop healthy relationships with others. Since they no longer project their needs onto others, they are capable of functioning independently and of honoring others as unique entities. Thus, anchored in a relationship with the Self, these individuals are more tolerant of others, more responsible for personal behavior, and no longer afraid of being possessed by others (Singer, 1972). As such, they are willing to delegate work, to empower others, and to be empowered. Consequently, the organization develops a sense of community that supports healthy interpersonal relationships, while preserving individuality. When this becomes pervasive in organizations, a great deal of dysfunctional behavior is eliminated.

To the extent that an organizational environment is supportive of an individual's change, the process is likely to be more positive, and the benefits for both the individual and the organization more expeditiously realized. The organization must not only acknowledge the individual's need for growth, but also alter its utilization of the individual in recognition of her/his growth.

Elliott Jaques' Stratified Systems Theory

Elliott Jaques' Stratified Systems Theory (SST) (1996) provides a way to foster a healthy organizational environment by focusing on the organization's structure. Instead of creating an environment that limits the full utilization of an individual's potential capability, Jaques provides a framework that acknowledges individual growth, not only accommodating it, but also encouraging it. Within the organization, Jaques' SST provides a strategic model for a hierarchical system of managerial layers to optimally utilize employees' talents.

Well-defined roles enhance the organization, in part by supporting the staffing of positions with people who possess the required mental complexity to perform in such roles. With the right individuals in the appropriate roles, it is easier to grant the authority and accountability necessary to perform effectively. By assessing the role requirements, the structure provides a system that enables people to develop and flourish by providing work that allows them to apply their potential capability. Organizations will be enhanced if individuals who value their work are provided the freedom to actualize their full potential. In an organizational environment emphasizing the importance of teams, Jaques' SST can be a true asset as it enhances team effectiveness by empowering individuals to realize their full potential (Jaques, 1996).

Jaques (1965) recognizes that work, given its centrality to our existence, is an essential element in the determination of an individual's self-worth. Successful implementation of SST supports individuals in their spiritual quest, removing barriers that otherwise obstruct the effort to fully actualize their potential. Providing a vehicle to align one's capabilities with her/his role, as well as the opportunity for both to grow in unison, is, indeed, conducive to spiritual growth.

Conversely, failure to provide conditions in which individuals are able to work at a level consistent with their capacity and values can be destructive to the individual and the organization. In addition to causing resentment and anger against the organization, inhibiting an individual's development can give rise to inner turmoil that manifests itself in a variety of non-productive ways, including loss of self-esteem (Jaques, 1965). Through its inattentiveness, the organization can create an environment where an individual's spirit may be lost. This can be both destructive to the individual and the organization. Enabling individuals to work at their full capacity will provide an environment conducive to healthy and productive individuals and, as a result, a healthy and productive organization. Therefore, the aim of Jaques' approach is to build a system that fully employs an organization's human resources through the recognition and utilization of the employees' capabilities (Jaques, 1996).

Potential Capability (PC)

In formulating his framework, Jaques posits that at any given stage in life individuals possess a mental capacity that determines their potential capability (PC) to handle a certain level of complexity (Jaques & Cason, 1994). The organization can measure this potential capability to more effectively align individuals and their roles. In addition, one's PC is assumed to mature with age, producing an increasing capacity to deal with complexity of mental processing and role complexity (Jaques, 1996). The perspective provided by SST enables an organization to anticipate an individual's increasing capacity and to accommodate and benefit from it. This organizational acknowledgment that individuals are growing and therefore require continuous effort to align roles with individual capabilities is conducive to the reality of change associated with an individual's spiritual journey.

Through the recognition of an individual's current and future development of PC, an organization can provide an environment that has the prospect of fully utilizing its human resources (Jaques, 1965). Thus, an individual placed in a role that matches her/his level of PC has the opportunity to realize her/his full potential. Of course, whether or not individuals actually achieve their PC is also a function of their level of commitment. If they are distracted, adrift, or spiritually bereft, their ability to function at their potential capability will be severely constrained. If individuals yearn for the opportunity to be fully challenged by work that they value, then the perception of value is an important element of how much of a person's potential will actually be applied to work. Hence, if through self-reflection, individuals are able to assess the extent to which they value their work, and are able to identify the work that is consistent with their capacity and value system, then they will be able to achieve to their full potential.

The nature of the organization's structure in terms of the extent to which it acknowledges and responds to an individual's values and capabilities is key to organizational health and prosperity. The organization possesses a powerful capacity to influence and be influenced by the individuals within it. If there is a discrepancy within the organization between individuals' potential capabilities and the level of complexity in their assigned roles, then both internal and external stress and conflict will occur. Enabling individuals to reach and work at their full capacity, regardless of their background, creates a structure that provides a healthy organization by minimizing conflict and frustration (Jaques, 1965).

Theoretical Integration

Individuals moving toward reconciliation of Self are increasingly able to satisfy their potential capability and therefore are better able to make a valuable contribution within the organization. To the extent that the organization enables individuals to derive satisfaction through spiritual development and to function consistently with their full capabilities, the organization can achieve optimum performance from its human resources.

In our increasingly complex environment, effective utilization of human resources is becoming vital for an organization's health. One element of that challenge, which is often not actualized, is the ability to harness the organization's latent human potential. By understanding and acting upon the theoretical concepts that we have set forth, the organization has the capacity to support the spiritual growth of its members and, as a consequence, unleash its potential. The organization can maximize the energy present in the dreams, skills, and aspirations of those who make up its reality.

In this vein, creativity and innovation are considered to be significant contributors to an organization's competitive advantage. Yet, creative insights are not readily forthcoming from those who lack a sense of self-worth. This means that until individuals truly acknowledge and embrace the Self within, the organization will be unable to realize its full creative potential. The more it restricts input, knowingly or otherwise, the more latent potential will never be realized. Conversely, if the organization encourages spiritual development, and thus enables individuals to achieve their individual wholeness, they are far more likely to make a truly valuable contribution to the organization. Of course, facilitating and sustaining what will develop within the organization is, to say the least, challenging. O'Connor (1996), in "The Spiritual Journey of the Corporate Warrior," concluded that to do so, organizations must possess "an understanding of the nature of 'spirit'; an ability to recognize, encourage, and reward potential; and, the capacity to continually integrate the emerging potential into the normal processes of business." We believe that an understanding of the theories of Jung and Jaques enhances the prospect of achieving these objectives.

Maximizing the realization of an organization's capability involves career planning to allow individuals to develop their capacity, and ensures that roles are aligned with the current and future potential of employees. Jaques' SST provides a framework for defining those roles and a methodology for ascertaining individual potential in order to achieve that alignment. Both its assumptions about the individual and the nature of its implementation support spiritual growth.

Conclusion

Two frameworks have been presented to assist individuals and organizations in facing a world of permanent white water. Although the two theories are distinctly different, together they provide a framework for supporting the growth of the individual. The theories of Jung were offered to foster understanding of what prompts individuals in their quest for the complete Self, including how the success or failure of that effort may manifest itself. Through the individuation process, individuals achieve integration of the Self and the full maturation of their potential.

Jaques' Stratified Systems Theory provides an organizational framework for acknowledging and supporting the realization of individuals' potential capabilities. In this manner, Jaques' structure can contribute to the fulfillment of an individual's spiritual quest. Not only is this desirable, but it has been suggested that to do otherwise, to frustrate one's capacity to grow, can create an emotional response that inhibits the individuation process. Thus, in a sense, the organization has a social responsibility to stimulate and support this process of social growth.

Both theories are based on concepts that can help individuals find meaning and purpose in their lives and provide a new level of spirituality. They support individuals in their development into fuller, more complete human beings, and, in doing so, allow individuals and the organization to flourish. Awareness and understanding of Jaques' model provides organizations with a system for enabling individuals to apply their full potential, while Jung's model provides an understanding of individuality and its relation to meaningful work. The combination provides a foundation for integrating the discovery of Self with work deemed to be meaningful and purposeful. Hence, the integration of Jaques' and Jung's models can assist in providing an organizational environment that releases the unique creativity, imagination, and growth of individuals as they follow their spiritual paths to wholeness. The organization's ability to foster and benefit from their journey will, in turn, enhance its own health. To the extent that both models contribute to achievement of that end, mutual benefit is derived and a new level of spirituality is attained.

References

Conger, Jay A. (1994), *Spirit at Work: Discovering the Spirituality in Leadership*, Jossey-Bass, San Francisco.

Covey, Stephen R. (1989), *The 7 Habits of Highly Effective People*, Simon & Schuster, New York.

Csikszentmihalyi, Mihaly (1990), *Flow: The Psychology of Optimal Experience*, Harper Perennial, New York.

Eddinger, Edward F. (1972), *Ego and Archetype: Individuation and the Religious Function of the Psyche*, G. P. Putnam's Sons, New York.

Harding, Esther M. (1965), *The I and the Not I: A Study of the Development of Consciousness*, Princeton University Press, Princeton, NJ.

Jacobi, Jolande (1965), The Way of Individuation, translated by R.F.C. Hall, Harcourt, Brace & World, Inc., New York.

Jaques, Elliott (1965), *A General Theory of Bureaucracy*, Heinemann Gower, New Hampshire.

Jaques, Elliott (1996), *Requisite Organization: A Total System for Effective Managerial Organization and Managerial Leadership for the 21st Century*, Second Edition. Cason Hall, VA.

Jaques, Elliott, & Cason, Kathryn (1994), *Human Capability*, Cason Hall, Fall Church, VA.

Jung, C. G. (1933), *Modern Man in Search of a Soul*, Harcourt Brace Jovanovich, New York.

Jung, C., & von Franz, M. L. (1964), *Man and His Symbols*, Doubleday Inc, Garden City.

King, S., Solomon, G., & Winslow, E. (1996) Entrepreneurial Leadership: An Interrelationship Among Adult Development, Leadership and Organizational Life Cycle, *Journal of Management Systems 8(1–4)*, 39–49.

Mitroff, Ian I., Mason, Richard O., & Pearson, Christine M. (1994), "Radical Surgery: What Will Tomorrow's Organizations Look Like?" *Academy of Management Executive 8(2)*, 11–21.

Morris, Tom (1997), *If Aristotle Ran General Motors*, Henry Holt and Company, Inc., New York.

Neal, Judith A. (1997), "Spirituality in Management Education: A Guide to Resources," *Journal of Management Education 21(1)*, 121–139.

O'Connor, B. (1996), "The Spiritual Journey of the Corporate Warrior." Presented at Massey University, Albany Campus, Auckland, NZ.

Patterson, R. B. (1997), "Religion or Spirituality: A Distinction," *Self-Help & Psychology Magazine*. Pioneer Development Resources, Inc.

Peck, M. Scott (1993), *Further Along the Road Less Traveled: The Unending Journey Toward Spiritual Growth*, Simon & Schuster, New York.

Roof, W. C. (1993), *A Generation of Seekers: The Spiritual Journeys of the Baby Boom Generation*, Harper Collins, San Francisco.

Singer, June (1972), *Boundaries of the Soul: The Practice of Jung's Psychology*. Doubleday & Company, Inc, Garden City, New York.

Stein, Murray, & Hollwitz, John (1992). *Psyche at Work: Workplace Applications of Jungian Analytical Psychology*, Chiron Publications, Wilmette, IL.

Vaill, Peter (1989), *Managing As a Performing Art: New Ideas for a World of Chaotic Change*. Jossey-Bass, San Francisco, CA.

SPIRITUALITY FOR MANAGERS:

CONTEXT AND CRITIQUE

Gerald F. Cavanagh, S.J.,
University of Detroit Mercy

There has been a dramatic upsurge in interest in spirituality among those who study, teach, and write about business management. This new interest is also apparent among practicing managers. Spirituality in the workplace helps many. However, the trend is disturbing to others. Among proponents, the need for spirituality is stated simply: "The modern focus on objectivity and the separation of science and spirituality, taken to fullness, leaves people separate from one another, separate from nature, and separate from the divine" (Whitney, 1997). Those who find it disturbing fear that spirituality in the workplace will lead to coercion and favoritism in the workplace. This potential for divisiveness will be addressed later.

Need for Spirituality in Business

The needs that businesspeople often feel are a separation from other people, alienation from their work, and a lack of meaning in their lives. They often experience their work, family life, and faith to be in separate compartments—50 to 70 hours per week at work, an hour on weekends for worship, and the time left over for family. This separation leaves one feeling dry, unfulfilled, and unhappy, and is often experienced as a profound absence or vacuum in one's life.

Parker Palmer finds a basic unconscious fault with many leaders. He calls it "functional atheism—the belief that ultimate responsibility for everything rests with *me.*" According to this view, if anything useful is going to happen, I cannot expect God's help. I alone am the one who must make it happen (Palmer, 1994). He goes on to point out that functional atheism leads to dysfunctional behavior on every level of our lives: workaholism, burnout, lack of attention to people in our lives, broken families, and even violence. Note how functional atheism and the resulting narrow view of life and work trap one into a lifestyle and behaviors that are not only not spiritual, but are not even human.

This new movement is triggered by several occurrences that affect people in business, according to Judith Neal, a pioneer participant and scholar in the spirituality in business movement. She sees three major causes for this new interest:

1. The baby boomers, who came of age during the idealistic 1960s, are now reaching middle age. The mid-life journey, which is sometimes a mid-life crisis, occurs at this age. As she puts it, "Many look at their lives and calculate the time they have left. They ask . . . 'What do I want to do with the rest of my life?' 'What is my purpose?' 'Have I accomplished what I set out to do?'"

2. Downsizing and employers' demand for additional hours in the workplace have also triggered reflection. Today people no longer have secure jobs, and that is unsettling and encourages self-examination.

3. Finally, the year 2000, like the New Year, birthdays, religious holidays, and other landmark events, encourages reflection and new commitments for the future (Neal, 1997).

While this new interest is clear, let us nevertheless obtain a more accurate measure of the extent of this concern for soul and spirituality.

Measure of Increased Interest

There are several indications of a dramatic increase in interest in spirituality among both practicing managers and academics. Some of these indicators are: (1) The increased number of sessions at the Academy of Management annual meetings that discuss spirituality and religion; (2) New books and articles on religion and spirituality in business; and (3) The new courses on religion, spirituality, and contemplation that are being offered in business schools.

Academy of Management

The 1998 annual Academy of Management meetings in San Diego attracted 5,000 management teachers, scholars, and managers from around the world. The overall theme of the 1998 meeting was "What Matters Most?" At least seven sessions explicitly discussed spirituality and/or religion and its relation to leadership and work. Six of the seven sessions were jointly presented by two or more of the 22 separate divisions of the Academy of Management. These six sessions thus merited special notice in the program as "Showcase Sessions," and were listed prominently in the program and were repeated in the individual section portions of the program.

It should be noted that this number is out of a total of about 900 sessions, and so is a very small percentage of the total. However, if we include the sessions explicitly devoted to business ethics, corporate social responsibility, ecology, and service learning, it would constitute perhaps 10 percent of the total. Significant here is the fact that the number of sessions on spirituality and/or religion has grown from zero in the last five years.

Books, Articles, Journals, and Conferences

A bibliography distributed at a session on spirituality in the organization at the 1998 Academy of Management meeting lists no fewer than 72 books on the subject of spirituality and business. Showing the rapid rise in interest in this subject, 54 of these books have been published since 1992.

Many articles also have been published in recent years on spirituality and work, both in professional and in popular journals. Professional journals, such as *Personnel Journal* and *Training*, have carried articles, as have *Business Week* and *Fortune*. Even the *Wall Street Journal* (1998) carried a front-page article on spiritual direction.

There are at least two journals on spirituality: *Spirit at Work*,[1] edited by Judith Neal, professor of management, New Haven University, and *Business Spirit*.[2]

Conferences on spirituality at work abound, with 1998 conferences in Washington, D.C., Santa Fe, NM, Minneapolis, MN, Indianapolis, IN, Loveland, CO, British Colombia, Canada, and Puerto Vallarta, Mexico. The Puerto Vallarta conference attracted more than 500 attendees. Not suprisingly, some of the same people appear as

---

[1] *Spirit at Work*, P. O. Box 420, Manalapan, NJ 07726. Journal is 6 issues per year for $35. The journal contains articles, lists of resources, book reviews, and commentary.

[2] *Business Spirit* is published 6 times per year by The Message Company, 4 Camino Azul, Santa Fe, NM 87505. Subscriptions are $29 per year.

presenters at these conferences. Some are also consultants, who are trying to sell their services.

Courses on Spirituality and Contemplation

Several courses were offered in schools of business on spirituality at work and on contemplation in Fall, 1998. The courses were held at University of Scranton, University of Detroit Mercy, and Chapman. One of the more notable was at Santa Clara University and is designed by Andre L. Delbecq, McCarthy University Professor, Leavey School of Business and Administration. Delbecq was awarded a year-long fellowship by the American Council of Learned Societies to develop this course. He offered it to eight active chief executive officers (one commuting from Boston) and eight graduate business students. This course discusses substantive and very important issues of: business leadership as a calling; listening to the inner voice in the midst of turbulent business environments; the need for self-integration; discernment and senior business leadership; approaches to prayer and meditation; challenges of leadership power; the spiritual challenges of wealth vs. poverty of spirit; contemplative practices; and the mystery of suffering. Toward the end of the course the group will do a weekend retreat together.

Delbecq has superb credentials to initiate this course. He has done extensive consulting with CEOs, is past dean of the Santa Clara School of Business, is the author of many dozens of professional books and articles, and is a Dean of Fellows of the Academy of Management. Initial reports on the course reveal that it is very successful.

This interest in spirituality embraces diverse traditions. The influence of the Koran on his business decisions and activities is cited by Farooq Kathwarai, CEO of Ethan Allen Interiors. Ranwal Rekhi, CEO of CyerMedia, speaks of how Sikhism affects his management style. *Forbes,* in July 1998, quoted these executives and many others on how their religion and spirituality affects them and their businesses.

Mark Belton, Vice President of General Mills, led a seminar at the National Black MBA Convention in Detroit entitled "Jesus in Blue Jeans." Belton cites the instability that the global economy and downsizings have brought as being one cause of the current interest in religion and spirituality in business. Work and jobs are no longer a source of security. As Belton puts it, "People are beginning to ask, Upon what rock will I build my future? Most are smart enough not to bet on their jobs" (*Detroit Free Press*, 1998).

Content of New Spirituality

This new spirituality in business means many things to different people. On the one hand, to many people spirituality means a search for personal meaning and a relation to the Supreme Being that many of us call God. For some religious executives and entrepreneurs, it means an affirmation of God and the Gospels in the workplace. On the other hand, to others it contains much that is "New Age" religious movement fad. For them, it is little more than acknowledgment of the importance of feelings and a "new consciousness."

Definitions

Proponents and those who practice spirituality in the workplace are not always clear in defining their efforts. However, in a 1998 "All Academy Symposium" that was addressed to the entire Academy of Management, Ian Mitroff, Professor of Management at the University of Southern California, defined spirituality as "the desire to find ultimate purpose in life, and to live accordingly."

Others define spirituality loosely as energy, meaning, knowing, etc. Some authors rely heavily on Taoist, Buddist, Hindu, Zen, and Native American spiritualities. These authors correctly claim that these non-Western societies are better in integrating personal life, work, leisure, prayer, religion, and other aspects of one's life.

Another aspect of this movement is the growing number of "Christian capitalists," that is, believing Christians who are entrepreneurs. These entrepreneurs and managers make their faith known explicitly to their employees, customers, and others with whom they deal. They often encourage prayer groups among employees—often meeting an hour or so before work. This movement is made up largely of "born-again" Christians, and they tend to be conservative in their views and the causes they support (*U.S. News & World Report*, 1995).

These entrepreneurs are often Christian evangelicals, and they are committed to particular religious, social, and political beliefs. Their blending of religion and the workplace is made possible because they are the owners of the firm. This is difficult or impossible for a manager in a large publicly held firm.

The older religious traditions also have significant influence. For example, currently there is an upsurge in interest in spiritual direction. The *Wall Street Journal* (1998) ran an article about business and professional people seeking out a regular spiritual director. Cited in the article were national programs to train spiritual directors in Los Angeles at Loyola Marymount and in Omaha at Creighton University. The author cited the importance of the director listening and discerning, and she acknowledged that this was in the best tradition of Catholic spiritual direction.

Mitroff, at the above symposium, cited sobering data about people's attitude toward spirituality and religion. He estimates that 60% of people, at least in the United States, are positive toward spirituality but negative toward organized religion. He says that 30% of people are positive toward spirituality and religion, while only 10% are negative toward both. While these figures may merely reflect Mitroff's perception, this suspicion of organized religion has had an impact on how interest in spirituality has developed. In addition, for those who live in a pluralist society, where there is no one dominant religion, there is thus no single religious tradition that is able to lay claim to spirituality. Hence, spirituality in the workplace generally is not tied to a specific religious tradition.

Spirituality and Religion

Spirituality historically has been rooted in religion. However, its current use in business and in the workplace is most often not associated with any specific religious tradition. There are several reasons for this separation: (1) Most Western societies are pluralistic; that is, there is no one dominant religious tradition that can be used as a foundation; (2) If used as a basis for a firm's vision and mission, depending on a specific religious tradition is not energy giving, but divisive, since people do not share that religious tradition; (3) Use of religion in the public forum can encourage distrust, dislike of outsiders, and suspicion, and that, in turn, can lead to the breakdown of democracy, and sometimes even to revolutions and war; (4) The nineteenth century European Enlightenment has made Westerners distrustful of religious values. Religion is judged to be opposed to rationality and science and the source of superstition and the irrational.

The above attitudes have been criticized, most notably by Stephen Carter, Professor of Law at Yale, in his best-selling book-length analysis, *The Culture of Disbelief* (1993). Carter points out how Western peoples seldom have an outright hostility to religion. Nevertheless, they do tend to trivialize religion, to treat it as a hobby or an unproductive emotional outlet. For most, it is acceptable to make reference to God as a formality; but, and especially for Americans, it is not acceptable to allow religious beliefs to enter into national public policy discussions. Then Carter goes on to make an excellent case of how religion is an essential part of most people's lives, and how they depend upon religious values and beliefs in both personal and public actions.

In spite of the fact that it is difficult to develop depth in any spirituality without a religious foundation, nevertheless spirit, spirituality, and even "the corporate mystic" have received considerable attention in recent years. And most of this emphasis has been severed from religious roots. Moreover, the basic issues are not new. O. H. Ohman in his classic, "Skyhooks," first published in the *Harvard Business Review* but often reprinted, makes a strong case for spirituality (Ohman, 1955).

Most of the books, articles, talks, and consultants who speak of "spirit at work," or "spirituality in the workplace" do not depend upon or make reference to any specific religious tradition. The objective of these efforts, in the words of an ad for a set of six taped talks that would help one to become a "corporate mystic," is to form "a higher level of consciousness . . . a spiritual perspective—which gives greater insight, creativity, and productivity—awakening new levels of joy, energy, opportunity, and personal satisfaction." Forty dollars will bring you six lectures that will enable you to become a "corporate mystic"![3] In the next section of this paper, we will examine the spirituality in business movement from the standpoint of Christian traditions.

Spirituality and Judeo-Christian Traditions

The spirituality in business movement is to some extent a descendent of the New Age Movement. It is difficult to critique either, because both are complex and diverse. The older and more widespread New Age Movement is criticized as egocentric, fringe, and somewhat unorthodox by the mainline Christian churches (Saliba, 1993). The cited article is from the spirituality journal, *The Way* (1993), which devoted an issue

---

[3] Ad mailing from Nightengale Conant in Niles, IL.

to the New Age spirituality. The spirituality in business movement is more focused, and thus does not merit the same criticism.

The spirit in business movement is becoming more popular, so it is fulfilling a need. Many of those who embrace spirit in business have felt that the mainline religions have not responded to their needs. In addition, many of these people are simply not aware of the wide variety of profound and time-tested spirituality traditions within Christianity.

God, Prayer, People, and Sustainability

There are many positive features of the spirituality in business movement. The following aspects of the movement are of help to men and women and also congruent with traditional Judeo-Christian traditions:

- People in the movement generally have a belief in God.
- Emphasis on quiet, prayer, and contemplation in one's life.
- Emphasis on the centrality of people and listening to others. This generally results in better relations with family and colleagues.
- A commitment to better relations among peoples, and to help bring greater peace and harmony in the world.
- The movement is also optimistic about the perfectibility of human nature and business culture; they are convinced that people and the world can become better.
- Commitment to a sustainable environment, to pass on a better world to future generations. This aspect of the movement is sometimes called eco-spirituality and has its own literature.

Two major figures in eco-spirituality are Catholic priests. The pioneer and prime inspiration for the theological reflection on God and the environment is the Jesuit Pierre Teilhard de Chardin (1959). Thomas Berry (1988) is a Passionist who has devoted himself to theology and ecology.

Limitations of Business Spirituality

While most of the spirit in business movement is beneficial, there are some elements with which Christian theologians find fault. Spirit in business advocates are often pantheistic, that is, they see the Supreme Being as existing in all things. Such a God is not transcendent and is not a personal God. Thus, they are less likely to have faith in a loving God whose grace is essential for our salvation.

The New Age Movement has received vehement criticism from fundamentalist and evangelical Christians, sometimes even calling it Satanic and a product of the Antichrist. Yet both New Age and evangelical Christians share many common attitudes. Both find society in crisis. Both have a new enthusiasm for God and prayer. And both find traditional churches deficient. One critic comments:

> Evangelical Christianity (and other contemporary religious fundamentalism) and the New Age Movement are in fact sibling rivals sharing at least similar (if slightly eccentric) presuppositions about history and salvation. (Woods, 1993)

Another element that both evangelical Christianity and the spirituality in business movements share is a person-centered individualism. In the old American tradition dating back to the observations of Alexis de Tocqueville (1946), both groups find that it is *my* fulfillment and *my* relationship to God that is essential. There is little conviction of the important role of organizations of any kind, and less realization of the importance of the common good.

Another limitation of the spirituality in business can occur when a particular religious tradition is espoused by a chief executive officer (CEO). Some CEOs are so enthusiastic about their own spiritual beliefs that they seem to demand that others embrace the same religious faith. There is then a danger of coercion for some and, for others, favoritism to those with similar beliefs. If handled well, common religious and spiritual beliefs in an organization can be fruitful. But if not handled well, they can lead to divisiveness and even lawsuits.

Business Ethics, Spirituality, and Religion

Business ethics has become a major concern of most business-people over the last few decades. Yet the spirituality in business movement has developed largely independent of this related movement. This lack of connection is not suprising in our fractured culture; but it is ironic, since the two movements could support one another, and there are many parallels in goals and inspiration. For example, both movements are: (1) focused on personal integrity and moral growth; (2) concerned with making the work and business environment more humane; (3) led by more visionary business executives; (4) Concerned with the physical environment and a sustainable future for all; and (5) growing in popularity with new books, articles, conferences in both the popular and academic circles. One reason for this may be that religion, which is a stimulus and source for traditional spirituality, has historically not been a significant resource for business ethics. A recent attempt to demonstrate the contribution of religious thinkers to business ethics is a special issue of *Business Ethics Quarterly* (1997). The editor of this special edition, Stewart Herman, sought contributions from representatives of Judaism, Roman Catholicism, and Protestant Christianity. He limited contributions to these religious traditions in order to "keep the project manageable in scope." The articles in this issue are widely read, very well received, and widely cited. The editor-in-chief of the journal, Dr. Patricia Werhane of the University of Virginia, says that she has had more requests for this issue than any other issue of the journal. Many have asked for another special issue, perhaps examining other traditions, such as Orthodox Christianity, Islam, Buddhism, Confucianism, and Hinduism. Another attempt to bridge the gap is the compilation of 150 articles on the influence of Christianity on economics and business, *On Moral Business: Classical and Contemporary Resources for Ethics in Economic Life* (Stackhouse et al., 1995).

In conclusion, the spirituality in business movement helps the businessperson to become more centered on the important things in life: God, people, family, and a physical world that can be passed on to our children. It enables the business person to gain a better sense of the role of God and other people in our world. Let us now examine in greater detail the meaning of this movement for businesspeople.

Implications for Business and Practicing Managers

Rich experiences need not be relegated to experiences outside of work and the firm. Many people would be much happier if their broader aspirations and desire for service wouldn't have to be left out of their business life. Many current leadership books, both scholarly and popular, cite the fact that our world is fragmented and that there is a "new search for purpose and meaning." Real leaders are most often proud of "their own feelings of inspiration, passion, elation, intensity, challenge, caring, and kindness—and yes, even love" (Kouzes and Posner, 1995).

Ford Motor and Service

Ford Motor Co. began a new three-day training program in 1998 for all upper and middle managers called the Business Leadership Institute. Most of the program is focused on "increasing shareholder value," but on the last day of the program Ford managers are asked to do a half-day of service work in the city. This work involves helping at a soup kitchen, homeless shelter, or building homes with Habitat for Humanity. The rationale for this half-day of activity, in which the managers, time is fully paid by Ford, is articulated by a Ford executive, in a written response to a participant:

1. It is the company's fundamental responsibility to the community in which it exists. This community is the source of our sales and we have a responsibility to give back to the world in which we live. This is not about selling cars. It is about being good corporate citizens.
2. We can learn from people in these agencies who have tremendous drive, teamwork, leadership, and organizational values. Most of these agencies accomplish great results on a shoestring. They know how to get things done with limited resources. As a company we need to emulate these traits. We can learn from them.

Ford has a comprehensive program for trying to bring spirit to its managers. But Ford is not alone.

Spirit Brings Vision and Innovation

Executives, workers, and often the companies they are with, attempt to bring quiet, wholeness, spirit, and even contemplation and prayer into their lives. Boeing has enlisted poet David Whyte (1994) to read poems and stories to executives in order to encourage their creativity. Lotus Development has a "soul committee" that tries to build a strong culture and to aid teamwork. AT&T sends middle managers off for a three-day training that is aimed at helping managers better understand themselves and be able to listen to their employees (*Business Week*, 1995).

In addition, . . . corporations like Chase Manhattan Bank, DuPont, AT&T, Apple Computer and others have tackled the subject of contribution by including a new question in their search for vision, "What is our higher purpose?" (Channon, 1992: 58)

DuPont agricultural products division created a vision topped by a banner headline: "A New Partnership with Nature." Such vision can create energy, enthusiasm, and creativity within the firm.

In searching for a source for such a new vision, some have turned to explicit spirituality. The source of much of that spirituality comes from "the great founders of the world's religions: Jesus, Moses, Buddha, Zoroaster, Mohammed, Krishna. . . . their core values are always there: inner peace, truth, right-conduct, nonviolence, and above all, love" (Miller, 1997). Love of others is certainly the core of the teachings of Jesus Christ. A book that provides wisdom and a model for managers examines the life of Jesus, and how he as a leader dealt with his followers and others (Jones, 1995). Laurie Beth Jones takes passages from the Gospels and finds remarkably up-to-date messages for contemporary managers among the sayings and actions of Jesus. The book was so popular that it reached the national best-seller lists.

The spirit in business movement can bring vision and enthusiasm to a work environment. An executive who takes spirit seriously will be able to more readily lead and articulate vision for the firm. Tom Chappell, founder and CEO of Tom's of Maine, is an excellent example of such an executive. In his popular book, *The Soul of the Corporation*, he describes how his firm grew from a small natural soap and toothpaste firm to one that marketed nationally in supermarkets. But in the process, he found that he and others in the firm had lost a sense of personal mission and common purpose.

Looking for new insights, Chappell enrolled at Harvard Divinity School, and while there resolved to use his role as CEO to bring soul back to the firm. Chappell realized that "common values, a shared sense of purpose, can turn a company into a community where daily work takes on a deeper meaning and satisfaction" (Chappell, 1993).

Robert Greenleaf is an early pioneer of this movement. Decades ago he founded the now widespread "Servant-Leader Movement." Greenleaf's career was at AT&T, and after doing much management development work there, he reflected on the task (Greenleaf, 1973). Greenleaf's inspiration came from Jesus in the Gospels. His description of the effective leader is one who is a servant of those he leads.

Greenleaf and the Greenleaf Center[4] have had an immense impact on business executives and other leaders over the past decades.

Several top managers of firms have articulated the overtly Christian vision that guided them as chief executive officers of their respective firms. Max DePree was chairman and CEO of Herman Miller. The firm was regularly listed on Fortune's list of "best managed" and "most innovative" companies during DePree's tenure. Max DePree spelled out his humane and religiously based philosophy of management (DePree, 1989). James Autry, who had been CEO of Meredith Communications, does much the same (Autry, 1991).

Agenda for Business Schools

Schools of business are now challenged to bring some of the rich dimensions of vision and spirituality into business education. This challenge should be more fully and easily met by universities with religious roots, since religion and spirituality is generally contained in the university and the business school mission.

Accreditation Demands Mission

The current accrediting criteria of both university-wide regional accrediting agencies and the American Assembly of Collegiate Schools of Business (AACSB) are heavily dependent upon each school's unique statement of their mission. The AACSB accrediting standards require that each school demonstrate that it is fulfilling its own self-declared mission. This statement of mission, plus the evidence that it is being fulfilled, is absolutely essential if a business school is to be accredited.

In their mission or vision statements, religiously rooted universities speak in terms of, for example: "service of faith and the promotion of justice," "compassionate service of persons in need," "concern for the dignity of the person and for the common good of the world community," "integration of the intellectual, spiritual, moral, and social development of students," "promotion of the understanding of religious, spiritual, and ethical dimensions of life," "educating to competence, conscience, and compassion," and "stewardship of resources." Such mission statements generally speak about religious and moral develop-

---

[4] Robert K. Greenleaf Center, 1100 W. 42nd St., Suite 321, Indianapolis, IN 46208.

ment of students, faith and justice, community, and helping those most in need.

Each business school then is required to demonstrate that it is accomplishing those goals. Over the coming decades, this focusing of efforts will have a profound effect on policies, practices, and hiring at religiously oriented business schools.

Service Learning

It is becoming common for business schools to offer courses that require undergraduate and graduate students to do service for those people who are less advantaged in the community. Faculty have described the results of such service learning at professional meetings for a decade. Volunteer work in the local community is done at more than two dozen graduate programs in the United States, including, for example, Stanford, Wharton, the University of Wisconsin, and the University of Maryland.

Service learning often has a profound influence on the student. Most MBA students have not done volunteer work among the very needy before. Such work generally has a positive impact on: their attitude toward the poor, recognition of the need to jump-start young people who come from broken families, poor schools, and disruptive neighborhoods, their view of the justice of the social and economic systems, and their own willingness to help the needy again in the future.

A critical factor in the success of service or volunteer work is reflection on the experience. Students can be asked to keep a journal and to reflect on such questions as: (1) What was the experience that you had? (2) What about the experience was most troubling? (3) What about the experience was most inspiring or empowering? and (4) How were you effected or changed by the experience? What did you learn? Such reflection is done in a group so that the experience of one can be heard by others, thus reinforcing each person's learning. Finally, students are asked to write a short paper with the above questions as a guide.

Faith That Does Justice in Jesuit Universities

The Society of Jesus (Jesuits) in 1975 asked that all Jesuit works focus on the call of Jesus and the special needs of the poor. In 1999 each of the Jesuit universities of the United States did an audit of the progress they made in their activities and policies on "the faith that does justice." The purpose was to examine the results of each individual university's work for social justice, stemming from the Gospels. For example, how have these efforts affected attitudes of students, faculty, staff, hiring, and other policies of each university? The individual university audit also included successes, failures, and the work that is yet to be accomplished.

Each university then sent representatives to regional meetings in 1999 and to an international meeting in 2000. These meetings will enable participants to gain further insight on how faith and the Gospels provide a foundation for an effective university vision and mission. In addition, the meetings will enable each university to see the results of a wide variety of programs for helping those in our society who are most in need, and to learn from the successes and failures of each university.

Spirituality in the Classroom

Bringing spirituality or soul into the classroom and the curriculum should be easier for religiously oriented business schools. Beginning class with a short prayer brings a sense of perspective. This prayer can be largely silence and/or can be said in a fashion that includes men and women of various religious traditions.

Business schools can also find opportunities for students to obtain a clearer sense of their own personal values and goals. Students can be asked to write out their own life goals and to prioritize their own personal values. One method is to ask students to specify their major goals in the areas of: career, personal relationships, leisure satisfactions, learning and education, and religion and spiritual growth. A student then writes a brief paper comparing her or his major life goals in each of the above areas with their top personal values (Cavanagh, 1998, pp. 33–36). In doing so, the student is often able to obtain new insights into their own values and goals. The process enables each person to highlight their own major goals, and to then take steps to better achieve those goals. This also enables a person to make changes in one's life, such as changing jobs, spending more time with family, or reestablishing friendships.

Business schools, like other professional schools, have been accused of teaching techniques of the profession and neglecting the larger historical, social, and ethical issues that undergird the profession. A university typically adds this dimension, and thus provides a broader and ultimately more useful education than do many secular or stand-alone professional schools. Encouraging students to examine the social and moral impact of, for example, global markets, mergers, speculation, downsizings, advertising, and the media, broadens a student's perspective. Larger issues, such as the historical roots of business values, how the values of a firm affect personal values, ethical behavior in business, and maturity and moral development of the person—all give a student a much wider lens with which to view and understand their own work and lives. This knowledge also enables the individual student to more easily establish their own personal goals and moral values, and to more easily cope with the difficult ethical choices with which that student will be confronted in their professional life.[5]

Conclusions

Spirituality enables a businessperson to gain a better perspective on one's firm, family, neighbors, community, and one's self. Furthermore, acknowledging dependence on God gives the individual manager a more stable and helpful vision. The manager then knows that her success also depends on someone beyond herself, so such a view also lessens stress. Such a vision also enables the manager to integrate one's life so that it is less segmented or compartmentalized.

There is much evidence of this new interest in spirituality in business. Business managers and firms now depend more on vision and spirituality in the workplace. This new movement is manifested in a wide variety of ways, and much of it is compatible with and supports Christian spirituality.

Religiously oriented universities are thus challenged to take a leadership role in helping all universities to integrate spirituality, religion, and religious values into their education. Business schools in religiously oriented universities have an important role to play, both in fulfilling the mission of their university, and also because spirituality provides a unique opportunity to make some of the most valuable elements of our heritage available to others.

---

[5] The substantive issues listed here, along with an evaluation of their influence on personal and organizational values, are the substance of *American Business Values with International Perspectives* (Cavanagh, 1998). The service learning project, along with the journal, group reflection, and paper, are described on pp. 104–105.

References

Autry, J. (1991), *Love and Profit: The Art of Caring Leadership*, Avon, New York, New York.

Berry, T. (1988), *The Dream of the Earth*, Sierra Club Books, San Francisco, CA.

Bolman, L., & Deal. T. (1995), *Leading with Soul: An Uncommon Journey of the Spirit*, Jossey-Bass, San Francisco, CA.

Business Ethics Quarterly (1997), Vol. 7, March.

Business Week (1995), "Companies Hit the Road Less Traveled," June 5, pp. 82–86.

Carter, S. (1993), *The Culture of Disbelief*, Basic Books, New York.

Cavanagh, G. (1998), *American Business Values with International Perspectives*, 4th ed., Prentice Hall, Upper Saddle River, NJ.

Channon, J. (1992), "Creating Esprit de Corps." in Renish, J. (ed.), *New Traditions in Business: Spirit and Leadership in the 21st Century*, Berrett-Koehler, San Francisco, p. 58.

Chappell, T. (1993), *The Soul of Business: Managing for Profit and the Public Good*, Bantam, New York.

Chardin, P. T. de (1959), *Phenomenon of Man*, Harper, New York.

Congar, J. (1994), *Spirit at Work: Discovering the Spirituality in Leadership*, Jossey-Bass, San Francisco, CA.

Detroit Free Press (1998), "Taking God to Work: Some Business Leaders Let Religion Influence Vision, Employee Policy," Oct. 2, pp. 1A and 9A.

DePree, M. (1989), *Leadership Is an Art*, Dell, New York.

Greenleaf, R. (1973), *The Servant Leader*, Greenleaf Center, Newton Center, MA.

Harman, W., and Porter, M. (1997), *The New Business of Business*, Barrett-Koehler, San Francisco, CA.

Hexham, I. (1992), "The Evangelical Response to the New Age," in Lewis, J., and Melton, G. (Eds.), *Perspectives on the New Age*, Albany, State University of New York Press.

Jones, L. B. (1995), *Jesus, CEO: Using Ancient Wisdom for Visionary Leadership*, Hyperion, New York.

Kouzes, J., and Posner, B. (1995), *The Leadership Challenge: How to Keep Getting Extraordinary Things Done in Organizations*, Jossey-Bass, San Francisco, CA.

Laabs, J. (1995), "Balancing Spirituality and Work," *Personnel Journal*, Vol. 74, No. 9, pp. 60–64.

Lee, C., and Zemke, R. (1993), "The Search for Spirit in the Workplace," *Training*, June, pp. 21–28.

Miller, W. (1997), "How Do We Put Our Spiritual Values to Work?" in Harman (Ed.), *New Traditions in Business*, op. cit.

Moore, T. (1992), *Care of the Soul: A Guide for Cultivating Depth and Sacredness in Everyday Life*, HarperCollins,New York.

Neal, J. (1997), "Spirituality in Management Education: A Guide to Resources," *Journal of Management Education 21(1)*, February, pp. 121–139.

Ohman, O. H. (1955), "Skyhooks," *Harvard Business Review*, May–June.

Palmer, P. (1994), "Leading from Within: Out of the Shadow, into the Light" in *Spirit at Work*, Congar, J. (Ed.), Jossey-Bass, San Francisco, CA.

Renesch, J. (Ed.) (1992), *New Traditions in Business: Spirit and Leadership in the 21st Century*, Berrett-Koehler, San Francisco, CA.

Saliba, J. (1993), "A Christian Response to the New Age," *The Way*, July, pp. 222–232.

Smith, H. (1958), *The Religions of Man*, Harper & Row, New York.

Stackhouse, M., McCann, D., and Roels, S., with Williams, P. (Eds.) (1995), *On Moral Business: Classical and Contemporary Resources for Ethics in Economic Life*, William Eerdmans, Grand Rapids, MI.

Tocqueville, A. de (1946), *Democracy in America*, Knopf, New York.

Thich Nhat Hanh (1995), *Living Buddha, Living Christ*, Riverhead Books, New York.

U.S. News & World Report (1995), "The Christian Capitalists," March 13, pp. 52–63.

Wall Street Journal (1998), "After Their Checkup for the Body, Some Get One for the Soul," July 20.

Whitney, D. (1997), "Spirituality as an Organizing Principle," in Harman, W., and Porter, M. (Eds), *The New Business of Business*, Barrett-Koehler, San Francisco, CA.

Whyte, D. (1994), *The Heart Aroused: Poetry and Preservation of the Soul in Corporate America*, Currency Doubleday, New York .

Woods, R. (1993), "What Is New Age Spirituality," *The Way*, July.

WHAT DOES SPIRITUALITY MEAN TO ME?

Abbass F. Alkhafaji,
Slippery Rock University

ABSTRACT

Spirituality in the workplace is a new concern for management in modern businesses. Many people believe that religion, or God, should be left outside the workplace. Today, there seems to be a changing attitude toward spirituality by some business leaders. How would management or any employee in the organization react if they see or hear someone praying or meditating next to them? This is starting to become common practice in some corporations. John D. Beckett, the president of R.W. Beckett Corporation, believes that spirituality and business should be brought together.[1] This paper will review the benefits of spirituality in the workplace. It will discuss this important issue from the point of view of a Muslim.

Introduction

Spirituality isn't merely practicing your religion; it's about the search for something bigger that connects you to a higher power that can energize you to perform your job better. You can't go to work every day without believing there's a good reason to do it. People set career goals to attain fulfillment from their job. Today people use their spirituality to help to get them through problems, to gain new perspectives, and to deal with ethical situations. Many people think that spirituality should not be part of the workplace, but for others "business as usual" is changing. The infusion of spirituality is catching on worldwide. These people are moving toward a new set of social values and a strong sense of inner peace.

---

[1] Braham, J. (1999, February 1). "The Spiritual Side." *Industry Week*, Vol. 248, Issue 3, pp. 48–56.

Socrates taught the goodness of humanity. Because of his beliefs, he was forced to drink poison by the Greeks. He died for telling the truth and what he believed. Socrates, Buddha, and Confucius taught good morality. They taught ethical orientation, the importance of spiritual belief, and the belief in God and the hereafter. Some of the people who wrote about those individuals claim that they must have a divine message like messengers of God before them and after them (Abraham, Moses, Jesus, and Mohammed). All of those messengers stressed the coordination of spiritual aspects of life.

On the contrary, the two major groups of people, the rationalists and traditionalists, have ignored their call for this balance. For example, those who call for the mind embodied (rationalists) have ignored the spiritual dimensions of life—so much so, that they deny that there is such a thing as a soul. However, they make the best use of their mind in satisfying the craving of their bodies, the demands of sex and other necessities. The second group is called the soul embodied (traditionalists). They play down the demands of their bodies and are almost totally preoccupied with the concern of their spirit. In this regard, they go to such extremes that they do not utilize their brains fully.

These two groups in various societies have often been in conflict throughout history. This conflict has only been to the extent of debates, unless some rationalist has infiltrated into the other groups to master their support to hoodwink the masses. Even without any obvious or subtle infiltration, the traditionalists have by their uncaring attitude toward material well-being often allowed the rationalists to usurp the worldly rights of the traditionalists and their blind followers.

Mind Embodied	Traditionalists
- Materialism: Do not believe in Soul. - Rationalists: Explain their behavior and use their mind. -Take advice of religious people. - Mostly are corporate people. They are knowledgeable and they run the show. - Less socially responsible.	- Mostly religious people. - Often do not use their brain and allow the rational people to run the country. - They don't care about worldly demands.—They are overspiritualists. - Pre-equipped with their spiritual aspects. - Often do not use technology or politics of the world. - They do not have a good idea of what is happening in the world.

There, however, has been an exception to this rule in the form of divine prophets, smaller in number than the other groups. The message of this group has been consistent and persistent throughout the ages and challenging to cultures for both intellectual and spiritual myopia. This influential and consistent message is one for the life of the submission to the providence culminating in the advent of the prophet Mohammed (peace be upon him).

Spirituality: Definition and Meaning

Spirituality is any effort that helps to lift individuals up and make them feel connected with a Supreme Being (the creator) in the sense of righteousness and accountability, at the same time remaining down to earth. One should not be overspiritualistic in the workplace. To serve people's needs properly is part of spirituality. It does not mean that we are neglectful of our worldly responsibilities for the absolute purpose of seeking the pleasure of God. (Our family, our friends, and our communities).

- It is the needed relationship with the unseen dimension of divinity.
- It is the awareness of the inner and direct relation with God Almighty.
- There is a feeling that we are here to worship and to please God, the Creator and Sustainer of the universe, because we will be facing him again in the hereafter.
- It is how to affiliate your life devotion with God that makes life easier.

In order to please God, it is important to control the material desire, greed, and injustice to others. Some people see spirituality different from religion, while others see them connected. A third group of individuals use religion and spirituality interchangeably to mean the same thing.

We can say that religion is usually associated with an organized structure—i.e., the pope, bishops, pastors or priest, etc. Some of these religions do not have a hierarchy structure—such as the religion of Islam. Islam allows individuals direct relationships with the creator. Religion people usually perform certain rituals collectively. Spirituality is a kind of attitude or an orientation toward satisfying the demand of the metaphysical dimension of life.—i.e., non-material, the demand of your spirit and not the body. Therefore, individuals can enhance their level of spirituality by constantly reminding themselves of the commandments of God through reflection on philosophical issues, and reminding themselves of their origin and duties and responsibilities toward fellow human beings, other forms of life, and the environment.

Recently, some people started taking comfort in religion and talking about soul, mind, spirit, and God. They came to realize the importance of a relationship with God. This is especially the case with those who experienced crises in their life or witnessed their friend's crises. They started being open about their religious practices at home and in the office. For example, after the incident in Jonesboro, Arkansas, people attended Sunday service in record numbers.

Spiritual practices were private and usually conducted in a silent tone. Nowadays, people are more open about their spiritual interests and practices. Spirituality also has an important role in the workplace. Many people at work are attempting to discover their true selves and find a higher purpose and meaning to their lives.

The writer remembers a debate that he had 15 years ago with a corporate officer, who told the author that he will not expand his business to the Middle East or any Muslim country because the workers take time to pray five times a day. He, like many others, did not understand why Muslims pray together. The reason is the quest for unity and direction. The perception that Muslims take time off for prayers during working hours is itself wrong. In reality, no time during the work is utilized for prayers. Prayers are carried out either at home or during the lunch break. The morning prayer is done at home before sunrise, the noon prayer is done during lunch break, and the other three prayers are carried out at home in the evening and night. Friday in the Muslim country is a holiday and people work on Saturday and Sunday. On Friday they gather for a mass prayer in the mosque.

Management's Role

In today's organizations, management is faced with the challenge of understanding and respecting the employee's spiritual right. They need to know how relevant the spirituality of the worker is to their effective performance in the company. The company must encourage these spiritual practices while not compromising the organization's objectives and work requirements. Management should first recognize that this is an important issue and then realize that some people like to practice spirituality privately. Management must make it clear that employees have the right to be spiritual as long as it will not interfere with their job. Make sure that the organizational environment is a tolerant one so that co-workers will understand and respect each other. Management concern should be with doing the job right the first time. Encourage people to work in a team environment, which requires the full understanding and appreciation of every member's capability and involvement.

In today's organizations, there seems to be a changing attitude toward spirituality by top-level management. For example, Jon Huntsman is the CEO of a privately held chemical company that emphasizes family values and spirituality but not a specific religion. He was also a leader in the Church of Jesus Christ of Latter-Day Saints. Huntsman feels that employees are entitled to their spirituality. He preaches that being a good mother or father is more important than the workplace. Apparently his ideas work. His privately held chemical company is the largest in the United States.

Another example is David L. Steward, the CEO of World Wide Technology Inc. This company was founded in St. Louis by Steward and has grown to an estimated $210 million. Steward promotes spirituality in his company. He keeps a Bible in his desk drawer and reads it daily. Steward has built a good relationship with his employees based on trust and integrity. A third example is Jeffrey H. Coors, president of ACX Technologies Inc. Although this is a public company, Jeff Coors still brings spirituality into the business. He regularly talks to his employees about his faith. He encourages people to be spiritual and to do their best in their job. He also believes a company might grow better if God is the focal point.

Spirituality on an Individual Level

- Spirituality is unique to every individual and therefore it is hard to measure.
- It is a level of awareness and sensitivity that surpasses the physical condition.
- It is the awareness of the existence of the source and the oneness of this universe and the oneness of God. Everything in this universe is interconnected.
- It is how to discover comfort to make your life more meaningful.

Spirituality and religion are connected, but you can have one without the other. For example you belong to an organized religion, but you do not practice or attend services regularly. Or, you meditate or do yoga, but do not belong to a particular religion. The usual case, however, is that you have a religion and are spiritually motivated. Religion, however, is a more recognized part of a person's life. How people feel and think has a lot to do with their spirituality and religion.

Would you consider the following a spiritual practice?
* I am a Muslim.
* I pray five times a day.
* I read the holy book (*The Quran*).
* I read inspiration literature.
* I sometimes write my thoughts about religion.
* I tape myself or write poetry about some aspects of religion.
* On a continuous basis I explore how to live a more spiritual life.
* I attend some Friday prayers in congregation.
* I apply my religion to be a guideline for my daily life.
* I provide services to my communities in a variety of aspects.
* I review my practices to improve my lifestyle on a regular basis.
* I pray at work. A reminder of being good and obeying God.
* I praise God in the highest and the greatest constantly.

I think that such a practice gave me the strength and the power to be better in everything I do. More specifically:
* Spirituality to me is personal growth.
* It is a commitment to be a better person.
• Honesty in dealing with others.
• It helps me to forgive and forget.
• It reminds me of my duty in the job and at home.
• It reminds me not to be biased or prejudice against others.
* It makes me more effective at my job.

• It constantly reminds me several times a day to be fair and just in dealing with others.
• It improves my decision-making skills.
• It improves my listening skills.
• It helps me to make ethical decisions.
• It helps me to be more tolerant of others.
* It teaches me how to be open and patient with others.

* My regular prayers every day at certain times make me disciplined. This discipline, in turn, makes me more productive and more effective in my job.

Conclusion

Any effort at spiritualism is commendable, especially in this day and age of consumerism and materialism. The test of the ultimate effectiveness of such efforts ought to be the bottom-line question as to what kind of societal structure the desired system seeks to establish, and what kind of individual that societal structure is expected to produce. Muslims believe that Islam offers the ultimate balance among various aspects of human personality, and caters to their demands in a manner that no other system has so far been able to do. Any spiritual exercises that contribute to this balance would be praiseworthy, but anything that interferes with this golden mean may only be an exercise in futility. Spirituality is a big part of people's lives and it is becoming popular in the workplace. Some of the corporate leaders today are more than willing to include spirituality and religion in the workplace. This is a corporate issue that needs to be highlighted. The more that people talk about the subject, the more it is going to be in the public eye.

The divine message calls for reforms and a balance of the soul (spiritual aspects), the mind (intellectual aspects), and the body (social and economic well-being). It all depends on, and must be started with, a clean consciousness and a clean heart. The spiritual part is the basis for everything else. If the conscious mind and heart are not clean, everything will fall apart. The genuine divine message has always taught followers in various times and places to strike a balance between the demands of soul, mind, and body.

References

Braham, J. (1999, February 1), "The Spiritual Side" *Industry Week,* *248(3),* pp. 48–56.

Miller, D. Patrick. "The Spirit of 9 to 5." *Yoga Journal.* Nov./Dec. 1997, pp. 73–79.

The San Diego Union-Tribune, "Spirituality on the Job." August 23, 1999.

CHRISTIAN SPIRITUALITY AND CONTEMPORARY BUSINESS LEADERSHIP

André L. Delbecq,
Santa Clara University

Introduction

There is always an interest in how an individual speaker defines spirituality. My definition is:

The unique and personal inner experience of and search for the fullest personal development through participation into the transcendent mystery.

It always involves a sense of belonging to a greater whole, and a sense of longing for a more complete fulfillment through touching the greater mystery (which in tradition I call *God*). My test of authenticity is the extent to which progress in the spirit of journey manifests itself in loving and compassionate service.

Since Robert Silvers asked each participant to speak from their individual spiritual traditions, I will discuss my interactions with executives in Silicon Valley with whom I have also shared religious reflection in the context of Santa Clara University as a Catholic and Jesuit institution. This is necessarily only my perspective and that of those executives I will report on. Christianity itself speaks with robust and diverse voices. Witness within the Catholic tradition diverse voices—

From the mountains: The Desert Fathers, John of the Cross, and the contemporary Carmelite Thomas Merion

From the valleys: St. Francis and the contemporary Teilhard de Chardin

From the City: Augustine, Aquinas, Ignatius, Newman, and the Contemporary Mother Theresa

There are also the great reformer voices of Christianity: Luther, Calvin, Wesley; black Christian spirituality (King); and feminist voices (Dorothy Day, Rosemary Ruether).

When I first began my intense study of Christian spirituality I was a bit taken aback by the diversity of the Christian voices. Then I reminded myself that God is infinite. So should there not be an infinite variety of voices speaking His language?

There is, of course, the common denominator among all the voices. God is love, and he who abides in God abides in Love and God in him. Love of God and Neighbor rests at the heart of Christian spirituality.

The Inspiration of Business Leaders

Let me forthrightly state that my interest in spirituality in the context of business leadership did not flow from my own inner inspiration. Rather it came from experiencing the intense spirituality of senior executives in Silicon Valley, and their selflessness of service flowing from the richness of their individual inner journeys.

How then do I perceive the Christian message informing executive leadership?

A few illustrations of themes

Robert J. House and I first interviewed many of these executives as part of a leadership study of CEOs dealing with rapid-change environments in the 1980s. As I have come to know these individuals more intimately in subsequent years, there are some common themes from their Christian spiritual tradition which inform their individual journeys as senior executives.

Theme 1. *The Christian perspective on "calling" as an orientation to work that adds a sense of vitality and purpose to their leadership journey.*

The first and overarching theme is that business leadership for these individuals is a calling to service, not simply a job or a career.

They share the pivotal Christian belief that all creation is redeemed and good, and therefore being involved in co-creation through industrial enterprise can be an act of love.

They see their own role and the function of their business enterprise as a form of service, in this case the design and provision of goods or services which meet important societal needs.

Theme 2. *The integration of their spirituality with their work rather than the separation between a "private life of spirit" and a "public life of work."*

These individuals share the "Ignatian" ethos of being contemplatives in action; the Rahnerian notion of finding God in the everydayness of their organizational challenges.

They see business as a dominant social institution at the turn of the 20th century. They are aware that the vast majority of individuals in modern societies find the expression of their individual talents within the private-sector organization, that community will or will not be experienced primarily within these organizations, and that human solidarity will be impacted by the practices of these organizations. Therefore, to them leadership in the private-sector organization is a role worthy of the highest form of servant leadership.

This parallels the Ignatian notion of looking where God is at work at a time in history, and selecting a contemporary institution as a place for service.

Let me mention three examples

Retailing: The chairman and CEO of a retailing organization who created one of the healthiest organizational communities I encountered during my early years in California. A man growing up in very modest circumstances, he established a major firm to provide quality and fashionable goods at modest prices for people of limited means, and employed and trained individuals with modest social-economic backgrounds to manage his organizations. Within the company he established a culture of generous service to the customer, and a mature and respectful internal organizational ethos among a very diverse work force. He exemplifies the Christian beatitude: clothe the poor, through creating a remarkable corporation that does so, and employs the poor as well.

Data Systems: Another of my heroes is a computer scientist who formed one of the earliest firms providing databases to a variety of consumer and scientific groups. He believed that knowledge should be shared, so a worker in Kenya should have the same knowledge resources as a scholar at Oxford. With enormous courage, overcoming many technical and market obstacles, he created and modeled the potential for sharing information through computer technology truly being a contemporary "educator/missionary" across national boundaries.

Bioengineering: I think of a woman executive in love with biological science, adding an NMA to her credentials in biology, who through creative financing of early-stage bioscience developments was as much of a medical missionary as Albert Schweitzer. She was filled with a passion to eliminate several diseases through her bioscience financial efforts.

Theme 3. *Courage to stay the course and survive with dignity the special challenges of executive leadership which are daunting to the best and the brightest.*

These leaders must continually strive to lead through a vision which is bold and courageous, yet remain flexible in order to accommodate continual change. This calls for detachment from what is comfortable and familiar, often taking them and their organizations into high-risk paths. For many of these executives (often introverts with scientific training in Silicon Valley) this requires excruciating public presence, with constant need to interface with diverse stakeholders.

Through personal reflection and meditation they manage to balance the dangers of over extension and burnout (illustrated by the "hero myths" as described in the work of Sonnenfeld).

In addition, they experience the hypercriticism, public scrutiny, hard times, uneven successes, and many other trials of senior leadership.

Two examples

Environmental Services: My MBA's favorite profile of executive courage is the CEO of an environmental services company twice facing bankruptcy due to changes in legislation and government support, who remained dedicated to developing a breakthrough technology for dealing with automotive emissions. His story of snatching success from the jaws of defeat through rededication and inspiration of his managerial team is one of overcoming the greatest of hardships. His courage to deal with these setbacks and ability to help the management team remain focused on how to solve an important environmental problem is truly inspiring.

Finance Services: A banking executive who created many of the enabling financial structures for both early-phase technology firms and urban reconstruction, who envisioned banking as a way of enacting the great works of mercy. Through his commitment to banking as a calling he managed to sustain his political position through four ownership transfers (in an era of mergers and turbulence) in order to sustain the financial arrangements he had put in place to serve his clients.

The Bonfires of Executive Vanity: Pride, Power and Wealth

Obviously the story of executive leadership is not always a story of unmitigated goodness. I find mischief and occasionally evil in the executive state as in all institutional sectors. However, for many Christian executives, I perceive and they report that their spirituality provides protection against the many pitfalls of executive leadership.

As identified by executives at a NASDAQ conference, the major cause of leadership failure is hubris. Or as Richard Hagberg, the consultant on leadership failure, writes, pride leads to executive failure because it leads to impatience, an unwillingness to build consensus, the inability to receive criticism, and the unwillingness to endure periods of trial and uncertainty. Humility as a Christian virtue looms large in the stories told by these executives.

Conclusion

Let me conclude these brief remarks by pointing out that in the contemporary business context illustrated by these brief vignettes of executives from Silicon Valley, I often listen to executives who tell me they find inner strength and wisdom in their Christian tradition which informs their leadership. It provides them with wisdom to discern and to reach toward noble goals, with contagious passion and courage that captivates their own and the energies of their colleagues, with the ability to sustain concentration and commitment in the face of daunting problems, with discipline which allows them to reduce their own egos and free themselves of debilitation obsessions, and with compassion that leads to a recognition of their own unity with their fellow men in all the stakeholder roles associated with business. For these executives, their spirituality is the integrative force enabling them to engage in business leadership as a form of human service, thus transforming it as part of the path for attaining their own union with The Transcendent Mystery. Nor do they expect that this path will always lead to success, and they are certain it does not allow them to avoid personal suffering. Thus, spirituality is a quiet but powerful force in their lives, not accounted for in most of our current management literature.

Of course I do not claim that only Christian spirituality matters. I have found Taoist Buddhist, Jewish, and Hindu executives with a similar centeredness transforming their leadership, but my task was to speak to Christian tradition, whose impact I find to be a major motivational element in the journeys of many Christian executives.

Reference

Sonnenfeld, Jeffrey A., (1991), *The Hero's Farewell: What Happens When CEOs Retire*. New York, Oxford: Oxford University Press.

MANAGING WITH AHIMSA AND HORSE SENSE:

A CONVERGENCE OF BODY, MIND, AND SPIRIT

by Grace Ann Rosile
"Horse Sense At Work"

*Note: Portions of this article are drawn from "Managing with Ahimsa and Horse Sense," published in March 1999 on the web site www.spiritatwork.com.

I have been teaching management courses for 20 years at the undergraduate as well as graduate levels. During this same time, I have been a student of Jain philosophy as presented by Gurudev Chitrabhanuji, as well as a lover of horses. Looking back, I see that these three distinct aspects of my life—the physical, mental, and spiritual—were not integrated very well. It was like three compatible strangers living as me. I even had totally different clothing for each activity.

Then my former husband (also a management professor) and I decided to combine my interest in horses with our business skills. We sold our suburban home and bought a beautiful horse stable with a run-down 100-year-old farmhouse. We spent over 10 years owning and operating a "full-service" horse business.

Soon stories of raising and training horses began to creep into my management lectures. Then one day Gurudev Chitrabhanuji and his Pittsburgh students all met for an enjoyable afternoon picnic at my farm. Everyone loved the closeness to nature and the beauty and gentleness of the horses. I was proud of the loving and peaceful aura I had established throughout my farm. Yet afterward, I began to examine how the standard practices of a horse business might look through the eyes of these people. I questioned how well I had applied Ahimsa and Jain philosophy to my practices with horses and with this business. My current work on "Managing with Horse Sense" emerged from the convergence of these three areas, representing body, mind, and spirit.

This chapter offers some examples of how my horses helped me to develop this integration and see the spiritual in my daily physical and mental work.

Horse Sense and Ahimsa

For me, the term "horse sense" refers to what I learned about life, relationships, and management, from over 10 years of training horses. It is what the horses have taught me. And many of you may know that Ahimsa is the concept embraced by Gandhi, which is at the core of the Jain (from India) philosophy. Ahimsa* (see endnote) comes from a Sanskrit word which means "non-harmfulness." Ahimsa is not a religion; rather it is a daily spiritual practice of enhanced mindfulness and awareness. In the process of living, we cannot help but cause some harm. The spiritual path of Ahimsa asks that I constantly strive to minimize the harm I do in the world.

But what does horse sense have to do with Ahimsa? Horse sense is based upon my ability to understand how my horse thinks and feels. Since a horse does not speak, I had to develop a heightened awareness of subtle cues, body language, and the look in the eye, to know what a horse is "saying." In addition to understanding the horse, I learned to be understood, by using many verbal and non-verbal means of getting my message across to the horse. The skills I developed through this combination of "listening" and "speaking" to horses allowed me to avoid inadvertently harming or frightening, allowed me to build trust, and allowed me to overcome fear (my own and the horse's). Ultimately, I learned to "connect" with horses by establishing a loving, trusting, and understanding environment. This "connecting" goes beyond mere communicating. For me, it is a very spiritual experience, perhaps the essence of spirituality.

I realized my horse-related skills worked with people too, especially when I consciously applied them. This conscious application to human relationships at work can yield the same benefits of greater trust and understanding, and yes, even love, in the workplace.

Here is one story of how my young Arabian stallion Nahdique (pronounced nah deek) taught me something about practicing Ahimsa. He taught me that showing reverence for life can be the simple acknowledgment of that life, and that the absence of that acknowledgment can be very painful to others. It happened like this.

It was during a period when I was even busier than usual, teaching full-time at the university, running my horse business, and training my three Arabian stallions every day. To fit everything in I was riding Nahdique at 6 or 7am. On these chilly Pennsylvania mornings I would enter his stall, put his halter on his head, lead him into the concrete aisle, and tie him in place. I would quickly begin to groom and then saddle him. I began to notice that each day he was becoming more restless, acting like he might kick me, and beginning to snap at me. As he was getting worse, I was getting less patient. We had WORK to do!

One morning I was again issuing another sharp "no!" and I was about to smack him on the neck to get his attention so he could "hear" my message. Suddenly I stopped, and I realized HE had been trying to get MY attention. That morning, an awareness began. I paused to really look at Nahdique. I saw his body, tense and prepared to dodge the slap which he was clearly expecting. I saw his eyes, looking rebellious and resentful. I stopped, went to his right side, and looked into his eye. He watched me warily. I said slowly, "I'm sorry, buddy. I SEE you. I'm glad you're here." I put a hand out, then hugged his neck. I stepped back and saw the anger fade from his eyes, leaving some righteous resentfulness. Then his look said, "well okay, I guess I'll accept your apology." I stroked his neck again, and then he looked calm and content. The "apology" took only a minute. We continued our work with no further problems. After that, each morning I would look in this eyes and feel that connection for just a second. Then I would pat him and say "Hi buddy, how are you this morning?"

One morning a few weeks later, as I walked into his stall I was worried about some other issues. Without thinking about what I was doing, I stood motionless and I sent a mental message, "Hi buddy, can I have a hug this morning?" To my surprise he did something he never had done before. He calmly lifted his head from the hay he was munching and he gently rested his chin on my shoulder.

What did I learn from this? I had wanted that "connected" feeling of wondrous joy at communicating with one of God's most beautiful creations, the horse. In this insidious culture of productivity, speed, and efficiency, I had allowed my work to overshadow the importance of my relationships. Ironically, both the relationship and the work suffered. It took a horse to get my attention, to bring me back to awareness that my ultimate reason for working with horses was to experience that connected feeling. And then, when the relationship worked, the work was better too.

If such small gestures can be so important to "even" a horse, how much more important might they be to a person? Nahdique taught me that in business and in life, Ahimsa can be the simple acknowledgment of a fellow living being. A simple greeting can become a joyous affirmation of the connectedness of all life. One connection at a time is what it is all about. It's just horse sense.

To use horse sense to best promote understanding and enhance spirituality in the workplace, I recommend the following three strategies:

1. That we incorporate direct experience as a preferred methodology, relegating written texts to the role of serving the cause of direct experience
2. That we deepen the centuries-old practice of looking to nature to understand our world from a spiritual perspective
3. That we use horses for the opportunity they offer us, to have a direct experience of Nature, which is a close parallel with interpersonal relationships in the workplace

I will address each of the above three points in turn.

Direct Experience as Part of Learning

The concept of "direct experience" was explicitly identified as a component in the theoretical model of learning widely popularized by Kolb and others in the 1960s and 1970s (see Kolb, 1984). However, learning through direct experience is still rather rare in our educational systems.

How can we reap the benefits of direct experience without giving up the value of collective knowledge? I suggest that narratives can serve this purpose.

Narratives are the communication medium of experience. Historically, one thing we see from cultures which are non-literate is that narratives play an important part in their learning and understanding. These narratives are stories, which means they have action, plot, characters, and some underlying theme or "moral" (Boje and Dennehy, 1994). In other words, narratives vicariously convey direct experience.

The Direct Experience of Nature as a Way of Learning

We commonly think of Thoreau when we think of great philosophers who recommended the benefits of a direct experience of the natural environment. One recent study found that most respondents cited time spent outdoors in nature as the most common source of spiritual renewal. Warren Grossman (1999) presents a new twist on this old idea. He suggests that the earth's energy field truly operates as a nourishing mother. He presents evidence that direct physical contact with the earth (for example, standing barefoot on the ground) provides great physical, emotional, and spiritual healing.

Steingard and Fitzgibbons (1999) call for organizational studies in the new millennium to integrate both intellectual and experiential approaches, and to incorporate "a greater understanding of our relationship to the natural world" (p. 537). This relationship would not be based on dominating or transcending the natural world, but rather being an integral part of it, beyond the man/nature false dualism. They call this approach "Integral Organizational Studies."

Ivan Illich (1993) (and many postmodernists, among others) studied the way language has affected our ways of knowing. His book, *In the Vineyard of the Text*, examines some of the ways written language distanced humans from nature and shifted our focus from personal experience, which was personally conveyed, to written texts.

Learning, Spirituality, and Horses

We have seen that direct experience offers us something unique and irreplaceable in the learning process. The direct experience of nature is acknowledged to be a common path to greater spiritual awareness. Given that we can learn about humanity and spirituality from nature, I suggest that working with horses provides an opportunity for learning which is spiritually grounded and also uniquely relevant to our relationships in the workplace. I use the language of direct experience (that is, narrative) to offer my experiences in this area. I ask that the reader remember that the value of the story lies in your ability to make it your own. I offer my interpretations only as a starting point, because some of what I learned from these experiences I know I can only convey with you, me, and a horse all present. This I do in my work-shops called "Horse Sense" (copyright 1999). These workshops offer experiences with obvious, direct, practical relevance to the workplace, while being personal and spiritual.

People have different definitions of what is spiritual to them. My stories offer personal insights, gained not through some mystical process or spiritual experience but through common daily interaction with horses. If you agree with me that shoveling manure is an enjoyable meditative process (I truly love it), then this is a spiritual experience also. Feeling a connection with a horse as we work together is an experience which is spiritual, physical, mental, emotional, aesthetic, and practical all at once.

Some people may have explicitly spiritual experiences with animals, as reported by Mannes:

> The stories I collected from people who have had spiritual experiences involving animals almost always involved personal insights, often occurring in the most private realm of dreams, and often so personal the storyteller could not even say what the experience meant, only that it was meaningful. (Mannes, 1997, p. 67)

I do not consider my experiences to be directly "spiritual" as such. I cite Mannes' quote here, because my daily work with horses often leaves me feeling that I do not know what these experiences have meant, yet I am completely convinced that they are deeply meaningful. I encourage you to allow yourself the gift of such experiences.

A Final Story

At a conference of prominent academics in the field of discourse and organizational change, I took a big risk and told my "horse stories." The main point of these stories was (and is) to demonstrate the management implications of the best kind of horse and human partnerships. I believe these partnerships work best when characterized by mutual respect, mutual empowerment, and mutual trust. (With horses, you also need mutual liking or love. Whether that is true in human organizations is a story for another time.)

After telling several of my stories, I was responding to questions. A gentleman with a French-sounding accent asked, was I not perpetuating hierarchical notions of worker/manager with my horse/rider analogies, since the horse and rider could never change places? I explained that my main point was exactly the opposite, that only outsiders falsely perceived the rider to be completely dominant; my point was that the partnership was more that of equals. He did not agree.

After several attempts to convince him that he had misunderstood my message, the gentleman still argued that I was promoting a managerialist view. Running out of both time and counterarguments, I said "YOU sit on that horse and tell me you are in control!" And everyone laughed.

My final response was not just a clever retort. It reflects the main reason I use my "horse stories." These stories are direct experience. The learning I received from those experiences can be only partially conveyed through language. It is the concrete, physical experience which adds a different dimension to our understanding. When I have told this story to other expert riders, they nod knowingly at that non-horse person's views. They assume a non-rider will not understand what they have learned through experience. Still, many people may be able to vicariously experience the events I recount and gain their own insights. So I work to be better at telling the stories, and I recommend my workshops or your own "field research" for direct learning experiences.

I have always liked what I once heard: that we are not physical beings learning to be spiritual; rather, we are spiritual beings learning to be physical.

I believe we can be physically spiritual.

Horses can teach us some of these lessons.

Note

*Ahimsa, or reverence for life, means respecting the right of all living things to live. For Jains (and for me), it means being vegetarian and not eating meat, fish, or poultry, and avoiding animal products like leather and silk. Ahimsa means non-violence. Practicing Ahimsa means living in such a way as to minimize the inevitable violence we commit every day, thanking even the plants for giving their lives to nourish us. Typically, Jains would not engage in any animal-related businesses. Elsewhere, I have a long explanation of what this means to me as a rider. In brief, such concerns have led me to leave the horse business and to restrict my riding to that which is mutually beneficial to myself and to the horse (we provide exercise for each other). I continue to question my relationship to horses, to make it as non-exploitive as possible.

In the Jain philosophy, the attitude of non-violence must extend also to non-violence in thoughts and beliefs. Thus, Jains do no missionary work. They believe that trying to persuade another that their ideas are wrong does violence to that other person's beliefs. In summary, Ahimsa is not a religion, but is a way of living (and managing) with a heightened awareness of the implications of our actions.

References

Boje, D., and Dennehy, R. (1994), *Managing in the Postmodern World*. Dubuque IA: Kendall Hunt Publishers.

Grossman, Warren (1998), *To Be Healed by the Earth*. Cleveland, Ohio: The Institute of Light.

Illich, I. (1993), *In the Vineyard of the Text*. Chicago: The University of Chicago Press.

Kolb, D. (1984), *Experiential learning: Experience as the Soures for Learning and Development*. Englewood Cliffs, NJ: Prentice Hall.

Mannes, Christopher (1997), *Other Creations: Rediscovering the Spirituality of Animals*. New York: Doubleday.

Steingard, D., and Fitzgibbons, D. (1999). "R/E-volution in Organizational Theory: Organizational Science, Organizational Studies, and Integral Organizational Studies" in Biberman, J., and Alkhafaji, A. (eds.), *Business Research Yearbook*, Vol. VI, pp. 534–538.

Organizational and Societal Issues
and Applications

HOSPITABLE TO THE HUMAN SPIRIT:

An Imperative for Organizations

Dorothy Marcic,
Vanderbilt University

We are entering uncharted waters, a new world. The old rules and structures don't work as well as they used to. We are in the midst of a change of consciousness of what organizations are all about. Twenty-five years ago when I began my career, I would suggest to my MBA students and attendees in management training programs that if they treated people with care and respect, they would likely end up with a more motivated workforce. The word that describes their reaction to me is: ridicule. "Treat them nice?" they would ask incredulously. "Why, we pay them! It's their job to work hard."

Nowadays I don't hear that much from managers anymore. There is a general awareness, unfortunately not often put into practice, that treating employees decently makes better workers. So why aren't we using this knowledge more? Why don't we implement these ideas everywhere? The reason was given by a Pratt & Whitney manager, who described the problem as: "Our structure has not caught up with our consciousness."

We instead fall back on the traditional way of management-top-down, hierarchical, more vertical than horizontal, and characterized by control. It is the best of what we might call a rational system and might be characterized by the magazine *Fortune* (Richard Daft, personal communication, 1998). In times of relative stability and predictability, as it used to be 40–50 years ago, this structure worked well. Twenty years ago (and still today), this is what we taught in business schools. Finance, accounting, and strategy were more-or-less predictable fields of study. Long-range planning was 10–25 years. But in current times of cut-throat international competition, globalization, transformation of whole industries from the information age, and the reduced product cycle time (as one Wall Street manager noted, long-range planning for him is four hours), a more organic, fluid, and horizontally oriented structure works best. This is typified by the newer magazine, *Fast Company*.

Hundreds of books have been published in recent years describing all the new changes in management and how to implement them. We know the words well, but we don't always know how to achieve what they represent: vision, empowerment, accountability, commitment, and customer orientation. This article presents the perhaps radical notion that these goals are achieved through love and spirituality.

Most of the moves from the old management to the new involve changing to a more spiritual foundation. For many managers and management theorists, this is a new way of looking at things. Yet once we open our minds to the perspective of spirituality, it becomes very clear: all the new management concepts that fall under the umbrella of "new management" are, at their core, outward manifestations of managers acting with love and spirit. They are a set of behaviors, attitudes, decisions, and policies that reflect the organization's spiritual essence. They are the workplace versions of spiritual virtues.

What is happening, then, is a sweeping change toward a new model, though we can as yet see it dimly. These changes have been predicted by religious prophets throughout the ages. The Holy Bible speaks of the days when wars and contention will cease, arguably meaning an age of collaboration.

More recently, radical changes in the world were predicted more than a century ago by Baha'u'llah (1817–1892), founder of the Bahá'í faith. He wrote:

> The world's equilibrium hath been upset through the vibrating influence of this most great, this new World Order . . . the like of which mortal eyes have never witnessed. (Baha'u'llah, 1976, p. 136)

Some Bahá'í writings early in the 20th century described what was to come. Shoghi Effendi, a central figure of the Bahá'í Faith, wrote in 1938 that we "would see . . . an organic change in the structure of present day society, a change such as the world has not yet experienced . . . [and] no less than the reconstruction and demilitarization of the whole civilized world . . . to remold its institutions in a manner consonant with the needs of an ever-changing world. (pp. 41, 43)

The changes may be coming, but we still have far to go. Rather than values- or spiritually-based organizations, too many firms today are toxic to the human spirit (Pfeffer, 1995; Webber, 1998), causing demotivation, lack of loyalty, and alienation. Instead, why not create organizations hospitable to the human spirit?

The "Cover Your Asset" Based Management Style

Until very recently, most organizations used asset-based management (Rosenfeld, 1998, personal communication). The real value was in tangible, often immovable, commodities. In agricultural times assets were land, jewels, and precious metals. From the industrial revolution until the very late twentieth century, the asset was money, which was often invested in factories and means of production. Under the above conditions, employees were incidental to the wealth of a company or a person. Certainly, they were needed, but it was more for brute force work or domestic servant chores, neither requiring high levels of education or complicated training. Therefore, workers were more-or-less replaceable and not seen as having any real value to the enterprise. In those times, managers had some real control over the firm's assets.

Enter the information age. Capital for investing in ventures is no longer a scarce commodity. When internet giants Yahoo! and Amazon can be started with almost no capital financing and they can become some of the largest United States corporations, you know that capital has lost its edge as the major force for creating successful enterprises.

Today we have a growing segment of employees called knowledge workers. More and more organizations are dependent on the skills, intelligence, and wisdom of these people. Robots and assembly lines have replaced the need for manual labor, but what is needed are smart, hardworking employees. They are the real assets of modern companies. And unlike in past ages, those assets can walk out the door if they don't like how they are being treated.

The trend today is toward a more respectful, consultative, encouraging, and ethical system of management system whose goal is to maximize customer satisfaction. Although widely accepted, this notion is not yet widely practiced. We remain stuck in the obsolete if more familiar "material world" and "rational view" models. As a result, many organizations espouse the values of this new management, but have yet to put them into effective practice. Often, when they try, they fail because they are still operating according to old ways of thinking, seeing organizations within a merely material framework. All too often, the changes undertaken prove to be superficial. They fail to deal with the deeper issues of spirit and love, the essential ingredients to achieve true customer satisfaction. Without embracing these, reforms deliver little. The "new" organizational scheme becomes constrictive, made to yield, like a rubber band, only by force. Sometimes efforts to change derive from motivations that are less than genuine. No amount of rhetoric can tune out hypocrisy or double standards. To be real and lasting, change must be real and fundamental.

Dimensions of Organization

If, instead, we could view companies from a broader perspective, we would see that spiritual values inspire a new way of doing business, from the basic spiritual virtues of unity, justice, integrity, respect, and service. In order to achieve this, all five of an organization's dimensions must be addressed. These are: material, intellectual, emotional, volitional, and spiritual. The material dimension concerns such issues of physical life as buildings, equipment, comfort, safety, adequate pay, and financial viability.

The intellectual includes the collective intelligence of employees, plus their continuing drive for development and learning, as well as the ability to use available resources effectively and plan productively to stay abreast of the latest developments—to be on the "cutting edge" of technology in their fields.

The emotional dimension embraces the work environment and how well people get along with one another, and how effectively they can work as a team. Effective teams require members who are concerned with maintaining the needed skills, who can foster mutual understanding, listen well, and get and give positive feedback, along with an absence of defensiveness in their dealings. In short, effective teams have members possessing mature emotional development.

The volitional dimension refers to the desire or will to improve. We may know that some other behavior is healthier, for example, but lack the will to adopt it. The ability to change, after all, demands the willingness to do things differently.

Finally, there is the spiritual dimension. It concerns such moral issues as justice and respect, involves empathy, and accepts each colleague as unique, to be treated with dignity. However, most organizational change focuses on just the material and intellectual dimensions. Some attention is given to volitional change, but the emotional and spiritual tend to be ignored. The resulting lack of balance almost guarantees only limited success at best, and often failure.

But most organizations today are concerned primarily with financial well-being and increasing shareholder wealth. These may be necessary goals, of course, but they are insufficient to provide long-term viability and success. To achieve that, we must look at all aspects of organizational life and improve each of them, and not merely the financial and material. In fact, of the 200 CEOs studied by Toney and Oster (1998), those who used religious principles in their daily decision making had more successful companies than those who did not. This was because while some CEOs might be motivated by personal reward or greed, those who reflected back to their Holy Books often chose "service" as the principle they would apply, and that, paradoxically, led them to greater corporate and personal wealth.

"A Better Life for Our Customers"

There are organizations which deem all the dimenions important. Consider a retail chain located in small towns and poor urban areas. Stores are relatively small, plain, and simple, with tile floors and bright fluorescent lights, giving the feeling more of a 1950s Woolworth's or Ben Franklin than their competitor Wal-Mart. Most customers have family incomes below $25,000 (Berner, 1998). The average sale is $8, and they like it that way, not wanting poor folks to spend too much in their stores.

Though this might not seem a recipe for success, Dollar General has defied conventional wisdom to become the most successful publicly held retail chain in the United States for five years running (Wiegold, 1998). And it's growing by a billion dollars a year (Milana, personal communication, 1999). During the decades Cal Turner, Jr., has run Dollar General (which was founded by Cal Turner, Sr.), the retail industry went through a traumatic shakedown unlike any other. The secret of his success is his solid business sense coupled with a deep and abiding belief in God and trust in good people.

"Our strategy is to hire ordinary folks, those with moral integrity, give them a sense of mission and then get out of their way. Good people in pursuit of mission need the least amount of policies and controls," he explained with the exuberance of a young boy hitting his first home run. "Values and mission are the greatest control factor for getting everyone to work towards common goals. It's the values that control them, not rules" (Turner, personal communication, 1998).

As comfortable in a navy suit as he is in plaid shirts and jeans, Turner also feels strongly about serving those less fortunate. Most five-and-dime stores charge odd-numbered amounts such as $.99, $1.99, or $2.49, but not Dollar General, where prices are in even amounts of $1, $1.50, or $2. Wouldn't the previous prices induce people to buy more, since it is easy to lose track of how much you are spending?

"My daddy and I talked about that," says Cal, Jr., in his relaxed, down-home style. "We thought poor and uneducated people might have problems adding up what they bought, making overall money management more difficult for them. So we decided to make it easier for them." Compare this to Wal-Mart, which aired a live Garth Brooks concert at Christmastime, in order to extend the customers' time in the stores. Or, as the National Association of Recording Merchandisers says, "The longer [retailers] keep you in the store, the greater the chance you'll leave with more items" (Nelson, 1998, p. B1). Cal, on the other hand, really believes in the first sentence of the Dollar General's mission statement: "A better life for our customers."

His compassion is not limited to customers. Employees are special, too. Prospective employees see a short video of Cal, Jr., describing just how Dollar General considers its workers "an honored and valued asset" of the organization. Each year the company pays out millions of dollars in employee bonuses tied to corporate performance. Recently I had lunch with one of the newer Dollar General executives, HR VP Susan Milana, and I asked her if Cal's message and values are taken seriously in the company, or whether it was, as in so many other companies, just so much corporate hype (personal communication, 1999). As a rising start in companies such as PepsiCo and T. J. Maxx, Milana has two decades of HR experience to draw on. When she started in Dollar General, she wondered if it would live up to its people-oriented promise. She has not been disappointed. In many meetings, she reported, managers are moved to tears—not out of frustration or pain, but rather from the empathy and positive connection there is between the company and its customers.

Many companies nowadays have value statements and those are hung proudly on the wall for all to see. But here is where Dollar General stands out. In another setting, the values might be espoused, but what happens when a promotion decision has to be made, when there are two candidates (Milana, personal communication, 1999)? One of them has strong interpersonal skills, good ethics, shows promise as a leader, but has not been the "star" in terms of sales or other performance measures. Candidate B is not so great with people, maybe even is self-centered, but recently made a momentous sale. If, as happens in many companies, the winner is candidate B, then they might as well rip the value list off the wall, because those espoused ideals have just been violated.

Dollar General maintains its values base by constantly challenging itself with policies and behaviors to see if they fit in with the values. Yet this is done in a supportive, collaborative mode. Milana told me they never "criticize" one another's ideas. They listen and try to build on them. Each of the 28 senior managers writes a development plan once a year and meets for an entire day with Turner, Milana, and sometimes another executive. Managers are evaluated on their vision, their ability to work in teams to achieve their goals, and how well they know and work with their employees, all the way down the line. If store supervisor Mary Schmidt's mother was in the hospital three months ago, the executive is expected to know the mother's name and condition.

Recruitment is important to the success of this, for it is easier to maintain the company culture if people are hired who share common values and aspirations. Visibly moved, Milana told me of how humbled she is after reading the development plans of co-workers, who are actively involved with family, church, and community, trying their hardest to make the world a better place.

I regularly visit a number of Dollar General stores and ask the clerks if they like their jobs. This is a question I often ask hotel maids, waitresses, and workers at car rental agencies. Rarely do I get the kind of positive response I uniformly get from Dollar General employees. It is proof to me that the policies from above permeate to the lowest level of the organization. The difference between Dollar General and other companies who hang their values on the wall is that Dollar General started living out its values from day one and only recently wrote them down on paper.

Because the right people are hired, values are so intentionally operationalized and scrutinized, and rewards match the mission, the values Dollar General started with have been fully integrated into the company. And despite the $1 billion growth per year, the values and culture are being maintained and replicated in about 700 new locations a year (for a total of 4,700 locations in 2000). Will the culture outlast Cal Turner, Jr, the keeper of the flame? Milana believes it will, because the values are such a fundamental part of the culture and are better integrated than any other organization she has seen.

In order to succeed at Dollar General, Milana had to forget everything she learned in her previous executive positions, for she is evaluated in a totally different standard, as shown in the chart below:

Other Major Corporations	Dollar General
Individual contribution	Team contribution
Ability to make independent decisions	Ability to take partners to resolve problems
Conviction in expressing ideas, and strength of persuasive skills	Collaboration in expressing and listening to others' ideas

Managerial Evaluation Criteria of Dollar General

Compared to other large corporations (Milana, personal communication, 1999), Turner is a self-proclaimed strategist and penny-pincher, trying simultaneously to be Scrooge and Santa Claus (Kennedy and Fulmer, 1998). In order to give better value to customers, he holds down costs on amenities in stores. "In Scottsville," he noted, referring to his hometown and the company's headquarters until it moved to Nashville in 1987, "we think ambience is something you ride to the hospital in" (p. 9). Turner is more of a people-based rather than asset-based manager, as discussed in chapter one. More like Gandhi than Genghis Khan, he realizes satisfied workers are pivotal to success. In order to hire the kind of employees who can get excited about Dollar General's mission and serve their customers, the HR department has devised an unusual interview process, which includes candidates writing their own personal mission statement (Milana, personal communication, 1999).

Cal Turner, Jr., runs one of the U.S.'s most successful retail operations. He lives his life according to principles learned long ago at his place of worship. Love of God is integral to his life and his work. Following the straight and "right" path has become natural to him. Earlier in the century, or hundreds of years ago, he might have been a priest or social reformer, working for abolition of slavery, temperance, or civil rights.

Our modern religious activist, though, is a CEO. As a young person, Turner felt the "calling" to go into business (personal communication, 1998). Having a burning desire to enter the ministry, he went through much soul searching and a crucial talk with his own pastor, finally laying aside a life of "sequestered goodness" in favor of taking over the family business. Rather than have only a few hours of impact on several hundred in a congregation, he now has forty hours a week of influence over 40,000 employees and has made life richer for 40 million low-income customers, most of whom live in crime-ridden inner cities or poor rural areas.

Make no mistake, though—Cal is a tough-minded businessman, but one who realizes the centrality of people to what he does, and proclaims, "Our two most important assets are people and merchandise, in that order" (p. 10). For Cal, however, the big profits do not seem to be the most important draw. He uses work to develop people—and lets everyone enjoy the process. "Work is the venue and fun is the catalyst"(Turner, personal communication, 1998).

Spirituality in Organizations. Spiritual principles relate to our inner part, our soul or core, the part of us that transcends "material man." Our spiritual nature craves a purpose in life. It is the part of us that deals with love, kindness, generosity, understanding, forgiveness, peace, and harmony.

There seems today to be a spiritual reawakening of organizations around the world. We are experiencing the marketplace adjustments and awareness of what Harman and Horman (1990) discuss as the fundamental fact—that we are spiritual beings inhabiting a spiritual universe, and that denying this is an error condemning any social structure to failure (p. 141). If so, we are in a world based on spiritual principles and laws, as well as the more familiar physical principles and laws. These we ignore at our peril. For example, I put my hand in a fire and it burns. If I test gravity by walking off a roof, I fall.

The consequences of violating physical laws is swift and clear. But spiritual laws are different. They are easier to ignore (at least in the short term), for the consequence is not always as quick, and it may also be less obvious. But, clearly, if I lie and cheat, people sooner or later will stop trusting me and I shall suffer the unpleasant consequences of being regarded with suspicion. If I am unkind or unjust, people will eventually react in ways that I may regret. So even though the result of breaking spiritual laws may not be immediately obvious, eventually it will come. Breaking a spiritual law has outcomes as predictable as breaking a physical law.

A Sample of Spiritual Laws from the World's Religions

Law	Religious Foundation
Be trustworthy	Thou shalt not bear false witness against thy neighbor. *Holy Bible, Exodus 20:16* The gift of truth excels all gifts. *Buddhist, Dhammapada 354* But in torment the soul of the liar shall surely be. *Zoroastrian, Gathas: Yasna 45–7*[1]
Be detached, remove ego	. . . give up pride. *Buddhist, Dhammapada 221*
Do not live in anger	Absence of anger, . . . indignation [and] of enmity; [this is] approved conduct for men in all stations of life. *Hindu, Apastamba Dharma Sutra, 8:1*
Live rightly	Right views, Right aspirations, Right speech, Right conduct . . . Right effort, Right mindfulness. *Buddhist, Buddha's First Sermon.* Led by . . . Thy Love, led on by thoughts and words and deeds of Truth. . . . *Zoroastrianism, Gathas: Yasna 47–1.*
Live in service	For the sake of the welfare of all, carry on thy task in life. *Hindu, Bhagavad Gita, 3:20* Again, is there any deed in the world that would be nobler than service to the common good? This is worship: to serve mankind. *Baha'i, Paris Talks, p. 177*
Love others	Hate is not conquered by hate. Hate is conquered by love. This is an eternal law. *Buddhist, Dhammapada, 177* . . . love your enemies, bless them that curse you . . . love thy neighbor as thyself. *Christian, Matthew 5:44, 19:19*

The company that violates spiritual laws may suffer in the long run through the alienation of its workers, the dissatisfaction of its customers, and the loss of community respect. Companies that follow spiritual principles and are competent, on the other hand, will be long-term winners. Companies adopt codes of conduct and statements of values for similar reasons—to increase the firm's prosperity.

The new management results not from some mass awakening, but from success. The infusion of spiritual principles in organizations

---

[1] Most of the quotations from Zoroastrianism are taken from either *Sacred Books of the East*, vol. 31, *The Zendavesta*, or Farhang Mehr's *The Zoroastrian Tradition*.

occurs because it has made companies more productive and more profitable. We are talking about what we have called the strengthening of an organization's spiritual dimension, putting the business on a firm foundation of ethics, integrity, and honor. Despite positive material results, however, the quest for profitability is an insufficient motivation. Spiritually oriented companies, as we have described them, adopt that orientation because it is *the right thing to do.*

Indeed, when the overarching goal of an organization is profit and shareholder wealth, it is difficult to create a spiritual framework because, if the bottom line becomes threatened, love goes out the window. For love and spirituality to work, material goals *must* embrace the spiritual—such as service to customers and suppliers, contributions to the community, development of employees, creating a sense of community within the organization, and, overall, convergence of the material and spiritual.

The motto of Thomas Masaryk, the first president of Czechoslovakia (1918–1935), was that "truth will prevail." Many people compare the moral courage of Masaryk with that of Vaclav Havel, the current president of what is now the Czech Republic. Havel has updated Masaryk's motto by saying that "truth *and love* will prevail *over lies and hatred.*" Despite a lack of overall morality in the present short term, the Czech Republic possesses a heritage of moral courage reflected in these two democratic presidents. This is one of many reasons why the Czech Republic is today, and at this stage in its adjustment to democracy and market economics, the most successful of all the former Soviet bloc countries.

I would venture about business, as Masaryk might say today of his country, truth will yet prevail.

References

Baha'u'llah (1976), *Gleanings from the Writings of Baha'u'llah*. Wilmette, IL: Baha'i Publishing Trust.

Berner, Robert (1998), Penny pinchers propel a retail star. *Wall Street Journal*, March 20, p. B6.

Effendi, Shoghi (1938), *The World Order of Baha'u'llah*. Wilmette, IL: Baha'i Publishing Trust.

Harman, Willis, and John Horman (1990), *Creative work*. Indianapolis: Knowledge Systems, Inc.

Kennedy, Jim, and William E. Fulmer (1998), *Dollar General Corporation (A) Abridged*, University of Virginia, Darden Graduate School of Business, UVA–BP–0388.

Nelson, Emily (1998), Retailing: Wal-Mart's Garth-Quake may spur sales, *Wall Street Journal*, Nov. 2, p. B1.

Pfeffer, Jeffrey, (1995), "Producing Sustainable Competitive Advantage Through the Effective Management of People. Academy of Management Executive, 9 (1), 55–69.

Toney, Frank, and Merrill Oster (1998), The leader and religious faith, *Journal of Leadership Studies, 5 (1)*, 135–147.

Webber, Alan M., (1998), "Danger: Toxic Company, Fast Company." 19, November, 152–155.

Wiegold, C. Frederic (1998), Sharehold scorecard: The quest for shareholder value. *Wall Street Journal*, Feb. 26, pp, R1–R17.

THE FOURTH WAVE:

THE SPIRITUALLY BASED FIRM

Fraya Wagner-Marsh,
James Conley,
Eastern Michigan University

Alvin Toffler (1980) foretold the technological "third wave." We suggest that an organizational fourth wave is mounting, the spiritually based firm. The movement toward spiritualizing the organization has apparently caught on, in both theory and practice, even if not yet universally acknowledged as the wave of the future. To stretch the metaphor, as we socially seem to be in a state of "permanent white water" (Vaill, 1989), business leaders are searching for an anchor to help provide stability in the workplace (Bailey, 1998). Our observation is that a great number of highly diverse firms are moving ahead with attempts to instill a spiritual approach to their corporate cultures: Tom's of Main, Herman Miller, TDIndustries, Lancaster Laboratories, Wetherill Associates, Toro Company, Sisters of St. Joseph Health System, Med-tronic, Townsend and Bottum, Schneider Engineering Corporation, Bank of Montreal, etc.

The intent of this paper is to suggest and explore certain basic attitudes and practices that appear to be essential for success in maintaining a spiritually based corporate culture. Six key concepts have been selected for this paper based on our review of the literature, professional observations, and in-depth personal interviews with leaders of spiritually based corporations: honesty with self, articulation of the corporation's spiritually based philosophy, mutual trust and honesty with others, commitment to quality and service, commitment to employees, and selection of personnel to match the corporation's spiritually based philosophy.

Honesty with Self

The first basic attitude that seems to be a key element to the successful transformation or development of a spiritually based firm is how the leaders view themselves. A genuine sense of humility and a sense of higher purpose without "ego" or pride seem to be prevalent characteristics of these leaders. In *The Living Organization— Spirituality in the Workplace*, William Guillory states that "leadership begins with self . . . a sufficiently in-depth knowledge of ourselves that our external activities naturally carry commitment and passion" (Guillory, 1997, p. 108). Leaders of spiritually based firms tend to know their personal mission before they engage others in pursuing the organization's mission (Jeffries, 1998). The importance of the leadership's personal development and self-awareness are identified as keys to the corporation's success.

Usually, those who "take over" top management of an organization or those who start their own organization make moves to try to remake or form the organization after their own image. Whenever there is some trouble sensed within the organization, there is typically an inclination to say that it is the organization itself that needs fixing. But many of the leaders of successful, spiritually based firms embrace Robert Greenleaf's servant-leadership philosophy. Servant leaders view every problem as originating inside, rather than outside, themselves. "To remedy any 'flaw in the world,' the process of change starts in the servant, not 'out there'" (Lee and Zemke, 1993). The servant leader is one who asks if the one who needs changing might be his or her self. In Bothwell's *The Art of Leadership* (1983) he describes a leadership technique: "The World's Worst-Kept Secret: How to Change Every Single Person You Know." His rule is simply that "the way that you change every single person that you know is to . . . change yourself" (p. 231).

The importance of inner reflection and self-awareness is also emphasized in Stephen Covey's writings on management, which are also embraced by many leaders of spiritually based firms. Covey believes that self-awareness enables leaders to examine their paradigms, "to look at their glasses as well as through them," to think about their thoughts, to become aware of the social and psychic programs that are within them, and to enlarge the separation between stimulus and response. "Self-aware, we can take responsibility for reprogramming or rescripting ourselves out of the stimulus-response mode"(Covey, 1994).

The concept of true humility is also a connecting attitude to self-awareness and servant leadership. Bill Bottum, of Townsend and Bottum, a large construction firm, has written: "Unless we are humble and open to new truth we will be unable to learn anything new. We must be open and teachable" (Bottum, 1993, p. 4). Covey is also an advocate of humility. He considers humility "the mother of all virtues: the humble in spirit progress and are blessed because they willingly submit to higher powers and try to live in harmony with natural laws and universal principles"(Covey, p. 3).

Articulation of the Organization's Spiritually Based Philosophy

A second practice or behavior that we have found in our research is that the firms committed to spirituality are extremely forthcoming in declarations of their philosophical commitment, with both their employees and anyone else with whom they do business. As an example, the president of WAI (Wetherill Associates, Inc.), a highly successful auto parts distribution firm, specifies that its field representatives hand over and discuss with potential customers an attractive piece of literature called a "Quality Assurance Manual." The manual sets forth the various aspects of the firm's offerings. But even the slightest perusal of the document reveals that the intent is also to communicate the spiritual basis for the firm's existence.

The WAI manual states that it is a company that operates on the basis of certain principles articulated by its founding chairman, the late Richard W. Wetherill. The firm, the manual declares, tries to "avoid all the nasty personality situations which tend to make people's working lives miserable." Basic to the operating philosophy of WAI is the "principle of right action." This principle is summed up as follows, "Whenever an action is known or felt to be right, the action is to be taken. Whenever [an] action is known or suspected to be wrong, the action is not to be taken." Interestingly, at the conclusion of the manual, which does indeed give a history of the company and presents the many services it provides, there is the statement, "We . . . feel privileged to have shared a small portion of Mr. Wetherill's writings with you." (Bothe, 1995)

Another outstanding example of a company articulating the spiritual principles the organization stands for would be Tom's of Maine. Tom Chappell, CEO of Tom's of Maine and author of *The Soul of a Business* (1993), in an interview in *Business Ethics* (1994), explained that the company originally thought their spiritually based values were things "we could place in the workplace, but when it came to either selling to our trade customers or developing an advertising and promotion strategy, we didn't have the courage to think that we could bring our values to those" areas. But in the end the values message worked. Tom's successfully used an advertisement that talked about both the products and the corporate philosophy. It invited people into the ad through its sharing of values.

> Several spiritually based firms incorporate spiritual values in their employee development and training programs. For example, Boatmen's First National Bank in Kansas City, Missouri includes spiritually oriented materials into its monthly, half-day leadership conferences for the bank's executive group. Martha A. Lynn, vice president for organizational development and employee development states that she has been given instructions from the CEO, Bill Nelson, to "emphasize spiritual values in the leadership conference" and the firm expects to extend this emphasis to lower levels in the organization in the near future. (Brandt, 1996)

> TDI Industries is among *Fortune's* 100 best companies to work for in America (Branch, 1999) and they have used servant leadership as the core principle for their leadership development for over 25 years in order to help reinforce a trusting corporate culture (Lowe, 1998). Xerox managers attend weeklong retreats where vision quests and council meetings based on a Native American model help Xerox professionals see their work in a more meaningful way (Oldenburg, 1997). Other examples include Exxon U.S.A. of Houston's two-day spiritually geared component to its management training program and Bank of Montreal's spiritually oriented materials used in employee training for its 36,000 employees from all levels of the company. (Brandt, 1996)

As further evidence of articulating the spiritual principles of the organization, we can look at the numerous CEOs and leaders of corporations who have gone so far as to write books and articles elaborating on their spiritually based philosophies on leadership. Examples include Max DePree, former CEO of Herman Miller and author of *Leadership Jazz* (1992), Kendrick Melrose, CEO of Toro Company and author of *Making the Grass Greener on Your Side: A CEO's Journey to Leading by Serving* (1995), Earl Hess, former CEO of Lancaster Laboratories and author of an article entitled "Character in the Marketplace" (Hess, 1995a), and Tom Chappell, CEO of Tom's of Main and author of *The Soul of a Business* (1993).

Mutual Trust and Honesty with Others

A third basic attitude or practice that the authors have observed about spiritually based firms is that they value mutual trust and honesty. These firms are extremely up front with their employees, customers, and suppliers. They are careful to make it clear that honesty is not only the best policy, it is the *only* policy. A lot of firms profess to embrace these principles, but the spiritually based firms constantly reaffirm and emphasize the importance of these cornerstones.

One company that epitomizes an emphasis on honesty and integrity is Wetherill Associates (WAI). "We don't tell lies here, and everyone knows it. We are specific and honest about quality and suitability of the product for our customers' needs, even if we know they might not be able to detect any problems. People trust us and this works well for us on both sides of the business, the sales side and the supplier side." Honesty is also a key element in dealing with employees at WAI. "We believe we have demonstrated beyond a doubt, that when people function in an atmosphere of absolute honesty, they feel safe, they are happier, they suffer no stress. And as a result, they are more productive and have a positive effect on everybody they deal with" (Bothe, 1995).

One reported incident at Lancaster Laboratories illustrates that the firm's value statement incorporating mutual trust and honesty is a live document, not just something "gracing our literature file or boardroom walls." A client required that all employees working on a certain project be subject to drug and alcohol testing. When Lancaster prepared to comply, there was a release form for each employee to sign which included some legal "hold harmless" language. A group of employees came to the team leaders carrying the release in one hand and Lancaster's value statement in the other. It was agreed that the two were not consistent and the release form was modified (Hess, 1995). In fact, Earl Hess always wore a company name tag with a note that said "If I'm not living our values, challenge me" (Hess, 1995b).

Bill George, CEO of Medtronic, strongly emphasizes the importance of being honest and discussing all issues. His view is that "no problem is so difficult that we can't solve it if we talk about it. The big risk is that things are going on that we don't know about." Medtronic recently had to fire the head of one of their international companies because the manager was not honest about certain operations and then tried to cover up various activities. The actions did not violate the Foreign Corrupt Practices Act, but they set a climate of dishonesty. Such a strict policy of mutual trust and honesty becomes even more complicated when a company operates globally and the tendency is often to say that compromises are necessary to market successfully in some countries. Medtronic has a worldwide standard of ethics. In fact, George states that Medtronic decided to pull out of one country because the organization couldn't tolerate some of the practices there (*Business Ethics*, November/December, 1993).

Commitment to Quality and Service

Spiritually based firms put quality and service at the forefront while still being profitable and highly competitive. Wetherill Associates is forceful in emphasizing that there is an *ethical* basis for quality. They believe that when there is an overall organizational commitment to a value system that is "ethics affirming," then quality of product and effectiveness of service will follow. WAI's Quality Assurance Manual states that, "Quality Assurance is the end result of a series of right actions," and "behavioral problems are largely responsible for poor-quality service." In fact, the company's phenomenal growth in the face of industry stagnation is accounted for by the company's intense focus on customer service. As an employee stated, "We are not in competition with anybody. We just do what we have to do to serve the customer." WAI is looking for long-term results. "If we are out of something, for example, we'll tell them our competitor's part number. We try to help our customers out in any way we can" (Bothe, 1995).

Another example of putting service and quality ahead of profits would again be Medtronic. The mission at Medtronic is to "help people live fuller lives." Bill George, CEO, states that the business world is "still too much of a mind that our role is to maximize shareholder wealth. That cannot be a basis for a company's existence." In fact, Earl Bakken, the man who built Medtronic and is now over seventy years old, meets with every new Medtronic employee all over the world and tells the history and mission of the company and gives everyone a medallion incorporating a representation of the mission statement. He says, "Put it on your desk, and when you look at it when you are working, it will remind you that you are not here just to make money. But you're here to help people lead full lives." As George explains, "we do have to have profits and we reward our shareholders very well, but serving our customers comes first. If the employees feel they really have a worthwhile mission themselves and are a part of carrying out that mission, then the result is that the company makes a lot of money. However, if you do it the other way around with profits being the mission, you can't sustain it. The company loses its soul" (*Business Ethics*, November/December, 1993).

Another believer in putting service before profit is Wayne Schmidt of Schmidt Associates Architects, Inc. Schmidt believes that the "bottom line is there if people are working effectively with an attitude of serving others. That's the reward. Don't distract people with what the bottom line needs to be. Let them concentrate on serving others, doing their job well, being the best they can be, and allowing them to be successful. The bottom line's there." Schmidt states that Schmidt Associates focuses on customer service by becoming "the facilitator" for the customer's success. "We design a facility that's totally responsive to their need, not necessarily ours. So the first, most important thing we can do is serve the customer. That's servanthood. We allow their criteria to become our criteria" (Frick, 1995, p. 269).

Quality and service are also key components to the mission statement of Lancaster Laboratories. Earl Hess, former CEO of Lancaster, believes that it is significant that the mission was formulated to define not only "what we do, but how we are committed to doing it. The *how* part of the mission statement committed us to the provision of quality service with a client focus, to conduct ourselves ethically, in a spiritual way." To encourage and maintain a commitment to quality, all full-time employees at Lancaster receive total quality training and must have at least one quality goal in their annual professional development plans (Hess, 1995b).

Commitment to Employees

Spiritually based firms value their employees as individuals and are committed to the development of their employees, far beyond just their professional development. One of the keys to the servant-leadership philosophy is the question: "Do those served grow as persons? Do they, while being served, become healthier, wiser, freer, more autonomous, more likely themselves to become servants?" (Greenleaf, 1977, p. 14). Servant leadership teaches that human beings have a value in their own right. Max DePree, former CEO of Herman Miller, says, "I see authenticity as an inherent value or right, we're authentic before we get to the workplace," and must be treated accordingly when we arrive there. Greenleaf's view explains that the "business exists as much to provide meaningful work to the person as it exists to provide a product or service to the customer" (Kiechel, 1992).

A company's commitment to employees is often seen in their programs and value statements. One example would be Toro Company's "Pride in Excellence" program which was developed by the entire management group. This program is a credo of employee empowerment and is aimed at creating a culture based on mutual respect and the worth of each employee, or "owner" (the term used by Ken Melrose, CEO). The cornerstones of the program include teamwork and win-win partnerships, giving power away, and respect for one another (Osborne, 1995). Another example would be TDI Industries' Basic Values Statement that begins with "concern for and belief in individual human beings." TDI let their actions reflect their words in 1990 when it came time to lay off employees ("partners" in company parlance). One year after the layoffs, the company received the highest scores on its annual morale survey of employees since it began polling over a decade ago. These scores were evidence of the company's compassionate and caring approach to the downsizing (Kiechel, 1992).

Townsend and Bottum's (T&B) experience with downsizing also provides another example of a company's strong commitment to employees as individuals and an attempt to follow Greenleaf's servant-leadership principles. "We found using an outplacement specialist to be in the spirit of servant-leadership. During our downsizing, we established two ground rules. One was that each supervisor was responsible for finding another job for each of his or her people who had to be outplaced. The other was that if there was a choice of who should originally tell the employee the bad news, the one who finds it the most traumatic and heart-rending should do it. You can't fake compassion." Many of the outplaced workers stay in touch with the company. According to Bottum, "the bond between us is permanent and lasting and transcends the name on the paycheck. They want to come back when it's possible, and some already have" (Frick, 1995, p. 273).

Another way of showing commitment to employees is providing competitive wages and an attractive benefits package that includes family-friendly benefits. One corporate example would be Wetherill's generous compensation package that includes a lucrative bonus program based on year-end profitability, health benefits, and a matching 401K plan. Another firm exemplifying extraordinary commitment to employees would be Lancaster Laboratories. Lancaster started a child care program in 1986 and has since added an adult day-care center to serve employees with elderly or handicapped adult members. The two centers are physically linked and there is continuous intergenerational programming. Lancaster has also built a Family Center to provide various wellness and fitness facilities for all employees and their families (Hess, 1995b).

Selection of Personnel to Match the Corporation's Spiritually Based Philosophy

In spiritually based firms there is a pronounced emphasis on selecting persons who are most likely to be comfortable and productive in a spiritual corporate culture. Bill George, CEO of Medtronic, explains that Medtronic is very up-front with the corporation's purpose. "We're trying to create an environment for our employees so that they can find the fulfillment they are looking for in their lives through their work here and a congruence between the corporation's objectives and their objectives." Medtronic, like many spiritually based firms, believes in employee empowerment and has eliminated all special perks for executives. George believes their spiritually based philosophy helps them recruit a different kind of person. "If prospective executives do not buy into our policies, this isn't the place for them. I'm not trying to put that person down. If status is your thing, it's better to go to a place where status is more highly regarded than it is here" (*Business Ethics*, November/December, 1993).

Wayne Schmidt, principal of Schmidt Associates, Inc., an Indianapolis architectural/engineering firm, explains that potential staff go through several interviews. The first is to determine if they are technically competent. The second interview is to determine if they have an attitude for serving others. Every new staff member is required to read Robert Greenleaf's *Servant Leadership* (1977) and Stephen Covey's *The 7 Habits of Highly Effective People* (1989). New people are given a mentor who helps nurture the servant leadership attitude and they are also given a "sherpa." A sherpa is someone who has about two more years' experience than the new person and can help them understand what the organization is about and how things really work (Frick, 1995, pp. 266–267).

Carol Miller, Human Resource Manager for Lancaster Laboratories, stated that some ten years ago their organization learned to hire on the basis of what people can contribute to the whole organization, not just what people know technically. Earl Hess, founder of Lancaster Labs, says, "We always needed committed people, not just good chemists. People really like to work here so word gets around, and soon you are dealing with lots of applications from very good, committed people. Furthermore, the staff turnover at Lancaster is extremely low since people tend to stay" (Hess, 1995b).

At Wetherill Associates the hiring process is fairly extensive in order to hire people who can support their Right Action Ethic and withhold support of wrongdoing. The organization looks for those who fit in rather than those with higher skills and more experience. They look for sincerity and the right attitude. New employees have several formal opportunities to learn about the company's behavioral expectations including a one-hour session every week for nine weeks based on Mr. Wetherill's book, *Management Techniques for Foremen*, (1946). Employees who come to Wetherill from other companies "have to be deprogrammed because they seem to be driven to get an order. We don't pressure our people to get an order. We are specific and honest about quality and suitability of the product for our customers' needs" (Bothe, 1995). Wetherill employees are trained to take right action to the best of their ability, rather than to make profits or avoid losses.

Summary

Although we do not claim to have identified all the characteristics of spiritually based firms, we are certain that the concepts discussed in our paper are central and universal to the firms we examined. We also appreciate that there are other firms, not mentioned, that exemplify the characteristics we identified. Executive honesty with self, up-front articulation of the organization's operational philosophy, a pervasive commitment to mutual trust and honesty with others, commitment to quality and service, commitment to employees, and selection of personnel to match the corporation's operational philosophy are not radically new concepts. But what we observe is that the spiritually based firms we have examined exhibit three added dimensions to those basic concepts. First, they absolutely put their philosophy first. It is not an add-on, certainly not an afterthought. In fact, as in the extreme case of WAI, we have a group organized *around a philosophy*, which sought out a business to support them so they could stay together. It is the philosophy that is all-pervasive. Second, these organizations present a distinct aura of spirituality, often quite overtly acknowledged, that provides a dimension of life together that goes beyond successful business operations. Life enhancement is all-important. This peculiar infusion stands in need of much further investigation, but we have found that when one talks with representatives of these firms there is a "fourth-dimensional quality" that penetrates everything that goes on. And third, these firms have put it all together and have been steadfast in their clearly articulated beliefs. Some firms practice one or more of the key concepts discussed in this paper, and some firms do them very well. However, we must point out that frequently other firms do them in response to a crisis that has developed and they quickly change their philosophies as other perceived priorities move in to push them aside. Our fundamental conclusion, then, is that the six attitudes and practices cited in this paper are indeed foundational for the maintenance of a spiritually based corporate culture. Subsequent to this, there is perhaps the lesson that business leaders might want to first examine their *commitments* rather than their *competencies*, in order to experience a more fulfilling business career.

References

Bailey, R. (1998), "Taking God to Work," *Detroit Free Press*, October 2, 1998, pp. 1A and 9A.

Bothe, M. (1995), Personal interview between Marie E. Bothe and James Conley, August, 1995.

Bothwell, L. (1983), *The Art of Leadership*, Prentice-Hall, Englewood Cliffs.

Bottum, C. (1993), "Lo, I am with you always: Sequel to 'Within your Reach.'" Text of speech made by Mr. Bottum.

Bottum, C. (1995), Personal interview between Bill Bottum and Fraya Wagner-Marsh, August, 1995.

Branch, S. (1999), The 100 Best Companies to Work for in America," *Fortune*, January 11, 1999, pp. 118–144.

Brandt, E. (1996), "Corporate Pioneers Explore Spirituality," *HR Magazine*, April, pp. 82–87.

Business Ethics (1993), "Interview with Bill George: In Care of the Company Soul," November/December, pp. 17–19.

Business Ethics (1994), "Interview with Tom Chappell: Minister of Commerce," January/February, pp. 16–18.

Chappell, T. (1993), *The Soul of a Business*. Bantam: New York.

Covey, S. (1989), *The 7 Habits of Highly Effective People*. Simon & Schuster: New York.

Covey, S. (1994), "Center on Principles," *Executive Excellence*, February, pp. 3–4.

DePree, M. (1992), *Leadership Jazz*. Dell Publishing: New York.

Frick, D. (1995), "Pyramids, Circles, and Gardens: Stories of Implementing Servant-Leadership," in Larry C. Spears (Ed.), *Reflections on Leadership*, John Wiley & Sons, Inc., New York, pp. 257–281.

Greenleaf, R. (1977), *Servant Leadership: A Journey into the Nature of Legitimate Power and Greatness*, Paulist Press, New York.

Guillory, W. (1997), *The Living Organization—Spirituality in the Workplace*. Innovations International, Salt Lake City, Utah.

Hess, E. (1995a), "Character in the Marketplace," in Don E. Eberly (Ed.), *The Content of America's Character: Recovering Civic Virtue*, Madison Books, pp. 267–280.

Hess, E. (1995b), Personal interview between Earl Hess and James Conley, August, 1995.

Jeffries, E. (1998), "Work as a Calling," in Larry Spears (Ed.), *Insights of Leadership*, John Wiley & Sons, Inc.

Kiechel, W. (1992), "The Leader as Servant," *Fortune,* May 4, pp. 121–122.

Lee, C., and Zemke, R. (1993), "The Search for Spirit in the Workplace," *Training,* June, pp. 21–28.

Lowe, J. (1998), "Trust: The Invaluable Asset," in Larry Spears (Ed.), *Insights of Leadership*, John Wiley & Sons, Inc: New York.

Melrose, K. (1995), *Making the Grass Greener on Your Side: A CEO's Journal to Leading by Serving,* Berrett-Koehler Publishers, Inc.

Oldenburg, D. (1997), "The Spirit at Work," *Detroit News*, May 7, 1997, pp. 1E and 6E.

Osborne, R. (1995), "Company with a Soul." *IW*, May 1, pp. 21–26.

Spears, L. (1991), "Robert K. Greenleaf: Servant-leader," *Friends Journal*, August, pp. 20–21.

Toffler, A. (1980), *The Third Wave*. Morrow Publishing: New York.

Vaill, P. (1989), *Managing as a Performing Art*. Jossey-Bass: San Francisco, CA.

Wetherill, Richard W. (1946), "Management Techniques for Foremen: Questions and Answers for All Supervisors." New York: National Foreman's Institute.

LESSONS FROM OZ:

BALANCE AND WHOLENESS IN ORGANIZATIONS

Jerry Biberman,
University of Scranton

Michael Whitty,
University of Detroit-Mercy

Lee Robbins,
Golden Gate University

Introduction

Organizations worldwide have begun to show an increased interest in spirituality and spiritual values (e.g., Brandt, 1996; Galen, 1995; Labbs, 1995; Vicek, 1992). Consultants and business writers are urging organizations to pay more attention to spiritual values (e.g., Bolman and Deal, 1995; Gunn, 1992; Russell, 1989; Schechter, 1995; Scherer and Shook, 1993; Walker, 1989). Perhaps the most mainstream business title bringing the good news is Novak (1996). Novak, a leading conservative Catholic, suggests spirituality is vital to a fulfilling life in business. One scenario which we believe can be achieved shows a harmonic convergence between old values reaffirmed—work as a calling or duty—and an evolving consciousness which has stirred the soul in the modern workplace.

By contrast, authors such as Schaef (1987), Schaef and Fassel (1988), Kets deVries and Miller (1984), and Harvey (1977) described business organizations in the United States as "addictive," "neurotic," and "phrog farms." Tom Peters shifted from discussing "excellent" organizations (Peters and Waterman, 1982; Peters and Austin, 1985) to contending there are no excellent organizations after the leading corporations he previously had cited as being excellent rapidly deteriorated (Peters, 1987). Leading companies aggressively market

217

their wares while concealing evidence of severely damaged products (from silicone breast implants to asbestos to defective condoms). Global tsunamis in the financial markets leave devastated economies and the starving and unemployed in their wake. The United States subsidizes third world exports of the same tobacco products which bear government health warnings at home. Leaving "things as they are" risks an early end to healthy human enterprise.

While popular organizational consultants such as Stephen Covey (1989) urge inner/outer victory for individual managers in large systems, other leading business writers and leaders recommend a paradigm shift in basic organizational values. Both individual and systemic changes are needed for the future evolution of work on a spiritual plane. Stephen Covey makes great use of story telling in his trainings. In this essay we will take our inspirational lessons from *The Wizard of Oz* (Baum, 1899). On our journey through our work lives we must find ourselves and our true work. We believe there is a sacred dimension to our daily work.

Holistic thinking is a leading metaphor for an integral work culture. We believe that for organizations and individuals the key to spiritual change lies in transformation which must come from within. Using *The Wizard of Oz* as a metaphor, we explain how an organization can balance its intellect, emotionality, and sense of purpose; and we recommend steps organizations can take in each area to achieve this balance.

We then suggest the beginnings of a different organizational paradigm. Preconditions for transformational or paradigmatic shift have been described (Robbins, 1992; Robbins and Stevenson, 1988) as repeated experiences of frustration, hope, and the emergence of a new model. Continuing social, economic, and ecological disasters can be the repeated experiences of frustration which lead to reexamination of basic assumptions. Unlike the single sharp crisis which leads to stronger attempts to implement the same paradigm—"more of the same, harder" —such repetitious experiences provide the foundation for the fundamental reexaminations and massive shifts described in Kuhn's (1970) seminal study and in Gersick's (1991) examination of punctuated equilibrium. Hope is found in the human spirit and activated through such cultural stories as that of Oz. An alternative model, which we describe later, involves questioning the single-pointed pursuit of profit maximization—which requires reexamining organizational processes and values of higher education as well as those of corporations.

A Question of Balance

Every spiritual tradition emphasizes the importance of being in balance or balancing one's energies as a means for spiritual transformation. These energies are often described in terms of "masculine" (or assertive) and "feminine" (or receptive) energies. Examples include the familiar yin and yang symbols, and the (perhaps less familiar) description in Kaballah or Jewish symbolism of the three pillars or columns of masculine, feminine, and center or balanced pillar. This emphasis on balance has found its way into the popular culture through such media as the Karate Kid films (with Mr. Myagi's teaching of, and emphasis on, learning balance, not just in karate but in all of life) and the Star Wars trilogy (with the Jedi philosophy of the force), the various Star Trek television and film series (illustrating balancing emotion and intellect—as illustrated by the interplay of Mr. Spock and Dr. McCoy, and in Data's wanting to express human emotions), and in the music of the Moody Blues (including their "Question of Balance" album). In each case, the balance is of energies, and the balance occurs within each person, so each person has both masculine and feminine qualities within her or himself; the task is to balance these qualities within one's self. The balance and subsequent transformation must be initiated by and performed from within the person, though, paradoxically, this occurs in response to contact with external forces, ideas, or teachings. Organizations too must discover the inner power to balance their energies and to transform themselves into more humane systems.

On this "yellow brick road" to organizational transformation, we have all encountered many cultural, political, and even technological obstacles. Toxic stress, selfish competitiveness, and inequity in the name of profit have created an economic and organizational world out of balance (Shaef and Fassel, 1988). Large systems and organizational processes have been undermined through cultural pathologies, addiction, and shadow. Sadly, the currently dominant paradigm contains much of addiction and shadow.

Chappel (1993) has developed a practitioner's model for integrating values, beliefs, and business. This type of integration is what we mean by organizational balance. Biberman and Whitty (1997) catalog some of the ever-expanding literature on spirituality and organizations. It is also helpful to apply the principles of transpersonal psychology to organizational transformation and the possible future. Readers may wish to refer to Shaef (1987) and LaBier (1989). In addition to the trend in business philosophy, a similar trend is occurring in economics and public policy. This drive for integration, wholeness, and balance applies not only to organizations and systems undergoing constant change but also to global society seeking new paradigms for balanced change. The foremost thinker along these lines has been Korten (1996).

Sharing Visions and Experiences by Means of the Metaphor of *The Wizard of Oz*

Telling and retelling the story of *The Wizard of Oz* has allowed our Western/world culture to understand what it is to be a balanced and integrated person. Folk tales often feature insights or some form of morality story for individuals and national cultures. *The Wizard of Oz*, in the book by L. Frank Baum, the MGM movie, and later incarnations, has served this purpose for readers and viewers over the past hundred years. A search by the authors for articles and books using *The Wizard of Oz* theme and story has found books that use the story as a metaphor for personal spiritual growth (Stewart, 1997), for survival as a spiritual orphan (Kolbenschlag, 1988), and to convey the principles of managerial and organizational accountability (Conners, Smith, and Hickman, 1994). Schlesinger (1997) used the Oz fable as a metaphor for helping subordinates to work and learn under different types of bosses. In this article, we intend to expand the metaphor to describe spiritual transformation of organizations at the macro level. Our goal in utilizing the story of *The Wizard of Oz* is to encourage the reader to go beyond securing personal balance at work to explore the steps needed to contribute to organizational balance from the individual in the basic work unit to the macro organization and all its stakeholder environments.

The characters of the Oz story illustrate the strengths and challenges we all face, individually and collectively. We intend to show the necessary choices required to humanize organizations by commenting on the story and major characters of the Oz story.

The Story

In this article, we refer mainly to the story and characters depicted in the MGM movie. The story begins in Kansas, where Dorothy yearns to leave her farm home and all of her perceived problems to go far, far away, "somewhere over the rainbow." A tornado sends Dorothy and her dog Toto to the land of Oz, where her house kills a wicked witch and she inherits the witch's ruby slippers. Dorothy meets the munchkins, the wicked witch's more wicked sister, and Glinda, the good witch of the story. No sooner does Dorothy get to Oz than she wants to return to her home in Kansas. She is told the Wizard of Oz can help her: the way to get to the Wizard is to follow the Yellow Brick Road. Along the road, Dorothy and Toto encounter the Scarecrow, Tin Woodsman, and Cowardly Lion. The characters then overcome a series of crises culminating in the killing of the Wicked Witch, the realization the Wizard is a fraud ("humbug"), and a further realization that each character has indeed demonstrated the quality each believed her or himself to be lacking. Finally, Dorothy learns she has always had the power to return home, but had to realize it for herself. We will examine Dorothy and each of the other characters, and their organizational counterparts, in more detail in the next section. In this section, we explore possible interpretations of the story.

On the simplest level, the story can be viewed as an exciting and humorous children's adventure tale, with the moralistic conclusion that "there's no place like home." On the psychological level, the story could be interpreted as a coming-of-age story for Dorothy and her companions or a series of initiation trials to be completed before Dorothy could return home. The story could be further seen as the importance of using all of your abilities (represented by each of the characters Dorothy encounters). Jesse Stewart (1997) described how the story serves a metaphor for balancing energies and reclaiming of personal power, resulting in personal spiritual growth and transformation.

The Unbalanced Value System of the Modern World

The Oz story offers an allegory of the interconnectedness of all things—humankind and the natural world. The human condition stands as a witness and mirror to the natural world. Humankind and its inventions including human organizations are part of the natural world. Organizations and human society are part of the transformational process in much the same manner as individuals. When the Oz characters are out of balance, nature reflects this crisis. Without the tornado, Dorothy would not have learned her lessons. Chaos and crisis are part of all life. Everyone and everything is our teacher. For example, the cowardly lion seems to represent aspects of our self-doubt or low self-esteem. Yet, each of us and our human creations, such as complex organizations, has the potential for empowerment, confidence, and high self-esteem. Organizations—and the researchers who study them and the academics who teach about them—can create a work culture supporting these potentials. Even the animal kingdom has an important role to play in saving the corporate planet through the cultural myth containing animal helpers, guides, and archetypes. Witness the supportive role of Toto and the messages from nature and the spirit kingdoms in the Oz story.

The story could also be looked at as a metaphor for the struggles of modern life and work. On that level, the Good Witch/Bad Witch could be seen to represent the two faces of twentieth century organizational life—on the one hand, bringing the grace of wealth/growth/technology, etc., but often at the expense of humanity, soul, and nature. Work and work structures have brought both light and darkness to humanity.

With the creed of greed threatening both ecology and human justice, it seems humankind has resigned itself to worship the false god of conflict and destruction. Spirituality seems so unscientific. The bad witch seems to have the upper hand. As Shaef and Fassel (1988) demonstrate, organizational pathology dominates office politics. The Wizard is in charge. He (and we mean He) rules via mass media. All the initial coping methods produced rigid rules, paternalism, bureaucracy, and crisis management. These methods, initially useful in creating the economic development of the earlier industrial revolution and checking the earlier liabilities of feudalism and mercantilism, achieved much of their ends. These same methods in a wired world allow heightened control of the munchkins and the other inhabitants of Oz both at work and in politics. Their excesses can lead to a world out of balance.

As crisis mounted, Dorothy and her allies from all walks of life discovered personal transformation led surprisingly to the transformation of organizations and whole systems such as the land of Oz. Perhaps the metaphor of Oz can apply to any system or imposed structure. All reactive management is like the politics of the Wizard. Change steps were needed. Let's examine each of the characters of the story in more detail, and explore counterparts and implications for the organization.

The Characters in "Oz" and What They Symbolize

Scarecrow. The Scarecrow represents intellect. The Scarecrow, who has no brains, is the problem solver of the story. On the organizational level, an organization that is not using its head does not plan. It usually operates using crisis management. An organization that makes full use of its brainpower uses a balance of rational (left hemisphere) and intuitive (right hemisphere) thinking and problem solving, uses strategic planning, and often finds creative solutions to problems. Change steps to develop this capacity include providing challenges, brainstorming and other creativity techniques, encouraging decision-making opportunities, and group problem-solving sessions including training in statistical process control tools, strategic planning, and team skills. A smart organization thinks with heart and head.

Tin Woodsman. The Tin Woodsman represents emotions. The Tin Woodsman, who has no heart, is the most emotional character in the story. On the organizational level, an organization that is not using its heart runs on bureaucracy, paternalism, and rigid rules, operating as if its mission were purely defined by objectively measured profit maximization. An organization that uses its heart encourages emotionality with celebrations and reward ceremonies. It encourages change by providing challenges, rewards, and recognition, and uses story telling, envisioning, revisiting its mission, and service projects, while providing positive reinforcement and training in communication and conflict management. The organization must discover its soul. It seeks to discover broader values externally by serving the larger economic and community systems with which it is interdependent, and internally by responding to the needs of its own employees. Soulful leadership is needed for this breakthrough in corporate culture.

Cowardly Lion. The Cowardly Lion represents the will to act. The Cowardly Lion, who has no courage, overcomes his fears to demonstrate great courage in the story. On the organizational level, an organization that has no courage is afraid to take risks, is compliant, and manages by reacting. Argyris and Schön (1976, 1978, 1993) and Senge (1990, 1994) demonstrated that organizational learning requires accepting error as an opportunity to learn, challenging assumptions of the existing paradigm, and acting with a belief in organizational robustness. All of these require courage. An organization that demonstrates courage takes risks, is proactive, and is socially conscious. It encourages change by providing challenging assignments and projects while providing training in survival training, ethics, and social justice.

The Wizard, the two wicked witches, and Glinda each represent an outside agent or external force to which the characters in the story initially attribute the ability to create change, i.e., the ability to exert power over them. The power which is attributed to each of them produces a sense of fear and results in compliance by the inhabitants of Oz. As Connors, Smith, and Hickman (1994) point out, this combination of blame and attribution of power to the Wizard and the witches serves to disempower the other characters in the story, and allows the inhabitants to act as victims who elude accountability. Each of these characters has counterparts in business firms. The balance of rights and responsibility requires vigilance and heightened self-awareness. Trust, integrity, courage, and compassion bring much needed balance to organizational power and politics.

The Wizard. The Wizard represents power in the organization. At the beginning of the story, this power is attributed to a specific magical person, but by its end, the Wizard is revealed to be a "humbug" or fraud, and the power and accountability are reclaimed by Dorothy and her companions. Similarly, on the organizational level, an organization that attributes power to a single charismatic leader disempowers itself in the long run. An organization that reclaims its power and accountability empowers all its internal resources, trusts its processes, and uses empowering techniques such as envisioning and process consultation. It encourages change by providing experiences and opportunities for spiritual growth, while providing training in self-awareness, community building, creativity, meditation, even the cultivation of basic virtues such as discernment. This will help bring life to work in its full human potential.

The Witches. The witches represent the opposing forces or energies of power that operate in the story, in each of us, and in organizations. At the beginning of the story, these forces or energies are, again, externalized and split, and are attributed to a "good" witch (Glinda) and to two "bad or wicked" witches. By the end of the story, Dorothy and her companions, through their shared experiences in overcoming the challenges they encounter, have reclaimed and balanced these energies within themselves. It is by reclaiming these energies that Dorothy realizes how to use her power and return home. On an individual psychological level, killing the wicked witch represents the psychological work of reclaiming one's "shadow," as Carl Jung called it, or accepting and integrating one's "dark side," or, as John Pierrakos (1987) refers to it, reconnecting one's lower human emotions (like anger and rage) with one's higher or spiritual self. A recurring theme of science fiction and myth is that we need both our so-called good and evil natures in order to be complete persons, and how, indeed, our darker, angrier side often contributes decisively to leadership and action. On the organizational level, such an energy split is manifested in the kinds of organizational defenses and pathology described by Schaef and Fassel (1988) or by Kets de Vries and Miller (1984). An organization can encourage the balancing of its energies by exorcizing its pathologies, while providing training in conflict management and incorporating the self-help philosophy of the various twelve-step programs (Robbins, 1992; Robbins & Stevenson, 1998).

Dorothy. Dorothy symbolizes all the various energies and forces of the story. She reclaims her personal balance and power, resulting in her spiritual transformation. The Oz characters, Dorothy and her friends, achieved inner victory over their darker sides as well as outer victory in attaining their goals. While the changes come from within, it is their integration of their experiences along the path that allows these changes to occur. Organizations need to balance recognition of their inner strengths with responsiveness both to ideas and to shifts in their environments. An organization that undergoes a spiritual transformation will exhibit the characteristics described at the beginning of this article. It will empower all of its members and celebrate their diversity. Its members will feel that they are in balance with their natures and are "home."

Conclusion

We hope our use of the Oz metaphor puts a human face on organizational theory. Institutions need to practice self-analysis ["inventory"] just as people do. Evolving organizations need to develop closer relationships with their feelings, culture, intentions, and mission. Learning organizations must take the initiative to evolve toward their highest and most creative possibilities. The recovering organizations at the turn of the century are overcoming much of this pathology in work, inch by inch, day by day. Hopefully, our story telling with the Oz metaphor gives encouragement to courageous leaders from all walks of life to face their witches and confront their wizards and contribute to the spiritual future of work.

L. Frank Baum, the author of *The Wizard of Oz*, was a forerunner of transpersonal psychology in his story telling of trusting the basic goodness of our earthly destinies. He saw humankind weaving back and forth between the wizard and the witch. Our human organizations, which reflect our consciousness in evolution, must contain a balance between masculine and feminine, the light and dark, levity and gravity

—all with the final aim of partnership in creation. For the organizational psychologist or cultural anthropologist, the non-integrated soul of the modern organization is represented by the Scarecrow, the Tin Man, and the Lion. The combination of these outside "higher powers" and the higher self resulted in positive evolution to solutions on the yellow brick road. The oncoming organizational myth makers, heroes, and heroines will be those who balance the dualities of work life with the organic destiny of the human enterprise. We believe the unfolding of a servant heart within future business leaders will produce the organizational consciousness necessary for a breakthrough to a new business paradigm. How might they apply these perceptions to the modern business firm? Moving along the path from organizational addiction to organizational transformation and developing work processes where people matter is a spiritual journey. In this journey the firm comes to recognize not just its particular mission but a broader mission of serving humanity, ourselves. Thus, this new work paradigm is one of balance, which likely will require deviations from the "lower" objective of profit maximization.

Without spirituality the normative goal of business is profit, an objective which has shown demonstrable effectiveness in increasing industrial output. In this paradigm income distribution is only a side effect, wagged by the output maximization goal. While the lack of attention to distribution is recognized (e.g., regulations to deal with the internal and external diseconomies and moral hazard), such adjustments fail to fully correct specific effects and deal weakly with the perception of profit as the proper legitimate goal. The impact of such a one-pointed goal, which readily comes to be seen as the goal rather than just a means to an end, expands. Concepts and behaviors based on the goal of profit maximization become embedded in organizational cultures and in the measures used in academic research to evaluate management techniques.

From the multiple goals advanced for spirituality, an increase in variety seems requisite just as Dorothy found multiple characteristics necessary in her journey home. Multiple criteria, rather than the single criterion of profit or profit's cousins, growth, and market share, are required. Spiritual alternatives mean widening the focus of business objectives including recognizing different and potentially conflicting criteria for, on the one hand, production, and, on the other, distribution. A set of more extensive normative criteria helpful for widening our concepts of the purpose of business can be found in the schema of

Russell Ackoff (1981). Maintaining that we are a species in search of ideals, he contends we have developed five recognizable foci (with each corresponding body of theory and academic disciplines in parentheses) as follows: Truth (Science), Beauty (Aesthetics), The Good (Ethics, Philosophy), Plenty (Economics), and Justice (Law). The ideals are the governing variables, the indicators of success, of the associated disciplines. Management is not included in Ackoff's list of disciplines; the prevailing paradigm we have discussed seems to imply that the purpose of business, its ideal, is simply Plenty, the domain of economics. Profit becomes a constraint, a necessary condition to achieve multiple objectives, rather than a single varied objective to be maximized. Even with multiple criteria, the problem of balance remains. Focusing on any of these ideals without attending to the others produces a bad result. Only Good and Justice (distribution) produces the problems of socialism with a potential for equity, but, as recently seen, too little to distribute, and the sterility of "socialist realist art." Only Truth produces science, but not necessarily sufficiency or ethics or fairness. Only Beauty produces neither food nor social concerns nor a search for truth—including medical progress. And only Plenty (abundance) produces an ugly, unjust society with little attention to truth or compassion.

Robbins (1992) suggests how a balanced firm might look with semi-autonomous units of limited size, minimal coercive pressures, recognition of error as a source of learning, and other characteristics. The Brazilian firm, Semco, which fits many of these characteristics, went from near financial disaster in 1980 to a position as Brazil's largest food-process machinery manufacturer and one of Brazil's fastest-growing companies in 1988, and, despite recent difficulties in Brazil, continues to thrive (Semler, 1989, 1995). Spirituality seems based more on questions than on proscriptive answers—the search for meaning in the ordinary business of life. Without spirituality the normative purpose of business is profit. If we choose to develop more spiritual organizations, we must use multiple criteria such as those suggested in Ackoff's model and develop organizational designs which support such criteria. This new paradigm contains many of the features of the Oz story in which all the characters have an awakening.

Both individuals and organizations work best with awakening, joy, meaning, and commitment in the work process. Richards (1995) calls this a centered organization—one which will produce environments where commitment is the norm, where people strive to be perceptive, receptive, and expressive and where people are involved in work that is congruent with the requirements of their own spirits and souls. Dorothy and her friends learned we are born with this potential if we only can wake up to its reality in our lives.

As the post-modern organization struggles to turn chaos into creativity, it is coming to grips with the necessity of integrating its soul and spirit. Dorothy and the dynamics of spirit may herald the coming of a new work community. A basic workplace spirituality can be the common ground for the new work community. Working people and human evolution itself are constantly seeking meaning, purpose, and a sense of contribution to work life. Reframing the meaning of work has the support of the servant leaders worldwide, who see that a life of service best fits the basic human need for relevance, recognition, meaning, and self-transcendence. Jesse Stewart (1997) is convinced that our human culture has the map for the modern spiritual journey. This journey runs through all of life at every level. In an age of economics where corporations rule the world, this journey has a most important passage through the world of work. From this universal folk tale and modern morality play, maybe we may some day reinvent work and transform human organizations in a way that will make the world more humane. We believe the experiences of the Scarecrow, Tin Woodsman, and Cowardly Lion, along with Dorothy and Toto, represent the challenge to everyone on this planet. We have the ability not only to heal ourselves but also the organizations within which we work.

We all have the opportunity to be servant leaders of the next breakthrough of human organizational evolution. There is a certain urgency for humanity to develop the consciousness needed to meet the new and diverse challenges arising on the planet. As they neared the Emerald City, Dorothy and her "fellow travelers" said to each other, "Well come on then. What are you waiting for?" "Hurry! Hurry!" "You can't rest now—we're nearly there" (Stewart, 1997, p. 174).

References

Ackoff, R. (1981), *Creating the Corporate Future*, John Wiley & Sons, New York.

Argyris, C. (1993), *Knowledge for Action: A Guide to Overcoming Barriers to Organizational Change*, Jossey-Bass, San Francisco.

Argyris, C., and Schön, D. (1976), *Theory in Practice: Increasing Professional Effectiveness,* Jossey-Bass, San Francisco.

Argyris, C., and Schön, D. (1978), *Organizational Learning: A Theory of Action Perspective*, Addison Wesley, Reading, MA.

Baum, L. (1899), *The Wizard of Oz*, Random House, New York.

Biberman, J., and Whitty, M. (1997), "A postmodern spiritual future for work," *Journal of Organizational Change Management 10 (2)*, pp. 130–188.

Bolman, L., and Deal, T. (1995), *Leading with Soul: An Uncommon Journey of Spirit*, Jossey-Bass, San Francisco, CA.

Brandt, E. (1996), "Corporate Pioneers Explore Spirituality: Peace," *HR Magazine*, Vol. 41, No. 4, April, p. 827.

Brisken, A. (1996), *The Stirring of Soul in the Workplace*, Jossey-Bass Publishers, San Francisco, CA.

Canfield, J., and Hansen, V. (1996), *Chicken Soup for the Soul At Work: 101 Stories of Courage, Compassion and Creativity in the Workplace*, Health Communications, Deerfield Beach, FL.

Chappel, T. (1993), *The Soul of a Business: Managing for Profit and the Common Good*, Bantam, New York.

Connors, R., Smith, and Hickman (1994), *The Oz Principle: Getting Results Through Individual and Organizational Accountability*, Prentice Hall, Englewood Cliffs, NJ.

Covey, S. (1989), *The Seven Habits of Highly Effective People*, Simon and Schuster, New York.

Fisher, R., and Ury, W. (1981), *Getting to YES: Negotiating Agreements Without Giving In*, Houghton Mifflin, Boston.

Galen, M. (1995), "Companies Hit the Road Less Traveled," *Business Week*, No. 3247, 5 June, p. 824.

Gersick, C. (1991), "Revolutionary Change Theories: A Multilevel Exploration of the Punctuated Equilibrium Model," *Academy of Management Review*, Jan. 1991.

Glanz, B. (1996), *Care Packages for the Workplace: Little Things You Can do to Regenerate Spirit at Work*, McGraw Hill, New York.

Gunn, B. (1992), "Computeruism: Ideology with a Sustainable Future," *Futures*, Vol. 24, No. 6, July/August, pp. 559–575.

Harvey, J. (1977), "Organizations as Phrog Farms," *Organizational Dynamics*, Spring 1977, American Management Association, New York.

Heerman and Barry (1997), *Building Team Spirit: Activities for Inspiring and Energizing Teams*, McGraw Hill.

Kets de Vries, F. R., and Miller, D. (1984), *The Neurotic Organization*, Jossey-Bass, San Francisco, CA.

230 WORK AND SPIRIT

Kolbenschlag (1988), *Lost in the Land of Oz: Befriending Your Inner Orphan,* Crossroads, New York.

Korten, D. (1996), *When Corporations Rule the World,* Berrett Koehler, San Francisco, CA.

Kuhn, T.(1970), *The Structure of Scientific Revolutions,* University of Chicago Press, Chicago, IL.

Labbs, J. J. (1995), "Balancing Spirituality and Work," *Personnel Journal,* Vol. 74, No. 9, September, pp. 60–76.

LaBier, D. (1989), *Modern Madness: The Hidden Link Between Work and Emotion,* Addison Wesley, Reading, MA.

Novak, M.(1996), Business as a Calling: Work and the Examined Life, *The Free Press,* New York.

Peters, T. (1987), *Report Card on American Competitiveness: Are There Any Excellent Companies?",* Tom Peters Group, Palo Alto, CA.

Peters, T., and Austin, A. (1982), *A Passion for Excellence,* Warner Books, New York.

Peters, T., and Waterman, R. (1982), *In Search of Excellence,* Harper and Row, New York.

Pierrakos, J. C. (1987), *Core Energetics: Developing the Capacity to Love and Heal,* Life Rhythms, Mendicino, CA.

Richards, D. (1995), *Artful Work,* Berkeley Books, Berkeley, CA.

Robbins, L. (1992), "Designing More Functional Organizations: The 12 Step Model," *Journal of Organizational Change Management,* 1992, Vol. 5., No. 4.

Robbins, L., and Stevenson, W. (1998), "Counter-Intuitive Approaches to Leadership: Implications of 12-Step Methodologies for Leadership Education," *Journal of Management Systems,* Vol. 10, #2, p. 27–42.

Russell, P. (1989), "The Redemption of the Executive," *Leadership and Organization Development Journal,* Vol. 10, No. 3, pp. i–iv.

Schaef, A. W. (1987), *When Society Becomes an Addict,* Harper & Row, San Francisco, CA.

Schaef, A. W., and Fassel, D. (1988), *The Addictive Organization,* Harper & Row, San Francisco, CA.

Schechter, H. (1995), *Rekindling the Spirit at Work,* Barrytown, Ltd., Barrytown, NY.

Scherer, J., and Shook, L. (1993), *Work and the Human Spirit,* John Scherer Associates, Spokane, WA.

Schlesinger, Les (1997), "It Doesn't Take a Wizard to Build a Better

Boss," *Handbook of the Business Revolution Fast Company*, Boulder, CO, p. 20–25.

Semler, R. (1989), "Managing Without Managers," *Harvard Business Review*, September–October 1989, p.76–84.

Semler, R. (1995), *Maverick*, Warner Books, New York.

Senge, P. (1990), *The Fifth Discipline: The Art and Practice of the Learning Organization*, Currency/Doubleday, NY.

Senge, P., et. al. (1994), *The Fifth Discipline Fieldbook*, Doubleday, New York.

Stewart, J. (1997), *Secrets of the Yellow Brick Road,* Sunshine Press Publications, Hygiene, CO.

Vicek, D. J. (1992), "The Domino Effect," *Small Business Reports*, Vol. 17, No. 9, Winter, pp. 21–25.

Walker, R. G. (1989), "The Imperative of Leaders to Create Leader," *Directors and Boards*, Vol. 13, No. 2, Winter, pp. 21–25.

MAINTAINING AN ORGANIZATIONAL SPIRITUALITY:

NO EASY TASK

Gregory N. P. Konz, S.J.,
Francis X. Ryan, S.J.,
John Carroll University

Introduction

"Something spiritual is creeping into the workplace, and it seems to be gearing up to be more than a trend" (Laabs, 1995: 60). Spirituality in general and in the workplace in particular has become an important topic in recent years, reaching even the front page of the *Wall Street Journal* (Miller, 1998). Spirituality in the workplace is more than a passing fancy (Brandt, 1996). The nature of work appears to have changed fundamentally. Work has ceased to be an endeavor totally removed from personal development. Work has been transformed into the forum in which individuals develop themselves. People are searching for meaning in work that transcends mere economic exchanges between isolated, autonomous individuals. People are searching for a way to connect their work lives with their spiritual lives, to work together in community, to be unified in a vision and purpose that goes far beyond making money (Miller, 1998).

As the nature of work has changed, so has the relationship between managers and their subordinates. Managers, at one time, were seen as order givers whose role had no influence on the personal development of their subordinates. Managers now are seen as guides who help create meaning and purpose for their subordinates (Leigh, 1997). Organizational forces also drive this transformation of the manager's role. As Thomas McKenna (1997) points out, it is possible and beneficial to combine spirituality and business. Spirituality grounds people in their work and allows them to connect with the transcendent in all they do.

The shift in the nature of work is leading to a shift in the nature of organizations. Spirituality has traditionally been an individual concern, and the same would be said about spirituality in business (Neal, 1997). People as individuals found meaning in their work. As the concern for finding meaning in work became greater, managers moved into the role as aids to the search for meaning in the workplace. Managers, especially top managers, also brought their spirituality into the workings of the organization. Organizations are slowly evolving from arenas of purely economic and social activity into places of spiritual development.

No transformation is easy, especially one as significant as the role shift from manager to spiritual guide. The purpose of this study is to explore the difficulties that may be encountered by leaders and their organizations as they make this transition. We begin by reviewing the spirituality in business literature to briefly trace the transition from spirituality as an individual journey of discovery to an endeavor in which organizational leaders are called to play a significant role as guides. A brief review of the organizational culture literature will highlight the difficulties organizations and their leaders may encounter as they attempt to create organizations with distinctive spiritualities (McGee, 1998). The mission statements of the 28 Jesuit universities in the United States then will be used to demonstrate how difficult it is to develop and maintain organizations with distinctive spiritualities. We finish with a discussion of our findings.

Spirituality in Business

No agreed upon definition of spirituality in business exists (Kahn-weiler & Otte, 1997; McGee, 1998). As Jennifer Laabs (1995) points out, it is much easier to explain what spirituality in business is not than it is to define what spirituality in business is. Such difficulty is not surprising given the intensely personal nature of spiritual experience. Spiritual experiences, however they may be defined, take place at a much deeper level than do our "normal" experiences. The experience is no less real to the individual, yet it is very difficult to objectify or explain to others. It is even more difficult to enunciate the experience when it pertains to the workplace (McGee, 1998). Much of the writing on spirituality in business has focused on describing spiritual experiences in the workplace and the effects these experiences have had on people (see Neal, 1997, and McGee, 1998, for a complete review).

John Barnett (1985), for example, proposed a model of personal growth that attempts to integrate workplace experience with spiritual experience. Barnett sees an individual's business career as a path of spiritual growth. The model is based on two life concepts. The first comes from the Hindu tradition in which the householder establishes a foundation for spiritual growth by providing for the physical welfare of her dependents. The second life concept is based on the Native American Medicine Wheel in which an individual engages in self-discovery as he moves from a state of innocence to a state of enlightenment. A career becomes more than a series of steps to be climbed. A career becomes a path to personal enlightenment leading through the mastery of material skills to spiritual growth and self-knowledge.

Organizations have not gone unchanged by this fundamental shift in the way careers and the workplace are viewed. Organizations that provide their employees opportunities for the spiritual development perform better than those that do not provide these opportunities. Christopher Neck and John Milliman (1994) found that spirituality positively affects organizational performance. Other researchers also report increases in creativity, satisfaction, team performance, and organizational commitment in organizations that attempt to promote the spiritual development of their members (Leigh, 1997; Mirvis, 1997; Brandt, 1996; McCormick, 1994). At the same time, leaders are more willing to use their personal spiritual values to make business decisions. The leaders' values become the standard against which all organizational activities are measured (Conger et al., 1994; Whyte, 1994; Chappell, 1993).

As the expectations individuals have about the workplace have changed, so have their expectations of their leaders. Leaders must do more than bring their personal spiritual beliefs to their decisions and actions. Leaders are being called to facilitate the spiritual development of their followers (Dehler & Welsh, 1994). Individuals are expecting organizations designed to promote their search for meaning or transcendence.

Organizational Culture

This change in expectations puts managers and organizations in a difficult position. Being a spiritual guide is not part of any manager's training. Managers traditionally are trained in four functions: planning, organizing, leading, and controlling. They are selected, promoted, and rewarded according to their ability to perform these four functions according to the needs of their organizations. Being a spiritual guide is a responsibility for which managers are totally unprepared. How managers should be prepared is beyond the scope of this study. How organizations would evaluate managers as spiritual guides is also beyond the scope of this study.

A third difficulty presented to managers and organizations by this change in worker expectations is within the scope of this study. In recent years, having a spiritual guide has become increasingly popular (Miller, 1998). Because spiritual development traditionally has been an intensely personal journey, individuals have chosen guides who match their personal spirituality. The difficulty faced by managers is the diversity of spiritual traditions and spiritual experiences individuals bringing to the workplace (McCormick, 1994).

Trying to recruit and develop organizational leaders who can serve as spiritual guides is impossible if the individuals, and the managers, bring a variety of spiritual traditions and experiences to the organization. The only practical way organizations can meet the challenge of having managers who can serve as spiritual guides to employees is to allow managers and employees to self-select which organizations they wish to join. The spirituality of the organization would become one of the criteria by which potential employees choose the organization they wish to join. This would require organizations to develop specific spiritualities. A potential employee would be able to determine the spirituality of an organization the same way a potential employee now can determine the culture and values of an organization.

For the purpose of this study, spirituality is defined as the particular way the human person in all its richness, the relationship of the human person to the transcendent, the relationship between human persons, and the way to achieve personal growth are envisioned. For an organization to have a spirituality, the spirituality must be enunciated; it must be presented in terms that can be readily understood by all organizational members. Individuals must know what behaviors and beliefs are congruent with the spirituality of the organization. The organization's spirituality would be the foundation of the culture (cf. Schein, 1985; Trice & Beyer, 1993; Allinson, 1998, for the role of values in organizational culture).

Visualizing organizations that embody particular spiritualities is relatively easy (Delbecq, 1998; Kane, 1998; Silvers, 1998; White, 1998). Translating these visions into concrete organizations is difficult.

Completely changing the culture of an organization is very difficult (Frost et al., 1985). Cultural change means much more than changing the surface representations of the cultural. Changing the culture of an organization requires changing the basic assumptions, values, and norms held in common by all the members of the organization. These deep structures are highly resistant to change (Konz & Katz, 1996). Leaders attempting to develop an organizational spirituality would face the same difficulty. The varied spiritualities of the organization's members would form a deep structure that must be changed. Given the intensely personal nature of spirituality, it is reasonable to assume people would resist strongly any attempt to change their spirituality.

Maintaining the culture of an organization is also difficult. The deep structures already in place do make it easier to maintain a culture than to change it. Having deep structures in place, though, does not guarantee that an organization's culture cannot change (Konz & Katz, 1996). The same holds true for an organization's spirituality. It is easier to maintain the established spirituality of an organization than it is to change an organization's spirituality. At the same time, it is not easy to maintain an organization's spirituality.

As stated earlier, the key to maintaining an organizational culture is the philosophy and values of the organization's leaders. The leaders' values determine their focus, their decision making, and their actions. In their role as leaders, they concretize their values in the culture of their organizations. The same could be said of an organization's spirituality. The spirituality of the leaders is the key to maintaining the organization's spirituality. The leaders' spirituality should guide what they do, so through their actions, they bring their spirituality to life.

The leaders' spirituality also influences the selection of employees. An important part of managing an organization's culture is attracting and choosing those individuals who share the same values as the organization (Trice & Beyer, 1993). Studies have shown consistently that individuals who join organizations that share their values are more likely to remain with the organization, be more satisfied with their employment, and be more productive. These employees also are more easily socialized into the specific organizational culture (Riordan et al., 1997; Kraimer, 1997). The same should hold for organizational spirituality. Individuals will tend to self-select those organizations that have spiritualities matching their personal spirituality. At the same time, the organization would seek out those individuals whose spiritualities match the organization's spirituality.

Finally, the spirituality of the organization's leaders maintains the spirituality of the organization through its influence on the socialization of new employees. Socialization can be seen as a mutual proactive learning process. Individuals joining the organization are seeking information about the organization's philosophy and values. At the same time, the organization is seeking information about the philosophy and values of the new member (Reichers, 1987). The demonstrated values of the organization leaders are a prime source of information for new employees (Holton, 1996). The spirituality of the organization's leaders, as enunciated and as lived, determines the organization's spirituality, the spirituality into which the new employee is socialized.

The mission statement of an organization is an important source of information on the values of the leaders of an organization (Riordan et al., 1997; Kets de Vries et al., 1994). In the mission statement, the organization's top managers enunciate their vision for the organization. The mission statement details the philosophy and values of the organization. The statement also explains the goals of the organization, as well as the acceptable means of achieving these goals. Philosophy, values, goals, and means are spelled out in language understood by the members of the organization. All members of the organization should readily understand terms with organization-specific meanings. In short, the mission statement represents the enunciated culture of the organization. For an organization with a spirituality, the mission statement would be the enunciated spirituality of the organization.

The mission statement can serve as the enunciated culture of an organization because all members of the organization have agreed upon the meaning of the terms or ideas used in the statement (Riordan et al., 1997; Kets de Vries et al., 1994). The same would hold true for an organization with a spirituality. All members of the organization would need to agree upon the terms or ideas used in the statement. Confusion over the terms or ideas would point to confusion in the spirituality of the organization. A method for studying how well an organization had maintained its spirituality would be to examine its mission statement. If it uses terms that are not understood by the members of the organization, then the organization is having difficulty in maintaining its spirituality.

Jesuit Universities

A difficulty in studying how well an organization can maintain its spirituality is finding organizations that have an enunciated spirituality. Jesuit universities in the United States form a group of organizations with an enunciated spirituality. Jesuit universities have a the particular way of envisioning the human person in all its richness, the relationship of the human person to the transcendent, the relationship between human persons and the way to achieve personal growth (O'Malley, 1993). This spirituality should be presented in terms that can be readily understood by all organizational members. Individuals joining Jesuit universities should know what behaviors and beliefs are congruent with the spirituality of the organization. The spirituality of the Jesuit universities should be the foundation of their organizational culture. An examination of the mission statements of the 28 Jesuit universities in the United States should reveal if the universities have been able to maintain their spirituality successfully.

The 28 Jesuit colleges and universities in the United States operate with different corporate frameworks, with a variety of organizational relationships to the Society of Jesus, the Jesuits. In most, the by-laws demand a president who is a Jesuit; many of the universities mandate that a certain number or percentage of their trustees belong to the Society; in some, the ultimate corporate authority with power to refuse the election of trustees resides with a group of Jesuits. All work closely with the Jesuit regional superiors, provincials, and the superior general of the Society in Rome.

The Jesuits, as what might be usefully termed the sponsoring body of these universities, possess an ancient, lively, and articulated spirituality. One ascetical path among many in the Catholic Church, the Jesuit vision of the Divine and the world is of no recent origin. The Society, dating from an informal group of students in Paris in 1534, takes its own vision from a program of thirty days of silent contemplation and mediation called the Spiritual Exercises (Loyola, 1997). All Jesuits undertake the Exercises at least twice, at the beginning of their religious career and before final approval as members of the Society. In addition, members of the order make an abbreviated retreat each year with the structure of the Exercises adapted to the brevity of the period. These Exercises provide the font of an articulated and clearly annunciated spirituality, a particular way to be open to the communication of the transcendent.

This spirituality is often called "Ignatian" after Ignatius of Loyola, who was the founder of the order and who distilled the Exercises from his personal spiritual journey. In full form, the Exercises require thirty days with five or six hour-long periods of prescribed prayer each day. They have been adapted in many forms (eight days, three days, or even a year-long "retreat" made during everyday life) for the convenience of those unable to make such an ambitious time commitment, but who are eager to follow the Jesuit spiritual path. Many employees of Jesuit universities have undergone one or many of these forms of spiritual quest, and the executives of the universities are supportive of such efforts. The Spiritual Exercises can be called the foundation of the organizational culture and spirituality of American Jesuit universities. The spirituality of the Jesuits has been elaborated and studied over the four centuries that the order has existed and administered educational institutions (de Guibert, 1964). Attempts to develop and maintain Jesuit spirituality in universities have not rested with academic studies. The highest assembly of the worldwide Society of Jesus, its General Congregation, published in 1995 the decree "On Cooperation with the Laity in Mission," mandating both cooperation with laity and further efforts to promote Jesuit spirituality among them (Society, 1995). The direction of the General Congregation is explicit and clear.

> Each such work [of the Jesuits] must be guided by a clear mission statement which outlines the purposes of the work and forms the basis for collaboration in it. This mission statement should be presented and clearly explained to those with whom we cooperate. Programs are to be provided and supported (even financially) to enable lay people to acquire a greater knowledge of the Ignatian tradition and spirituality and to grow in each one's personal vocation. (Society, 1995:163)

A professional association of the Jesuit universities, the Association of Jesuit Colleges and Universities (AJCU) encourages and supports the propagation of Jesuit spirituality within the member institutions. The journal, *Conversations on Jesuit Higher Education*, fosters discussions on Jesuit spirituality in the context of higher education and the world of scholarship. It is "jointly sponsored by the Jesuit Conference Board [the national organization of American Jesuit Provincials] and the Board of the Association of Jesuit Colleges and Universities" (*Conversations*, 1998: 2). The AJCU has produced through St. Louis University a series of three videotapes outlining the origin, transformation, and transitions of Jesuit spirituality in academic institutions under their sponsorship *Shared Vision: Jesuit Spirit in Education*. These videotapes are used to orient new employees and to advance the knowledge of those who have worked in the universities for some time. An association of Midwestern Jesuit universities, the Heartland Conference not only hosts occasional conventions of employees from the member universities, but has local committees which host various activities that nurture discussion of spiritual affairs integral to the Jesuit education. The listing of various organizations and activities might well go on, but the point is made that the Jesuit educational establishment has devoted not a little effort, organization, and investment to sharing their well-developed spirituality with their co-workers.

Unlike most managers, Jesuit presidents, for example, are carefully trained and officially licensed through their ecclesiastical faculties as priests to serve as spiritual guides. The vocation to the ministerial priesthood might well be termed their primary profession. The same is true of the many Jesuits who serve in other managerial capacities in their universities: as chancellors, provosts, vice-presidents, deans, department chairpeople, and committee heads.

There is in the Jesuit universities, then, an enunciated spirituality which can be clearly and readily understood and which is officially promoted. This vision is the foundation of the organizational culture, which will be seen in the various mission statements, which builds upon the lived tradition of some five hundred years of involvement in education and over two hundred years of experience in American higher education. The larger population of employees in these institutions is composed of Catholics and non-Catholics, believers and non-believers, constituting a fund of goodwill. It would seem, then, that the Jesuit universities stand in an enviable position to promote an organizational spirituality whose maintenance would be relatively easy.

The mission statements of the Jesuit universities, as published in their catalogs and bulletins, illustrate in the language through which they express their organizational spirituality how difficult it is to develop and maintain a specific path to the transcendent. The various published mission statements represent the language of institutional self-identification and spirituality. We have chosen university catalogs and bulletins because they are published for external use and widely distributed to the universities' various stakeholders: students, parents, faculty, staff, trustees, benefactors, and alumni.

Only one institution, Marquette University, had not published a mission statement in its undergraduate bulletin for 1996–97. Language similar to many other mission statements is found in the description of its University Ministry, and it offers a letter from the president affirming its historical identity "as a Christian and Catholic institution" (Marquette, 1996–97: 3). Seattle University replaces a mission statement *per se* with a section entitled Purpose and Scope (Seattle University, 1996). A number of universities make no explicit mention of the name Jesus Christ or the term Christian in their statements: Boston College, Canisius College, University of Detroit Mercy, Fairfield University, Fordham University, Georgetown University, College of the Holy Cross, John Carroll University, Loyola College in Maryland, Loyola University of Chicago, Loyola University of New Orleans, Loyola Marymount University, Regis University, Rockhurst College, St. Joseph's University, Saint Louis University, University of San Francisco, Santa Clara University, Spring Hill College, St. Peter's College, and Xavier University. The omission illustrates the difficulty of self-identification and definition of spirituality within organizations that desire to promote pluralism, especially since the foundation of Jesuit spirituality, the Spiritual Exercises, focuses upon the life, passion, and resurrection of Jesus Christ.

Those organizations mentioning Jesus Christ in their mission statements do so in phraseology that highlights the difficulty of specifically defining a spirituality. Gonzaga University, for example, sees itself as "inspired by the vision of Christ at work" (Gonzaga University, 1997–99: 1). LeMoyne College understands that its Jesuit tradition calls for a "special recognition to . . . the message of Jesus Christ as a way to frame a meaningful philosophy of life" (LeMoyne College, 1997–98: 7). Seattle University defines itself as a "community inspired with the spirit of Christ" (Seattle University, 1996: 6).

The same diversity of language appears in the self-identification as Catholic. Seattle University does not use the term in its Purpose and Scope statement (Seattle University, 1996). Saint Louis University "strives for excellence under the inspiration of the Catholic faith" (Saint Louis, 1995–97: 5); Santa Clara University educates "within the Catholic . . . tradition" and affirms "its Catholic identity" (Santa Clara University, 1996–97: 13). The University of San Francisco "affirms its close relationship and commitment to the educational mission of the

Roman Catholic Church" (University of San Francisco, 1993–94: 2). Regis University sees itself as "standing within the Catholic and United States [sic] traditions" (Regis University, 1996–98: 17). The terms Jesuit and Society of Jesus are found in all the institutional self-identifications, but with different characterizations and varied degrees of linguistic distance. It should be noted that two universities, Detroit Mercy and Loyola Marymount, are not exclusively Jesuit institutions but are sponsored with other religious orders who possess their own spiritualities, so their self-definitions will not be considered under this heading. Loyola College in Maryland denominates itself rather distantly as "under the aegis of the Society of Jesus" and its core curriculum as one of the "hallmarks of a Jesuit education" (Loyola College, 1996–97: 6). Seattle University mentions itself as "conducted under the auspices of the Society of Jesus" (Seattle University, 1996: 6).

Often the term Jesuit tradition appears in various forms adopted without much more specification than excellence or tolerance. Fordham University sees "the Jesuit tradition" as informing "every aspect" of its education. It goes on to define this tradition in terms that are very different from what might be characterized as spiritual language in the Jesuit mode: "This tradition is characterized by excellence in teaching and by the care and development of each individual student" (Fordham University, 1997–98: 4). Boston College, however, uses a level of specificity employed by a number of universities. Defining itself as a Catholic and Jesuit university, "it is rooted in a world view that encounters God in all creation and through all human activity" (Boston College, 1998–99: 5). The College of the Holy Cross defines its mission as a Jesuit college: "As such, Holy Cross seeks to exemplify the longstanding dedication of the Society of Jesus to the intellectual life, the service of faith and promotion of justice" (College of the Holy Cross, 1995–96: 1).

Conclusion

The examination of the mission statements of the 28 Jesuit universities in the United States demonstrates the difficulty of maintaining an organizational spirituality. The Society is a unified body with a specific spirituality. Since the Jesuits are the sponsoring body of the universities, every university should share the same spirituality, enunciated in the same basic manner. Such does not appear to be the case with Jesuit universities. Terms essential to a characterization of organizations founded upon a specific spirituality are sometimes absent and sometimes redefining in remarkably different ways. For example, almost all of the universities declare themselves to be Jesuit, yet the term goes undefined or is defined differently by each organization.

If the mission statement were the enunciated spirituality and culture of an organization, then the terms referring to the spirituality should be spelled out in language understood by the members of the organization. The mission statement of an organization also serves as an important source of information on organization to potential members. The mission statement represents the enunciated culture of the organization. For an organization with a spirituality, the mission statement would be the first place potential employees would look to determine if their personal spirituality fits the organization's spirituality. As seen earlier, a close fit between personal and organizational spirituality is very important.

No doubt, much of the redefinition or lack of specification reflects the pluralistic nature of universities that incorporate students and employees of many, and no, spiritual traditions. This is the problem faced by any organization as it attempts to become a spiritual organization. Even with considerable spiritual tradition of the Jesuits, the clear articulation of this tradition through five hundred years, the commitment of the Society to promoting its spirituality among the members of its universities, and the investment of resources and talents, the development and maintenance of an organizational spirituality is no easy task.

References

Allinson, R. E. (1998), Ethical values as part of the definition of business enterprise and part of the integral structure of the business organization, *Journal of Business Ethics*, Vol. 17, Nos. 9–10, p. 1015.

Barnett, J. H. (1985), A business model of enlightenment, *Journal of Business Ethics*, Vol. 4, No. 1, p. 57.

Boston College (1998–1999), Bulletin.

Brandt, E. (1996), Corporate pioneers explore spirituality peace, *HR Magazine*, Vol. 41, No. 4, p. 82.

Canisius College (1996–1997), Academic Undergraduate Catalog.

Chappell, T. (1993), *The Soul of a Business: Managing for Profit and the Common Good*, New York, Bantam Books.

College of the Holy Cross (1995–1996), Bulletin.
Conger, J., & Associates (1994), *Spirit at Work: Discovering the Spirituality in Leadership*, San Francisco, Jossey-Bass.
Conversations (1998), Vol. 1, No. 13, p. 2.
Creighton University (1997–1999), Undergraduate Bulletin.
de Gilbert, J. (1964), *The Jesuits: Their Spiritual Doctrine and Practice; A Historical Study*, trans. W. J. Young, Institute of Jesuit Sources, Chicago, IL.
Dehler, G. E., & Welsh, M. A. (1994), Spirituality and organizational transformation: Implications for the new management paradigm, *Journal of Managerial Psychology*, Vol. 9, No. 6, p. 17.
Delbecq, A. L. (1998, August), What matters most: Senior leadership revisioning–A Christian perspective, Paper presented at the Academy of Management, San Diego, CA.
Fairfield University (1997–1998), Undergraduate Catalog.
Fordham University (1997–1998), Undergraduate Bulletin.
Frost, P., Moore, L., Louis, M., Lundberg, C., & Martin, J., eds. (1985), *Organizational Culture*, Sage, Beverly Hills.
Georgetown University (1995–1996), Undergraduate Bulletin.
Gonzaga University (1997–1999), Undergraduate Catalog.
Holton, E. F. (1996), New employee development: A review and reconceptualization, *Human Resource Development Quarterly*, Vol. 73, p. 233.
Kahnweiler, W., & Otte, F. L. (1997), In search of the soul of HRD, *Human Resource Development Quarterly*, Vol. 8, No. 2, p. 171.
Kane, K. R. (1998, August), A restoration of spirit through the shaman's path, Paper presented at the Academy of Management, San Diego, CA.
Kets de Vries, M., Loper, M., & Doyle, J. (1994), The leadership mystique, *Academy of Management Executive*, Vol. 8, No. 3, p. 73.
Konz, G. N. P., & Katz, J. A. (1996), Hyperlongevity in entrepreneurial endeavors: Deep structures and the lessons of religious orders for very long-term survival, *Journal of Management Systems*, Vol. 8, Nos. 1–4, p. 51.
Kraimer, M. L. (1997), Organizational goals and values: A socialization model, *Human Resource Management Review*, Vol. 7, No. 4, p. 425.
Laabs, J. J. (1995), Balancing spirituality and work, *Personnel Journal*, Vol. 74, No. 9, p. 60.

Leigh, P. (1997), The new spirit at work, *Training and Development*, Vol. 51, No. 3, p. 26.

LeMoyne College (1997–1998), Catalog.

Loyola College in Maryland (1996–1997), Undergraduate Catalog.

Loyola Marymount University (1997–1998), Undergraduate Bulletin.

Loyola University, Chicago (1997–1998), Undergraduate Studies Catalog.

Loyola University, New Orleans (1997–1999), Undergraduate Bulletin.

Marquette University (1996–1997), Undergraduate Bulletin.

McCormick, D. W. (1994), Spirituality and management, *Journal of Managerial Psychology*, Vol. 9, No. 6, p. 5.

McGee, J. J. (1998, August), The emergence of "secular" corporate spirituality, Paper presented at the Academy of Management, San Diego, CA.

McKenna, T. F. (1997), Vincent de Paul: A saint who got his worlds together, *Journal of Business Ethics*, Vol. 16, No. 3, p. 299.

Miller, L. (1998, July 20), "After their checkup for the body, some get one for the soul," *Wall Street Journal*, pp. A1, A6.

Mirvis, P. H. (1997), "Soul work" in organizations, *Organization Science*, Vol. 8, No. 2, p. 193.

Neal, J. A. (1997), Spirituality in management education: A guide to resources, *Journal of Management Education*, Vol. 21, No. 1, p. 121.

Neck, C. P., & Milliman, J. F. (1994), Thought self-leadership: Finding spiritual fulfillment in organizational life. *Journal of Managerial Psychology*, Vol. 9, No. 8, p. 9.

O'Malley, J. W. (1993), *The First Jesuits*, Harvard University Press, Cambridge, MA.

Regis University (1996–1998), Bulletin.

Reichers, A. E. (1987), *Academy of Management Review*, Vol. 12, No. 2, p. 278.

Riordan, C. M., Gatewood, R. D., & Bill, J. B. (1997), Corporate image: Employee reactions and implications for managing corporate social performance, *Journal of Business Ethics*, Vol. 16, No. 4, p. 401.

Rockhurst College (1997–1998), Bulletin.

Saint Joseph's University (1996–1997), Catalog.

Saint Louis University (1995–1997), Undergraduate Catalog.

Saint Peter's College (1996–1998), Undergraduate Bulletin.

Santa Clara University (1996–1997), Undergraduate Courses and Degrees.

Schein, E. H. (1985), *Organizational Culture and Leadership*, San Francisco, CA, Jossey-Bass.

Seattle University (1996), Undergraduate Bulletin of Information.

Silvers, R. (1998, August), And it harm none, do what ye will: A neopagan revisioning of organizations, Paper presented at the Academy of Management, San Diego, CA.

Society of Jesus (1995), On Cooperation with the Laity in Mission, *Documents of the 34th General Congregation of the Society of Jesus*, The Institute of Jesuit Sources, St. Louis, MO.

Spring Hill College (1996–1997), Bulletin of Information.

Trice, H. M., & Beyer, J. M. (1993), *The Cultures of Work Organizations*, Englewood Cliffs, Prentice Hall.

University of Detroit Mercy (1991–1993), Undergraduate Catalog.

University of San Francisco (1993–1994), General Catalog.

University of Scranton (1993–1994), Undergraduate Catalog.

Wheeling Jesuit University (1997–1998), University Bulletin.

White, J. (1998, August), How Buddhist principles might be embodied in organizations, Paper presented at the Academy of Management, San Diego, CA.

Whyte, D. (1994), *The Heart Aroused: Poetry and Preservation of the Soul in Corporate America*, Currency Doubleday, New York.

Xavier University (1996–1998), Catalog.

SPIRITUAL THEMES OF THE "LEARNING ORGANIZATION"

Stephen J. Porth,
John McCall,
Saint Joseph's University

Thomas A. Bausch,
Marquette University

As markets become more globally competitive and technology more advanced, many organizations have found it increasingly difficult to sustain a competitive advantage. Witness the fall of some of the corporate icons of American business success, including Sears, IBM, Westinghouse, and General Motors (Drucker, 1993). With markets more dynamic and competitive advantage more fleeting, organizations have been exhorted to develop the capacity to produce an ongoing flow of innovation to achieve and sustain a competitive advantage (Werther & Kerr, 1995; Liedtka, 1996).

The capacity to achieve ongoing organizational innovation requires a fundamentally different approach to managing employees than the centralized, control-oriented approach of Frederick Taylor. The new role of top management, according to Bartlett and Ghoshal (1995), "is to unleash the human spirit, which makes initiative, creativity, and entrepreneurship possible" (p 132). The learning organization model has been espoused as the type of organization in which the human spirit may be unleashed. Building a learning organization is a critical challenge for top managers since it depends on establishing an organizational climate that allows the human capacity for innovation and creativity to flourish. The learning organization seeks to tap into the fullness of human potential. Only by developing a thorough understanding of the nature of the human person may this be achieved.

The purpose of this study is to examine the spiritual themes of the learning organization. We begin by defining a learning organization and describing its characteristics. The learning organization model is based on a set of underlying assumptions about employees and organizations. These assumptions find resonance with many aspects of traditional spiritual teachings about the nature of the human person. These points of convergence are identified and described.

We believe that finding these points of convergence and agreement is of great importance for two very fundamental reasons. First, the only source of sustainable competitive advantage for any organization over the long term is the commitment of qualified employees to the mission and vision of the organization. Technological advances, product innovation, marketing or finance activities, and other sources of value-added are all replicable or can be surpassed, as the history of so many once successful organizations demonstrates. Development of the learning organization is arguably one path to building the sustainable commitment of qualified employees. Second, we believe that the fields of philosophy and theology are a rich and time-tested source of wisdom for organizational leaders. Learning from these sources will not only help organizations achieve business objectives, but will allow human beings to flourish within the organization.

We begin with a few caveats. First, the social teachings underlying the world's spiritual and religious traditions are enormously rich and complex. This would include teachings from philosophers, religious leaders, and theologians from all major world religions, representing both Eastern and Western world-views. It is beyond the scope of this study to adequately represent all or even most of these spiritual traditions. We recognize and appreciate the important contribution each of these traditions can make to our discussion of management. However, our focus is primarily on the Judeo-Christian tradition. We acknowledge that this is just one of many perspectives with a contribution to make to this discussion and we emphasize that our reliance on the Christian social teachings is a reflection of our knowledge, experience, and expertise. We leave it to future researchers with expertise in other spiritual and religious traditions to establish the contributions of those traditions to the field of management.

Given our primary emphasis on Christian social teachings, we have a second caveat. Even today arcane practices, such as a stubborn refusal to use inclusive language, unnecessarily detract from the underlying riches of these documents. Thus, in the quotations we use in this paper we will use appropriately inclusive terminology.

The Learning Organization

The concept of a learning organization has been popularized by several recent authors, most notably Peter Senge, author of *The Fifth Discipline* (1990). Since the early 1990s, research on the learning organization has proliferated (Easterby-Smith, 1997). Indeed, a bibliographic review by Crossan and Guatto (1996) found as many academic papers on organizational learning in 1993 as in the entire decade of the 1980s.

According to David Garvin (1993), a learning organization is "an organization skilled at creating, acquiring, and transferring knowledge, and at modifying its behavior to reflect new knowledge and insights" (p 80). Similarly, Easterby-Smith (1997) describes the learning organization as an ideal type of action- and change-oriented enterprise in which learning is maximized.

One reason for the growing interest in the learning organization is its suitability for today's fast-paced, global business environments. Anderson (1997) argues that from a strategic perspective, the learning organization is especially important in highly competitive situations because it builds the capacity to change strategies, to be creative, and to avoid a narrow and rigid dependence on the status quo (p 28). Baldwin, Danielson, and Wiggenhorn (1997) likewise claim that "the dynamics of rapid change, heightened global competition and advancing technology mean that organizational success will be increasingly dependent on learning" (p. 47). Similarly, Liedtka (1996) argues that the ability "to continuously build new capabilities is at the heart of competitive advantage" (p. 21). This capacity to innovate is sustained by organizational learning.

Characteristics of a Learning Organization

Thus, change and innovation are the hallmarks of a learning organization. But change and innovation are outcomes, the result of various processes and characteristics that are embedded in the organization. What are these characteristics and processes that foster the change and innovation that distinguish the learning organization?

A review of the literature suggests that different authors stress different aspects of the learning organization. Indeed, Easterby-Smith (1997) did an extensive search of the organizational learning concept and found six disciplinary perspectives on the topic, each with its own distinct contributions and viewpoints. Stepping back from the differing perspectives, however, and accounting for differences in terminology but similarities of meaning, at least three characteristics of a learning organization consistently emerge: (1) employee development and continuous learning within the organization, (2) information-sharing and meaningful collaboration, and (3) team-building and shared purpose.

Employee Development and Continuous Learning

One of the six disciplinary perspectives described by Easterby-Smith (1997) is the psychology and organizational development (OD) view. The central theme of this perspective is "human development within the organizational context" (p. 1087). This theme focuses on topics such as how individuals learn, stages of the learning process, cognitive styles, and obstacles to learning. Implicit in the theme is the understanding that organizational learning depends on employees who are growing and developing on the job.

Information Sharing and Collaboration

A second perspective on organizational learning described by Easterby-Smith (1997) emphasizes the theme of information processing and sharing. This theme is also one of the principles of learning identified by Baldwin et al. (1997). These authors stress that organizational change is a shared responsibility and that innovation and change require employee participation and involvement. "Innovation is much more likely to occur when people participate in the solution rather than having it handed to them" (p. 50).

This inclusive approach to planning brings new voices, new perspectives, and new energy to the process. It allows the organization to tap into the knowledge of its people, a key to competitive advantage, according to Bartlett and Ghoshal (1995):

> In the emerging information age, the critical scarce resource is knowledge . . . (not capital). The implications for top-level managers are profound. If front-line employees are vital strategic resources instead of mere factors of production, corporate executives can no longer afford to be isolated from the people in their organizations. (p. 142)

Team Building and Shared Purpose

Anderson (1997) speaks for many contributors to the organizational learning research stream when he claims that team building and a strong sense of community are fundamental to the learning organization. "When there is no community, trust and respect are hard to maintain and performance is even more difficult to reinforce" (p. 39).

Creating a sense of shared purpose, an esprit de corps, is a view aptly stated in *The Fifth Discipline Fieldbook* (Senge et al., 1994):

> Thus, at the heart of building shared vision is the task of designing and evolving ongoing processes in which people at every level of the organization, in every role, can speak from the heart about what really matters to them and be heard—by senior management and each other. The quality of this process, especially the amount of openness and genuine caring, determines the quality and the power of the results . . . a true shared vision cannot be dictated; it can only emerge from a coherent process of reflection and conversation. (p. 299)

The Learning Organization and Employment Policies

This emphasis on employees, however, raises questions about whether there are specific corollary employment policies that are necessary for, or at least increase the probability of, successful introduction of the learning organization approach. In particular, questions arise about the scope of team authority (is it merely consultative or is it substantive decision making), the degree of employment security, and the shape of compensation programs. Happily, there is both theoretical and broadly empirical evidence (case studies, surveys, and performance-related data sets) that helps answer these questions.

Theoretical Evidence

Human resource theorists increasingly believe that achieving the benefits of the team concept will require an interrelated set of employment policies. Moreover, they argue further that these employment policies are unlikely to produce the desired effect if introduced piecemeal (see, for example, Kochan and Osterman, 1994). Rather, recent scholarship suggests that successful implementation may demand a fundamental restructuring of workplace rules. Job security and pay are just two of the areas where theoretical speculations have significant implications for the learning organization approach.

Job Security

The learning organization model poses risks for the employees who work under it. Clearly, employee suggestions that increase productivity will also the raise the possibility that the demand for labor will decrease and that employees will be laid off. There are similar risks present in the efforts employees make in acquiring cross-functional but potentially firm specific skills. Rational agents cannot be expected to assume these risks unless there is some conditional promise by the firm to avoid layoffs and to soften the impact of any layoffs that prove unavoidable (perhaps by promising severance packages) (see Butler and Walwei, 1993; Gerhart, Milkovich, and Murray, 1992; Marshall, 1992; Kochan and Osterman, 1994).

Additionally, as Levine and Tyson (1990) suggest, the free flow of ideas and information will be chilled by fear of reprisals unless there is an additional guarantee that employees will be dismissed only for cause. The key in both the for-cause dismissal policy and the promise to avoid layoffs is that the corporation and its management provide credible expressions of commitment to and respect for employees. Osterman (1992) argues that this mutuality seems a necessary condition for the emergence of trust and loyalty among employees.

Pay

The success of the learning organization model depends on the development of group cooperation and cohesiveness. Mitchell, Lewin, and Lawler (1990) claim that since substantial differences in pay scales are likely to produce frictions among teams, one could theorize team cohesiveness might dictate small differentials in base wages among team members, perhaps with variation in compensation coming from seniority or learning additional skills (pay for knowledge). The latter also provides incentive for employees to engage in the process of continuous skill improvement.

Moreover, the demand for mutuality would argue for a sharing of any gains produced by the team concept. Gain sharing based on measurable performance outcomes might also provide a powerful incentive for improving productivity, as might profit sharing (although profits are contingent upon many variables over which employees have little control and hence may provide a less certain incentive mechanism).

Empirical Evidence

The theoretical arguments on job security and compensation provoke thought about what employment practices are needed for the learning organization model's success. Assessing the wisdom of those arguments, however, requires that we have empirical evidence of what works in practice. Case studies, surveys, and data sets relating performance and work organization have by and large corroborated the theory about the specific employment practices that best "fit" the learning organization.

Case Studies

Case data show that not all attempts at reorganizing workplaces succeed. Some experiments with introducing team processes or employee participation have failed. There have also been notable successes, however. And the success stories reflect a common pattern.

The commonly cited Saturn, NUMMI, Xerox, and Corning Glass examples (see Osterman, 1992, 1993; Kochan and Osterman, 1994) of successful team production and flexible job assignments, as well as a detailed case study of a paper mill (Ichniowski, 1992), reveal that all had a set of employment practices characterized by employment security pledges, some element of contingent pay tied to performance measures, and opportunities for training and development. Perhaps the most telling aspect of these case studies is that some of these same firms lost the benefits associated with team production and committed employees when they abandoned some of the corollary employment practices, especially the avoidance of layoffs (Kochan and Osterman, 1994). Recent events at Saturn may prove a topical case in point.

Broader Empirical Evidence

Some authors try to go beyond the obvious limitations of individual case studies for drawing conclusions. Levine and Tyson (1990) review

47 different empirical studies (ranging from case studies to econometric analysis to field experiments) in an attempt to clarify the relationship between employee participation and productivity. Their assessment of the evidence is that employee participation is more likely to have significant positive impact on productivity when it is substantive (as in direct team-based decision making), when it extends to "shop-floor" issues, and when it is combined with profit or gain sharing, employment security pledges, and guaranteed individual rights.

Kochan and Osterman (1994) also review the performance of a variety of firms that have experimented with innovations such as self-directed teams, cross-functional work, and flexible job assignment. They argue that to sustain such innovations, three specific human resource practices are required: a conditional commitment to employment security, investment in extensive training opportunities for employees, and a fair compensation scheme that includes a sizable share of any corporate gains. Finally, MacDuffie and Krafcik (1992) reach similar conclusions in their assessment of the performance of a large number of auto assembly plants from across the globe.

Thus the theoretical and empirical evidence both indicate that the levels of employee commitment and trust upon which the learning organization model depends are unlikely to emerge unless employees are treated with respect and are provided job security, a share of the economic benefits that accrue to the firm, significant opportunities for skill development, and substantive participation in decisions.

Spiritual Themes and the Learning Organization

Based on the preceding discussions, it is possible to identify themes common to spiritual teachings and the learning organization approach. The organization's goal is to create a sustainable competitive advantage. This is achieved through an ongoing stream of organizational innovations. Innovation, in turn, is driven by the energy and resourcefulness of dedicated, qualified employees who are committed to a shared vision of the organization. The climate for creating this cadre of dedicated employees is fostered by the learning organization, built on the pillars of continuous learning, meaningful collaboration, and shared purpose.

The learning organization's emphasis on the primacy of human intellect that produces ongoing innovation has many affinities with social teachings from the Christian and Judaic traditions.

For instance, the Christian tradition's prescriptions about employment derive from its understanding of human nature as body, mind, and spirit (i.e., the whole person) and its perennial emphasis on the dignity of each individual person. Consistently present in these teachings are themes about the social dimension of work and about labor as a co-creative activity. These themes reflect a perspective that employees are co-equal partners in the productive process and should be seen as common stakeholders with rights both to participate in decision making and to a fair share of the gains of enterprise. These principles of religious ethics have led Catholic religious leaders to conclude:

Whereas at one time the decisive factor of production was the land, and later capital—understood as the total complex of the instruments of production—today the decisive factor is increasingly the person, that is, one's knowledge, especially one's scientific knowledge, one's capacity for interrelated and compact organization, as well as one's ability to perceive the needs of others and to satisfy them. (*Centesimus Annus*, 32)

[The Church's] teaching also recognizes the legitimacy of workers' efforts to obtain full respect for their dignity and to gain broader areas of participation in the life of industrial enterprises so that, while cooperating with others and under the direction of others, they can in a certain sense "work for themselves" through the exercise of their intelligence and freedom. (*Centesimus Annus*, 43)

The Catholic tradition even expresses a belief in the micro-economic efficiency of attention to personal development that is strikingly similar to the learning organization model's emphasis on the source of sustained competitive advantage in team processes:

The integral development of the human person through work does not impede but rather promotes the greater productivity and efficiency of work itself, even though it may weaken consolidated power structures. (*Centesimus Annus*, 43)

The U.S. National Conference of Catholic Bishops has also issued statements about work and the economy that echo themes from contemporary management about both employee development and job security:

Work . . . embodies the distinctive human capacity for self-expression and self-realization. (U.S. Catholic Bishops, 1985: 97)

At a minimum, workers have a right to be informed in advance when such decisions [layoffs and plant closures] are under consideration, a right to negotiate about possible alternatives and a right to fair compensation and assistance with retraining and relocation expenses should these be necessary. (U.S. Catholic Bishops, 1985: 291)

Some find similar emphases on the ethical and spiritual importance of work in Jewish thought. Pava (1998) asserts that Jewish aspirational thought sees economic life as directed toward "building a just and caring society in which the best of human and spiritual values might flourish" (p. 81). Green (1987), in comparing Jewish thought on ethics with a Catholic bishops' pastoral letter, finds great similarities. In particular, he emphasizes the common themes of both interdependence and the value of work. Finally, Leiser (1982) suggests that an obligation to provide severance for employees derives from the historical tradition of Rabbinic courts and interpretations of passages in *Deuteronomy*.

Common Ground

These spiritual teachings are fundamentally consistent with the learning organization model regarding the importance of teamwork, participation, and providing opportunities for full development of human talents in the workplace. And the specific employment practices recommended as essential for sustaining transformed workplaces (e.g., job security and sharing in corporate gains) have echoes in a religious ethic's insistence on fair distribution of the burdens and benefits of work and on placing the human needs of employees before the interests of capital.

Differences

While there are striking parallels between the spiritual themes and some contemporary management theories, especially in their insistence on paying attention to the whole person, those similarities should not obscure the significant differences that remain. Chief among these is that the advice of management theories is meant as a contingent, strategically instrumental tool for competitive markets. Religious prescriptions, on the other hand, are closer to categorical moral imperatives dictated by a demand to treat all human persons with dignity.

Another significant practical difference involves the range of employees and workplaces that the respective prescriptions of religions and the learning organization model cover. Religions intend to speak to the morality of workplace practices generally. The learning organization model, at least under its usual interpretation, is offered for businesses whose environment is the hypercompetitive international market or whose production process is high-tech. As Kochan and Osterman (1994) note, their "mutual gains" principles are not necessarily appropriate for all firms. In fact, they suggest that it might be more efficient for some firms to adopt low-skill, narrowly defined, Taylorist principles of work organization.

Conclusion

Notwithstanding the differences between the spiritual and business perspectives, we believe that there is the possibility of expanding the scope of management theories beyond their limiting contingencies. There is a substantial benefit to be gained from a loyal and committed workforce even in the lower-tech service industries. In those industries, success depends on satisfying customers. It is unlikely that a dispirited, uncommitted, unengaged, and untrained staff of employees will generate customer satisfaction. That is precisely the staff a firm might expect to have unless it shows reciprocal loyalty and respect to its employees. (See Duska, 1985, for a *reductio* of the belief that firms can expect loyalty without showing reciprocal loyalty toward employees.)

We all possess anecdotal evidence of experiences with businesses in the service industry where employees are unhelpful, surly, or even rude, and other encounters where employees are enthusiastic, responsive, and helpful. These experiences are not merely the result of individual employee personalities; they have much to do with the values embedded in the organization's culture, and the levels of training and the degree of respect accorded the workforce.

It would appear then that a significant portion of the employment practices recommended above could be generalizable to a variety of strategic contingencies. If these speculations are valid, there is reason to believe that the spiritual themes and learning organization model converge even further than it seems at first glance. It may be that contemporary management thought gives new credibility to the old saw that "good ethics is good business." Nonetheless, that old saw has its dangers, too often being interpreted to mean that anything that is profitable is therefore morally acceptable. Those dangers should caution us not to minimize the potential conflicts between religious ethics and contemporary management theory.

References

Anderson, C. (1997), "Values-based management," *Academy of Management Executive*, Vol. 11, No. 4, pp. 25–46.

Baldwin, T. T., C. Danielson, & W. Wiggenhorn (1997), "The Evolution of Learning Strategies in Organizations: From Employee Development to Business Redefinition," *Academy of Management Executive*, 11 (4), pp. 47–57.

Bartlett, C. A., & S. Ghoshal (May–June 1995), "Changing the Role of Top Management: Beyond Systems to People," *Harvard Business Review*, pp. 132–142.

Butler, F., & U. Walwei (1993), "Employment Security and Efficiency: Assumptions in the Current Debate and Empirical Evidence from West Germany." In *Employment Security and Labor Market Behavior*. C. Buechtemann, ed. Ithaca, NY: ILR Press.

Crossan, N. M., and Guatto, T. (1996), Organizational learning research profile, *Journal of Organizational Change Management,*, Vol.9, No. 1, pp. 107–112.

Duska, R. (1985), "Whistleblowing and Employee Loyalty," In *Contemporary Issues in Business Ethics*, 1st ed. J DesJardins and J. McCall, eds. Belmont, CA: Wadsworth Publishing Company.

Drucker, P. F. (Feb. 2, 1993), "A Turnaround Primer," *Wall Street Journal*, p. A14.

Easterby-Smith, M. (1997), "Disciplines of organizational learning: contributions and critiques," *Human Relations*, Vol. 50, No. 9, pp. 1085–1106.

Garvin, D. A. (July–August 1993), "Building a Learning Organization," *Harvard Business Review*, pp. 78–91.

Gerhart, B., G. Milkovich, & B. Murray (1992), "Pay, Performance and Participation," In *Research Frontiers in Industrial Relations and Human Resources*. D. Lewin et al., eds. Madison, WI: Industrial Relations Research Association.

Green, R. (1987), "The Bishops' Letter—A Jewish Perspective." In *The Catholic Challenge to the American Economy.* T. Gannon, S.J., ed. New York: Macmillan Publishing Company.

Ichniowski, C. (1992), "Human Resource Management and Productive Labor-Management Relations," In *Research Frontiers in Industrial Relations and Human Resources.* D. Lewin et al., eds. Madison, WI: Industrial Relations Research Association.

Kochan, T., & P. Osterman (1994), *The Mutual Gains Enterprise.* Boston, MA: Harvard Business School Press.

Leiser, B. M. (1982), "The Rabbinic Tradition and Corporate Morality." In *The Judeo-Christian Vision and the Modern Corporation.* Oliver Williams and John Houck, eds. South Bend, IN: University of Notre Dame Press.

Levine, D., & L. D'Andrae Tyson (1990), "Participation, Productivity and the Firm's Environment." In *Paying for Productivity.* Alan Blinder, ed. Washington, DC: The Brookings Institute.

Liedtka, J. M. (1996), "Collaborating Across Lines of Business for Competitive Advantage," *Academy of Management Executive*, Vol. 10, No. 2, pp. 20–34.

MacDuffie, J. P., & J. Krafcik (1992), "Integrating Technology and Human Resources for High Performance Manufacturing: Evidence from the International Auto Industry," In *Transforming Organizations.* T. Kochan and M. Unseem, eds. New York: Oxford University Press.

Marshall, R. (1992), "Work Organization, Unions and Economic Performance." In *Unions and Economic Competitiveness.* L. Mishel and P. Voss, eds. Armonk, NY: M.E. Sharpe, Inc.

Mitchell, D., D. Lewin, & E. Lawler (1990), "Alternative Pay Systems, Firm Performance and Productivity." In *Paying for Productivity.* Alan Blinder, Ed. Washington, DC: The Brookings Institute.

Osterman, P. (1992), "Internal Labor Markets in a Changing Environment: Models and Evidence." In *Research Frontiers in Industrial Relations and Human Resources.* D. Lewin et al., eds. Industrial Relations Research Association, Madison, WI.

Osterman, P. (1993), "Pressures and Prospects for Employment Security in the United States." In *Employment Security and Labor Market Behavior.* C. Buechtmann, ed. Ithaca, NY: ILR Press.

Pava, M. (1998), "Developing a Religiously Grounded Business Ethic: A Jewish Perspective," *Business Ethics Quarterly*, Vol. 8, No. 1, pp. 65–83.

Pope John-Paul II (1981), *Laborem Exercens.*

Pope John-Paul II (1991), *Centesimus Annus.*

Pope Leo XII (1891), *Rerum Novarum.*

Senge, P. M (1990), *The Fifth Discipline: The Art and Practice of the Learning Organization.* New York: Doubleday/Currency.

Senge, P. M., C. Roberts, R. Ross, B. Smith, & A. Kleiner (1994), *The Fifth Discipline Fieldbook: Strategies and Tools for Building a Learning Organization.* New York: Doubleday/Currency.

U.S. Catholic Bishops (1985), *And Justice for All: A Pastoral Letter on the U.S. Economy.*

Werther, W. B., & J. L. Kerr (May–June 1995), "The Shifting Sands of Competitive Advantage," *Business Horizons,* pp. 11–20.

SPIRIT AND COMMUNITY AT SOUTHWEST AIRLINES:

AN INVESTIGATION OF A SPIRITUAL VALUES-BASED MODEL

John Milliman,
Jeffery Ferguson,
University of Colorado, Colorado Springs

David Trickett,
The Jefferson Circle

Bruce Condemi,
University of Colorado, Colorado Springs

Introduction

Recently there has been increasing interest in spirituality in business. One of the challenging aspects about spirituality is that it seems to mean different things to different people, making it difficult to give a universal definition of this dynamic concept. Nonetheless, in all cases it appears to involve deeply held values. Some of the fundamental ideas that individuals typically posit in spirituality include (1) Who am I? (2) What is my purpose in life?, and (3) What is it that I have to offer? (Block, 1993; Hawley, 1993; Neal, 1998). An active spiritual life can help individuals find meaning and purpose in their lives and live out deeply held personal values. These values often reflect a desire to make a difference and to help create a more meaningful world (Block, 1993; Ray, 1992). However, much of what is written focuses on the concept and philosophy of spirituality rather than its implementation. This leads to two important questions.

First, what might spirituality look like if it were manifested in an organization (Neck & Milliman, 1994)? We do not have many examples of how spirituality is demonstrated throughout an organization. For instance, how do organizational spiritual values simultaneously impact different types of people such as managers, employees, and customers? How does spirituality affect organizational practices such as strategy, human resource management (HRM) practices, and customer service?

A second key question is what would be the impact on both individuals and the organization if spirituality were manifested in the workplace? In investigating its impact, some observers view spirituality as a "soft" approach that either benefits individuals only, or has a neutral or possibly negative impact on organizations—such as threatening the traditional business goal of maximizing profit. These observers question whether creating a spiritual environment for employees is truly compatible with a profit-making objective. In contrast, others believe that having a strong set of deeply held values not only benefits employees, but can also positively impact organizational performance (e.g., Neck & Milliman, 1994). As an example, in *Built to Last*, Collins and Porras (1994) note that all the visionary companies in their study have posted exceptional long-term financial performance and have as their primary goal something other than maximizing profit. For instance, at Merck the purpose is "to preserve and improve human life" and at H-P it is to "make technical contributions for the advancement and welfare of humanity." Although Collins and Porras do not use the term *spirituality* to describe these corporate statements that focus on a deeper purpose, they are excellent examples of how an aspect of spirituality, namely, the concept of "contributing to the greater good," is articulated in these firms.

We believe that the issue of whether spirituality can have a positive impact on both employees and organizations is particularly important because many chief executive officers (CEOs) will not justify a practice unless it favorably impacts the bottom line. Thus, we believe that researching whether and under what conditions spirituality can have a positive impact is not only an important academic question, but also is relevant for practice. Such research is needed if we are to create a paradigm shift in CEOs so that they incorporate spiritual principles into their organizations.

One key to creating such a paradigm shift is to show how spirituality is actually manifested throughout all areas of an organization. Using such a case study approach is also consistent with the newness of the field of spirituality in business where an inductive approach (Glaser & Strauss, 1967) is appropriate in assessing and developing theory. We selected Southwest Airlines (SWA) for our case study because it appears to have a strong sense of spiritual-based values guiding its organizational goals and practices. In addition, the company has an established track record of excellent organizational performance as well as high employee and customer satisfaction. In profiling SWA we certainly do not want to imply that it is a perfect example of living spiritual values; it has its problems and limitations like other firms. Despite this, there seems to be a genuine sense of spirit and affection in both SWA employees and customers (Levering & Moskowitz, 1993).

The purpose of this article is to (1) examine the ways spirituality is manifested within SWA and (2) assess the impact of spirituality on SWA employees, customers, and organizational performance. Because spirituality is reflected through values such as making a contribution to humankind, we have adapted a model of spiritual values–based management as a framework for our analysis. The use of such a framework minimizes concentration on anecdotal evidence and forces a more comprehensive analysis of spirituality in organizations. First, we articulate a four-step model of spiritual values–based management which addresses both the development and the implementation of spiritual values in organizations. Second, we summarize the literature on SWA to identify the manner and extent to which spiritual values are exemplified in its organizational practices. Third, we discuss lessons learned about how business organizations can employ a spiritual approach to gain benefits for both its employees and the bottom line. Finally, we make suggestions for a preliminary contingency framework of spirituality in business and suggest propositions to guide future research in this emerging field.

Spiritual Values–based Model

A model of how spiritual values are proposed to affect an organization is shown in Figure 1. This figure is based on an integration of the literature on spirituality in business with two models— Anderson's (1997) values-based management model, which focuses on the impact of values on top management strategy, and Schuler and Jackson's (1987) strategic human resource management framework, which focuses more on the implementation of organizational strategy. The combination of these frameworks provides an integrated approach for analysis of spirituality in organizations.

Figure 1

At the top of Figure 1 are the organization's core spiritual values which represent the philosophical views of the organization as well as its priorities and sense of purpose (Anderson, 1997). In a real sense, these values represent the "soul" of the organization (Blanchard & O'Connor, 1997) and reflect its sense of spirituality and purpose. The higher purpose of an organization is reflected in its values which directly influence the organization's mission, goals, and objectives (Channon, 1992) and ultimately provide the foundation for corporate practices and the context into which employees think, act, and make decisions (Brown, 1992; Collins & Porras, 1994; Rosen, 1992). However, it is important to note that for these values to truly have an impact, they must reflect the inner needs, beliefs, and aspirations of the employees (Collins & Porras, 1994). As such, a central question in spirituality in business concerns is how can organizations and employees put their spiritual values to work (Miller, 1993) so that they can find their higher purpose and meaning in life (Ferguson, 1993; Mandel, 1993; Miller, 1993; Sanford, 1993).

As shown in the right-hand side of Figure 1, the organization's core values shape its business plans and individual employee plans (Anderson, 1997). The business plan determines the organization's various businesses and states specific directions, time frames, and goals. In turn, these business plans define individual and team plans at the operational level (Anderson, 1997; Schuler & Jackson, 1987).

Many organizations have lofty values, but don't integrate them into daily practice. Thus, an important challenge for an organization is to ensure that its employees align their work habits with the core values of the firm (Blanchard & O'Connor, 1997; Schuler & Jackson, 1987). This is why it is important that spirituality be examined at both the organizational and individual levels. As illustrated at the bottom of Figure 1, human resource management (HRM) represents the fundamental way an organization develops and motivates its employees so that they exhibit the behaviors and high productivity needed to help the company accomplish its business plans (Schuler & Jackson, 1987) and value-based goals. The successful attainment of the company's strategy then reinforces the company's spiritual values and purpose as shown in the upper left-hand side of Figure 1. Therefore, the model shows an iterative cycle of how spiritual values can be integrated throughout the organization. We now use this model to examine spirituality and organizational behavior at SWA.

SWA Spiritual Values

SWA is widely viewed as having a very strong set of values which shape its corporate culture. As we shall see, many of these values are manifestations of spirituality. First, SWA has a strong emphasis on community (Godsey, 1996; Tyler, 1998). Teamwork, serving others, and acting in the best interests of the company are central aspects of this community value at SWA (Caudron, 1997). There is a strong feeling among the employees that they are part of a family and that the employees take care of each other as well as their customers. Even though SWA places a strong emphasis on customers, it states that its employees always come first (Freiberg & Freiberg, 1996; Levering & Moskowitz, 1993). Moreover, not only are employees encouraged to be part of the company, but so are their families who are often invited to participate in company activities and celebrations (Freiberg & Frieberg, 1996).

Second, SWA employees feel like they are part of a cause. SWA seeks to offer the lowest airfares, frequent flights, and a personable service characterized by fun and humor. When demand increases, SWA seeks to expand flights rather than increase prices. With this philosophy, SWA has frequently driven down the prices of other airlines and significantly increased the number of people who fly. To some degree, SWA seeks to give an opportunity to fly to people who ordinarily could not afford it. It is important to realize that this cause of cheap and fun air travel originated from the intense struggle SWA endured in setting up operations, and later in surviving an industry that was then dominated by restrictive regulations and large established airlines. SWA had to struggle for years to even earn approval to start operations. Later it had to work very hard to make its concept of low-cost, no-frills air travel succeed in the face of continued opposition from regulators as well as the large established airlines. For these reasons a sense of being a "rebel," independence, and liberty are associated with SWA's cause or mission of offering low-cost, fun air travel (Freiberg & Frieberg, 1996).

These aspects of SWA are consistent with the literature which states that the organization acting as a community and having a cause or important purpose are central interrelated aspects of workplace spirituality (Brown, 1992; Channon, 1992; Gozdz, 1993; Ray, 1992). These articles contend that people want to have something to believe in, have meaningful work, and feel like they can contribute to an organizational mission that makes a difference in others (Collins & Porras, 1994). In addition, the sense of community promotes the feeling of partnership with other employees and with the organization (Rosen, 1992) as well as a connection to something larger than oneself (Brown, 1992).

Another integral aspect of spirit at work mentioned in the literature is the empowerment of all employees (Jaffe & Scott, 1993; Ray, 1992). True empowerment involves several levels, including whether employees believe they can (1) really make change, (2) be a source of creativity, (3) behave in a self-managing way, (4) fully accept the values and culture of the organization, and (5) have input into corporate policies (Jaffe & Scott, 1993).

Many of these levels of empowerment are found at SWA. SWA employees, including flight attendants, customer service reps, and baggage handlers, are encouraged to take whatever action they deem necessary to meet customer needs or help fellow workers—even if it means breaking company policies (Noe et al., 1997). If employees make mistakes in judgment, the employees are not punished, but given feedback on how to improve the next time. In fact, errors are sometimes celebrated with the intent of turning failures into personal growth (Bruce, 1997). All of these practices work to reinforce the self-worth of employees.

A related aspect of empowerment is that employees are strongly encouraged to give suggestions to create continuous improvement of the company. To this end, employees and their unions are given many opportunities to influence the company's decisions and policies. In fact, at SWA the input of unions is often actively sought in company decisions. SWA also constantly surveys its employees and unions to identify their perceptions and solicit ideas about how to run the company (Sunoo, 1995).

Another core value of SWA is an emphasis not only on the intellectual and skill-based aspects of work, but also on emotional and humor aspects (Levering & Moskowitz, 1993). A portion of SWA's mission statement states that its customer service will be "delivered with a sense of warmth, friendliness, individual pride, and Company Spirit" (Southwest Airlines, 1988). This is manifested in two ways. First, the organization places an extraordinary focus on showing "heart"—caring for its customers and employees. While this may sound simplistic, SWA appears to live this idea actively. There are legendary stories about the extent to which SWA has gone to please its customers. For example, there are times when employees have driven customers to their destinations when they missed a flight, had a customer stay at their home when they were undergoing medical treatments in an unfamiliar city (Kelleher, 1998), taken care of a customer's pet when a customer had no other alternatives (Noe et al., 1997), or paid for a customer's ticket when they didn't have enough money (Freiberg & Freiberg, 1996). While every company has a few stories like this, at SWA they appear to happen on a much more regular basis. Although described as routine business practices, they are another manifestation of a commitment to a greater cause and a desire to serve humanity.

Second, SWA highly values humor and enthusiasm (Levering & Moskowitz, 1993). For instance, the CEO, Herb Kelleher, is famous for his humorous and eccentric behavior, such as singing and entertaining at company functions and playing jokes (Levering & Moskowitz, 1993). He has been known to help flight attendants serve drinks and peanuts (Malloy, 1996), sing at company picnics, wear costumes on holidays, play pranks, and belt out rap songs at press conferences (Levering & Moskowitz, 1993; Sunoo, 1995). Not just Kelleher but also the employees dress up in costumes at Halloween and during casual dress days, produce rap videos, and perform songs and dances at company celebrations. Flight attendants tell jokes and sometimes pop out of the overhead baggage compartments (Noe et al., 1997). One employee noted that at a previous company she was told that she laughed too loud, but at SWA she states, "Now I can laugh in the hall as much I want to. . . . They [SWA] allow each person to really be themselves" (Levering & Moskowitz, 1993, p. 413). In sum, the intent at SWA is to have personable, outgoing employees who display their spirit in humor, energizing emotion, celebration, and sheer fun while they work (Levering & Moskowitz, 1993; Sunoo, 1995).

These elements of SWA are consistent with the literature which states that an emphasis on enthusiasm and commitment (Rosen, 1992), emotional expression (Bracey, Rosenblum, Sanford, & Trueblood, 1993), and personal relationships (Miller, 1993) are all considered important aspects of spirit at work. Similarly, it has been stated that having employees who act fully alive (Ray, 1992) and have relationships that provide caring, nurturing, and cooperation (Harman, 1992) are considered as essential aspects of spirituality in business.

While SWA values community and having fun, it also has a strong work ethic. Employees at SWA are expected to work hard and be flexible so that they can reduce staffing requirements below their competitors (Levering & Moskowitz, 1993). Both employees and managers are expected to work different jobs (Kelleher, 1998). At SWA, top managers as well as pilots sometimes help with boarding passengers or loading the plane. This hard work appears to be based to a large extent on the pride of being part of a company that stands for something. For SWA employees, working hard and having fun are not at odds with each other. The culture at SWA reflects the view of having "people who take their jobs seriously, but not necessarily themselves" (Levering & Moskowitz, 1993, p. 413). The philosophy is that happy and relaxed employees are also more productive (Noe et al., 1997; Sunoo, 1995).

These elements of the work ethic at SWA are in line with the view that a healthy company contains employees who are hardworking, enthusiastic, eager to share their ideas, and committed to the organization (Rosen, 1992). Together these values of work ethic, community, having a company cause, empowerment, and expression of emotion form the spiritual core of SWA and in turn play an integral part in shaping its business plans and goals (LeBarre, 1996).

SWA Business and Individual Plans

As discussed earlier, SWA's philosophy is to make flying "cheap, fast, and fun" (Stewart, 1998) by providing low airfares, frequent and dependable flights, and high-quality, friendly, and humorous service (Levering & Moskowitz, 1993; Noe et al., 1997). While this philosophy certainly seeks to fill a strategic niche within the airline industry, it also seems to reflect a genuine desire to provide customers with low prices and a unique brand of high-quality service (Freiberg & Freiberg, 1996).

SWA's business practices include the use of only one type of aircraft to reduce maintenance, inventory, and training costs. The company also has flights of short distance with frequent service between destinations, a limited food and beverage service policy, no advance seating, and no baggage or ticket exchange with other airlines. All of these practices are specifically geared to help SWA fulfill its low-cost, no-frills, but highly personable service niche (Noe et al., 1997). To provide for successful execution of these values-based business plans, SWA's employees work hard and frequently perform multiple job functions (Godsey, 1996; Tyler, 1998). As stated previously, employees are (1) empowered to make decisions, (2) instructed to consistently provide high-quality service, and (3) encouraged to add fun and humor in their interactions with customers. These employee goals and behaviors are specifically encouraged and nurtured by the company's HRM practices, which are discussed next.

SWA HRM Practices

Other airlines have sought to imitate many aspects of SWA's strategy, but few of these airlines have survived, illustrating how difficult it is for organizations to successfully execute their philosophy over time. A major reason for SWA's longer-term success is its HRM practices which are carefully designed to provide "conditions that energize and inspire people" (Stewart, 1998) and to implement the company's core values and strategy (Noe et al., 1997). We now briefly discuss several aspects of these HRM practices.

SWA places the highest importance in its selection process on employee attitudes and values, rather than technical abilities. This philosophy includes all employees, including pilots (Caudron, 1997). To test for behaviors such as a sense of humor, ability to work with others, and friendliness, SWA's interview process includes group interviews where applicants tell jokes and role-play a variety of situations to demonstrate teamwork, a sense of humor, and the capacity to act spontaneously. Frequent flyers and peer employees participate in interviewing candidates to provide a deeper perspective and to further emphasize teamwork (Noe et al., 1997; Sunoo, 1995). Because of its reputation for being an excellent place to work, SWA can be very selective as it receives an extremely large number of job applicants without active advertising (Kaydon, 1998).

Once employees are hired, they are immediately given a celebration greeting into the company (Tyler, 1998). Customers are brought in to provide their perspective to new employees, more senior employees are assigned as mentors, employees are oriented to think independently, and training includes humorous videos and skits to teach employees about the company's culture of teamwork and fun. SWA's casual dress policy and its allowance of employees to wear costumes to work are intended to reinforce its fun, relaxed, and spontaneous atmosphere (Levering & Moskowitz, 1993).

SWA asks a lot of its employees and in return provides them with a wide range of financial and non-financial rewards. These rewards are consistent with the literature that states spiritual-oriented organizations give much back to their employees, including respect, growth (Rosen, 1992), and intrinsic value through their work as well as extrinsic rewards such as ownership and security (Brown, 1992; Mollner, 1992). The company, which has never had a layoff (Noe et al., 1997), recently announced that it has officially adopted a no-layoff policy (Branch,

1999). SWA has a strong policy allowing lateral transfers and promoting from within (Joinson, 1997). They offer profit sharing (McNerney, 1998), bonus, retirement savings policies, and stock option plans (Levering & Moskowitz, 1993). As a further demonstration of this kind of community attitude, the CEO agreed to freeze his pay when SWA's pilots accepted a stock option plan in lieu of an annual pay increase for 5 years (Cimini, 1995; Noe et al., 1997).

SWA also offers many non-pay rewards, including merchandise, travel, celebrations for specific organizational and employee accomplishments, as well as just for the fun of it (Gruner, 1998). Deal and Key (1998) note that SWA is a model company in providing both frequent spontaneous praise (acknowledgment) on *current* behaviors as well as having formal recognition programs which reward *past* behaviors.

SWA Employee and Organizational Outcomes

SWA's core values and its implementation of those values through its various HRM practices appear to generate strong employee, customer, and firm results. SWA has consistently been named to the list of 100 best companies to work for in America (Levering & Moskowitz, 1993) and in 1998 was voted the number one company at which to work (Levering & Moskowitz, 1998). A typical comment found in random employee surveys in this selection process of the 100 best companies was: "Working here is truly an unbelievable experience. They treat you with respect, pay you well, and empower you. They use your ideas to solve problems. They encourage you to be yourself. I love going to work!" (Levering & Moskowitz, 1998, p. 84).

As a result of this high employee satisfaction, SWA employees have one of the lowest turnover rates (6%) in the airline industry (Levering & Moskowitz, 1998). At the same time, SWA consistently has one of the lowest labor cost per miles flown of any major airline (Lederer, 1995) and its employees are credited with being primarily responsible for SWA's various quality awards (Laabs, 1998). Employees are also actively involved in community-based service projects. In addition, they demonstrated their support for each other by setting up a catastrophe fund to support employees during personal crises (Noe et al., 1997).

Many researchers assert that this high employee satisfaction and productivity play a major role in SWA's profitability (Freiberg & Freiberg, 1996; Nirenberg, 1997; Stewart, 1998). At least the following is clear. The company won the triple crown of air travel with the highest on-time arrival, best score on baggage handling, and fewest customer complaints five times in the 1990s. SWA has been profitable every year except one since it began in 1971 (Levering & Moskowitz, 1993) despite the high volatility of the airline industry (Sunoo, 1995). In one year in the early 1990s, it was the *only* major U.S. airline to make a profit. It has also been able to accomplish this while maintaining strong growth. SWA currently employs almost 25,000 people, having created almost 5,000 jobs during 1996–98 (Levering & Moskowitz, 1998). In 1998 and 1999, it was the only company named to the top ten list of most admired companies as well as best companies to work for in the U.S. (Branch, 1999; Brown, 1999; Levering & Moskowitz, 1998; Stewart, 1998).

Discussion

In this paper we have sought to make several contributions to the emerging literature on what is being called spirituality in business. First, we have proposed a spiritual values–based model to systematically illustrate how spirituality can be manifested in an organization and influence its performance. Using this model as a comprehensive framework for assessment, the complexity associated with implementing spirituality throughout an organization is highlighted, for it is not enough merely to integrate spirituality into the mission statement. Instead, these ideas need to be woven into business strategies and practices. Second, while SWA certainly has its limitations, we believe that its values of a sense of cause, community, empowerment, work ethic, and rich emotional expression can provide important insights into the conditions when spirituality can benefit both employees and organizations.

In terms of implications of spirituality for both employees and companies, we can relate our analysis of SWA in several important ways to recent findings which link a highly satisfied workforce (a core aspect of a spiritual-based company) to organizational financial performance. First, Grant (1998) found that in order for the "best" (from an employee satisfaction perspective) companies to be profitable, workers must see a connection between their jobs and the company's mission. Further, in support of the earlier contentions of Collins and Porras's (1994) *Built to Last*, it was found that this sense of mission is not making a profit, but involves some notion of making a real difference in the world or personal betterment of the company's customers (Lieber, 1998). Concerning this point, SWA's core values of a sense of community and cause directly relate to SWA's business strategy of offering low-cost air travel to customers who ordinarily couldn't afford to fly. In addition, the emphasis SWA places on emotional expression and humor directly connects to offering an extremely personable and fun-oriented brand of service quality.

Based on this research, we believe that companies that engage not just the minds, but also the hearts and emotions of their employees, will be more profitable. In other words, an organization that earnestly treats its employees as part of its community and emotionally engages them in a company purpose which makes a difference in the world will obtain a higher level of employee motivation and loyalty—and ultimately higher organizational performance (Brown, 1998). SWA's treatment of its employees as part of its family and focus on relationships, caring, and emotional expression taps an entirely deeper level of employee spirit, motivation, and satisfaction. In contrast, most companies seek only to engage the workers through pay or through workers' minds and intellect. This leads to the following proposition:

1. Company spiritual values that tap both the mental and emotional aspects of employees will be more positively related to employee work and spiritual attitudes and organizational performance than company values which only tap the mental aspects of employees.

    Second, Grant (1998) found that workers must believe that they are consistently given the opportunity to perform their best and that their opinions must count if there is to be a relationship between employee satisfaction and organizational performance. An important spiritual-based principle at SWA is the empowerment and involvement of its employees. SWA employees are actively encouraged to make the best decisions for customers, break company rules when necessary, and give active input (often via unions) into company decisions and practices. Based on this, we propose the following moderator proposition:

2. The degree to which employees are truly empowered to have input into company decisions moderates the linkage from organizational spiritual values to employee attitudes and organizational performance. Specifically, firms that highly empower their employees will experience a stronger positive

linkage of the company's spiritual values, employee work and spiritual attitudes, and organizational performance.

Third, it was found that employees in the "best" (from an employee satisfaction and financial perspective) companies believe that their fellow workers are also strongly committed to high quality (Grant, 1998). SWA's HRM practices are all carefully designed to align employees with the company's values and goals. SWA's practices are applied consistently across all job levels (e.g., top managers and pilots as well as mechanics and flight attendants). While other organizations may have some similar values, SWA's HRM practices help make its values a daily reality for all of its employees over the long run, which is key to integrating spirituality throughout an organization. This leads to the following moderator proposition:

3. The degree to which the company's HRM practices are aligned with the company's spiritual values moderates the linkage of the company's spiritual values to employee attitudes and organizational performance. Specifically, firms that highly align HRM practices with the company's core values will experience a stronger positive linkage of the company's spiritual values, employee work and spiritual attitudes, and organizational performance.

We believe that these propositions provide a starting point for a preliminary contingency perspective of the conditions when a company's spiritual values can enhance both employee spiritual and work attitudes and organizational performance. In addition, this inductive research effort illustrates the need for future research to empirically test and refine the spiritual values–based model and these propositions. This research should probably involve some type of qualitative component to ensure that the notion of spiritual values and employees' reaction to them are assessed on an in-depth basis. Such systematic research is needed if we are to create a paradigm shift in CEOs so that they incorporate spiritual principles in their organizations. It is clear that we need to conduct more rigorous theory-based research on spirituality in the workplace if organizations are to create a higher level of social and economic performance and to offer employees an opportunity to find a greater sense of meaning in their work

References

Anderson, C. (1997), Values-based management, *Academy of Management Executive*, Vol. 11, pp. 25–46.

Block, P. (1993), *Stewardship: Choosing Service Over Self-Interest*, Berrett-Koehler Publishers, San Francisco.

Blanchard, K., & O'Connor, M. (1997), *Managing by Values*, Berrett-Koehler Publishers, San Francisco.

Bracey, H., Rosenblum, J., Sanford, A., & Trueblood, R. (1993), *Managing From the Heart*, Dell Publishing, New York.

Branch, S. (1999), The 100 best companies to work for in America, *Fortune*, January 11, pp. 128–144.

Brown, J. (1992), Corporation as community: A new image for a new era, in Renesch, J. (Ed.), *New Traditions in Business*, Berrett-Koehler Publishers, San Francisco, pp. 123–139.

Brown, E. (1999), America's most admired companies, *Fortune*, March 1, pp. 68–73.

Bruce, A. (1997), Back to the fundamentals, *Human Resource Focus*, Vol. 74, p. 11.

Caudron, S. (1997), Hire for attitude: It's who they are that counts, *Workforce Staffing: Hire for Attitude Supplement*, August, pp. 20–26.

Channon, J. (1992), Creating espirt de corps, in Renesch, J. (Ed.), *New Traditions in Business*, Berrett-Koehler Publishers, San Francisco, pp. 53–66.

Cimini, H. (1995), Southwest Airlines agreement, *Monthly Labor Review*, Vol. 118, p. 74.

Collins, J., & Porras, J. (1994), *Built to Last: Successful Habits of Visionary Companies*, Harper Business, New York.

Deal, T., & Key, M. (1998), *Corporate Celebration: Play, Purpose and Profit at Work*, Berrett-Koehler Publishers, San Francisco.

Ferguson, M. (1993), The transformation of values and vocation, in Ray, M., and Rinzler, A. (Eds.), *The New Paradigm in Business*, G. P. Putman's Sons Publishers, New York, pp. 28–34.

Freiberg, K., & Freiberg, J. (1996), *Nuts! Southwest Airlines' Crazy Recipe for Business and Personal Success*, Bard Books, Austin, TX.

Glaser, B., & Strauss, A. (1967), *The Discovery of Grounded Theory: Strategies for Qualitative Research*, Aldin, Chicago.

Godsey, K. (1996), Flying lessons: 10 Southwest strategies to apply to your business, *Success*, Vol. 43, pp. 24–25.

Gozdz, K. (1993), Building community as a leadership discipline, in Ray, M., and Rinzler, A. (Eds.), *The New Paradigm In Business*, G. P. Putnam's Sons, New York, pp. 107–119.

Grant, L. (1998), Happy workers, high returns, *Fortune*, January 12, p. 95.

Gruner, S. (1998), Have fun, make money, *Inc.*, Vol. 20, p. 123.

Harman, W. (1992), 21-st Century Business: A Background for Dialogue. In J. Renesch (Ed.) *New Traditions in Business*, pp. 11–24. San Francisco: Berrett-Koehler.

Hawley, J. (1993), *Reawakening the Spirit in Work: The Power of Dharmic Management*, Berrett-Koehler, San Francisco, CA.

Jaffe, D., & Scott, C. (1993), Building a committed workplace: An empowered organization as a competitive advantage, in Ray, M., and Rinzler, A. (Eds.), *The New Paradigm in Business*, G. P. Putnam's Sons, New York, pp. 139–146.

Joinson, C. (1997), Multiple career paths help retain talent, *HR Magazine*, Vol. 42, pp. 59–66.

Kaydon, D. (1998), Riding high, *Sales and Marketing Management*, Vol. 150, pp. 64–69.

Kelleher, H. (1998), Customer service: It starts at home, *Secured Lender*, Vol. 54, pp. 68–73.

Laabs, J. (1998), Southwest airlines credits employees for winning quality award, *Workforce*, Vol. 77, pp. 13–14.

LaBarre, P. (1996), Lighten up, *Industry Week*. Vol. 245, pp. 53–54.

Lederer, J. (1995), Equity based pay: The compensation paradigm for the reengineered corporation, *Chief Executive*, Vol. 102, pp. 36–39.

Levering, R., & Moskowitz, M. (1993), *The 100 Best Companies to Work for in America*. Penguine Books, New York.

Levering, R., & Moskowitz, M. (1998), *The 100 best companies to work for in America*, *Fortune*, January 12, pp. 84–95.

Lieber, R.B. (1998), Why employees love these companies, *Fortune*, January 12, pp. 96–98.

Malloy, A. (1996), Counting the intangibles, *Computerworld. The 100 Best Places to Work Supplement*, June, pp. 31–33.

Mandel, T. (1993), Giving values a voice: Marketing in the new paradigm, in Ray, M., and Rinzler, A. (Eds.), *The New Paradigm in Business*, G. P Putnam's Sons, New York, pp. 164–170.

McNerney, D. (1998), Creating a motivated workforce, *HR Focus*, Vol. 72, pp. 1–4.

Miller, W. (1993), How do we put our spiritual values to work? In Renesch, J. (Ed.), *New Traditions in Business*, Berrett-Koehler, San Francisco, CA, pp. 69–80.

Mollner, T. (1992), The 21st century corporation: The tribe of the relationship age, In Renesch, J. (Ed.), *New Traditions in Business*, Berrett-Koehler, San Francisco, CA, pp. 95–108.

Neal, J. (1998), Research on individual spiritual transformation and work, Symposium presented at the *Academy of Management Conference*, San Diego, CA, August.

Neck, C., & Milliman, J. (1994), Thought self-leadership: Finding spiritual fulfillment in organizational life, *Journal of Managerial Psychology*, Vol. 9, pp. 9–16.

Nirenberg, J. (1997), Mean business, *International Journal of Organizational Analysis*, Vol. 5, pp. 212–216.

Noe, R., Hollenbeck, J., Gerhard, B., & Wright, P. (1997), *Human Resource Management: Gaining a Competitive Advantage*, Irwin, Chicago.

Ray, M. (1992), The emerging new paradigm in business, in Renesch, J. (Ed.), *New Traditions in Business*, Berrett-Koehler, San Francisco, CA, pp. 25–38.

Rosen, R.H. (1992), The anatomy of a healthy company, in J. Renesch (Ed.), *New Traditions in Business*, Berrett-Koehler, San Francisco, CA, pp 109–120.

Sanford, C. (1993), A self-organizing leadership view of paradigms, In Renesch, J. (Ed.), *New Traditions in Business*, Berrett-Koehler, San Francisco, CA, pp. 193–208.

Schuler, R., & Jackson, S. (1987), Linking competitive strategies with human resource management practices, *Academy of Management Executive*, Vol. 1, pp. 207–220.

Southwest Airlines (1988), Southwest Airlines Corporate Mission Statement, January, Dallas, TX.

Stewart, T. (1998), America's most admired companies, *Fortune*, Vol. 137, No. 4, pp. 70–82.

Sunoo, B. P. (1995), How fun flies at Southwest Airlines, *Personnel Journal*, Vol. 74, pp. 62–73.

Tyler, K. (1998), Take new employee orientation off the back burner, *HR Magazine,* Vol. 43, pp. 49–57.

INTEGRATING SPIRITUALITY INTO MANAGEMENT EDUCATION IN ACADEMIA AND ORGANIZATIONS:

ORIGINS, A CONCEPTUAL FRAMEWORK, AND CURRENT PRACTICES

Sandra King,
California State Polytechnic University, Pomona

Jerry Biberman,
University of Scranton

Lee Robbins,
Golden Gate University

David M. Nicol,
Frostburg State University

Introduction

Spirituality engenders questions more than normative prescriptive answers. As such, it is better approached in a formative rather than summative terms. We suggest a simple but comprehensive definition of spirituality—*the search for meaning in the ordinary business of life.* Thus, our goal in this paper lies not in judging the practice or assessing the literature of spirituality in the managerial environment, but in exploring aspects of the topic to raise questions and increase attention to relevant issues.

The first section suggests factors that appear to be producing increased interest in spirituality for businesses and among managers, drawing upon the literature in spirituality and work and an empirical survey. The survey of academics, managers, and consultants was conducted to determine the extent to which the topic of spirituality is of growing interest in the workplace, and why. The second section explores other frames that may be more consistent with today's spiritual concerns. In the third section, we demonstrate how course design and pedagogy can support the development of a spiritual dimension in the organizational workplace.

Roots of Rising Interest in Spirituality in the Workplace

A growing interest in the relationship between spirituality and the prospect of a healthy, productive workplace is increasingly evident in the broad spectrum of attention being devoted to this topic. In a relatively short time frame, it has become the central focus in such diverse locales as academic conference sessions (e.g., the national meeting of the Academy of Management), an extensive array of paid workshops, published texts, and the syllabi of university courses. Within academia, we have seen the topic of spirituality included in sections of a wide variety of courses and, less frequently, as stand-alone course offerings. A scan of the internet reveals numerous web sites addressing spirituality and the workplace, while a topical review of the literature quickly demonstrates the heightened interest in this topic. This groundswell of interest is driven by the tentative exploration of the question: Is the incorporation of spirituality in the workplace, in fact, of potential benefit? The application of spirituality in the workplace is increasingly the object of discussion among consultants, academics, and the business community (Neal, Lichtenstein, & Banner, 1998). What seems to be driving this interest? A review of the literature suggests the answers to be multi-faceted, a function of the level of analysis—be it the environment external to the organization, the organization, or the individuals in the organizations.

External Environment: Organizational and Individual Levels

We are living in a world characterized by an accelerating rate of change (Vaill, 1989), one in which individuals often feel as though they are unable to achieve a sense of balance and stability in their lives. Through technological innovation, we have access to instant communication and previously unfathomable masses of information requiring us to process increasing amounts of data. Often, this produces information overload and consequent anxiety (Russell & Evans, 1992).

Fifty years ago, families typically stayed in one place for all of their lives. Today, a large portion of the population has become transient, with the consequent loss of connection to communities, extended families, and, often times, their religious anchors. Concurrently, relieved of many of the external anxieties previously associated with war or economic depression, growing up in a work environment that supports fragmentation and specialization, baby boomers have focused on individual achievement (Briskin, 1996). Without the linkages present in the past, individuals often look to their immediate families and/or to their work for a sense of connection to others (Conger, 1994). Increasing change, unsettling overload, community fragmentation, and disconnection characterize the largest percentage of our working population—the baby boomers, who are reaching the age at which individuals often experience mid-life crisis (Neal, 1997). Not surprisingly, as baby boomers reach mid-life, their drive for achievement and the associated consequences are often subjected to scrutiny in an effort to assess merit and meaningfulness.

On the organizational level, we have witnessed the downsizing and restructuring of numerous organizations with the consequence that many employees have been laid off (Noer, 1993; Pulley, 1997). Not only is there a sense of loss for those who have been laid off, but also an intense residual element of uncertainty and fear within the organization. Though the layoff may create an opportunity for some, for others, it is a disaster. For both those directly affected and their wary colleagues it prompts reexamination of their lives and their organizational duties.

Briskin (1996) suggests that the legacy of focusing on efficiency, being driven by pursuit of profit maximization, has diminished corporate sensitivity to the core human values of its members. In such a climate, individuals often find it difficult to perceive meaning in their work. Many organizations fail to establish and/or maintain a sense of collective purpose, prompting individuals to be disinclined to exercise initiative, instead becoming dependent on the managerial hierarchy to make all decisions. By not providing individuals with a sense of purpose in their work, organizational creativity is suppressed, if not eliminated (Mitroff et al., 1994). The individualistic emphasis of our society is reflected in a desire for personal accomplishment and the freedom to pursue it. Unfortunately, this drive often conflicts with the organization's efforts at control, thereby contributing to a sense of distrust within organizations (Conger, 1994). The absence of trust has created unproductive competition between individuals, organizational departments, and the employer and employee. Ironically, in organizations initially constructed to achieve a common purpose, the breakdown and fragmentation of individual relationships within them actually creates a lack of community and a dysfunctional work environment. In order to rectify the problems and counter the fragmentation that has occurred, various types of team management processes have been implemented. Many individuals, however, feel the processes merely create an illusion of involvement (Argyris, 1993). In essence, many organizations often fail to walk their talk (Richards, 1995; Secretan, 1997). This results in widening the distance between the organization and its members.

In order to compensate for their sense of deprivation within the organizational setting, many, particularly at the managerial levels, are looking to the spiritual in their quest for meaning. For example, Jerry Harvey (1996) recently observed that when he asks CEOs about their prayer life, they often become so engrossed in the conversation that they will offer to drive him to the airport to continue talking until the last minute.

For many leaders, the growing distinction between religion and spirituality has also created an opening for finding a way to implement spirituality in the workplace. With this latitude, a number of businesses (e.g., Mary Kay, Service Master, Tom Chapell, and Chick-Fil-A) are attempting to integrate spiritual values as the foundation for their corporate mission (Conger, 1994). The turmoil of organizational change, employee alienation, and the absence of collective purpose prompt interest in integrating spirituality into the workplace to enhance organizational performance. At the individual level, a variety of factors have prompted the increased focus on spiritual connections. Individuals have an innate thirst for understanding and direction, heightened in times of confusion and uncertainty. Management theorists (e.g., Mary Parker Follet and Abraham Maslow) have argued that individuals are driven toward self-actualization. A sense of discomfort arises from the discrepancy between an individual's potential capability and the level of work in which s/he is engaged, impelling her/him to search for spirituality in the workplace (King & Nicol, 1998). Even as individuals achieve positions of leadership, thereby fulfilling material (and even ego) goals, they are beginning to acknowledge that they need more— driving organizations toward attentiveness to issues of value, meaning, and spirituality.

To supplement and refine the perspective of our review of the literature, we conducted a survey of academics, managers, and consultants to confirm the growing interest in the topic of spirituality in the workplace, as well as the reasons for such interest. The survey was distributed through academic conferences and an on-line snowball (networking) technique. It requested that the respondents describe: (1) how and why they became interested in the topic of spirituality in the workplace; (2) whether they are aware of a growing interest in this area in general; (3) what factors they believe are driving it; and (4) how they have formally, or informally, included the topic of spirituality in any of their classroom and/or training sessions. To develop a greater understanding of how individuals are integrating spirituality into their courses, we also collected syllabi from those respondents who were offering a course in management and spirituality and/or incorporating the topic in other courses. Over fifty people completed our exploratory survey. We found that the predominant theme mentioned from our respondents was that their interest in spirituality in the workplace was derived from their personal spiritual evolutionary experience and a desire to integrate their personal and professional lives. This is not inconsistent with Maslow's hierarchical perspective. With increasing affluence and the widespread satisfaction of "lower-level" needs in Western societies, individuals are inclined to progress toward self-actualization, and with that, confront what constitutes meaning in their lives. Thus, their emerging spiritual values, whether theological or psychological, become blended into their work life. Most of the participants wrote about how the process was a natural evolutionary one.

A majority of the participants reported an increased interest, both among their colleagues and their students, in the topic of spirituality and management. Many believe this increase has occurred as a direct result of societal insecurity. For example, many of the participants mentioned that the world was becoming more "messed up" (e.g., increasingly rapid rate of change, increased information and technology overload, loss of family life and community, general loss of security). In addition, there were a number of individuals who suggested that the large number of baby boomers reaching mid-life, beginning to reexamine their work life, are driving the increased interest in spirituality in the workplace. These "boomers" are increasingly questioning the meaning of their work, with the consequent search for work that will enable them to integrate their personal values within their work in the organization.

A predominant number of the academic respondents reported that they are including spirituality in their teaching, either formally or informally. A review of the syllabi and the course titles makes it immediately evident that the topic of spirituality and work is being integrated into courses through a number of different avenues. Among the more explicit course titles were: HRD: Spiritual Values; Self-Leadership; Ethical, Moral, and Spiritual Issues of Management; and HRD: The Meaning of Work. Although some conduct entire courses in spirituality and management, the majority report incorporating the concepts within the context of more established courses. To assist in this effort, many are using recent texts that have been written on the topic of spirituality in the workplace. Many remain unsure as to how to effectively implement it in their management courses.

The Spiritual Perspective: Its Legitimacy in the Workplace

Although the survey and literature demonstrates strong interest among academics and managers to integrate spirituality and work, we believe a major impediment remains. Managers need a clear framework for spiritual leadership and decision making, distinguishing between activities that are and are not "spiritual." Discussions of management and spirituality are addressed primarily at the individual level. Today, texts, articles, and conferences addressing management and spirituality help incline individuals toward a recognition of critical uncertainties, of unresolved issues. Managers are prompted to bring their inner spirituality, their concerns for value and meaning, through the doors of their offices, rather than leaving them at the enterprise gate. However, without a framework of organizational theory, such arguments may fail to persuade, or, on the other hand, may persuade those inclined to zealotry that will then run roughshod over those with differing beliefs.

Less is said at the organizational level. Increased attention to a conceptual framework for choosing directions for the spiritually attentive business enterprise is needed. To begin, we might inquire into the basic assumptions in the current paradigm of business. In this paradigm, what is the purpose of business organizations? In the still prevailing hierarchical firm, power and decision making are concentrated at the top and trickle down through delegation. Priorities, reward structures, agendas of discussion, and data selected to guide decisions all depend upon certain basic assumptions and assumed purpose. When asked about purpose, leaders of firms can proudly respond by pointing to their carefully crafted *Mission Statement*, which generally fails to address the responsibility of the business as a social system. Rather, the purpose is declared in the categorization of the firm as being "for-profit," without further qualification. Though some hold profits to be the sole objective, others suggest that profits should be conceived solely as an enabler for businesses to fulfill their social obligations. The purpose, as argued by economists from Adam Smith to Milton Friedman, is to fulfill the desires of the marketplace, wherein profit is but the mechanism driving the invisible hand.

In the current era, growth and market share have been accorded preeminence as objectives. Instead of focusing on the extent to which the firm has successfully provided value to its stakeholders, we tend to embrace these markers of magnitude, embracing the narrow and quantifiable, rather than the holistic and qualitative. This does not bode well for encouraging organizational innovation, for supporting employee development, for promoting actions that serve the social good, etc. When market share or growth, or "the bottom line," are used as the sole or primary measures of success, we implicitly reinforce the perception that they are the only ultimately worthy ends to be pursued. Rather, we need to acknowledge that organizations serve multiple stakeholders, not just the stockholders. As such, they must balance competing ends to achieve a common success. Hence, being socially responsible, fostering participative decision making, responding to changing consumer demands, and operating profitably is all necessary and appropriate for success; yet none is sufficient by itself. We do not exist in a vacuum, though we may perceive that to be the case in the short term. For too long, we responded to only one of our stakeholders. Now we must acknowledge and be responsive to the needs of others.

Of course, we are habitual animals. Hence, we tend to assess our progress in the form of past measures. Thus, we ask if increased worker satisfaction, heightened productivity, or enhanced creativity resulted in an increase in market share. R&D in firms is functionally evaluated not for its contribution to human welfare, however laudable medical research, for example, might seem, but for its contribution to the welfare of the firm as measured by profit or growth. These approaches to assessment of research, innovation, or general effectiveness are further promulgated in textbooks and classrooms, reinforcing the paradigm for succeeding generations of managers.

Are these criteria sufficient to produce better societies? Will these criteria decrease suffering? Are these the criteria we need? Despite optimism about the invisible hand reinforced by recent comparative production successes in market economies (at least until the recent

"Asian crisis"), longings and recognition of the need for something more are increasingly evident. As John Dunning (1998) points out, cooperation must play a larger role in the "global capitalism" of the current era. As the problem of production becomes less pressing, problems of distribution, of equity, of natural and person-created beauty rise in relative importance. Profit, as the guiding mechanism for the invisible hand, has become inadequate.

Choosing different measures of business success would mean that research, practice, and business education would produce different processes for firms, and different content, and perhaps an educational process, in our business schools. Spirituality seems more about questions than about prescriptive answers—*the search for meaning in the ordinary business of life*. If we choose to develop more spiritual organizations, we must use multiple criteria and develop organizational designs that can support such criteria. Further work is needed, but a critical beginning is to recognize both the limitations and the enormous impact of using profit alone as the criterion of success.

Bringing Spirituality in the Workplace into the Classroom

We will now examine how the needs driving the interest can be taught to students who will be the future leaders for our businesses. At the end of the 20th century, a new paradigm for business management and business education has been emerging in response to the world business community's need for a different educational product. The main components of this emerging new paradigm for business education, as well as for business management, include a need to connect people's public selves with their personal or private selves. As Parker Palmer (1998) suggests in *The Courage to Teach*, leaders of any kind—including teachers—must begin to find ways to teach the whole person, to consider intellectual, emotional, and spiritual needs, as well as the practical demands of career training. In our recent survey of management educators, finding work that integrates the whole self was mentioned from both students' and teachers' perspective. The inclusion of spirituality and spiritual techniques in management higher education parallels similar trends that are occurring in schools at all levels in several countries—including medical schools (Mangan, 1997), seminaries (Niebur, 1997), public schools in the United Kingdom (Neumark, 1997), and in undergraduate psychology of women classes (Power, 1995). Tools and techniques which enhance a person's ability to become self-aware, to learn and to grow, have been increasingly accepted in business training (Senge, 1990). These new ways of learning require business educators to revamp their approaches to include psychological and spiritual approaches to classroom teaching. The content areas in which spirituality at work can be, and has been, discussed include self-awareness, decision-making, power and politics, ethics, creativity, intuition, problem solving, stress management, leadership, and diversity.

In the course of personal and professional development, the authors have studied techniques and have been experientially involved in a variety of spiritual disciplines—such as Jesuit spiritual exercises of Ignatius of Loyola; the Kaballah; and Vipassana Buddhist, Hindu, and Chinese philosophy and meditative and prayer techniques. We have found the regular practice outside of our classrooms of some spiritual discipline (yoga and tai chi) to serve as a ground for our classroom innovations. Our experiences with these spiritual traditions have demonstrated the similarity underlying all of the spiritual or mystical traditions, regardless of their religious background (Biberman & Whitty, 1997).

Despite differences in culture and specific language or terminology used, the philosophies of all of these spiritual traditions describe spiritual transformation, the awareness and experience of one's higher self, and the interconnectedness of all people with each other and with divine creator, source, or energy. The second author of this paper teaches management courses at a religious institution. The religious nature of the institution provides a natural lead-in and context for him to raise spiritual issues within his classes. He is able to show how the spiritual philosophies of the traditions described above parallel the emerging new paradigm of personal empowerment and group collaboration in business and organizations. We have shared with our students the spiritual teachings and philosophy from mystical traditions of the major world religions, including teachings from Ignatius of Loyola, Buddhist, Hindu, and Chinese philosophy, Zen and Taoist readings, vedic wisdom, Kaballah and Jewish mysticism, and Catholic and other Christian readings. Specific processes and techniques that have been used in class include: explaining the benefits of, and then teaching, various kinds of prayer, relaxation exercises, meditation (including mantra meditation), journalizing and other writing, active imagination, guided imagery, drawings, spiritual exercises, hatha yoga and other stretching, tai chi, breathing exercises, music, dance, and movement.

Two of the authors have used Lee Bolman's and Terrences Deal's text, *Leading with Soul*, as the basis for class discussion and papers in a MBA and EMBA courses. This book describes the personal journal and organizational impact of a CEO's search for meaning. Our use of spiritual techniques and philosophies in our teaching has met with acceptance, not only from our students, but also from our colleagues and superiors. In our experience the use of spiritual philosophies and techniques can lead to physical, cognitive, and spiritual benefits for both teacher and student, on both the individual and class levels. It can also lead to a transformed classroom climate. Classroom meditation has been observed by both the authors to produce increased physical relaxation in our students, as well as anxiety and stress reduction. Cognitively, we believe it enhances mental clarity, empathy, stamina, and confidence. In addition, the use of creative visualization, movement, drawing, music, and story telling in our classes has enabled our students to learn to trust and use their intuition and to improve their creative problem-solving abilities. Examination of alternatives to the single-variable profit model of corporate success has created lively discussion and considerable interest from students, examining a wider range of behaviors and the potential for increased congruence between organizational goals and their individual searches for meaningful work.

As for explicit spiritual benefits, as a consequence of the authors' experiences related to the classes, our students have reported experiencing an expanded sense of wholeness, a renewed sense of purpose and meaning in their lives, and a sense of well-being predicated on contact with their essential natures. A great benefit we have observed when using spiritual philosophies and techniques, has been the transformation of the class climate into that of a learning community. We have observed behavioral changes in our students and in the classroom climate consistent with concepts typically found in models of learning organizations (Senge et al., 1994), such as dialogue; attention to raising questions and to experiment; openness and trust; and consensus seeking. We would argue that a company experiencing similar behavioral changes would become less structurally constrained, more inclusive, less committed to power distance, more holistic, and more process-oriented (focusing on both the means and the ends). To that end, spiritually attentive organizations might be: emotional, smaller, and place emphasis on the role of work organizations as communities as well as production systems.

Conclusion

Through heightened understanding of the driving forces underlying interest in the linkage of spirituality and management in the workplace, we can begin to uncover the implications for our role as educators. In this is the prospect for developing a framework that will provide the basis for a new organizational framework. Our review of the literature, in conjunction with our own research, suggest, that the sources that are driving the need for change are multi-faceted, associated with different levels of analysis—be it the environment external to the organization, the organization itself, or the individuals that make up the organization. Although the survey and literature demonstrate strong intentions among academics and managers to bring spiritual perspectives to classrooms and work organizations, we believe that a major impediment remains in the lack of a clear framework to do it. In order to address the issue, we have noted the limitation of the singular focus characterizing blind adherence to the bottom line, or alternatively, growth or market share.

Finally, we have listed and briefly discussed teaching methods and techniques derived through our research and extensive experience. Through our own experience, and a review of the syllabi that we have gathered, we have suggested specific content areas, as well as techniques, in which spirituality at work can be discussed. We have also described anecdotal results and benefits that we have observed resulting from the use of these philosophies and techniques. We have only provided an initial probe into what we hope will become a major body of knowledge related to spirituality in the workplace. It is our belief that by fostering an education perspective that includes attention to spirituality in the workplace, we will not only help to produce a healthier society, but will unleash phenomenal energy and creativity for individuals and the organizational environment.

References

Ackoff, R. L. (1981), *Creating the Corporate Future.* New York: John Wiley & Sons.

Argyris, C. (1993), *Knowledge for Action: A Guide to Overcoming Barriers to Organizational Change.* San Francisco: Jossey-Bass.

Biberman, J., & Whitty, M. (1997), A post-modern spiritual future for work. *Journal of Organizational Change Management,* 10(2), 130–136.

Bolman, T., & Deal., T. E. (1995), *Leading with Soul : An Uncommon Journey of Spirit*. San Francisco: Jossey-Bass.

Briskin, A. (1996), *The Stirring of the Soul in the Workplace*. San Francisco: Berrett-Koehler.

Conger, J. (1994), *Spirit at Work: Discovering the Spirituality in Leadership*. San Francisco: Jossey-Bass.

Covey, S. (1989), *The Seven Habits of Highly Effective People: Restoring the Character Ethic*. New York: Simon and Schuster.

Dunning, J. (1998), Presentation: Capitalism at Golden Gate University. San Francisco, CA, Nov.

Harvey, J. (1996), Conversation at the George Washington University; Washington, D.C.

King, S., & Nicol, D. (1998), Individual and organizational change: Jacques and Jung's contribution to spiritual growth. In Biberman, J., & Alkhafaji, A. (Eds.), *Business Research Yearbook: Global Business Perspective: Vol. 5* (pp. 803–807). Michigan: McNaughton & Gun.

Mangan, K. S. (1997, March 7), Blurring the boundaries between religion and science/medical school programs on the healing role of spirituality. *Chronicle of Higher Education*, 43, 14, 26.

Mitroff, I. I., Mason, R. O., & Pearson, C. M. (1994), Radical surgery: What will tomorrow's organizations look like? *Academy of Management Executive*, 8(2), 11–21.

Neal, J. (1997), Spirituality in management education: A guide to resources. *Journal of Management Education*, 21(1), 121–139.

Neal, J., Lichtenstein, B., & Banner, D. (1998, August), What matters most in transformation: Economic and spiritual arguments for individual, organizational and societal change. Paper presented at the meeting of the Academy of Management, San Diego, CA.

Neumark, V. (1997, February 14), Cards on the table. *Times Educational Supplement*, 201, S1.

Niebur, G. (1997, April 12), At Jewish Theological. *New York Times*, 25, 146.

Noer, D. (1993), *Healing the Wounds: Overcoming the Trauma of Layoffs and Revitalizing Downsized Organizations*. San Francisco: Jossey-Bass.

Palmer, Parker (1998), *The Courage to Teach: Exploring the Inner Landscape of a Teacher's Life*. San Francisco: Jossey-Bass.

Power, R. (1995, Summer–Fall), A class that changes lives. *Women and Therapy*, 16, 2–3.

Pulley, M. L. (1997), *Losing Your Job–Reclaiming Your Soul*. San Francisco: Jossey-Bass.

Richards, D. (1995), *Artful Work*. San Francisco: Berret-Koehler.

Roth, G. (1997), *Sweat your Prayers*. New York: Jeremy Tarcher.

Russell, P., & Evans, R. (1992), *The Creative Manager*. San Francisco: Jossey-Bass.

Secretan, L. H. K. (1997), *Reclaiming Higher Ground*. New York: McGraw-Hill.

Semler, R. (1989, September–October), Managing without managers. *Harvard Business Review*, 76–84.

Semler, R. (1995), *Maverick*. New York: Warner Books.

Senge, P. M. (1990), *The Fifth Discipline: The Art and Practice of the Learning Organization*. New York: Doubleday.

Senge, P. M., et al. (1994) *The Fifth Discipline Fieldbook: Strategies and Tools for Building a Learning Organization*. New York: Currency, Doubleday.

Vaill, Peter (1989), *Managing as a Performing Art: New Ideas for a World of Chaotic Change*. San Francisco: Jossey-Bass.

LINKING COMMUNITY AND SPIRIT:

A COMMENTARY AND SOME PROPOSITIONS[1]

Sandra A. Waddock,
Boston College

**"Conscious community concern is at the
heart of human morality."**

Frans De Waal, *Good Natured* **(1996)**

Economists have tried to tell us for years that what matters most is the economy, economics, money, and of course the things that money can buy. As the 1996 election refrain went, "It's the economy, stupid!" The only thing that really matters (in this view) is self-interest and personal gain. This slogan translates to the organization level as "maximize shareholder wealth." Make as much as you can as quickly as you can. Get the goods and forget the good. Common good? What's that and what's it got to do with me?

But we know better. It's *not* "the economy, stupid." Not really. Or at least not only. Other things also matter, whatever the economists say. For example, one other thing that matters is developing community, that is, caring, belonging, trust, working with others in a joint enterprise that is bigger than oneself, that makes a contribution, and allows us to co-exist in our world successfully. This paper will argue that even in an individualistic society such as the United States, some form of community is important. Community, however, is built on collaboration and not just competition, and derives from the fundamental symbiosis or

---

[1] This paper is based on a presentation entitled "Community Matters Most," given in an all-academy symposium entitled "What Matters Most in Management Scholarship: Nature, Community, Spirituality, and Character," 1998 Academy of Management Annual Meeting, San Diego, CA.

interdependency that biologists now tell us that organisms have with other organisms. It is premised not solely on independence and autonomy, or dependence and hierarchy, but as well on connectedness and a healthy *inter*dependence. Expressed this way, developing community is an exercise of spirituality. It is part of what Wilber (1996) calls the "left-hand" side, the internal, expressive side of life, as opposed to the external, empirically measurable and observable aspects of the world. Community is a part of organizational life that, like other "left-hand" elements like feelings, aesthetics, intuition, awareness, and meanings, has been largely ignored or discounted, in their collective expressions.

The term *society* implies community at its essence. In this use, community implies care, joint meanings, mutuality, and commonality of purpose, of history, norms, and values. It is community in this sense, I argue, that people need to fully develop as human beings, to be integrated wholes and for our societies to be integrated wholes. It is this sense of community that needs to be valued if we are to reintegrate the expressive and consciousness elements of being with the empirically observable. Yet it is exactly these subjective and intersubjective aspects of community that are too frequently ignored in our objectivist mindset. This paper will explore the importance of creating a sense of community that inspires individuals' commitment to a set of goals encompassing the common as well as the individual good. By implication, this enhancement of community allows for a degree of spirituality in our common enterprises.

We are in the United States, as numerous scholars have pointed out (e.g., Lodge, 1975; Bellah et al., 1985), individualists. Yet it may well be a deep sense of loss or absence of community (and an attempt to understand that loss) that has made Robert Putnam's 1995 "Bowling Alone" the most cited article in recent history. Despite the decline of formal associational activities documented by Putnam, Wolfe (1998) finds that people *do* find or build community in a variety of places, especially in the modern world through work organizations. Indeed, a dissertation based on the data in Wolfe's study (Poarch, 1997) finds that work organizations are replacing other types of communities in many Americans' lives. So even if people in the United States have started bowling alone or do watch too much television (Putnam, 1995, 1996), they still care deeply about creating communities that help shape meaning and purpose in their lives. They—we—still seek engagement and involvement not just with self, not just with the "goods," but with others.

In direct contradiction to the need to evoke community at work, however, there is now significant evidence that many organizations, especially businesses, are experiencing diminished capacity to build successful communities and meaningful work. Layoffs, downsizings, re-engineering, and restructurings of all sorts combine in a devaluing of locational communities, not to mention community among employees. These activities are visible features of the modern corporate landscape, highly rewarded by Wall Street and the business press. Further, despite years of attention to "participative management," the quality "revolution," and decentralization to "empower" employees, too frequently jobs are still structured to provide the most control for management and the least for those who actually perform the work. And now there are numerous virtual organizations where people interact less frequently than in traditional organizations, where telecommuting, temporary offices, and contingent workers are becoming all too common means of cost containment. These shifts arguably occur at some cost to community.

Forces in the global economy thus work in direct contrast to Poarch's (1997) finding that with the loss of other types of community found in earlier years in churches, neighborhoods, and civic organizations, people now develop their sense of community at and through work. Processes of modernization and industrialization have vast potential to shift community dynamics as developing nations attempt to become "world class" (Kanter, 1995) without regard for the impacts of those globalization processes, their inherent materialism, and the homogenization of values and culture on local community (see also Korten, 1995; Barber, 1995).

Given the global realities described briefly above, it may well be an imperative that our institutions, market-based, public, and civil, recognize and deal with this need for community and spirit if they hope to be successful in the future and tap the best of human energies. Perhaps because many companies are not prepared to overtly acknowledge community's importance to their own success and even survival, many people seem to be experiencing a tremendous loss of community. Many people live in suburbs, not knowing their neighbors, working 50–60 hours a week in what is too frequently meaningless work, where "face time" is as important as real contribution, and where pressure to do more substitutes for teamwork. This loss of community relates back to a perceived loss of civil society in a nation characterized as having been "wilded" or as having become a "corporation nation"(Derber, 1992, 1998). Others, looking globally, suggest the term "McWorld" (Barber, 1995) to indicate the homogenization and cutthroat competition characterized by a "race to the bottom" (Korten, 1995; Henderson, 1996) resulting from wage and low-cost producer wars (Greider, 1998) imposed by forces of globalization (Kanter, 1995). This dynamic may be somewhat counteracted by strenuous, but unfortunately not always friendly or civil, attempts to sustain or develop a form of community that one scholar has labeled "Jihad," which represents a form of struggle to sustain community identity (Barber, 1995). Further, these countervailing forces exist in a world that is increasingly "one" whether we are ready or not (Greider, 1998).

Integrating the Unobservable

Generally speaking, issues such as spirituality, emotion, and community have received little attention in management thinking, research, and practice, at least until quite recently. Attention has largely been placed on analytical and readily quantifiable subject matters, particularly those that can be expressed in monetary, or at least quantifiable, terms. In fact, as suggested above, in many cases community may be being systematically destroyed in the modern corporation's effort to compete in what appears to be a constantly changing, highly competitive, and even chaotic environment, where dog-eat-dog competition appears to rule over the "softer" elements of living (cf. D'Aveni, 1994). As management scholars, teachers, and consultants hoping to influence practice, it is time that we ask why so little attention has been paid to people's need for community and spirit in our modern organizations.

Part of the answer lies in the "Cartesian split" (Overton, 1998) that characterizes much of Western thought. This split has brought us the distinction between mind or spirit and body, between the ineffable and what Westerners perceive as the "real," or, alternatively, between the subjective and the objective, the material and immaterial. In some respects, we may have reached the point where we can scarcely believe in the reality of anything, such as consciousness or community, that cannot be empirically measured, touched, tasted, or seen. Yet consciousness and subjective matters of all sorts, as Wilber (1996) points out, things that are of the "spirit" broadly conceived, are not measurable or physical things. If the essence of things such as community is to be shared at all, they must somehow be interpreted in words (or other ways) shared between at least two people (Wilber, 1996). These things of spirit, such as community, are things we cannot measure. Because what gets measured is what gets attention, they have been given short shrift in management thought. Yet as anyone who has ever experienced community, felt a strong emotion, had an idea or a dream knows, the fact that these things are of the "spirit," of the "heart," or of the "head," does not make them any less real—or valuable—than the material goods pursued so vigorously in the modern world.[2]

"Crits" or critical theorists and others have argued, as I am arguing here, that we need to bring back into our thinking what has been called the "ghost in the machine," the presence of consciousness and collective energy that is not readily quantifiable or observable. In research, in teaching, and in decision making, this is the "I" and "we" of deliberate choices, of questions to ask and answer, of perspectives that shape the "realities" explored. In research, it is, if we acknowledge it, the reason why we choose "this" subject rather than that one: because at some level the question tugs at our minds, hearts, and souls. This "I" and "we," the subjective, brings altogether different subject matter to our attention than does positivist science, focusing as it does on the objective ("it" and "its" [Wilber, 1996]) generally permits, embedding the consciousness of the researcher directly into the work. If we wish to know something fully, we need to explore all four realms (Wilber, 1996).

In Western science, we are most familiar with the objective and inter-objective elements, i.e., the exterior-individual or "it" dimension typically measured in the hard sciences, and the exterior-collective dimensions or "its" addressed generally in the social sciences. We are less familiar with and tend to ignore in Western studies, the subjective and inter-subjective elements, the interior-individual "I" in which consciousness, emotion, sensations, perceptions, ideas, and spirituality are to be found, and the interior-collective "we" where cultural identities are found (Wilber, 1996).

Using a logic of both/and rather than our more typical either/or, we can perhaps accommodate all four realms of "knowing." The great

---

[2] Thus, this paper is an essay and commentary rather than traditional empirical research, in part because it presents an argument and a set of ideas rather than a set of "findings."

contribution of the critical theorists is (whatever other limitations their work might have) to make us aware, in the words of Wilber (1996, p. 8), that:

> [T]he so-called "empirical" world is in many ways not just a *perception* but an *interpretation*. . . . [T]he allegedly simple "empirical" and "objective" world is not simply lying around "out there" waiting for all and sundry to see. Rather the "objective" world is actually set in subjective and inter-subjective contexts and backgrounds that in many ways govern what is seen, and what *can* be seen in that "empirical" world.

Recognition of *both* the subjective (and intersubjective) and objective (and interobjective) contexts suggests that a profoundly different way of experiencing our worlds—as organizations, and in our teaching, research, and management practice—is needed to honor all of these domains. As Wilber (1996, p. 9) indicates:

> The fact that both of these approaches—the exterior and the interior, the objectivist and the subjectivist—have aggressively and persistently existed in virtually all fields of human knowledge ought to tell us something—ought to tell us, that is, that both of these approaches are profoundly significant. They both have something of incalculable importance to tell us. And the integral vision is, beginning to end, dedicated to honoring and incorporating both of these profound approaches in the human knowledge quest.

We have with our organizations and in most of our teaching and research about management honored primarily the objective, empirically observable "realities," ignoring the subjective and inter-subjective. The rising popularization of "spirituality" in organizations suggests increasing recognition of the need for more integrative approaches.

So, if we hope to influence teaching, scholarship, and practice, and if community is one of the elements on the subjective side of life that reflects spirit, then we need to make it acceptable in our teaching to build small communities, e.g., of inquiry (Fisher and Torbert, 1995) or practice (Wenger, 1998), where spirit and community can flourish. Common enterprise may allow and even encourage communities of practice (Wenger, 1998) to evolve within business organizations so that people within them can cope with today's complexities.

Such an integrated approach allows the expression of individual meanings, feelings, beliefs, aspirations, hopes, and dreams as acceptable elements of organizational life and allows for the feelings of working collaboratively that create a sense of community. Bringing mind, heart, soul, and body into union, individually and collectively, validating subjective as well as objective, can help our enterprises, public and private, acknowledge the importance of community as a basis on which success, even survival, is built.

The first half of this paper has attempted to make the connection between spirituality and community, and to show why management thought has devoted little attention to such issues. Now I would like to develop three propositions about community. The goal is to move management thinking slightly toward a more holistic integrative management that can serve both organizations and societies well into the 21st century, and, as well, incorporate elements of community into organizational life.

We All Seek Community and Contribution

The first proposition is that people need and want to belong to communities where they can make meaningful contributions that build a better world. This, I believe, is a fundamental human—and humane— need too frequently ignored. Many people discover that beyond a certain point more money isn't going to make their lives better, that there are other important things to which they need to pay attention. Getting more goods doesn't result in common goods or even family goods. These discoveries are at least in part realizations about the core importance of community, of relationship, of integration into something meaningful in people's lives, arguably, of spirituality. Of course, such longings may be expressed as framed here largely in privileged societies where people actually move beyond survival and subsistence levels. But then community may be the essence of less privileged societies, where living in tightly integrated units is essential to day-to-day survival, where the Cartesian split is not made. In more developed societies, we have different opportunities and constraints as we live and work largely through managed enterprises of various sorts.

As humans we are aware, conscious. Awareness at its essence makes us want to understand our context, to be part of something that goes beyond ourselves. Once our basic needs are met, as well as in the communal struggle to meet those needs, we seek something higher, beyond ourselves. That something higher finds its expression in community.

Modern organizations, particularly business organizations, however, too frequently fail to provide that "something higher," though there is evidence that those that do generate significant success (e.g., Collins & Porras, 1997). Turned off to work that is at its roots meaningless and in some cases even unethical, many people opt out of their organizations psychically, turning their productive energy and attention to family, civic matters, or self-development. Too many of those who remain engaged are engaged in an endless pursuit of "more," more material goods, more things. Community, where it can be found or created, can be a countervailing force to the stress, isolation, and anomie that characterizes organizations that have cut out too much of what was community in their efforts to become competitive.

Arguably, community, caring, being with others who care, working toward or being in something bigger than us, becomes as important as having more of the goods that are pervasive in developed societies globally. Arguably, it is the positive experience of community that brings out the best in us, that allows us to develop our own sense of connectedness, even of spirituality, that uncovers our deepest values and allows the expression of those values—and that counts for the organization and society as well (the dark side of the power of this experience, of course, is its capacity to imprison and subjugate). From the positive perspective that resonates well with the findings of Collins and Porras's *Built to Last*, Anderson recently noted pointedly:

> Community also provides a necessary counterpoint and precedence to financial goals, since it has a different appeal to basic needs, motives, and instincts; it enlarges the range of each person's competence, control, initiative, and commitment, which are root causes of economic success. . . . By itself, shareholder wealth provides an incomplete sense of identity and uniqueness, and does not motivate long-term creativity the same way community does. Coupling strong communities with high economic performance comes closer to assuring the overall health of the organization. Business success is grounded in a stable organization community. (1997, p. 34).

The question is: How and when will our business organizations recognize this fundamental fact of existence and structure themselves to accommodate these needs so that they are better in tune with the needs of the societies and stakeholders they serve? To the extent that community is built within our major organizations, they will have positive values that serve the needs of society. Hence the next proposition.

Prosperity Is Premised on Community

The second proposition is that organizational prosperity and even survival depend on organizations' capacity to build in structures and caring relationships that permit people to make meaningful contributions and fulfill the fundamentally spiritual need for community. Collins & Porras' (1997) seminal work on visionary companies again sheds some insight into this proposition. How much more meaningful would work and organizational life be if people were able, in fact, to bring their whole selves into work, to engage in personal "projects" (Freeman & Gilbert, 1988) in which they truly believed and that provided a source of shared purpose and identity? Isn't that, in fact, exactly what those visionary companies have in some respects accomplished? These organizations have not only survived long term but have greatly prospered in doing so. Further, recent work on stakeholder relations of these visionary companies (Graves & Waddock, 1998) suggests that they also pay more attention than their less visionary counterparts to primary stakeholders. One implication may be that because of the strength of their value systems and the roles that values play in developing a shared participation in enterprise development, visionary companies also do a better job at building community.

This proposition, then, raises a question. Do most business organizations today encourage people to meet their personal needs, to create meaning in their work? I suspect that the answer is no, probably because they are afraid of the anarchy that might result (and people may be afraid of the power of that total—even totalitarian—commitment).[3] But in the decentralized web structures that have evolved in today's technologically connected organizations, meaning and connectedness,

---

[3] I am grateful to Bill Frederick, University of Pittsburgh, for this insight which developed in an extensive e-mail discussion prior to a symposium at the Academy of Management, where early versions of these ideas were shared.

that is, community, arguably get created by the "glue" provided by vision, values, and culture. This "glue" allows people to form their own purposes, hopefully in congruence with those of their employing enterprise. And that congruence: (1) avoids anarchy; and (2) provides the potential for autonomy (decentralization, empowerment) within a context aimed at common goals that simultaneously holds the enterprise together through shared meanings and community spirit.

Let us take an example. What could be more "anarchic" than a university with its front-line personnel, the professors, each pursuing his/her own individual research, teaching, and perhaps personal agenda (Weick, 1976). Yet universities are not really anarchies. Classes get taught and faculty do work together in the common enterprise of creating and disseminating knowledge, each by her own lights. Faculty form themselves into communities of inquiry (Fisher & Torbert, 1995) internally within their universities through research and teaching projects and externally through professional associations. Other "communities" form within departments and colleges, as well as at the institutional level, each creating its own sense of meaning and coherence through the work being done. Business organizations are, arguably, moving closer to this model of organizing. Consider the emergence of web-like structures, electronic connectedness, highly decentralized structures, and multiple strategic and tactical alliances. These elements combine in entrepreneurial subunits to enable employees to get the work done in a flexible, fractal-like set of structures held together primarily by the vision and values of common purpose.

The proposition is that survival and success depend on community, caring relationships, and appropriately supportive structures, yet we find organizations devolving into decentralized units, purportedly managed by empowered employees. The rationale for the proposition is that empowered and autonomous individuals need to be held together by some sort of "glue" if they are to be productive for the organization or a community. Vision and values can create meaningful work within these autonomous units, and serve as a source of glue, and the contributions of employees at work can be acknowledged and recognized. This decentralized pattern, as we see it evolving, thus puts significant demands for performance on the empowered and relatively autonomous units, and even on individuals. Yet it also dramatically shifts both the fundamental hierarchical and power relationships toward a fundamentally more collaborative model. What it does to community is more debatable, for unless the vision and values promote positive association with the enterprise, people are likely to become more fragmented, more separated from each other. Positive values, arguably, can draw people into community; positive visions can unite them and provide that very sense of community that risks being lost in the empowerment process.

Perhaps here lies the fundamental reason that I disagree with Collins & Porras' (1997) conclusion that the content of the core ideology of firms doesn't matter: I think the content of core values does matter greatly. If we are to be able to "manage" people toward authentic goals with which they can actually agree, if their own dreams and visions and purposes and actions are to fit into those of the enterprise, collaboration and community are needed at multiple levels: person to person, group or team, organizational, and society to society. Working together toward common goals permits meaning and community to evolve. From shared meaning, from accomplishment, from common tasks a sense of community and spirit develops.

For example, if we looked at Philip Morris (despite that many, including me, would object to the marketing and selling of tobacco products), what we see are values that can be termed end values (Burns, 1978): the right to personal freedom of choice, winning, individual initiative, merit-based opportunity, and hard work and continuous self-improvement. These are values that people of character can buy into and that create a common culture and set of goals within an enterprise like Philip Morris. (This notion assumes, of course, that employees allow themselves to forget that what they are doing is actually selling products that kill people, which has to create authenticity—character— problems for some people at least.) Thus, the values also create a common core around which people join together in work. When shared, they create community spirit and a spirit of community.

Think of the generative power that could be released if organizations were able to incorporate wholeness, authenticity, shared meanings, and end values, and really give people equality, power, efficacy to serve the "common good" as well as profits. Then we wouldn't have to ask people to destroy their spirituality or character (their integrity, i.e., their capacity for integrated wholeness) or their communities or nature for that matter by making decisions that they know are unethical, harmful. Decisions that they would not make if their own kids were the ones being hurt in the interests of efficiency— or economizing, or power aggrandizement (Frederick, 1995). Then perhaps we (people) could be happier making our meanings with less of the "goods" and more of the "good" however we define it in community, spiritually, integratively.

Collaboration Generates Community—and Success

The third and perhaps most controversial proposition states that we need collaboration as much as, and perhaps more than, competition to survive as the interconnectedness of the world grows more apparent. The dominant management, business, market paradigm is one of cutthroat competition, even hypercompetition (D'Aveni, 1994), which is now being touted as a desirable way to force communities to become "world class" (Kanter, 1995). The logic of this perspective seems embedded in a sort of amoral winner-take-all competition or race (to the bottom, (Korten, 1995, and Henderson, 1996), among others, would suggest).

Eisler (1988) suggests that dominator societies and models of human interaction with which we are all too familiar today overtook societies that were premised in partnership and collaboration. Halal (1996) indicates that a new paradigm of organizing will bring more democracy to the workplace, partially through collaborative interactions with (vs. on) stakeholders. When, how, can we begin to take this new type of understanding and the role—the importance—of community and collaboration to our students, to societies, and to individuals/managers operating in the world? That's a puzzle.

Stakeholder theory (Freeman, 1984) helps somewhat because it is relational, especially when it is framed in terms of mutual collaboration and interaction, rather than in terms of a focal company that will somehow "manage," i.e., dominate, its stakeholders. In this view, stakeholder relationships involve entities embedded together in a web or interwoven context where the actions of any one person affect all the others (see also Capra, 1995). Despite the emergence of such relational and web-based ideas, the problems of fragmentation and atomization go deeply into our Western roots: we atomize relationships, looking for fundamental parts that don't exist, rather than focusing on the relationships themselves, which actually are the system; we focus, that is, on what is observable and empirical rather than what is intrinsic and related to awareness, meanings, or consciousness. And somehow, we have focused on dominance and competition, one outdoing the other, when it is cooperation—symbiosis—that forms the interstices of both meanings and relationships.

There is a countervailing view to the fully Darwinian "survival of the fittest" logic that generally prevails. This perspective would suggest that it is symbiosis, mutuality, or in organizational terms, collaboration and *inter*dependence on which success is built (Capra, 1995; Maturana and Varela, 1988). And this mutuality occurs at the biological, individual, organizational, and societal levels. This perspective contradicts the dominant values of business of aggressive competition, particularly related to power aggrandizement, and a market logic based on economizing and efficiency (Frederick, 1995). Yet this perspective, which is partially based on what Frederick (1995) terms the set of ecologizing values, suggests that success is achieved within a framework of interlinked, mutually supportive, and interdependent entities. Thus, natural scientists tell us quite directly that life derives from processes of symbiosis—collaboration and community—at least as much as from competition, as the philosophers would have it, "red in tooth and claw."

Symbiosis acknowledges interdependence among each other, a fundamental element of community. What holds community together, arguably, are the cultural norms and shared values, particularly end values (Burns, 1978). End values, I believe, provide the possibility of creating collective spirit—community and connectedness—by giving us something to believe in collectively, to work toward, a higher end, creating a sense of community. This sense of community is based on common interests, goals, and experiences together. The experience of collaboration and sharing needs to be structured so that it is safe for personal expression, so that people are allowed to share and not be punished for sharing, so that community based on authenticity can actually be built. That building process is fragile, I think, easily disrupted by old patterns, hierarchies, power differences, the need for the domination of some by others, competition, and opportunistic personal or organizational agendas.

Think, for a moment, of the traditional hierarchically structured "dominator" (Eisler, 1988) model of organization (and most modern societies). Imagine working on an assembly line or in the tortures of a clothing sweatshop. How many of us would then be able to live out our passions or create meaning in our work, be it spirituality or community? We do the bidding of others in such jobs, bringing very little of our whole selves to the work. Still, there are those rare individuals who rise above their circumstances and exhibit qualities of self-expression, fulfillment, and meaning, and create community around them, no matter what their work.

Csikszentmihalyi (1997), for example, suggests in his book *Finding Flow* that it is entirely possible to live daily life in what he terms "flow." He describes "Joe," an assembly-line worker who created a meaningful work environment by learning everything about all the machines and becoming a tremendous resource for his co-workers. Creating meaning and community that inspires and brings out the best in others—and by extension in organizations—thus can be done. Living this way requires a spirit and a passion that eludes many people, resulting in what Henry David Thoreau (in *Walden*) termed a life of quiet desperation! The very success of the visionary companies over long periods of time (Collins & Porras, 1997) attests to the survival and prosperity value associated with creating this sense of togetherness and community in companies, helping people to focus their energies on meaningful contributions to the work of the collectivity. Thus, the critical question is how can we transform our organizations so that more—all—of them permit this kind of individual self-expression, yet retain the context of the larger enterprise's meaning, purpose, and goal achievement? Creating these types of enterprises really pushes the edge of the both/and logic identified as crucial in the built-to-last companies (Collins & Porras, 1997).

Despite this evidence, one does have to wonder about anarchy if everyone really were able to pursue individually meaningful and community-based work. The world might then (another proposition?) be full of self-efficacious individuals who didn't need or want to be dominated by those who viewed themselves as superior by virtue of their position, power, or access to resources. Such an evolution would potentially generate real democracy in the workplace. Yet success in such democratically based organizations would, necessarily, result not from cutthroat competition but from cooperation and collaboration with other democratically based enterprises and units. Mind, heart, body, soul, all together—seeking a degree of integration, wholeness, rather than fragmentation; moving out of the Cartesian dualism that has so affected Western thinking.

Conclusion

If we want to create meaning in our own lives and want to help our students, clients, and managers create meaning and passion in theirs, then (my guess) we need to do much more to tap into their emotional and spiritual sides than the analytical approaches that dominate management education now allow. Living with passion in organizations requires bigger meanings and purposes, aimed at something beyond the "goods" contained in dollars and products, and something of the common good that is engendered in relationships of care and community, commonality, among all stakeholders in an enterprise. That is the goal of bringing spirituality—and community—into the work-place.

References

Anderson, C. (1997), "Values-based Management," *Academy of Management Executive*, 11 (4): 25–46.

Barber, B. (1995), *Jihad vs. McWorld*. Times Books/Random House, New York.

Bellah, R. N., Madsen, R., Sullivan, W. M., Swidler, A., and. Tipton, S.M. (1985), *Habits of the Heart: Individualism and Commitment in American Life*, Harper & Row, New York.

Burns, J. M. (1978), *Leadership*, Harper Torch Books, New York.

Capra, F. (1995), *The Web of Life*, Anchor Doubleday, New York.

Collins, J. C., and Porras, J. I. (1997), *Built to Last: Successful Habits of Visionary Companies*, HarperBusiness, New York.

Csikszentmihalyi, M. (1997), *Finding Flow: The Psychology of Engagement with Everyday Life*, Basic Books, New York.

D'Aveni, R. (1994), *Hyper-Competition: Managing the Dynamics of Strategic Maneuvering*, The Free Press, New York.

Derber, C. (1992), *Money, Murder, and the American Dream: Wilding from Wall Street to Main Street*, Faber and Faber, Boston, MA.

Derber, Charles (1998), *Corporation*, St. Martin's Press, New York.

De Waal, F. (1996), *Good Natured: The Origins of Right and Wrong in Humans and Other Animals*, Harvard University Press, Cambridge, MA.

Eisler, Riane (1988), *The Chalice and the Blade: Our History, Our Future*, HarperCollins, San Francisco, CA.

Frederick, W. C. (1995), *Values, Nature, and Culture in the American Corporation*, Oxford University Press, New York.

Freeman, R. E. (1984), *Strategic Management: A Stakeholder Approach.* Basic Books, New York.

Freeman, R. E., and Gilbert, D. R. (1988), *Corporate Strategy and the Search for Ethics*, Prentice-Hall, Englewood Cliffs, NJ.

Fisher, D., and Torbert, W. R. (1995), *Personal and Organizational Transformations: The True Challenge of Continual Quality Improvement*, McGraw Hill, London, England.

Graves, S. B., and Waddock, S. A. (1998), "Beyond Built to Last . . . An Evaluation of Stakeholder Relations in 'Built to Last' Companies," Boston College Working Paper.

Greider, W. (1998), *One World, Ready or Not: The Manic Logic of Global Capitalism*, Touchstone Books, New York.

Halal, W. E. (1996), *The New Management: Bringing Democracy and Markets Inside Organizations*, Berrett-Koehler, San Francisco, CA.

Henderson, H. (1996), *Building a Win-Win World: Life Beyond Global Economic Warfare*, Berrett-Koehler, San Francisco, CA.

Kanter, R. M. (1995), *World Class: Thriving Locally in the Global*, Simon & Schuster, New York.

Korten, D. (1995), *When Corporations Rule the World*, Berrett-Koehler Publishers, San Francisco, CA.

Lodge, George C., and Vogel, Ezra F. (1987), *Ideology and National Competitiveness: An Analysis of Nine Countries*, Harvard Business School Press: Boston, MA.

Maturana, H. R., and Varela, F. J. (1988), *The Tree of Knowledge: The Biological Roots of Human Understanding*, Revised Edition, Shambala, Boston, MA.

Overton, W. (1998), "Developmental Psychology: Philosophy, Concepts and Methodology," In R. M. Lerner (Ed.), *Theoretical Models of Human Development*. Vol. 1, *Handbook of Child Psychology* (5th edition), Editor-in-Chief: William Damon, Wiley, New York.

Poarch, M. (1997), "Civic Life and Work: A Qualitative Study of Changing Patterns of Sociability and Civic Engagement in Everyday Life." Boston University Doctoral Dissertation.

Putnam, R. D. (1993), *Making Democracy Work: Civic Traditions in Modern Italy*, Princeton University Press, Princeton, NJ.

Putnam, R. D. (1995), "Bowling Alone: America's Declining Social Capital," *Journal of Democracy*, January 6 (1): 65–78.

Putnam, R. D. (1996), "The Strange Disappearance of Civic America," *The American Prospect*, 24, Winter 1996 [http://epn.org/prospect/24/24putn.html].

Reich, R. (quote on society and economy).

Waddell, S., and Brown L. D. (1997), "Fostering Intersectoral Partnering: A Guide to Promoting Cooperation Among Government, Business, and Civil Society Actors," *IDR Reports*, Vol. 13, No. 3, 26 pp.

Weick, K. E. (1976), "Educational Organizations as Loosely Coupled Systems," *Administrative Science Quarterly*, March, Vol. 21, No. 1, pp. 1–11, 19.

Wenger. E. (1998), *Communities of Practice, Learning, Meaning, and Identity*, Cambridge University Press, New York.

Wilber, K. (1996), *A Brief History of Everything*, Shambala Publications, Boston, MA.

Wolfe, A. (1998), *One Nation After All: What Americans Really Think About God, Country, Family, Racism, Welfare, Immigration, Homosexuality, Work, The Right, The Left and Each Other*, Viking Press, New York.

Wood, D. J. (with Laquita Blockson, Craig Caldwell, Kim Davenport, Harry Van Buren). "Field-Mapping: Business School Approaches to Corporate Involvement in Community Economic Development." Unpublished Report to the Ford Foundation.

HOLISTIC HEALTH FOR HOLISTIC MANAGEMENT

Dennis P. Heaton,
Maharishi University of Management

What Is Holistic Health?

The World Health Organization (1999) defines health as "a state of complete physical, mental, and social well-being" and not merely the absence of disease or infirmity. Health is, by definition, a holistic phenomenon. Dictionary meanings of the word *whole* include sound, healthy, restored, healed. Definitions of *health* include hale, sound, or whole in body, mind, or soul. The words *health, whole,* and *holy,* in fact, share a common root word and are hyperlinked to each other in the *Webster's Dictionary* on the World Wide Web (*Webster's Dictionary,* 1999).

The term *holistic health* is used to refer to concepts and practices which in some respects are opposite of those of the paradigm of modern medicine. Modern medicine focuses on the health problem. Holistic health considers the whole person—including body, environment, relationships, purpose, and knowledge. It offers not only alternative treatments for disease, but an emphasis on primary prevention and health promotion. While disease care in modern medicine is dependent on institutions and professionals, holistic health is more oriented toward self-understanding, self-administered practices, and healthy living. Evidence of the limitations of modern medicine can be seen in the fact that while the United States has the highest per capita health care costs of any nation—approximately $1.2 trillion spent on health in 1999 (Smith, Heffler, Freeland, & the National Health Expenditures Projection Team, 1999)—it is estimated that over 100 million Americans suffer from at least one chronic disease, for which modern medicine can only offer palliation (Hoffman, Rice, & Sung, 1996).

The differences between conventional medicine and holistic health can be seen in how they approach cardiovascular diseases. When the structure of the heart and/or arteries become damaged by disease, modern medicine resorts to surgical procedures—including coronary

313

artery bypass grafts, heart transplant, or angioplasty (inflating balloons inside clogged arteries to expand their capacity). A more natural alternative to surgery is a program designed by Dr. Dean Ornish. This program, which involves the systematic use of low-fat vegetarian diet, exercise, and stress reduction in combination, can clear clogged arteries —promising large savings over the average $20,000–$50,000 cost of angioplasty and bypass surgery (Neergaard, 1999). Moreover, Ornish (1999) also recognizes that the health of the heart is very much related to our emotions and relationships. In *Love & Survival* he argues that personal intimacy and other aspects of emotional well-being motivate us to make better lifestyle choices and give us stronger immune systems, better cardiovascular functioning, and longer life expectancies.

Another natural alternative which has been tested for treatment and prevention of heart disease is the Transcendental Meditation® (TM)[1] program, the most thoroughly researched meditation practice—with more than 500 studies on its effects on mind, body, and environment (Murphy & Donovan, 1996; Schmidt-Wilk, Alexander, & Swanson, 1996; Sharma, & Alexander, 1996). A study on hypertension in elderly African-Americans found that Transcendental Meditation was twice as effective in reducing high blood pressure as progressive muscle relaxation and about equally as effective as medication, but without harmful side effects (Schneider et al., 1995). A further study found that Transcendental Meditation was more cost-effective in the treatment of hypertension than any of five classes of hypertensive drugs studied (Herron, Schneider, Mandarino, Alexander, & Walton, 1996). During the practice of the Transcendental Meditation technique there are reductions in heart rate and oxygen consumption, and increased electroencephalographic (EEG) coherence indicative of a state of profound restful alertness, distinct from eyes-closed relaxation or sleep (Alexander, Cranson, Boyer, & Orme-Johnson, 1986). The profound relaxation gained during the practice is said to dissolve mental and physical stress. Research indicates that practice of the TM technique leads to decreased anxiety (Eppley, Abrams, & Shear, 1989); reduced health insurance utilization (Orme-Johnson, 1987; Herron, Hillis, Mandarino, Orme-Johnson, & Walton, 1996); improved health, im-

---

[1] ® SM Transcendental Meditation and TM are registered trademarks licensed to Maharishi Vedic Education Development Corporation and used under sublicense.

proved productivity, and improved relations in business settings (Alexander et al., 1993; Haratani & Henmi, 1990; DeArmond, 1996).

A Tale of Two Workers

How holistic health practices can influence personal and professional fulfillment can be illustrated with the following tale about Beth and Joan, two recent college graduates working in professional positions.

Beth works for a company which is a pioneer in making solar energy feasible on a large scale. This work satisfies her personal mission to reduce the burning of fossil fuels. Beth enjoys taking care of her health. The food she eats is from organic natural food stores and restaurants. Her cottage is near the county park, where she gets some outdoor recreation just about every day. Beth's life routines maintain a balance of rest and activity. She retires and rises at an early hour and she practices meditation every day. Beth nourishes her senses with her hobby of photography. She nourishes her heart by spending time each week with her fiancé, her friends, and her family. She nourishes her mind with classes and readings about her interests in photography and about natural medicine. Beth is on a path of personal growth through which she is discovering more and more each day about how to attune herself with nature and unfold her limitless human potential.

Joan likes creating software and she likes the challenges and the successes of working in a high-growth industry. But lately, to meet the project deadlines at work, she has been pushing herself to work up to seventy hours per week. On many nights, dinner means grabbing some fast food or snacks and rushing back to her office and computer. Joan knows that she has been gaining weight and has resolved to join a health club to work out regularly, but she hasn't yet found the time. She is not aware that her restless sleep and her anxious nerves may be side effects of too many evenings on the computer. To relax at night, especially on the weekend, she has gotten into the habit of having a few alcoholic drinks. To get herself going again the next morning, she relies on caffeine. Somewhere in the back of her mind, Joan is beginning to wonder about the choices she has made and what her life is becoming.

Someone like Beth has her work life balanced with her other nurturing interests and routines. On the other hand, the tale of Joan represents a lifestyle with greater risk of developing a disabling health problem that would require significant health care expenditures and diminish her participation in the workforce. Because stress and illness hurt employers with worker absenteeism and health care expenditures, more and more employers are investing in health promotion and fitness programs for their employees (Harrison, 1999; Pelletier, 1999).

Beyond the impacts of health problems on expenses, absenteeism, turnover, and quality of individual life, we would expect that the health of workers also impacts the health of the world they help create through their work. Someone like Beth, who is attentive to the quality of food, water, and air which she puts into her body, would be more likely to eschew producing high volumes of pollutants or land fill. She would be as sensitive about the purity of her outer environment as she is about her inner environment. We would expect that someone like Joan, on the other hand, who is learning to live with strain, junk food, and chemical stimulants in her physiology, would tolerate more imbalance, strain, and waste products in her environment.

It can be argued that not only the beauty and health of our physical environment but also the quality of products and services sold and bought in society are expressions of the health of our workers. A worker who is growing in stress and "disease" might more readily act in ways that are damaging to the ethical quality of life in the workplace and the community-at-large. A healthy person, on the other hand, enjoying a natural state of vitality, mental clarity, and emotional well-being, would be less inclined to participate in producing and consuming the array of unnatural stimulations and escapes which clutter today's media and shopping shelves. Indeed, it is those members of society who have the greatest psychological health (Maslow, 1998) that tend to enrich society with innovative thinking, aesthetic creativity, and moral leadership. It would be interesting to see more systematic research exploring the relationship between holistic health practices and various values and behaviors at the workplace.

From Holistic Health to Holistic Management

As more and more individuals are pursuing holistic health in their personal lives, there is a parallel trend toward wholeness in the values and management principles of organizations. The field of management has seen the emergence of what Biberman and Whitty (1997) call a spiritual paradigm of work, which balances material objectives with values of meaning and community. A central element in this trans-formation, they report, is various types of meditation practices and spiritual disciplines (cf. McDonald, 1999). For Srinivas (1999), workplace spirituality is "a life-oriented quest for personal integration and meaning, a personal commitment to self-discovery and self-transformation and inner growth" (1999, p. 33). Biberman, Whitty, King, and Neal argue that "holistic management education that taps more of the human potential of both teacher and students will better prepare graduates for the unpredictable and ever-changing business world" (1999, p. 7).

The same quality of balance which characterizes individual health is essential to holistic management. Marcic explains, "A healthy organization would have a balance of material and physical development, intellectual growth, and a deep concerns for human issues" (1997, p. 28). Indeed it is by being balanced in one's personal life that a manager can bring a more balanced perspective to the tasks of goal setting and decision making for the organization (Covey, 1989). Meditation practices bring a profound experience of wholeness in the quest for holistic health (Schneider et al., 1997). This same experience is central to holistic management. Ray writes of a new paradigm of holistic management based on "wholeness and connectedness ... from our most profound inner awareness" (1993, pp. 4–5). Hagelin (1998) has argued the holistic intelligence of the unified field—the most basic level of nature according to quantum field theories—can be harnessed in the administration of human institutions by promoting the experience of one's own pure consciousness. Following Maharishi Mahesh Yogi's (1995) treatise on wholeness in management, Heaton and Harung (1999) have described characteristics of holistic management based on the full development of human consciousness, including: maximum achievement with least effort, spontaneous and frictionless coordination, doing well by doing good, and harmony with the natural environment. Each of these characteristics is described in the paragraphs which follow.

Maximum Achievement with Least Effort

Modern physics holds that all known laws of nature function through the principle of least action (Hagelin, 1998). In an organization grounded in nature's intelligence, things would seem to run almost by themselves. The members would display a high degree of personal self-sufficiency, full expression of individual creativity and intelligence, excellence in action, coherent social interactions, and frictionless progress without strain—in short, doing least and accomplishing most.

This relationship between healthy individuals and healthy industry has been expressed by Maharishi: "To maintain a strong, growing economy, all that is necessary is to utilize the infinite creativity and organizing power of Nature which is latent within everyone" (1996, p. 78).

Spontaneous and Frictionless Coordination

Simultaneous coordination of numerous elements is evident in systems in nature. Consider, for example, the vast number of automatic processes continuously taking place in our body—self-regulating homeostasis, respiration, cardiovascular activity, metabolism in each cell—and the synchronized movements of celestial bodies in the universe. In a similar way, holistic management in an organization will be expressed as all the parts spontaneously aligned in a coherent wholeness. Highly coherent physical systems are found to take on special properties such as superconductivity—where electrons aligned together create a powerful field that can reject any disruption from external magnetic influences—and superfluidity—a state of zero viscosity in which a liquid will continue to flow indefinitely once set in motion (Wallace, 1993). With growth of holistic health, work and communication within the organization become more like these coherent phenomena. Those working in such an organization will commonly experience fortuitous coincidences in which the work of others is found to spontaneously support what one is trying to accomplish.

Doing Well by Doing Good: Prosperity and Social Value

Wheeler and Sillanpaa (1997) describe a more holistic framework for business planning which considers how the business creates value for multiple stakeholders—including employees, managers, investors, local/global communities, government and civil society, suppliers and business partners, future generations, and the natural environment. There is an increasing appreciation that businesses which live by moral principles excel in the long run in simultaneously fulfilling the interests of investors, employees, and society (Collins & Porras, 1994). Steingard, Fitzgibbons, Heaton, and Schmidt-Wilk (2000) extend the stakeholder perspective by recognizing the significance of the experience and understanding of the unifying element of consciousness. They argue that awakening the inner intelligence of the members of a business is the key to fulfilling the social and environmental responsibilities of the business. They report on the experience of teaching a course on the consciousness-based stakeholder corporation, which informs students to evaluate how companies promote mind-body-spirit evolution for their employees and contribute to creating "Heaven on Earth."

Harmony with the Natural Environment

In recent decades, science and technology have extended the impact which human actors have on the natural environment of our planet but not without "unintended ecological degradation" (Shrivastava, 1995). The goal of environmental sustainability—doing business without harming the physical or social environment—is now becoming increasingly appreciated by corporations. Leaders in environmental management recognize, however, that sustainability requires a new educational approach to transform "human thinking . . . and . . . increase the rate of people's evolutionary consciousness toward a 'new mind'" (Gladwin, Kennelly, & Krause, 1995). Holistic management constitutes just such a "new mind"—realizing the spiritual depth of our being where we are one with Nature, enabling us to live in harmony with the natural world.

Holistic Management in Action at Sunshine Energy Systems

Let's come back to the tale of Beth and Joan and update the story, so as not to leave Joan on a path toward disease. The impulse to health is natural, innate, and difficult to resist. Joan heeded that impulse to health and by good fortune she got some opportunities to change toward a healthier life.

Joan was having dinner with her friend Laura on a Friday night and they got to talking about the passion for environmentalism that they both shared as undergraduate students. Laura suggested that Joan look into the possibility of finding a new job with Sunshine Energy Systems, a growing local business renowned for its environment-friendly practices.[2] Joan applied and was hired for a software position at Sunshine. She began to participate in a series of health promotion programs sponsored by her new employer. She took a course of meditation, and a course on diet and health. Her eating habits began to change as she enjoyed the delicious organic food available at the company cafeteria.

---

[2] The fictional case of Sunshine Energy Systems as an example of holistic management is adapted from Heaton, D., & Harung, H. S. 1999. The conscious organization. *The Learning Organization: An International Journal,* 6 (4).

As her social life shifted toward her new friends from Sunshine, gradually Joan's alcohol and coffee habits fell away. She joined exercise sessions offered at the worksite.

Joan began to recognize that the holistic health that was growing in her and the other members of her company was definitely related to the appealing climate, healthy products, and exceptional success which the company was producing. She enjoyed talking about this with Beth, one of the founders of the company, whom Joan had come to meet in a seminar at the company about holistic management.

Joan: I am very impressed with the waste management practices in this company. It appears that there are practically no by-products from manufacturing which end up dumped into the environment.

Beth: That's right. Our insulation research and development group has just developed an electromagnetic radiation shielding material with better performance and lower cost than anything we've seen before. And the source of the material is a by-product from the manufacturing of solar energy collection devices by our company and other manufacturers. Joan, it sounds like environmentalism is a pretty important value for you.

Joan: Yes, it sure is. I joined Sunshine to help move the world from fossil fuel–based energy systems to non-polluting solar power. I noticed that Sunshine has been expanding throughout the world because you are offering energy supply and distribution systems which are not just the cleanest, but also the least expensive. I wanted to be a part of what you are doing.

Beth: What is your experience of working here at Sunshine?

Joan: This is an exceptional place to work. I've really enjoyed the smooth coordination that I see between individuals and between departments.

Beth: It is a common experience here that we are thinking in ways that anticipate each other and will easily synchronize together.

Joan: Its seems to me that just as Sunshine creates low-resistance energy transmission systems, so also Sunshine has created a low-resistance culture, where people work together without friction or loss of energy.

Beth: We have been employing specific practices, including group meditation, to cultivate a coherent field of consciousness within our organization. This has paid off in achieving exceptional business results without wearing out our people. We liken our coherence to a laser which has great power with minimum expenditure of energy because the photons are in synchrony with one another.

Joan: This is sure different than my last job. There we all worked long hours, got tired, and almost always seemed to be in a crisis—rushing to put out one fire or another.

Beth: Do you find now that you are able to get enough accomplished without working such late hours?

Joan: I think I'm more productive now, even though working less hours. I find that daily meditation especially helps me to bring more clarity and creativity to my work, which enables me to solve problems more quickly and more simply. Like yesterday. I had started writing a software program which I thought would take about four days of work. After meditation last evening, a simpler way of writing the program came to me, and I was able to get the whole thing finished today, with about ten percent of the lines of code I had originally planned to use.

Beth: It is just this kind of creativity that is the basis of the success of our whole company. Our engineers have reported that detailed ideas for complete product designs bloom in their minds—like the experience that some musical composer has written about. These intuitive solutions, they report, turn out to become the most holistic, economical, error-free, environmentally friendly, and aesthetically pleasing products. We believe that we wouldn't be the world leaders in clean and economical energy systems unless we had attuned ourselves to natural law through holistic health practices, including technologies of consciousness. Nature is the most creative engineer and the most efficient manager. We can make products that are friendly to the natural environment because we as individuals and as a collective entity are friendly with nature within.

Conclusion

The beginning of the millennium presents us an opportunity to commit ourselves to creating the future we want for our individual lives and for the organizations in which we work. Many of us are like Joan—tired of an imbalanced life, and moving toward greater personal wholeness; tired of a more conventional workplace, and moving toward a more fulfilling organizational setting where we participate in enacting holistic management. Holistic health enlivens that inner intelligence that can facilitate the natural growth of our individual and collective capability to create a better world without accumulating strain. By adopting holistic health practices, we can help ourselves and our organizations to grow to new levels of efficiency, quality, pollution-free progress, prosperity, and fulfillment.

References

Alexander, C. N., Cranson, R. W., Boyer, R. W., & Orme-Johnson, D. W. (1986), Transcendental consciousness: A fourth state of consciousness beyond sleep, dreaming and waking. In J. Gackenbach (Ed.), *Sourcebook on Sleep and Dreams*, pp. 282–315. New York: Garland.

Alexander, C. N., Swanson, G. C., Rainforth, M. V., Carlisle, T. W., Todd, C. C., & Oates, R. (1993), Effects of the Transcendental Meditation program on stress-reduction, health, and employee development: A prospective study in two occupational settings. *Anxiety, Stress, and Coping*, 6, pp. 245–262.

Biberman, G., Whitty, M. (1997), A postmodern spiritual future for work. *Journal of Organizational Change Management*, 10, 2, pp. 130–138.

Biberman, G., Whitty, M., King, S., & Neal, J. (1999), Innovative management training: Combining the wisdom of East and West. *Chinmaya Management Review*, III, 1, pp. 5–13.

Collins, J. C., & Porras, J. I. (1994), *Built to Last: Successful Habits of Visionary Companies*. New York: Harper Business.

Covey, S. (1989), *The Seven Habits of Highly Effective People*. New York: Simon & Schuster.

DeArmond, D. L. (1996), Effects of the Transcendental Meditation program on psychological, physiological, behavioral and organizational consequences of stress in managers and executives. Doctoral Dissertation, Maharishi University of Management. *Dissertation Abstracts International*.

Eppley, K. R., Abrams, A. I., & Shear, J. (1989), Differential effects of relaxation techniques on trait anxiety: A meta-analysis. *Journal of Clinical Psychology*, 45, pp. 957–974.

Gladwin, T. N., Kennelly, J. J., & Krause, T. S. (1995), Shifting paradigms for sustainable development: Implications for management theory and research. *The Academy of Management Review*, 20, 4, pp. 874–907.

Hagelin, J. S. (1998), *A Manual for a Perfect Government*. Fairfield, IA: Maharishi University of Management Press.

Haratani, T., & Henmi, T. (1990), Effects of Transcendental Meditation (TM) on health behavior of industrial workers. *Japanese Journal of Public Health*, 37, 10, p. 729.

Harrison, L. (1999), Healthy profits. *Time*, November, 1.

Harung, H. S. (1999), *Invincible Leadership: Building Peak Performance Organizations by Harnessing the Unlimited Power of Consciousness*. Fairfield, IA: Maharishi University of Management Press.

Heaton, D., & Harung, H. S. (1999), The conscious organization. *The Learning Organization: An International Journal*, 6, 4, pp. 157–162.

Herron, R. E., Hillis, S. L., Mandarino, J. V., Orme-Johnson, D. W., & Walton, K. G. (1996), Reducing medical costs: The impact of the Transcendental Meditation program on government payments to physicians in Quebec. *American Journal of Health Promotion*, 10, 3, pp. 206–216.

Herron, R. E., Schneider, R., Mandariano, J. V., Alexander, C. N., & Walton, K. G. (1996), Cost-effective hypertension management: Comparison of drug therapies with an alternative program. *American Journal of Managed Care*, 2, 4, pp. 427–437.

Hoffman C., Rice D., & Sung H.-Y. (1996), Persons with chronic conditions: Their prevalence and costs. *Journal of the American Medical Association*, 276, pp. 1473–1479.

Maharishi Mahesh Yogi (1995), *Maharishi University of Management: Wholeness on the Move*. Vlodrop, Holland: Maharishi Vedic University Press.

Maharishi Mahesh Yogi (1996), *Maharishi Forum of Natural Law and National Law for Doctors*. India: Age of Enlightenment Publications.

Marcic, Dorothy (1997), *Managing with the Wisdom of Love: Uncovering Virtue in People and Organizations*. San-Francisco: Jossey-Bass Business and Management Series.

Maslow, A. H. (1998), *Maslow on Management*. New York: John Wiley.

McDonald, M. (1999), Shush. The guy in the cubicle is meditating. *U.S. News and World Report*, May 3, p. 46.

Murphy, M., & Donovan, S. (1996), *The Physical and Psychological Effects of Meditation: A Review of Contemporary Research with a Comprehensive Bibliography 1931–1996 (2nd ed.)*. Sausalito, CA: Institute of Noetic Sciences.

Neergaard, L. (1999), Medicare to offer diet to elderly facing heart surgery. SFGATE.com. http://www.sfgate.com/cgibin/article.cgi? file=/news/archive/1999/10/02/national0056EDT0415.DTL (October 29).

Orme-Johnson, D. W. (1987), Medical care utilization and the Transcendental Meditation program. *Psychosomatic Medicine*, 49, pp. 493–507.

Ornish, Dean (1999), *Love and Survival: 8 Pathways to Intimacy and Health*, New York: Harper Collins.

Pelletier, K. (1999), A review and analysis of the clinical and cost-effectiveness studies of comprehensive health promotion and disease management programs at the worksite: 1995–1998 update (IV). *American Journal of Health Promotion*, 13, 5.

Ray, M. L. (1993), Introduction. In M. Ray and A. Renzler (Eds.). *The New Paradigm in Business: Emerging Strategies for Leadership and Organizational Change*. Los Angeles: Jeremy P. Tarcher/ Perigree.

Schmidt-Wilk, J., Alexander, C. N., & Swanson, G. C. (1996), Developing consciousness in organizations: The Transcendental Meditation program in business. *Journal of Business and Psychology*, 10, 4, pp. 429–444.

Schneider, R. H., Staggers, F., Alexander, C., Sheppard, W., Ranforth, M., et al. (1995), A randomized controlled trial of stress reduction for hypertension in older African Americans. *Hypertension*, 26, 5, pp. 820–827.

Schneider, R. H., Charles, B. M., Sands, D., Gerace, D. D., Averback, R. E., & Rotherburg, S. (1997), The significance of the Maharishi Vedic Approach to Health for modern medical care and medical education. *Modern Science and Vedic Science*, 7, 1, pp. 299–318.

Sharma, H.M., & Alexander, C.N. (1996), Maharishi Ayurveda: Research Review. *Alternative Medicine Journal*, 3 (1): 21–28.

Sharma, H.M., & Alexander, C.N. (1996), Maharishi Ayurveda: Research Review-Part 2. *Alternative Medicine Journal*, 3(2):21–28.

Shrinivas, K. M. (1999), Workplace spirituality: An American affirmation. *Chinmaya Management Review*, III, 1, pp. 33–46.

Shrivastava, P. (1995), The role of corporations in achieving ecological sustainability. *Academy of Management Review*, 20, pp. 936–960.

Smith, S., Heffler, S., Freeland, M., & the National Health Expenditures Projection Team (1999), The next decade of health spending: A new outlook. *Health Affairs*, 18, 4, pp. 86–95.

Steingard, D., Fitzgibbons, D., Heaton, D., & Schmidt-Wilk, J. (2000), Awakening Students to Social and Environmental Responsibility Through "Transformational Stakeholder Management." Symposium for the SIM Track of the Midwest Academy of Management Annual Meeting, Chicago, April, 2000.

Wallace, R. K. (1993), *The Physiology of Consciousness*. Fairfield, IA: Maharishi International University Press.

Webster's Dictionary (1999), Definition of "Whole." http://machaut.u chicago.edu/cgi-bin/WEBSTER.sh?Word=Whole, (November 3).

Wheeler, D., & Sillanpaa, M. (1997), *The Stakeholder Corporation: A Blueprint for Maximizing Stakeholder Value*. London: Pitman Publishing.

World Health Organization (1999), WHO Definition of Health. http://www.who.org/aboutwho/en/definition.html. (October 29).

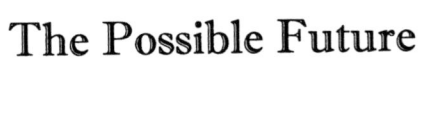
The Possible Future

DAWN

by Tom Brown

An infant bursts
From mother's womb,
Broad smiles illuminate the room.
Each birth a chance to celebrate:
Youth, aglow, anew!
Once more, a precious fireball rises,
Shimmering above the morning dew.

Who you are, what you do,
Each day's a dawn
If you stay true:
The fire's deep down inside of you.

Your days blazed fast
When you reprise,
How few the dawns
Since the dawn of you:
The day your lips spoke ooh;
The day you tiptoed through;
The day you learned in school
The thought you never knew.

Who you are, what you do,
Each day's a dawn
If you stay true:
The fire's deep down inside of you.

First dream first friend first kiss first fight
First job first home first speech first flight:
Every alpha, each aurora,
Those flags you made and flew,

In your mind, now folded carefully,
Locked away . . . they're you!

Who you are, what you do,
Each day's a dawn
If you stay true:
The fire's deep down inside of you.

Ticking ever older,
You ache; you mourn; you fear.
Life's quest? A welled-up tear?
All those dawns behind you:
Mere ghosts of greatness now;
Fleeting flecks of fire,
Smothered in the snow.

If mankind's urge is forward:
Ideas, then as now, the glue;
If your own emanations
Have shaped the life you grew;
If you yearn to peel away,
To find once more the new;
Then go again to where you've been:
It's *right there*, though out of view.

Who you are, what you do,
Each day's a dawn
If you stay true:
The fire's deep down inside of you.

—from *The Anatomy of Fire: Sparking A New Spirit Of Enterprise*
by Tom Brown ©2000 by MANAGEMENT GENERAL
http://www.mgeneral.com

A VALUE-BASED PARADIGM FOR CREATING TRULY HEALTHY ORGANIZATIONS

Mark P. Kriger,
Norwegian School of Management (BI),
Sandvika, Norway

Bruce J. Hanson,
Pepperdine University

Acknowledgments

An earlier version of this paper was presented at the 8th International Conference of the Society for the Advancement of Socio-economics (SASE) in Geneva, Switzerland, in July 1996. The authors wish to thank Andre Delbecq and Frank Elter for their early encouragement in the crafting of this paper as well as Barbara Gray and Oystein Fjeldstad for their timely and thoughtful comments which helped to shape the quality of the final version.

She: "What do you do for a living?"
He: "I work for a company that makes bottle caps, but it's not as exciting as it sounds."
—from an unremembered movie

"We are shaped and fashioned by what we love."
—Goethe

Today's organizations, both profit and not-for-profit, have to balance an increasing array of conflicting forces and values. Stakeholder demands are diverse and numerous. No individual is in a job without conflicting demands—for innovation *and* stability, for quality *and* efficiency, for goal clarity *and* flexibility, for short-term results *and* long-term effectiveness. How can individuals balance the outer demands of the workplace with their own inner needs and values?

331

What we propose in the following paper is that each of the major world religious traditions, having endured the test of time, contains a set of values which are relevant, indeed necessary, for organizations in the 21st century. Collectively these value systems provide an inner, often invisible, governance system which can allow individuals and their organizations to stay on course in turbulent times.

We argue that these values are necessary to enable both economic and spiritual ideals to thrive and grow. The values we have selected—truthfulness, trust, humility, forgiveness, compassion, thankfulness, service, and peace—are not intended to be exhaustive, for that would be beyond the page constraints of this paper. We also propose a set of supporting activities which we believe are necessary to foster these core values. These core values and beliefs constitute what a number of authors, including Ray Guenon and Aldous Huxley, have termed "the perennial philosophy" (Smith, 1991). Our overall intent is to shape aspirations—to identify and to articulate desirable values and behaviors, rather than reflect current reality. If this paper increases the awareness of what organizational leaders and members could or should aspire toward, then it will have achieved its aim.

Organizations are constantly being reengineered to achieve greater efficiency and effectiveness in economic terms. But can we also think about developing organizations to achieve greater closeness of fit with what is most human and, hence, health-creating in the long term? In the words of Maslow on spirituality in the workplace:

> Enlightened management is one way of taking religion seriously, profoundly, deeply and earnestly . . . for those who define religion (and spirituality) in terms of deep concern with the problems of human beings, with the problems of ethics, of the future of man, then this kind of philosophy, translated into the work life, turns out to be very much like the new style of management and of organization. (Maslow, 1998: 83)

When addressing spiritual values we are well aware that actualizing them daily, on a moment-by-moment basis, is enormously challenging. This is especially the case within the context of conflicting choices to be made in today's businesses, where individuals constantly are struggling to resolve the tensions between their own ideals and values and the economic realities of competition in a global marketplace. In this paper we present a case for eight values and seven supporting activities which we advocate as necessary for creating healthy organizations (see Table 1).

Table 1: Values and Activities for Creating Truly Healthy Organizations

Necessary Underlying Values:

1. Honesty and truthfulness
2. Trust
3. Humility
4. Forgiveness
5. Compassion
6. Thankfulness
7. Being of service
8. Stillness and peace

Supporting Activities:

1. Behavior consistent with values
2. Creating a climate where morality and ethics are truly important
3. Legitimizing differing viewpoints, values, and beliefs
4. Developing imagination, inspiration, and mindfulness
5. Letting go of expectations that are unrealistic
6. Acknowledgment of the efforts and accomplishments of others
7. Creating organizational processes that develop the whole person—not just exploiting current talents and strengths

The Current Challenge for Organizational Leaders

Working in organizations in these turbulent times is not easy for most people, including those who ostensibly are the "heads" of corporations. According to Greenleaf (1998): "The first order of business is to build a group of people who, under the influence of the institution, grow healthier, stronger, more autonomous."

There are enormous challenges for all of us, but especially for those who are in leadership roles. Some chief executives are beginning to boldly speak to this issue. For example, Vaclav Havel, the first President of the Czech Republic, states:

Those who find themselves in politics bear a heightened responsibility for the moral state of society, and it is their responsibility to seek out the best in that society, and to develop and strengthen it. (1992: p. 4)

The preceding statement by Havel applies equally well to those in leadership positions in business corporations, large, medium, or small—whether in the east or the west. The only substitution needed is to replace "those who find themselves in politics" with the phrase "those who find themselves in business leadership."

Is this too high a hurdle of moral responsibility to place before executive leaders in corporations? Currently there is a highly challenging state of affairs in the growing global society—an increased erosion of traditional values such as integrity, honesty, and compassion for others, continuing high levels of crime in both developed and developing nations, and increasing uncertainty facing workers at all levels in organizations. Given this, it is important that those talented in managing organizations constructively apply those talents as well as modeling those ideals for others (Kriger & Malan, 1993).

Some will find this challenge of balancing economic and human ideals not justifiable in financial terms or too moralistic. However, in even the most seemingly mundane events, those who find themselves in leadership positions must begin to give back to society forms of service that are commensurate with the social and economic privileges and returns they receive. If a collective sense of moral integrity and responsibility is not taken by those in leadership positions at all levels of society, then we shall see a continuing erosion and tearing of the social fabric in both profit and not-for-profit organizations (Greenleaf, 1998).

Each interaction with another is an opportunity to practice the virtues embodied in the list of advocated values and behaviors. Through constant practice we increase the likelihood that the proposed virtues will become a living reality in our own organizations. In this way each of us can become initiators of "deep change" at both personal and organizational levels (Quinn, 1996).

The aim of this essay is somewhat ambitious; to develop and to argue for the validity of a set of normative propositions for the establishment of truly healthy organizations in turbulent times. We shall attempt to address two questions:

1. Why are these particular values important for both individuals and organizations?

2. In what ways would the enactment of these values help to create not only more healthy, human workplaces but also more economically viable and sustainable organizations?

One meaning of *to be healthy* is to be "whole"; and to experience wholeness is the very essence of what it means to be spiritual. In this way of looking at things, what is spiritual, that is, wholeness, is not the exclusive province of any one of the world's religious traditions, but all of them. Wholeness is within the province of and central to the tenets of each of the world's religious traditions—when connection with the deepest values of what it means to be human is maintained and enacted. When our essential humanity is kept foremost, religious fanaticism in the name of spirituality will tend to lose its ability to warp the moral sensibility of the world community. In a now classic book on the religions of the world, Smith (1991) gives an excellent discussion of the connection and difference between spirituality and religion. He uses an analogy of a wheel where the center of the wheel is the Truth or Ultimate Harmony and Oneness. The circumference of the wheel is life and the spokes of the wheel are the differing religious traditions, each unique but all leading to the same Essential Oneness. In this view, each individual is traveling on his or her own path from the circumference of the wheel to the same essential Truth.

A fundamental issue in organizations is that "right" human relationships are essential for effectiveness in our work systems. Over-identification with our tasks and technology creates illusion and isolation. As socio-technical studies have found, the introduction of new technology can be detrimental to the human side of the organization (Pasmore, 1988). But it need not be so. Heidegger saw the "entrapping" nature of technology wherein we "become machines"; however, when a deeper connection with our work occurs, when technology enhances the connection between our internal and external worlds, then there is increased liberation of the human spirit. (Heidegger, 1977)

While striving for spiritual health and wholeness, the world religions have also examined the nature of spiritual disease. The fundamental causes of this disease are isolation of people from each other, the feeling of separation from the spirit, and illusion (*maya* in Buddhist thought). The diseases of isolation, separation, and illusion occur in the midst of our daily lives, and stem from fundamental lapses in our awareness. In Buddhism, the source of non-healthy states derives from illusion which prevents us from seeing things as they really are.

If unhealthy situations emerge from illusion and isolation, then creating healthy organizations is an issue of developing and maintaining relationships which bridge isolation and shatter the illusion of separateness. We then have the possibility of creating a fuller life where we appreciate the unique and the subtle within our work. Essential to this level of change is to see the task of the change agent as one of creating organizational cultures which foster the values and supporting activities in Table 1.

Propositions Concerning Necessary Underlying Values

Rokeach (1973) in his classic study, *The Nature of Human Values*, states:

> a *value* is an enduring belief that a specific mode of conduct or end-state of existence is personally or socially preferable to an opposite mode of conduct or end-state of existence" (p. 5) and that "values are multifaceted standards that guide conduct in a variety of ways (p. 13).

Values may be either terminal or instrumental, that is, ends in themselves or means toward desired behavior. In the following we discuss values which are intended to be terminal, desirable end-states in themselves, but which can also be instrumental in creating greater personal and organizational competence and increased long-term organizational health and effectiveness.

Honesty/Truthfulness

Proposition 1: *Organizational exchange and inter-organizational transactions are impossible without a pervading basic expectation that contracts and agreements are represented with honesty, in good faith, and with the intention of being honored.*

Truthfulness is one of the most difficult personal values to enact consistently in today's business world, where agreements are continuously being overturned or renegotiated depending on changes in the competitive environment or in one's personal preferences. How is an individual to be consistently honest when others do not feel beholden to such a standard? When a business norm of "strategic misdirection" is deemed necessary because of compelling competitive pressures, honesty is then perceived as naive, at best, in a world where only the strong and cunning are believed to have what it takes to prevail. Truthfulness is a fundamental dedication to see and to report events as they are.

Organizational transactions would come to an immediate halt if suppliers and buyers did not believe that there was an underlying level of honesty in relationships. After all, why would a firm perform a service or ship a product if it did not believe that the buyer was going to pay in good faith and in a timely manner? Similarly, if a buyer does not believe a seller's claims about their product or service, then there is no compelling reason to enter into the transaction in the first place. Thus, honesty and credible commitments are basic standards which allow transactions to be negotiated and consummated (Williamson, 1996).

Trust

Proposition 2: *Trust increases the ability to commit to and to engage in long-term effectiveness in organizational transactions.*

Some argue that trustworthiness can become a source of competitive advantage and can be treated as a form of "social capital" (Barney & Hansen, 1994). This is to denigrate trust to becoming simply a means for achieving instrumental ends. Trust depends to a great extent on the perception of truthfulness between parties and is the underlying basis for continuing business relationships and transactions, especially in turbulent times. Semler (1994) writes about his experience running a company in Brazil which succeeded in an economy with 1000% annual inflation. Most of his business colleagues utilized highly authoritarian management styles, creating a fortress mentality in which they attempted to isolate themselves from the negative forces of the economy. This was accomplished for a while, but at the high human cost of disenfranchisement. However, our fundamental being in the world rests on our ability to trust and to have faith in its continuity. When all is changing in a turbulent world, upon what are we to rely? It is our values and close personal relationships that allow us to transcend the forces of constant change and to define a deeper sense of meaning and existence.

How is trust created and what are its consequences? It takes time and is built via numerous interpersonal exchanges, complex signaling processes, and small acts which indicate a willingness to collaborate and work together with others (Gray, 1989). For example, Semler and his company succeeded by opening up the books and empowering their workforce, creating a deep trust through truthful relationships (Semler, 1994). Becerra and Gupta (1998) found that trust comes from integrity, benevolence, competence, and predictability of behavior. They report the consequences of trust to be: (1) lower monitoring costs; (2) faster decision making; (3) greater innovation and entrepreneurship; (4) faster knowledge transfer; and (5) a greater external focus on customers. Economic actors support one another because they believe that they form a community based on trust (Fukuyama, 1995). In short, trust facilitates the creation of both greater organizational effectiveness and an overall social fabric which, in turn, fosters interpersonal openness and exchange.

Humility

Proposition 3: *Without a modicum of humility, organizational relationships and routines will tend to be permeated with defensive behaviors and agendas, resulting in a high level of organizational ineffectiveness.*

Humility is a difficult personal quality to enact in an age of high-tech marketing where it is expected that organizations and individuals will actively promote their own accomplishments and aims to the detriment of others. There is a subtlety of feeling and graceful communication which is lost when messages contain excessive superlatives out of a fear that they will be lost in the cacophony of media-born messages. How is an individual leader to be a living example of humility when the norm has become one of self-promotion and self-aggrandizement? Humility places the self in the context of the whole, and is a recognition of our relationship to our community. The teachings of the sixth century B.C. Chinese philosopher/mystic, Lao Tzu, are appropriate here, despite the passage of over 2000 years:

> True self-interest teaches selflessness.
> Heaven and earth endure because they are not simply selfish
>   but exist in behalf of all creation.
> The wise leader, knowing this, keeps egocentricity in check
>   and by doing so becomes even more effective.

Enlightened leadership is service, not selfishness. The leader
grows more and lasts longer by placing the well-being of
all above the well-being of self alone.
Paradox: by being selfless, the leader enhances self.

—Lao Tzu (1972), *Tao Te Ching*

Forgiveness

Proposition 4: *Forgiveness is the letting go of our feelings and beliefs
about what others should have or could have done. Forgiveness
increases the likelihood that new initiatives will be undertaken and
decreases stress in organizational members.*

Several recent authors note that there is a strong tendency to resist
change at both the personal and organizational levels (Kotter, 1995;
Quinn, 1996; Daft & Lengel, 1998). When what occurs is different from
our expectations, we tend to become over-preoccupied with avoiding
error. As a result, we become overly risk averse and perform below our
capabilities. From the perspective of spiritual life, forgiveness is necessary if we are to avoid becoming enmeshed in false expectations.
Clinging to past errors disrupts our ability to be in the present. Individuals and organizations have a strong inertial tendency to retain
erroneous perceptions and negative feelings, which organizational
members are then forced to defend as in the Exxon Valdez oil spill
(Dutton et al, 1991). Clinging to past negative impressions is epito-
mized by the disastrous effect of bitter extended labor-management
disputes in the American steel industry over several decades. These
disputes were a major force behind the severe decline of the steel
industry by generating excessively formal work rules, worker roles, and
resulting noncompetitive labor rates (Iverson, 1998).

Forgiveness lies at the heart of the values and scriptures of
Christianity, Buddhism, Islam, and Hindism. Jesus' dying statement,
"Forgive them Father for they know not what they do," poignantly
illustrates this. In Buddhism all negative emotions (for example, hatred,
fear, anger, lust, impatience) are perceived as causing harm to others
and to ourselves. By forgiving we put an end to a vicious spiral of
erroneous perceptions leading to continued isolation which, in turn,
creates further false perceptions. But when we forgive others we
recognize the possibility that we can attenuate the cycle of isolation and

illusion, and choose to live in healthier relationships with others (Hanh, 1992, 1997).

Compassion

Proposition 5: *Compassion is the basis for the ability to feel what another is feeling and creates an enduring basis for collective action. It increases feelings of trust and the likelihood that organizational values will be realized.*

Bayrak (1985) lists 99 so-called "names of God" in the Islamic Sufi tradition. *Compassion* and *mercy* are the first two and the most primary of these. Also closely aligned with these virtues in this tradition is the valuing of inner surrender, so that we identify with and ultimately merge with "the beloved." We exist in relationship—with the physical environment, the plant and animal kingdoms, and within human communities—and cannot survive outside of relationship with these. In compassion, we extend the realm of what is central and important beyond ourselves. We come to recognize that it is our connection with the "apparently other" that makes us human in the deepest sense.

Similarly, Thich Nhat Hanh (1997) states that in a classical Buddhist text, the *Anguttara Nikaya*, the Buddha mentions eleven advantages of practicing meditation on loving compassion. The first two of these are: "1. The practitioner sleeps well, and 2. upon waking, he or she feels well and light in his heart" (Hanh, 1997: 17).

The Jewish tradition also extols the importance of practicing loving compassion as this story illustrates:

> When Reb Abraham Isaac Kook was asked why he loved those who were known to be sinners and anti-religious, he replied: It is surely better to err on the side of causeless love than on the side of causeless hatred. (Unterman, 1976)

This level of loving compassion is alien to many individuals and probably is excessive in the eyes of most. However, people in the workplace today are subjected to enormous amounts of stress due to concurrent levels of high uncertainty, pressures to meet numerous role demands to contribute to organizational effectiveness, and struggles to develop needed competencies. By practicing compassion toward others in the workplace, we can become more relaxed and at ease with both ourselves and the other. An individual is also better able to be aware of events as they arise and see more clearly what is needed to deal appropriately with the myriad of events because they are not assuming what they imagine to be the worst in others, but affirming what is best.

Thankfulness

Proposition 6: *Thankfulness creates the basis for healthy interpersonal relations by establishing norms of respect and positive regard for the needs and contributions of others.*

In organizations where the drive toward cost containment is held paramount, there is increasingly an overemphasis on a transaction cost orientation. This tendency results in the focusing on questions such as:

*   What will our firm or business unit get for what we give?
*   How will we profit from the relationship?
*   Who benefits and in what ways?

Thus, the orientation toward instrumental relationships increases the consideration of costs incurred for effort expended. This attitude permeates person-to-person and firm-to-firm interactions. Thankfulness reverses this instrumental dynamic and creates spaciousness between potential collaborators where a person becomes accepting and grateful for what another has given or created, not out of obligation but simply because it was freely given. To be not thankful is to invest energy in denying the present situation. Over time this can become quite exhausting. Furthermore, this pattern of denial of what is arising often becomes the foundation of inner emotional and eventually physical disease.

A fundamental attitude and practice in Buddhism is *gasho*, which is bowing to the other out of respect and gratitude. In the Judeo-Christian traditions the essence of prayer is thankfulness. Similarly, in Islam one of the 99 Names of God is *ya Shakur*, the Thankful One. The attitude and practice of being thankful creates a feeling of generosity that enables the givers to extend themselves and to invite others to break out of their isolation and enter a deeper relationship with others—friends as well as apparent enemies.

Service

Proposition 7: *Being of service to others in thought, feeling, and action creates a climate of generativity which fosters relationships with a full range of human qualities, rather than relationships mainly shaped by instrumental values of transaction cost and exchange.*

It is surprising how long it has taken for many businesses to rediscover the customer. For much of modern United States industrial history there has been an expectation that "if you build it someone will buy it." Recent exceptions are Saturn and Honda Motors in automobiles, L.L. Bean and Sears in retailing. The United States ideal of individualism built on the role model of business leaders such as Carnegie and Rockefeller eventually resulted in later years of philanthropy; however, there remains a strong tendency for executives to value themselves before others, including the firm. This self-orientation and narcissism has become almost epidemic in the last couple of decades. In contrast with this trend, a number of writers have been calling on organizations to be governed and based on the concept of *stewardship* (Block, 1993; Greenleaf, 1998). Ironically it is the service sector which is growing faster than the industrial, but the service sector of the economy often least exemplifies the importance of service. Self-servingness has a negative effect on human consciousness. It creates arrogance and a resulting isolation from both the environment and other people. Individuals cut themselves off from the wellspring of inner harmony when they are not of service to values and endeavors that go beyond themselves. Thus:

> (t)he purpose of a business firm is not simply to make a profit, but it is to be found in its very existence as a community of persons who in various ways are endeavoring to satisfy their basic needs and who form a particular group at the service of the whole of society. Profit is a regulator of the life of a business, but it is not the only one; the human and moral factors must also be considered, which in the long term are at least equally important for the life of a business. (Pope John Paul II in Maslow, 1998, p. 52)

Stillness and Peace

Proposition 8: *Stillness and peace increase the likelihood that organizational members will be satisfied in belonging to the organization and decrease the likelihood of burnout.*

Stillness and peace are the result of letting go of the barrier between our concept of ourself and the ground of our being. Peace is a value that is difficult to talk about, because our talk (particularly our inner dialogue) proceeds nearly incessantly, creating the opposite of stillness (Hanh,1992). The seeking of revenge can create feelings of hatred toward others which can last for centuries, as witnessed by ethnic crises around the world. Religious leaders that advocate revenge only perpetuate the very dynamics they claim they wish to eradicate.

The word *religion* comes from the Latin meaning "to reconnect." Thus, religious fundamentalists, of whatever denomination, who create conflict and discord rather than stillness and peace are creating the opposite of what the founders of their respective religions intended.

Lasting peace and inner stillness arise when the ego or 'false self' lets go of its obsession with attempting to fulfill desires that are inherently insatiable. Organizations built on a foundation of valuing stillness are rare and hard to find in a business climate which values the generating of endless data and information, but with little lasting deep knowledge or wisdom. There is a restorative function to stillness which creates clarity of mind and with practice provides a grounding for the other virtues. Along these lines, Kabat-Zinn (1994), one of the leading medical researchers in the growing field of stress reduction, has adapted techniques of meditation and mindfulness from the Buddhist tradition which have the effect of creating greater stillness and inner peace while at one's work.

In the preceding exposition of values we have referenced a mixture of both sacred and secular sources. What we are advocating is a process theory, something to be aspired to, rather than a variance theory (Mohr, 1982). The values and practices advocated here facilitate the creation of healthy organizations, but certainly they are not the only path. According to the Sufis, there are many paths to the Divine; each path to realization of what is highest and most real is unique but not intended to be exclusive. There are often subtle pressures to create agreement on universal values as the basis for economic order in the world, as Hans Kung and Vaclav Havel have stated in a recent world order meeting on economics and religion (Smith, 1998). These universal values are not the exclusive property of any one group or institution. They are a matter of human choice to establish the conditions necessary for creating vibrant communities at all levels of scale, from local neighborhoods to the global, each level having its own economic, religious, social, and environmental values embedded within their cultures.

Mere agreement on a minimal set of transaction-based values is not enough to create healthy economic communities, especially on a global scale. A deeper understanding and enactment of our inherent interconnectedness is needed. The previous eight values provide an inner governance structure which permeates both markets and hierarchies (Williamson, 1996). They are proposed as essential for the creation of truly healthy and enduring organizations. However, they are insufficient without practices that bring them to life and support them in the workplace. The following set of supporting activities is proposed to make this bridge.

Supporting Activities

1. Behavior consistent with values

It is an irony of human nature that people often behave opposite to and inconsistently with their values. There is a struggle that tends to occur between our values as aspirations and our day-to-day behavior. In essence, we become hypocritical without intending to. This is particularly true when we are trying to impress others with our self-importance. Values often appear noble and straightforward to implement until we attempt to enact them via consistent actions. Numerous authors have written about the importance for leaders to model the way and to "walk the talk" (see, for example, Kouzes & Posner, 1995; Quinn, 1996; Daft & Lengel, 1998; Iverson, 1998).

2. Creating a climate where morality and ethics are truly valued

It can be a daunting task for most people to begin to integrate the whole self, especially ethical and spiritual beliefs, in the workplace. We feel an inner mandate to incorporate our ethical values in our daily actions and decisions; however, individuals are rarely pure in their motives. Moralism is often invoked to identify the errors of others, but ethical piety can result in rigidity of beliefs. Carl Rogers (1961), perhaps more than any other modern psychologist, has advocated "valuing." Beyond simply espousing values, this involves the active appreciation of the other.

According to Badaracco (1997), there are times in each person's life when work choices and life choices become one—what he calls "defining moments." These moments are ultimately shaped by our personal values. Barnard (1982) states that the moral codes of a typical manager are "ingrained in him by causes, forces, experiences, which he has either forgotten or on the whole never recognized. Just what they are, in fact, can best be only approximately inferred from his actions, preferably under stress" (p. 267). Thus, how to make the right ethical choices, especially under stress, is an often daunting task requiring inner diligence and a clear understanding of one's true priorities.

3. Legitimizing differing viewpoints, values, and beliefs
    The writer F. Scott Fitzgerald once commented, "My definition of a true genius is one who can hold two seemingly contradictory ideas in their head at the same time, and not go crazy." The process theologian Bernard Loomer (1976) makes a similar point on the power of multiple perspectives where he defines "relational" power as the ability to hold two seemingly contradictory elements together until they become complementary. The reconciling power of multiple perspectives is often underestimated, even though it has been espoused and written about for over 2500 years. For example, in Taoism the principle of yin-yang consists of the inclusion of apparently opposing forces to form complementarities, wherein aspects of two opposing elements are enfolded within each other (Lao Tzu, 1972). More recently, Morgan (1986) established a legitimacy for multiple images of organizing which are complementary rather than simply competing. The continuing challenge is to hold on to the differing viewpoints or opposing values to discover the way of reconciliation.

4. Developing imagination, inspiration, and mindfulness
    Imagination, inspiration, and mindfulness are the bases for the ability to feel what another is feeling, to see what is about to be created out of the field of latent possibilities and, hence, the ground out of which all enduring collective action is made possible. "Mindfulness is the ability to appreciate new possibilities and new ways of thinking, to see the subtle forces, to see the potential in people as being more powerful than safety and control" (Daft & Lengel, 1998: 69). Imagining the ideal or picturing what could be is the first step toward creating an alternative future. Whole new organizations, new businesses, new in-

dustries begin with exercising the powers of imagination and inspiration.

In his commentary on the Zen story of the *Woodcarver's Tale*, Parker Palmer notes that the path of "right action" requires that people discern the nature of things and what their true potential is (1990). In the story, the Emperor commissions a master woodcarver to create a perfect bell stand. The woodcarver takes a long time to prepare himself and then sees the bell stand in the proper tree in the forest before taking any action of carving or shaping. While this is occurring his assistant gets very upset, saying that the master must directly and urgently take on the task, since the Emperor has demanded perfection and time is short. The death of the woodcarver will result if he is not able to see the totality of the bell which is yet to be. This story highlights the importance a vision can have in liberating what is not yet seen.

5. Letting go of expectations

It is important to let go not only of expectations but, at times, of concepts themselves. We wish to control so much in our world and much of the controlling is first attempted via our thoughts and expectations. The truly miraculous can occur when we let go of our pre-conceived notions, and of our need to control outcomes. Most people would like to have certainty in a highly ambiguous world of conflicting currents.

Managers are especially prone to getting attached to expectations. Organizations are largely socially constructed realities (Weick, 1979) that derive their identity from collective cognitions, agreements, and behaviors. It is difficult for managers to let go of expectations the higher they rise in the organization and the longer they remain with the organization because people tend to become routinized over time in their thinking, feelings, and behavior.

Thus, situational responsiveness is needed—responding to each situation with a "beginner's mind." One of the central stories of Zen is called "Taking an Ox to Market." It is essentially about the training and disciplining of the mind, until finally the seeker finds the *original mind*, which has been there all along, the mind of the beginner (Suzuki, 1970). In the Christian parables, Jesus stated that people must come to the Kingdom of God as little children. The type of situational spontaneity called for here is a simplicity which embraces complexity, in full awareness of the situation and context.

6. Acknowledgment of the efforts and accomplishments of others

It is indeed easy for us to get caught up in our own personal affairs and efforts such that we forget the larger work proceeding around us. If attribution theory is fairly accurate, that on the whole people tend to attribute success to themselves and failure to others and external forces, it is indeed difficult for people to acknowledge the work of others, particularly when there is success. It is important to be able to acknowledge the contributions of others, especially that which is positive and successful (Kouzes & Posner, 1995).

7. Creating organizational processes that develop the whole person—not just exploiting current talents and strengths

One of the effects of "right sizing" in the last decade has been the breaking of an implicit agreement that a person would have a job as long as the organization was reasonably successful. While this is at first interpreted as the breaking of a corporate promise of life-time employment, it also has a liberating effect. People are no longer "owned" by the organization and must prepare themselves for continuing employability. A career now usually spans several companies and most likely several disciplines or industries over the course of a lifetime. This implies that while an organization may have an agreement which is primarily economic with an employee, there is also the need for managers to develop supportive relationships with employees, and with each other, which respect and affirm the basic humanity of the individual.

Conclusion

Each of the preceding practices facilitates the bridging of the distance between ourselves and others in our search for collective humanity and shared truth. These actions, when embodied in work settings, can help us to see and to integrate our personal and organizational selves. They can also help us to find our connection with a fundamental basis of knowing and being which is alluded to in all the great spiritual traditions. What the values all have in common is their emphasis on letting go of delusions and aspiring to enact what is highest and most uplifting to the human spirit.

Regarding our aims, these values and qualities are cited in numerous secular and sacred commentaries; what appears most difficult is to enact them consistently in daily life. They have both sacred and secular interpretations. We suggest that both are necessary to create truly healthy workplaces. Regarding our second aim, the enactment of these values can create the basis for the continuity of our work in organizations through the creation of common understandings which spread into the larger communities we are part of.

Each interaction in daily life is an opportunity to increase the likelihood that our own lives and the organizations we work in will be more healthy, that is, more filled with trust, compassion, tolerance of others, and populated with people who have both clarity of mind and heart. It is important that we, as researchers, teachers, change agents, and as members of a wide range of communities, begin to dialogue with others and our own inner conscience concerning how to live consistent with these values and activities. What we thus see is the need for a process of deep organizational and societal transformation that bridges both personal and organizational levels. In this endeavor every moment is a new opportunity.

Would you sell the colors of your sunset and the fragrance
Of your flowers, and the passionate wonder of your forest
For a creed that will not dance?

—Helene Johnson

References

Badaracco, J. L. Jr. (1997), *Defining Moments: When Managers Must Choose Between Right and Right.* Harvard Business School Press, Boston, MA.

Barnard, C. (1982), *The Functions of the Executive*. Harvard University Press, Cambridge, MA.

Barney, J. B., and Hansen, M. H. (1994), Trustworthiness as a source of competitive advantage, *Strategic Management Journal*. Vol. 15, pp. 175–190.

Bayrak, T. (1985), *The Most Beautiful Names*. Threshold Books, Putney, VT.

Becerra, M., and Gupta, A. K. (1998), Trust within the Organization: Integrating the trust literature with agency theory and transaction cost economics. Paper presented at the 58th Annual Meeting of the Academy of Management in San Diego, CA.

Block, P. (1993), *Stewardship: Choosing Service Over Self-interest*, Berrett-Koehler Publishers, San Francisco, CA.

Bohm, D. (1980), *Wholeness and the Implicate Order.* ARK Paperbacks, Boston, MA.

Daft, R. L., & Lengel, R. H. (1998), *Fusion Leadership: Unlocking the Subtle Forces That Change People and Organizations.* Berrett-Koehler Publishers, San Francisco, CA.

Dutton, J. E., Dukerich, J. M., and Harquail, C. V. (1991), Organizational images and member identification, *Administrative Science Quarterly.* Vol. 39, No. 2, pp. 239–260.

Fukuyama, F. (1995), *Trust: The Social Virtues and the Creation of Prosperity.* The Free Press, New York.

Gray, B. (1989), *Collaborating: Finding a Common Ground for Multiparty Problems.* Jossey-Bass Publishers, San Francisco, CA.

Greenleaf, R. K. (1998), *The Power of Servant-Leadership* (edited by L. C. Spears). Berrett-Koehler Press, San Francisco, CA.

Hanh, T. N. (1992), *Peace in Every Step: The Path of Mindfulness in Everyday Life.* Parallax Press, Berkeley, CA.

Hanh, T. N. (1997), *Teachings on Love.* Parallax Press, Berkeley, CA.

Hans, J. (1989), *The Question of Values: Thinking Through Nietzsche, Heidegger, and Freud.* Southern Illinois University Press, Carbondale.

Havel, V. (1992), *Summer Meditations,* Alfred A. Knopf, New York.

Heidegger, M. (1977), *The Question Concerning Technology and Other Essays.* Harper & Row, New York.

Huemer, L. (1998), *Trust in Business Relations.* Borea Bokforlag, Umea, Sweden.

Iverson, K. (1998), *Plain Talk: Lessons from a Business Maverick.* John Wiley & Sons, Inc, New York.

Kabat-Zinn, Jon (1994), *Wherever You Go, There You Are: Mindfulness Meditation in Everyday Life.* Hyperion, New York.

Kotter, J. P. (1995), Leading change: Why transformation efforts fail, *Harvard Business Review,* March–April, pp. 59–67.

Kouzes, J. M., & Posner, B. Z. (1995), *The Leadership Challenge: How to Keep Getting Extraordinary Things Done in Organizations.* Jossey-Bass Publishers, San Francisco, CA.

Kriger, M. P., & Malan, L. C. (1993), Shifting paradigms: The valuing of personal knowledge, wisdom, and other invisible processes in organizations, *Journal of Management Inquiry,* Vol. 2, No. 4, pp. 391–398.

Lao Tzu (1972), *Tao Te Ching* (Gia-Fu Feng & Jane English, tr.). Vintage Books, New York.

Loomer, B. (1976), Two conceptions of power, *Process Studies,* Vol. 6, pp. 5–32.

Maslow, A. H. (1998), *Maslow on Management.* John Wiley & Sons, Inc, New York.

Mohr, L. (1982), *Explaining Organizational Behavior: The Limits and Possibilities of Theory and Research.* Jossey-Bass, San Francisco.

Morgan, G. (1986), *Images of Organization.* Sage Publications, Beverly Hills, CA.

Palmer, P. (1990), *The Active Life.* Harper & Row, San Francisco, CA.

Pasmore, W. (1988), *Designing Effective Organizations: The Socio-technical Systems Perspective.* Wiley, New York.

Quinn, R. E. (1996), *Deep Change: Discovering the Leader Within.* Jossey-Bass Publishers, San Francisco, CA.

Rogers, C. (1961), *On Becoming a Person.* Houghton Mifflin, Boston.

Rokeach, M. (1973), *The Nature of Human Values.* The Free Press, New York.

Semler, R. (1994), *Maverick.* Time-Warner, Burbank, CA.

Smith, H. (1991), *The World's Religions.* HarperCollins Publishers, New York.

Smith, P. (1998), Religious, cultural leaders urge new ethic for globalizing world, *Religion News Service,* 10/14/98. Prague, Czech Republic.

Suzuki, S. (1970), *Zen Mind, Beginner's Mind.* Weatherhill, New York.

Unterman, A. (1976), *The Wisdom of the Jewish Mystics.* New Directions, New York.

Weick, K. E. (1979), *The Social Psychology of Organizing.* Addison-Wesley, Reading, MA.

Williamson, O. E. (1996), *The Mechanisms of Governance.* Oxford University Press, New York.

Youngblood, M. (1997), *Life on the Edge of Chaos.* Percival Publishing, Dallas, TX.

A POSTMODERN SPIRITUAL FUTURE FOR WORK

Jerry Biberman,
University of Scranton

Michael Whitty,
University of Detroit-Mercy,

Acknowledgements

An earlier version of this paper was presented at the annual meeting of the International Academy of Business Disciplines in Orlando, Florida, April 1997. Many thanks to Krista Kepler for her assistance in preparing the article.

Introduction

A number of writers are predicting the end of work as we know it and a bleak jobless future as we head into the twenty-first century (e.g., Korten, 1995; Lerner, 1994; Rifkin, 1995). This article seeks to provide a more hopeful and humane paradigm for the future of work—a model based on spiritual guidelines and principles. In this article we will explore what these spiritual guidelines and principles might be and contrast them with the prevailing modernist paradigm. We will then explore how these principles could be applied to produce shared power in organizational settings.

The Changing Nature of Work

There certainly appears to be evidence that the kinds of jobs that most employees have grown used to having for more than the past 50 years are either changing dramatically or are disappearing entirely. Employees can no longer look forward to lifetime employment with the same organization, to eight-hour work days, or to generous benefit packages. Management theorists are predicting that the workers of the future will need to demonstrate to organizations how they can add value to the organization, that workers can look forward to doing this continuously with a number of organizations over a period of less than 20 years (Bridges, 1994), and that this will require continuous skills training and reeducation (Coates et al., 1990; Gordon et al., 1994). Academicians and professionals alike are noticing the increased stress and uncertainty that workers are already encountering as organizations downsize and demand ever-increasing amounts and hours of work from those workers who survive in the organization (Schor, 1993).

Many of the organization theorists who have predicted the above occurrences also claim that the future will provide many exciting opportunities for workers who are flexible and who can demonstrate they add value to organizations (e.g., Harari, 1993). They also point to a shift in organization structure and governance from the hierarchical mechanistic monolithic organization to smaller, more organic structures consisting of empowered leaderless work teams (Coates et al., 1990; Overholt, 1996). Such organizations could provide opportunities for professional development and empowerment of workers at all levels of the organization.

In this article, we contend that both scenarios of future work derive from a modernist paradigm of work that has been the prevailing paradigm for the past 100 years.

Two Contrasting Paradigms

Modern Paradigm

Most organizations have been designed and managed for the past 100 years using a paradigm based largely on a logical and mechanistic paradigm—a paradigm that values reason and "scientific" principles—that Boje and Dennehy (1994), among others, have called modernism, and that Fox (1994) has called the machine-era paradigm. The paradigm assumed that people can be scientifically measured and categorized based on intellectual and other characteristics they possess, and that certain people are meant to be leaders while others are meant to be followers—or other variations of superior versus inferior—and that organizations, and indeed the whole world, run on rational laws that, once discovered, dictate the only correct way for the organization to run. This paradigm has given rise to such organization practices as scientific management, employment testing, and job instructional training, and to an approach to management that this paper will call "autocratic paternalistic stewardship."

In this paradigm, rational decision making and logical thinking are encouraged, and emotions are to be avoided. Another major component of this paradigm is the belief in scarcity of resources—that is, that all resources, including financial and human resources, exist in finite quantities, and possession of a resource by one person or unit implies its unavailability to other persons or units. This belief has led to such personal and organization practices as competition, political manipulation, "padding" of budget requests, empire building, and lack of trust and cooperation between persons and units. In addition, this paradigm leads to a belief that the person or organization is separate from other persons or organizations, and that preservation of the self, even if it is at the expense of the other, is paramount to survival.

Spiritual Paradigm

Organizations and their executives both in Japan and in the USA are beginning to show an interest in spirituality and spiritual values (e.g., Brandt, 1996; Galen, 1995; Labbs, 1995; Vicek, 1992). A number of organizational writers are urging organizations and their members to pay more attention to spiritual values and spirituality (e.g., Bolman and Deal, 1995; Gunn, 1992; Russell, 1989; Schechter, 1995; Scherer and Shook, 1993; Walker, 1989).

Some authors have related spirituality to organizational learning processes. Mingin (1985), for example, describes how information-based technology will lead to "spirituality oriented fundamental abstractions." Vail (1985) proposes a "process wisdom" explanation of organizational transformation that involves four elements—grounding in existence, appreciation of the openness of the human spirit, understanding of human consciousness, and an appreciation of the spirituality of humankind. Hawkins (1991) relates the spiritual dimension in learning organizations to Gregory Bateson's concept of double-loop Level III learning.

Interest in organizational learning and creative thinking has also led to the increased use of certain spiritual practices—particularly meditation—among organization members, and an increased interest in intuition and whole-brain thinking in organization decision processes (e.g., Agor, 1989). Increasing numbers of executives and managers are turning to various types of meditation and spiritual disciplines as a way of coping with stress and for finding meaning in their turbulent work environments (Dehler and Welsh, 1994) and in dealing with recovery from job loss (Byron, 1995).

At the same time that organizations and managers are paying more attention to spirituality and to whole-brain thinking and learning, global competition and other conditions are bringing about increased attention to team development and employee empowerment.

When one examines the various descriptions of organizations using work teams (e.g., Levine, 1994), one is struck by the similarity of the values, behaviors, and processes that emerge from these teams to those described in relation to spirituality, creativity, and organization learning. Indeed, Poe (1991) points out that the Japanese, with their knowledge of Zen Buddhism, understood Deming's Plan-Do-Study-Act (PDSA) cycle as a spiritual discipline. As employees master this PDSA discipline, they continually trade information with each other until individual wisdom fuses into a powerful group intelligence. Poe says that excessive reliance on logic and reason led many Westerners to misunderstand this aspect of Deming's theories. Similarly, Fort (1995, p. 16) describes how total quality management's emphasis on fulfilling the needs of customers and stakeholders is a contemporary managerial articulation of what Pope John Paul calls solidarity, or the goodness of understanding the self in terms of the self's dialectical relationships with others. Fort asserts that "this expresses an overlapping wisdom that grounds a spirituality of connectedness in all aspects of life, including business."

What do these emerging trends have in common? It is our contention that they represent a postmodern management paradigm that is emerging—one that emphasizes spiritual principles and practices, as opposed to the current prevailing modern management paradigm.

Rose (1990) describes a new paradigm that is beginning to develop among managers and executives which incorporates ideas from quantum physics, cybernetics, chaos theory, cognitive science, and Eastern and Western spiritual traditions. It contains two main components —everything is seen as being interconnected, and there is a focus on empowering people. Rose attributes the vogue for Japanese management techniques, the spread of technology, and the spread of idealism as fueling the trend. Fox (1994) describes many of these same characteristics as depicting what he calls the green (sheen) era of Creation as Sacrament paradigm. James Redfield (1993, 1996) has summarized many of the components into the ten insights described in the Celestine Prophecy and the Tenth Insight, and Deepak Chopra (1994) has distilled the spiritual laws involved in this paradigm (from the Indian Vedic tradition perspective) into the Seven Spiritual Laws of Success.

It is our contention that this paradigm is continuing to emerge and will become more widespread in future years, and that the existing stress that managers and organizations are experiencing may actually produce the catalyst for organization spiritual transformation, in ways similar to that in which personal crises have led to personal spiritual growth and transformation (Grof and Grof, 1989).

The Two Paradigms Contrasted

The two paradigms can be contrasted on both the individual manager and organization level.

On an individual level, persons who ascribe to the modern management paradigm would be expected to have rigid attitudes and beliefs about the nature of themselves, other managers, their superiors, and their subordinates (similar to what McGregor described as Theory X), and a set pattern of behaviors in dealing with each of them. They would also be likely to establish and follow specific procedures or rules of behavior for themselves and others, and be resistant to change. They would attempt to base their decisions purely on logic and reason, and would frown on the use of intuition and the display of emotion. Their scarcity belief would be likely to lead to their not trusting other people, to the use of win-lose tactics in dealing with conflict situations, and to using a variety of power and political tactics to secure their own power base. They would also have a hard time delegating power to others.

Persons operating from a spiritual paradigm perspective would be open to change, have a sense of purpose and meaning in their life, appreciate how they are connected with a greater whole, and have individual understanding and expression of their own spirituality. In contrast to a scarcity belief, they possess what has been referred to as an "abundance" mentality—a belief that there are abundant resources available to all, so that there is no need to compete for them. They would also be more likely to trust others, share information and work in concert with teams and co-workers to accomplish mutual objectives, and empower their co-workers and people below them in the organization hierarchy. They would be more likely to use intuition and emotions in reaching decisions. They would also be more likely to use win-win collaborative strategies in conflict situations.

Organizations that operate from the modern paradigm possess rigid, bureaucratic structures and hierarchical chains of command. They are more likely to use formal communication channels and have very formal policy manuals and procedures for every activity and job title in the organization. They are more concerned with following policies and procedures than in pleasing either internal or external customers. The belief in scarcity of resources leads to competition between organization units for budget, personnel, and other resources, and leads to politics and power struggles between units.

In contrast, organizations that operate from the spiritual paradigm would be expected to have flatter organization structures and a greater openness to change. Their belief in abundant resources would lead to greater interconnectedness and cooperation between organization units, and empowerment of workers at all levels of the organization. Rather than believing in the preservation of the self at all costs, these organizations would be more concerned with existing in harmony with their environment, and would thus be more supportive of the ecology and environment, and more concerned with meeting the needs of internal and external customers. These organizations would be more likely to encourage creative thinking and the working together of organization units to establish and accomplish mutually agreed-on mission statements and objectives for the organization.

The Shift to the Spiritual Paradigm

It is important to point out that the characteristics we described above of persons and organizations operating from a spiritual paradigm perspective are not new. Many of the concepts advocated date back to the human relations movement of the 1950s, and organization development professors and consultants have been advocating many of these concepts for at least 40 years. What is new about these recent developments, however, is that they appear to be emerging from a different overall paradigm, and that environmental conditions are causing them to emerge much more rapidly than ever before.

It is our contention that the human relations movement, organization development, and its attendant concepts developed as a reaction to the prevailing modernist paradigm, and existed within it, rather than trying to create a new paradigm. Thus, the proponents of the human relations movement and organization development accepted most of the underlying tenants of the modernist paradigm—such as the belief in the scientific method—as true and as fact, and then attempted to use the methods of that paradigm to call for what were largely cosmetic changes in the way organizations were managed.

As we asserted earlier, we predict that more and more organizations and their workers can be expected to shift to this new spiritual paradigm in the coming years. This shift is not only likely to occur for the reasons Boje and Dennehy (1994) and others cite as pushing organizations into postmodern practices, but also because of the shift in the consciousness of workers and managers at all levels of organizations that is already beginning to occur as workers and managers seek to find more meaning in their work.

Spirituality and Shared Power

What the employee of the twenty-first century will need more than training is the opportunity to control more fully his or her economic destiny. This desired sense of control can only come with an expanded awareness. Part of this heightened consciousness is soulful or implicitly spiritual (Schechter, 1995). Spirit in the workplace can lead to greater kindness, fairness, even industrial democracy, also known as co-management or power sharing. An invitation to co-manage is an important step away from well-intentioned paternalism. An empowered employee increases the organizational strength and competitive energy necessary for global survival. The greatest empowerment comes from heightened consciousness of our highest self. This higher self is ultimately aware that the purpose of life and work is spiritual as well as material (Fox, 1994). The balance or integration of these two aspects will enhance the effectiveness of organizations and the people within them. This trend will expand in the century to come. Rekindling the spirit in work is not only good business but also subconsciously sought after by workers and managers alike.

Rekindling the Spirit of Community in Work

Organizational soul and the spirit of the workforce have been too often ignored or neglected. Nonetheless, the history of economic reform movements and the thread of social justice in philosophy and religion have long called for a basic change of heart in human behavior. This has always implied a more communal approach to organizational theory and practice as well as a more humanistic psychology for individual behavior. These democratizing concepts were often introduced by social democrats in alliance with unions. Liberal religion supported these community-building reforms.

Spirit-based organizational theorists might profit from further interdisciplinary research into aspects of all major work reform movements of the last 200 years. With the rise of modernism came a heightened materialism that marginalized sharing and caring. Industrialism weakened community and sidelined religion. Employees were often excluded stakeholders. Now a post-industrial age yearns for community and spiritual nourishment in both personal and organizational terms. Selfishness seems dysfunctional to many global thinkers. Only by reinventing work from the inside out will individuals acquire a sense of deeper purpose in work.

In the postmodern future, humankind's eternal search for meaning will require not only reinventing work and the workplace but also a renewed sense of the deepest intentions behind human activity. Spirit-based organizations might also profit from such an arrangement. Cooperation may be good for people's sense of shared destiny and good for the future of organizational culture.

Shared Power

Employee ownership and community involvement in partnership with local and regional employers could evolve into an advanced form of comanagement where all stakeholders share power with spirituality, forming the common ground for cooperation. The individual would be respected in a work world that values diversity and cooperativeness. The organization would recognize its global stewardship of all its resources. Environmental impacts for the long run would include not only the planet but also the spirit which gives it life and ultimate meaning.

A New Work Community: Spirit at Work

A basic workplace spirituality can be the common ground for the new work community. The philosophy of participation adopted from the team concept model can be expanded in the twenty-first century to involve human unity and higher consciousness as well as continuous improvement. This may require a fuller understanding that management makes decisions that have far-reaching impacts on the spiritual lives of employees. Work life reaches into the very soul of all working people. Employees in touch with their spirituality seek to have more input into those decisions. Rekindling the spirit in work will deepen these efforts. The final step would be a corporate attitude of servant leadership toward all stakeholders. Visionary groups such as the Greenleaf Center for Servant Leadership and the Noetic Sciences Institute have path-breaking conferences and workshops designed to encourage new paradigms in business. These groups believe that shared power will ensure that the future "borderless world" values diversity, embraces pluralism, and provides global servant leadership. Workplace unity and high purpose can create a service-learning atmosphere which will result in high standards, adequate competitiveness, and an agile business system for the century to come. A deepened form of organizational stewardship could evolve from reforms in organizational decision making.

Soul at Work

Working people and human evolution itself are constantly seeking meaning, purpose, and a sense of contribution to worklife. These needs are best served and deepened when a spiritual paradigm frames the intentions of all stakeholders. Real human nourishment is provided by the soulful organization.

The postmodern work organization can transform the purpose and meaning of work without excluding employee stakeholders. During the rest of our professional lives we can teach the wisdom and skills of organizational harmony and evolving. Reframing the meaning of work has support of the servant leaders worldwide who see that a life of service best fits the basic human need for relevance, recognition, meaning, and self-transcendence. The *Journal of Organizational Change Management* has become an academic source for new thinking on matters related to a people-centered approach to the future of work.

References

Agor, W. H. (1989), *Intuition in Organizations*, Sage, Newbury Park, CA.

Boje, D. M., and Dennehy (1994), *Managing in the Postmodern World: America's Revolution Against Exploitation*, 2nd. ed., Kendall/Hunt, Dubuque, IA.

Bolman, L. G., and Deal, T. E. (1995), *Leading with Soul: An Uncommon Journey of Spirit*, Jossey-Bass, San Francisco, CA.

Brandt, E. (1996), Corporate pioneers explore spirituality: peace, *HR Magazine*, Vol. 41, No. 4, April, pp. 82–87.

Bridges, W. (1994), *JobShift: How to Prosper in a Workplace Without Jobs*, Addison-Wesley Publishing Co., Reading, MA.

Byron, W. J. (1995), Spirituality on the road to re-employment, *America*, Vol. 172, No. 18, pp. 15–16.

Chopra, D. (1994), *The Seven Spiritual Laws of Success: A Practical Guide to the Fulfillment of Your Dreams*, Amber-Allen Publishing, San Rafael, CA.

Coates, J. F., Jarratt, J., and Mahaffie, J. B. (1990), *Future Work: Seven Critical Forces Reshaping Work and the Workforce in North America*, Jossey-Bass, San Francisco, CA.

Dehler, G. E., and Welsh, M.A. (1994), Spirituality and organizational transformation: implications for the new management paradigm, *Journal of Managerial Psychology*, Vol. 9, No. 6, pp. 17–26.

Fort, T. L. (1995), The spirituality of solidarity and total quality management, *Business and Professional Ethics Journal*, Vol. 14, No. 2, Summer, pp. 3–21.

Fox, M. (1994), *The Reinvention of Work: A New Vision of Livelihood for Our Time*, Harper San Francisco, San Francisco, CA.

Galen, M. (1995), Companies hit the road less traveled, *Business Week*, No. 3427, 5 June, pp. 82–84.

Gordon, E. E., Morgen, R. R., and Ponticell, J. A. (1994), *Futurework: The Revolution Reshaping American Business*, Praeger, Westport, CT.

Grof, S., and Grof, C. (Eds.) (1989), *Spiritual Emergency: When Personal Transformation Becomes a Crisis*, Jeremy P. Tarcher, Los Angeles, CA.

Gunn, B. (1992), Competruism: ideology with a sustainable future, *Futures*, Vol. 24, No. 6, July/August, pp. 559–579.

Harari, O. (1993), Back to the future of work, *Management Review*, Vol. 82, No. 9, September, pp. 33–35.

Hawkins, P. (1991), The spiritual dimension of the learning organization, *Management Education and Development*, Vol. 22, No. 3, Autumn, pp. 172–187.

Korten, D. C. (1995), *When Corporations Rule the World*, Kumarian Press, Inc., West Hartford, CT, and Berret-Koehler Publishers, Inc., San Francisco, CA.

Labbs, J. J. (1995), Balancing spirituality and work, *Personnel Journal*, Vol. 74, No. 9, September, pp. 60–76.

Lerner, S. (1994), The future of work in America: good jobs, bad jobs, beyond jobs, *Futures*, Vol. 26, No. 2, March, pp. 185–196.

Levine, L. (1994), Listening with spirit and the art of team dialogue, *Journal of Organizational Change Management*, Vol. 7, No. 1, pp. 61–73.

Mingin, W. (1985), The trend toward being: what's after the information age? *ReVISION*, Vol. 7, No. 2, Winter-Spring, pp. 64–67.

Overholt, M. H. (1996), *Building Flexible Organizations: A People-Centered Approach*, Kendall/Hunt Publishing Company, Dubuque, IA.

Poe, R. (1991), The new discipline, *Success*, Vol. 38, No. 6, August, p. 80.

Redfield, J. (1993), *The Celestine Prophecy: An Adventure*, Warner Books, New York.

Redfield, J. (1996), *The Tenth Insight: Holding the Vision*, Warner Books, New York.

Rifkin, J. (1995), *The End of Work*, G. P. Putnam and Sons, New York.

Rose, F. (1990), A new age for business? *Fortune*, Vol. 122, No. 9, 8 October, pp. 156–164.

Russell, P. (1989), The redemption of the executive, *Leadership and Organization Development Journal*, Vol. 10, No. 3, pp. i–iv.

Schechter, H. (1995), *Rekindling the Spirit at Work*, Barrytown, Ltd, Barrytown, NY.

Scherer, J., and Shook, L. (1993), *Work & the Human Spirit*, John Scherer & Associates, Spokane, WA.

Schor, J. B. (1993), *The Overworked American: The Unexpected Decline of Leisure*, Basic Books, New York.

Vail, P. B. (1985), Process wisdom for a new age, *ReVISION*, Vol. 7, No. 2, pp. 39–49.

Vicek, D. J. (1992), The domino effect, *Small Business Reports*, Vol. 17, No. 9, Winter, pp. 21–25.

Walker, R. G. (1989), The imperative of leaders to create leaders, *Directors and Boards*, Vol. 13, No. 2, Winter, pp. 21–25.

ON FINDING AN
INTEGRATED PATH

Elizabeth Guss
"Cohesion - Integrating Spirit and Work"

When we refer to workplace spirituality, we usually speak about organizational generalities and possible effects to the group. We can worry about religious or denomination pressure negatively affecting our workplace; we can rejoice at the many benefits that come when the human spirit is engaged. But I think we often overlook the truth that spirituality is essentially a personal choice and journey. While spiritually grounded people influence the work environment with presence and personal power, their positive influence is a result of their inner work. This article considers the individual perspective on integrating the spiritual into our lives at work.

Not at all about religion, spirituality really speaks to the deep sense of connectedness that we feel/know—to one's interior self, to one another, to nature, and ultimately, to the Source of all being—and how that connectedness manifests itself in our behavior. A deepening spiritual awareness results normally in calm, personal stability, re-siliency, and better decision making. It guides us toward wisdom—an attribute desperately needed in today's world (Guillory).

Developing wisdom is a dynamic process that affects how we think, what we do, what response we get, and how we respond, as well. Greater awareness leads to attitude and behavior change, in ourselves, and potentially, in others, too. But it depends on a growing under-standing of what we believe is most important and how our lives are shaped by those values. Wisdom guides us in the necessary and dynamic process of self-renewal—maintaining our essential identity while changing our external form.

Who am I? What am I about? What do I hold sacred? What affects me? How do I affect others? These start the process of looking at our inner world and seeing the congruence with our outer world. If we look honestly and openly at ourselves, we come to understand more, bringing that bigger perspective to the service of all whom we meet.

This deeply personal journey toward wisdom has a very public expression when we undertake it at and through our work. Facing the ongoing process of organizational self-renewal that is critical to survival today, we can tap into essential resources—stronger relationships, resiliency, greater calm—resources more important to this process than technical skills. We can have both a clear sense of core identity and an openness to the possible (Wheatley). It doesn't matter where we are in the organization, we can ground ourselves in our beliefs and make a difference; we can make a spiritual practice work (Richmond).

This ongoing process of attitude and behavioral self-examination is a practical expression of a twelfth century definition of theology—faith seeking understanding.[1] This type of deep seeking is a process best undertaken in a context of human community, with companions whom we trust and who help us make sense of events and decisions, as well as seeing opportunities that life presents. The spiritual journey, while still intensely personal, need not be a lonely one.

There is a longstanding tradition of this type of companionship that is increasingly being sought to help integrate our spiritual journey with our work. Variously called spiritual guidance or direction, it is a relationship of another's loving listening to us as we search for deeper understanding (Guenther, Wicks/Rodgerson). Historically seen in a context of personal growth and, often only within religious denominations, Spiritual Direction is now being recognized as relevant to workplace decisions and behavior. While far from common, this companioned searching for understanding about and through work was newsworthy enough to be reported by the *Wall Street Journal* in July, 1998. It would seem that Spiritual Direction is increasingly going to work.

From years in management training and leadership development, I have seen the hunger of people to connect their deeper spirit with their work. Prompted often with a desire to solve a specific problem (frequently stress-related), they begin meditation, yoga, chanting, etc., and find that those practices create a quiet space and centering that opens for them an awareness of deeper issues that need exploration. Those places

---

[1] Anselm of Canterbury (d. A.D. 1109) is credited with this definition as part of his contribution to the growing emphasis on merging reason with faith. This definition helped shape theological study and discourse from the twelfth century forward (McBrien, Richard. *Catholicism* (1994). Winston Press. p. 26).

of quiet and stillness are often where we meet the Sacred within who calls to us through all parts of our lives, including our work.

Becoming aware of and deepening our connection to the Holy is the essence of the spiritual journey. Our own spirituality flourishes as we more consciously participate with the mysterious Divine expressing itself in and through us. But we don't always see it because we are so close to it and that's where Spiritual Direction comes into the picture.

In this relationship of loving listening, the Spiritual Director looks with us at our lives and listens with us for the song of the Spirit that is breaking through our resistance and awakening us to new possibilities. In asking for deeper reflection on an event or feeling, the Spiritual Guide widens the space to let us see if (and how) Wisdom is speaking to us. In that space, we can perhaps recognize more fully where self, a hunger for meaning, and Divine Energy interconnect and then understand better this juncture of belief and its lived application. The long-term goal of Spiritual Direction is to be a companion to another in the ongoing process of discovering the Great Mystery present in our lives.

Training and development led me to personal coaching and then to formal studies in and the practice of Spiritual Direction. I now do team building, training, and coaching within the context of this type of companionship, weaving it into how I listen, facilitate meetings, and develop curricula. I have come to believe that it is impossible to separate sustained high performance from the enthusiasm of the engaged human spirit. Because I see the workplace as full of opportunity to liberate human potential, to make a meaning-filled difference, and to strengthen the fabric of our society, for me, the workplace is full of hope for everyone. But these incredible possibilities require that we see work in a new way—as perhaps a spiritual journey, certainly an opportunity to serve the greater good (Griffin). And many clients and work associates share this vision of the possible.

Who am I? What am I about? What do I believe matters? How do I live those beliefs? These questions lift us from the mechanics of performance improvement and reframe the issues, defining performance improvement in a context of living authentically. It is a breakthrough realization that changes our view of the world, and I illustrate it with these stories.

1. Through mutual employment, I met and came to know somewhat a very talented, driven, and accomplished salesman. As he faced a very difficult personal situation, he asked me to

listen and provide some perspective. His greatest need was for a safe place to explore his deep hurt. Knowing clearly that my role was not to advise, I suggested that he begin some meditation and allow the inner stillness to provide him with the answers he sought. Although he did not get the answer he wished, he did receive inner guidance that has, over time, opened his life to establish a balance that meets family and professional needs. His overall approach has moved from intellectual-only decision making to values-centering in his life. Now, a consultant who operates independently, he combines his new awareness into his work. His professional planning services gain him entrance into a company and he then works with top management to examine company processes and cultures to find ways to free the people to do their best—to find wholeness and satisfaction instead of frustration. Doing this work requires that he continually learn new skills and he sees work as a wonderful vehicle for his own growth and development. Always an energetic salesman, now he is an enthusiastic person.[2]

2. A colleague who moved from a speaking and training career into non-profit work with a marginalized population did so initially as a marketing strategy for her business and career. She quickly realized that the work itself "touched her heart"; she was energized by helping people realize their innate dignity and value. Believing that the path to a good future requires changing our attitude from "being victimized" to "being accountable," she encourages personal responsibility non-stop. Coming to know me after her organization was established but when she was becoming discouraged and weary, she found that it mattered greatly to her that someone could hear and understand how her heart was calling for this work to be done. Asking for help to make the organization more effective was ostensibly to develop better infrastructure and training programs, but it was also to affirm the value of what she was doing. She needed someone to hear how the Spirit of Life had enveloped her in and through her work; once heard, she could continue with enthusiasm. The organization's mission is to help

---

[2] The root of enthusiasm is "en theos," translated as the *Spirit of God within*—a radiating internal energy.

welfare women become economically self-sufficient, but her deeper purpose is cultivating "hope"—and it fills her heart with joy that she wants to share.

3. I met a woman through a professional association, who, on the heels of a serious emotional trauma, asked me to work with her as a personal coach to help her develop better personal/ emotional boundaries. Coaching questions invited her to look at her life, its influences, and her worldview, in general. In that process, she deepened her awareness of who she is and how she has viewed God, historically and currently. In the protected environment of a trusted conversation, she has begun to examine her spiritual and emotional wounds, treating them with loving, compassionate care. She is coming to like herself more, to care for herself more fully, and to face the future with more hope. The boundary issue is taking care of itself. This integrated, stronger person is becoming more aware of herself within her environment and much more effective in her teaching and training role.

For each of these people, and for many others, as well, work is an opportunity to reflect on what is important and come to new insights. Seldom are the insights earth-shaking, but they have a deep impact on the ordinary and on self-esteem (Wicks). We begin our conversations to accomplish some stated goal and, in the process, we do the work of becoming more integrated and whole. These conversations let the Spirit take center stage. Not a one-time fix-up, but an ongoing relationship— shaping the context to develop greater resiliency, wisdom, and peace.

When we are centered in our core values, we can adapt without losing our identity (Wheatley). We can be a contributing part of a system of growth and change, not lost in the seeming chaos. We are better able to integrate new information and to contribute to healthy organization/system development. Through our personal stability, we bring calm to our work environment, become a yeast for change, and influence good decision making. This path of wisdom comes from the conscious integration of spirit and work and provides needed navigation as we venture into the unknown.

I met each of these people through work. Not one found me in my role as a Spiritual Director and yet each has received Spiritual Direction. While they use different words to describe and name the Sacred, the One, the Divine Energy, they are all keenly aware of how they have been touched by the Holy in their lives. They are more alive today than before we began our conversations.

For me, this process has been and continues to be an exciting one. I began with a confident although vague belief that people are hungry to find meaning in their work. Now, I see evidence that people want to speak about how their work is part of their connection to the Mystery that we call God. In the workplace, we can explore new understandings of what it means to live fully, to live in hope, to make a difference. My own views have been stretched and challenged. My work and beliefs have become enriched with meaning. With clients and colleagues, I realize an unfolding awareness of the Divine becoming more visible through people and events, understanding that every place hosts the Sacred. This brings me back to my own issues, which include theology.

If theology is the process of seeking understanding, then to "do theology" requires that we ask the tough question, stretch out of our comfort zones, and look at things with new eyes. Theologians think boldly and imaginatively about what faith means (McFague). For too long, we have thought that theology was about proof texts of some stated dogma, missing the point that it is about how our beliefs about God inform the way we live. We are called to challenge our beliefs and our behavior until new understanding leads to new ways of being. Theology like this will inevitably take us from theoretical and conceptual statements to a values-centered way of living.

People shake their heads at me when I speak of the workplace as full of hope. It is bold, imaginative thinking to see business as celebrating the human spirit, unlocking potential, and illuminating the Sacred ever present in our lives (Novak). This is a vision of the possible (not the easy). As people look more deeply at themselves and their work, they often find a values center that gives hope and a vision that propels them forward. This is transformational thinking, the Good News bringing new life into the world of numbers and bottom line.

As I have walked with others on their search for meaning and peace, I have discovered my own spiritual path. Through the tools of training and development, of consulting and coaching, I have become a theologian of the workplace.

For Further Reading

Griffin, Emilie. *The Reflective Executive—A Spirituality of Business and Enterprise.* Crossroads Press, New York. 1993. A profoundly practical commentary on how to integrate management and scriptural resources to see God's presence in work, even in the details. Draws from 30 years of marketing, poetic wisdom of Christian mystics, and visionary business thinkers.

Guenther, Margaret. *Holy Listening—The Art of Spiritual Direction.* Cowley Publications, Cambridge, MA. 1992. A practical explanation of the incredible gift of spiritual direction—listening wholly to another, helping that person get his inner house in order and await the arrival of divine messengers who wait for an audience.

Guillory, William. *The Living Organization—Spirituality in the Workplace.* Innovations International, Salt Lake City, UT. 1998. Incorporating previous work on empowerment to understand the positive effect on an organization when people consciously embrace their spiritual selves and journey as part of their lifestyle.

McFague, Sallie. *Models of God—Theology for an Ecological, Nuclear Age.* Fortress Press, Philadelphia, PA. 1987. Let us not narrow God, but engage the imagination about this all-encompassing reality and free ourselves to a change in consciousness that can open us to new action to accomplish good.

Novak, Michael. *Business as a Calling—Work and the Examined Life.* The Free Press, New York. 1996. Winner of the Templeton Prize in 1996, Novak examines the concept of vocation—a calling to wholeness—and its deep integration with business.

Richmond, Lewis. *Work as a Spiritual Practice—A Practical Buddhist Approach to Inner Growth and Satisfaction on the Job.* Broadway Books, New York. 1999. The active, engaged side of Buddhism draws people into the creative, inspiring, and accomplishing that is necessary in our workplace world. Invites empowerment in all work.

Wheatley, Margaret. *Leadership and the New Science—Learning About Organization from an Orderly Universe.* Berrett-Kohler Publishers, San Francisco, CA. 1992. A synthesis of new understandings from science—systems, relationships, and that chaos is change toward a new order—that prompt us to look at organizations in a new way, seeing change as the impetus toward higher development and understanding.

Wicks, Robert, *Touching the Holy—Ordinariness, Friendship, and Self Esteem.* Ave Maria Press, Notre Dame, IN. 1992. A look at truth and our search for it through the simple, ordinary aspects of everyday life and relationship.

Wicks, Robert, and Rodgerson, Thomas E. *Companions in Hope—The Art of Christian Caring.* Paulist Press, New York. 1998. A companioning guide for those who wish to care deeply for another through presence and conversation.

INDEX

Accountability, 62, 143, 170, 192, 220, 224, 229

ACX Technologies Inc., 172

Ahimsa, xv, 77–79, 82, 84–88, 92, 93, 181, 182, 184, 187

Atomization, 306

Attribution theory, 347

Authenticity, xxxi, 33, 45, 64, 65, 81, 98, 175, 305, 307

Authority, 63, 143, 239

Baha'u'llah, 192, 201

Bank of Montreal, 203

Belonging, 33, 96, 175, 295, 343

Bioethics, 85

Boatmen's First National Bank, 206

Buddha, 160, 166, 169, 340

Business, xi–xxiii, xxv, xxviii–xxxii, 6, 9, 15–18, 19, 21–25, 27, 29, 32, 33, 35, 36, 38, 39, 42, 52, 53, 55, 56, 58, 60–65, 67, 70–76, 86, 87, 92, 95–97, 99, 101, 102, 105, 107, 109, 112, 125–127, 130, 131, 140, 142, 146, 149–166, 168, 171, 172, 175–177, 179, 180, 181, 183, 184, 187, 188, 191, 194, 195, 198, 199, 201, 202, 203, 205, 207–211, 213, 214, 217–220, 224, 226, 227, 229–231, 233–235, 244, 246, 265, 266, 268, 271–273, 276, 279, 281, 282, 286, 288, 289, 292, 293, 297, 301–304, 306, 307, 310, 311, 315, 317–320, 322–324, 334, 336, 337, 341–343, 348, 349, 351, 354, 357, 359–361, 366, 368, 369

Business ethics, xi, xviii, 62, 70, 72–74, 151, 157, 158, 165, 205, 208, 209, 211, 214, 244, 246

Business Leadership Institute, 159

Calling, 13, 67, 71, 73, 78, 140, 152, 157, 176, 179, 198, 214, 217, 230, 342, 366, 369

Cartesian split, 298, 301

Chappell, Tom, 62, 106, 160, 205, 207, 214

Chick-Fil-A, 284

Christianity, xxix, 114, 116, 156–158, 175, 176, 339

Collaboration, xv, xx, 60, 112, 125, 192, 198, 240, 295, 305–308

Community, xiv, xx, xxi, xxix, 38, 39, 45, 46, 60–62, 65, 69, 70, 72, 76, 80–82, 85, 87, 97, 100, 103, 107, 130, 159, 160, 162, 164, 177, 197, 200, 201, 223, 224, 228, 233, 242, 264, 269, 270, 272, 274–276, 279, 282–285, 290, 295–309, 311, 316, 335, 338, 342, 357, 358, 364

Compensation, 104, 211, 280

Competition, xix, 64, 77, 96, 101, 103, 191, 208, 283, 295, 298, 306–309, 332, 353, 354, 356

Competitive advantage, xiii, 52, 73, 145, 280, 281, 337, 348

Consciousness, xi–xiv, xvi, xviii– xxi, 7, 20, 23, 31, 35, 37, 38, 59, 64, 73, 75, 131, 141, 147, 153, 155, 174, 217, 225, 226, 228, 96, 298, 299, 306, 317–325, 342, 353, 357, 358, 369

Contemplation, 152, 156, 159, 239

Coors, Jeffrey H., 172

Corporate culture, xxviii, 129, 203, 206, 211, 213, 223, 269

Covey, Stephen, 147, 218

Culture, xii, xv, xviii–xx, xxvii, xxviii, 9, 12, 13, 22, 31, 45, 49, 53, 57, 60, 64, 66, 75, 87, 89, 95–97, 100–104, 118, 123, 124, 126, 129, 131, 155–157, 159, 161, 177, 183, 197, 198, 203, 206, 210, 211, 213, 218–220, 222, 223, 225, 228, 234–241, 244, 245, 247, 269, 270, 272, 274, 289, 297, 304, 305, 309, 320, 358

De Chardin, Pierre Teilhard, 156

Diversity, xiv, xxix, 37, 45, 49–51, 53, 91, 101, 115, 120, 176, 225, 236, 242, 289, 358, 359

Dollar General, 195–198, 202

Downsizing, xxviii–xxx, 29, 30, 45, 96, 99–101, 105, 107, 150, 210, 283

Ego, 35–37, 39, 122, 139–141, 147, 200, 204, 284, 343

Employee Attitudes, xx, 273, 277, 278

Employee development, 206, 245, 287, 322

371